Writing and Computers

Colette Daiute
Harvard University

ADDISON-WESLEY PUBLISHING COMPANY
Reading, Massachusetts · Menlo Park, California
Don Mills, Ontario · Wokingham, England · Amsterdam
Sydney · Singapore · Tokyo · Mexico City · Bogota
Santiago · San Juan

Illustration Credits: Photos on pages xxii, 41, 50, 70, 103, 129, 147, 148, 198, 202, 229, 248 and 282 by Sharon Bazarian; pages 4, 12, 169 and 281 by Colette Daiute; pages 213 and 232 by Bob Bickford; page 90 courtesy John Seely Brown and Richard Burton, Xerox Palo Alto Research Center (PARC). Drawing on page 145 by Ivan Wright. Back cover photo by Paula Rhodes.

Library of Congress Cataloging in Publication Data

Daiute, Colette.
   Writing and computers.

   Bibliography: p.
   Includes index.
   1. English language—Rhetoric—Study and teaching—
Data processing.   2. English language—Rhetoric—Data
processing.   3. English language—Composition and exercises—Study and teaching—Data processing.   4. Word
processing.   5. Authorship—Data processing.   I. Title.
PE1404.D35   1984   808'.042'02854   84-12458
ISBN 0-201-10368-0

Copyright © 1985 by Addison-Wesley Publishing Company, Inc.

ISBN 0-201-10368-0

ABCDEFGHIJ-HA-898765

For my mother and father

Preface: Learning to Write, Again

Writing changed for me when I began to use a computer. I like to write quickly, but I have to revise a lot. I have never had the money to pay typists for preparing neat drafts—and I have never been a good enough typist to recreate draft after draft efficiently—so I didn't spend as much time writing as I wanted to. The computer has changed writing for me because it helps me revise as much as I want, and it does the recopying.

Computers provide tools that respond to writers' instructions for changing texts. I found that once I had mastered the word processor and other computer writing tools, I had more time and energy for creating and critiquing texts than when I used pens and typewriters. I can, for example, make one type of change each time I read a draft without having to retype the entire text after every revision. Writing on the computer is also easier because it seems more like talking. The computer program responds to me: it carries out instructions, prompts me to keep to the point, highlights possible spelling mistakes, and offers a communication channel for corresponding with friends, colleagues, and strangers. I still use pencils and paper because they are more portable and more manageable than a computer, but the computer has taken a place among the other writing tools on my desk.

As the computer gave me increased power as a writer, I was struck by the value it could have for my students in English classes. I thought that computers would offer my students tools that would take some of the drudgery out of writing. With the computer, they could more easily take advantage of my suggestions such as "Let your writing grow. Discover what you have to say as you write." When they used the computer, they were more likely to believe such comments as "You aren't stuck with your first words. Even if they don't sound great, those first words will lead you to more interesting ones." Beginning writers are more willing to write when their tools help them out a little. They feel free to experiment when they don't have to face the consequences of endless retyping, and they enjoy writing when they can use it to communicate with their peers.

This book is about writing—a social, physical, and cognitive process—and it is about computers. In the book, I discuss the value of myriad tools for beginning and mature writers with different skills. I suggest applications of computer word-processing programs, electronic mail systems, prompting programs, text analysis programs, language exercises, and linguistic games. I also suggest how to integrate these computer tools with other writing tools—pencils, pens, and paper. Researchers have found that computers are helpful for some writers doing some types of writing, but there are situations in which the old tools are better or just as good. Therefore, I present the cons of using computers as well as the pros, so that teachers and parents can make decisions based on experience rather than on advertising.

Even though the computer is powerful, the writer still has to know what to say and how to say it. And the computer does present writers with some new problems. A writer who uses a computer has to learn to type, to use the hardware and software, and to cope with a machine that can gobble up texts. This book suggests ways to exploit the power of the computer while avoiding its drawbacks.

I wrote this book for all teachers—English teachers and social studies teachers alike—who want to make writing as easy and enjoyable as possible for their students. The book is also for parents who are interested in the impact of computers on their children's education. I suggest methods for using computers to make writing and writing instruction more meaningful and more fun, and I discuss how the computer can help you revive your own writing process.

Reading this book doesn't require prior knowledge of computers. As you read about the role of the computer in the writing process, you will learn basic computer terms and will gain a sense of what computers can and can't do, but I don't go into detail about the inner workings of the machine. Writing is the focus of the book, so readers who have already worked or played with computers won't feel that they are reading another book on "computer literacy." Even those who have already used computers extensively for math drills, science exploration, or programming will find ideas for applying computers to writing.

This book should stimulate readers to think about writing and computers in new ways. Computers, like other writing instruments, change the nature of written communication. The computer is a dynamic instrument that accepts the writer's words, carries out commands, and offers suggestions about texts. Such a writing instrument can blur the distinctions between thinking, talking, and writing in a way that the pencil and typewriter have not. Writers can use computers to emphasize the social nature of writing, because these machines provide communication channels for corresponding and collaborative composing. Both children and adults find writing to be more meaningful in social environments, and the cognitive difficulties of writing may be less trouble-some than they are when writers work with tools that are isolating. Of course, writing is lonelier than talking, but students who learn to write with computers may find it easier to make the transition from oral to written expression, because working on the computer is interactive—somewhere between talking and writing with a pen or typewriter.

The ideas presented in this book are based on research and experience. I am a psycholinguist studying the effects of computers and other writing instruments on oral and written language development. My colleagues and I have tried to determine why writing is difficult for some students but fun and fulfilling for others. We have been studying the ways in which writers of different ages guide their thinking and the interactions they have with computers as they write. In this book, I draw on the work of other cognitive scientists, writing researchers, and teachers, addressing such questions as "What writing activities are better done with computers than with pens or typewriters—and vice versa?" "Are the benefits of using the computer for writing and writing instruction worth the complication and expense?" "How does the computer affect writing quality?" and, finally, "How does the computer affect human thought and action?"

Some people doubt that the writing instrument makes any difference in the creative process. The writer has a big job, regardless of the instrument he or she uses, but just as the artist's brush affects the strokes and the overall look of a painting, the writer's tool can affect the text. Thinking about the writing instrument stimulates writers and writing teachers to consider the "how" of their craft as well as the "what" and the "why."

After an introductory overview of the uses of computers for writing, the chapters in Part I of this book offer a theory of writing instruction and computer use. These chapters highlight the social, physical, and cognitive factors in the writing process that are useful for teachers to think about—whether or not they use computers. Part II describes computer writing tools as they apply to various steps in the writing process. Part III discusses specific applications of computer programs for writers of different ages. Computers do not benefit all writers in the same ways, so a discussion of the different effects is useful. Part IV provides information for evaluating and selecting computer writing tools and designing learning environments in which students can work in harmony with peers, teachers, and computers. The Afterword highlights issues and concerns about the future of writing as it may be affected by technology. The book concludes with a bibliography, a directory of resources, and a glossary of terms.

Acknowledgments

During the years I was doing the research and writing for this book, I received support from colleagues, friends, and institutions. I am naming those who helped me here, so that they become part of the book in yet another way.

Several foundations supported the research that led to many of the ideas presented in this book. I am grateful to the Spencer Foundation, for their generous support of my initial work on the uses of computers for writing; to the National Institute of Education, for funding my earlier research on the psychology of writing; and to the Apple Education Foundation, for funding my studies of children's mastery of keyboarding. I am also grateful to the Harvard University Graduate School of Education and Columbia University Teachers College, where I did most of my work.

I thank Thomas G. Bever, Sarah Freedman, Lillian Bridwell, Bruce McCarty, Hugh Burns, Denise Potter, Cheryl Weiner, Karen Billings, Rachele Thomas, and Samuel Boothby, for reading and critiquing an early draft of this book, and I am grateful to Samuel Boothby for his help in preparing the resources and glossary sections. Also, Thomas Bever and Robert Taylor provided valuable advice on the research underlying the ideas in this book. Many research assistants, programmers, teachers, students, and subjects have also helped: Pegeen Wright, Sharon Liff, Sandy Mazur, Sharon Moore, Arthur Sheild, Peggy O'Brien, Wanda Bethea, Michelle Musacchio, Robin Geller, Janet Liff, Stephen Suckow, and Victor Muslin. My friends Rachele Thomas, Cathy Canzani, Karen Billings, and Sara Wright offered personal support. I also thank Peter Gordon of Addison-Wesley for his guidance and flexibility with this project, and I thank his staff for their creative assistance in bringing this book to print.

Special thanks go to my family—my mother, my father, Denise, John, and especially my husband, Patrick Wright—who kept me laughing even in the final stages of preparing this book for publication.

I also thank my readers in advance for sitting with me; I hope that you find this book stimulating as well as informative.

Contents

Introduction: The Computer Is a Language Machine

Writing is a dynamic process. It combines thinking, feeling, and talking silently to readers and to oneself. Writing is a process of discovery as writers develop ideas and create texts. Like all discoveries, the process of creating a text often surprises even the writers—who, after putting words on paper, see new ideas that lead them to refine a piece or start a new one.

People once "wrote" only in their minds. The ancients had to keep all information—facts and fiction—in mind if they wanted to use it or pass it on. The invention of writing gave societies external records of facts and cultural experiences, works of art, and a method for clarifying thought. Writing is an extension of thinking and talking, as ideas become written symbols on the page, but the writing process has also differed from talking because writing instruments have been cumbersome.

Writing tools have always affected the process of writing. People have written on cave walls, animal skins, clay, stone, papyrus, and paper. They have made their marks on these materials with animal hairs, sticks, chisels, quills, printing presses, pens, pencils, typewriters, and now **computers**.* While some writing tools require application of liquids or carbons to a surface, the "ink" for computer writing is electrons; the words appear as lights on the computer screen. The human voice can also be a writing instrument on experimental computer systems that translate speech sounds into written words.

In general, writing has become more dynamic—more like talking and thinking—as writing tools have advanced. Writing has become more like talking as the process of translating ideas into written symbols has become faster and as the written product has become more changeable. At certain times in history, writers have spent hours, even days, preparing their

---

*Boldface terms throughout the book are defined briefly in the text and in detail in the glossary.

instruments and surfaces before they actually began writing. Greek writers prepared papyrus and reeds for writing, so they had to develop the artisan skills of tool making as well as literacy skills. Cuneiform and hieroglyphic writing required preparation of clay tablets. Writers had to press letters onto the clay tablets and correct mistakes quickly, before the clay dried. Writing in the Middle Ages was similarly cumbersome, mostly because it functioned as art work dedicated to the glorification of God. Clerics spent years making a single copy of the Bible. All of these forms of writing were static because the methods were slow and changes were difficult, if not impossible, to make.

The modern styluses—the pencil and the pen—are easier to use because writers can buy them rather than make them and because paper quality makes erasing possible. Machines like the printing press and the typewriter have made the transcription process less time-consuming than it was when a writer had to draw each letter in each copy of a text. Printing and photocopying have spread writing to many readers, which increases the dynamism of writing as each reader experiences and interprets the text. Correction fluid and copying machines have made text increasingly transformable. Computer word-processing programs, screens, and printers, however, have made the process of translating ideas into printed words faster by far than any of the traditional methods. Text produced with a computer passes through the writer's mind and hand to the teacher or editor, to the publisher, and to the reader much faster than traditionally printed text can.

With the computer as the instrument, writing is more like talking. Writers interact with the computer instrument, while the pen and the typewriter are static tools. The computer enhances the communication functions of writing not only because it interacts with the writers but also because it offers a channel for writers to communicate with one another and because it can carry out a variety of production activities. Writing on the computer means using the machine as a pencil, eraser, typewriter, printer, scissors, paste, copier, filing cabinet, memo pad, and post office. Thus, the computer is a communication channel as well as a writing tool. The computer is a language machine.

When using a computer, people communicate with the machine, with other people, and with themselves as they carry on the internal dialogues necessary for writing. The following story will illustrate the value of a computer as a communication machine for writers.

I walked up to my office, a small room at the end of a long hallway, opened the double locks on the doors leading into my laboratory (computing equipment is expensive), shed my winter coat, and turned on the **microcomputer**. I stared at the television-like screen, and the **cursor**, the bright, blinking dot against the black video screen, reminded me that I was sitting in near-darkness. The blinking cursor was a message saying that the computer was ready for me to start writing. I would be using a variety of codes on the computer and then writing an article in English. I turned on the light and began what was to become a 3-hour writing session. During this time, I saw what my friends were doing on the computer, read and answered mail sent the day before, had a discussion with a friend, revised and printed a paper, sent it to an editor in California, responded to her comments, played a game, wrote a story with two third-graders and their teacher, and watched them talk, in writing, to a businessman in another city.

I was working on a microcomputer connected to a telephone line, so I could communicate with other writers working at their machines in the next office or across the country. I gave the communication program instructions to connect me to the outside world by typing instructions to call The Source **network** and **information utility**. Such information networks offer subscribers access to databases, programs, and connections to other people. First, I typed in a command telling the computer program to call The Source, and then typed in the telephone number.

I then typed in the identification number by which The Source computer in Virginia knew me:

ID BBI1977

And my password, HOPE. The computer responded by presenting on the computer screen a **menu** of options available on The Source.

I like to begin writing sessions by communicating, so I usually select the menu to check for mail first.

MAIL AND COMMUNICATIONS

1 MAIL
2 CHAT
3 POST
4 PARTICIPATE
5 MAILGRAM MESSAGES

Enter item number or HELP

I entered 1, which showed me a list of communication options:

MAIL

1 OVERVIEW
2 INSTRUCTIONS
3 MAIL CHECK
4 MAIL SEND
5 MAIL READ
6 MAIL SCAN

Enter item number or HELP

I checked the list of messages that had arrived in my electronic mailbox the previous day. To view a message from a former student who subscribed to The Source from Canada, I typed the proper number sequence to read her message, which the computer then displayed on the screen:

```
MSG: 5 <M> [ ] <23>
DATE: 11/30 6:10
TO: COLETTE DAIUTE
FROM: JANE BLUM
SUBJECT: READINGS
```

Please send me a copy of your reading list because I'll be teaching again next fall. By the way, I'm organizing a one month hike in the Rockies. Want to come with us? You need to get away from the East.

I wrote an answer to Jane and then gave the command telling the computer to bring it to her account so she would see it as soon as she checked her mail, which she did every day.

Then I wanted to send mail to four teachers with whom I was collaborating in New York. I wrote the message once and then typed the names and ID numbers of my colleagues. A copy of the message would be waiting for each of the teachers to read the next time they checked their electronic mailboxes.

After reading and sending more mail, I asked the program to show me a list of the other people who were using it at 9:00 Monday morning. The list appeared, showing me the ID numbers of people on the network. As I perused the list, I imagined what my friends were doing: Karen was writing, Ursula was playing a game, and Robert was being nosy, as I was.

I then used the CHAT program to talk, in writing, to Karen, a friend who was using The Source at the same time from her office on the other side of town. First, I typed the command CHAT and Karen's ID number; the computer responsed READY, and I typed:

I've been waiting for you to get back from your trip. Welcome home. I got the note you sent before you left and have found that April 1 is a good date for the meeting. What do you think about that?

As I wrote, Karen saw my message on her computer screen, since she had forgotten to tell the program that she didn't want interruptions. She answered:

Hi. I'm writing some letters that I have to get out this morning. Let's meet for lunch. I'll see you later at the usual place.

A few minutes later, someone I didn't know connected to my workspace via CHAT, and we had an extended conversation.

Talking in writing like this warms me up. After communicating with other people, I was more attuned to the potential audience of my formal writing—a magazine article that I was still polishing. I had used the computer in another language capacity—as a **word processor**—to compose the first draft of the article. As writers type texts on the computer keyboard, the **word-processing program** stores them in the computer **memory**—the space in the computer for processing programs and text. The program incorporates each change the writer makes by using word-processing commands and displays the latest version of the text on the screen. The writer can get a paper copy of the text if the computer is attached to a printer. Changes that would take about a week's turnaround time with a typewriter take only a day or two when a writer uses a word-processing program—if, of course, the writer knows the changes to make.

In half an hour, I made major changes in a seventy-page manuscript. I moved three pages from one section to another, added a few paragraphs, and tightened up the writing. Rather than cutting and pasting or scribbling between lines and in margins, I gave about fifteen word-processing commands to make these changes.

To understand what it is like to write using a word-processing program, imagine a letter of self-introduction you have written with a pencil. You decide to erase three words from the first sentence. As you erase, the rest of the words march up, close the gaps, and space themselves evenly on the page. You also decide you want to make your point sooner, so you pick up the tenth sentence and move it in front of the second. No crossings out, arrows, or scribbles interfere with the message in the letter; you merely nudge the tenth sentence in between the first and the second. The rest of the text moves down, and the words realign and format themselves. As you make each subsequent addition, erasure, spelling change, and reorganization, the page transforms itself. You have changed the letter five times, never having to recopy. This text on the computer is dynamic in a way that it is not when writers use pens, typewriters, or even pencils.

I wasn't happy with the opening section of my article, so I wrote two different opening paragraphs and gave commands to get one printout of each. After selecting the better version, I printed the manuscript so that I could scrutinize and improve it further. I made revision notes on the hard copy, entered the changes into the computer, and began the editing process to make more detailed improvements.

When I was finished, I connected to The Source again and sent the text to my editor, Sarah. She was 2,000 miles away, but she read my text within 15 minutes because I had told her it would be in her electronic message bin by 11:00 my time.

Then Robert, a third-grade teacher, arrived with two of his students to use the Apple computer in my lab for some extra help with spelling. I had been trying to convince Robert that the word-processing functions of the computer would help his students, but he thought they would gain the most from the computer by using it to learn grammar rules, since their writing was so weak.

I gave up—but only for a while. Robert started with a spelling drill, and the screen began to present instructions:

'Spelling Fun' Loaded

Press the space bar to continue

The kids played a few spelling games but then became bored and asked if there was anything else they could do. I gave them a program that is a **simulation** of a search for the New World. When children play problem-solving games together, they use their imaginations, they plan, and they often create stories—all essential activities in early writing. With the simulation program, the children play the roles of sailors using celestial navigation to guide their ship to the New World. The screen graphically shows the stars, the ocean's depth, and the sun's shadow as the crew journeys across the ocean. The children plot their course, plan the use of their meager provisions, and survive storms. The children collaborated, each working at a different computer. One child gave commands to the simulation program on one computer, while the other child typed a log of their trip into a word-processing program on the other machine. They began their story pro-saically—"Once upon a time . . . "—but soon became more involved in inventing and describing details of the trip. They took turns writing with the word-processing program. Their teacher and I added a word here and there.

Once upon a time we sailed across the sea. We were tired of the old country. Anyway we needed spices. The trip was fun but we didnt have room to carry too many cans of food, so we had to plan and we didn't have street signs so we used the stars. We had to figure out our movement by the angels of the stars. Then one night it was cloudy and rany and what a mess!!!!!!!!!!!!!!!!!!

The children debated over the spelling of *country*, course plottings, and a fair disciplinary action for a crew member who had taken extra food. They wrote an elaborate log, which they printed out and took home. One child's mother had an Apple II microcomputer at her office, so he took a copy of the diskette with the story on it to finish the next time he went to visit his mother at work. The other child used an Apple computer in math class to finish his version of the story.

Wondering about my article, I went back to my computer for an update on my mail. I had a message from the editor in California; she had already skimmed over the article and had written a few general comments about the style and content of the piece. I okayed a few changes and disagreed with others.

The children watched me read and write my message, and they then wanted to write something, too. I showed them that they could see the ID numbers of other people who were using The Source at the same time by simply typing **ONLINE**. Since they didn't know anyone who uses The Source, they decided to pick someone whose ID number had many 7s. They asked PQ7787 if she or he wanted to chat, but that person was busy, so they tried another who was interested in talking to them. The following is a transcript of the session (the children's comments appear in uppercase):

```
DO YOU WANT TO CHAT?
Ok.
HI.
I'm in Ohio and I work on The Source every day to do my business.
WE'RE KIDS AND WE JUST TRIED IT FOR THE FIRST TIME.
What grade are you in?
PLEASE GUESS.
I guess under fifth grade.
HOW DID YOU KNOW?
Since you said "Kids" I thought you must be under fifth grade.
Do you like computers?
YES, BUT WE CAN'T USE THEM VERY MUCH.
I'M NOT SURE I LIKE COMPUTERS.
What don't you like about computers?
WELL, WELL THEY MAKE YOU///ME DO EVERYTHING EXACTLY
AND THAT IS BORING. BUT, I DO LIKE COMPUTER GAMES. I BET YOU
DON'T. WHAT IS YOUR OPINION ABOUT COMPUTERS?
```

As they chatted, the children exchanged ideas about what to say to this "business guy" in Ohio. They didn't always agree on what to say, so, in some cases, they each wrote a response.

As these children played, they were spontaneously engaging in some of the classic lessons in a writing curriculum. They were learning about voice, audience, supporting details, planning a text, and spelling. They did this naturally because they were using writing as communication. They even changed their language slightly when they knew they were writing to a grown-up. They carefully considered the elements in their log/story and they even worried about spelling—perhaps because typing heightened their awareness of each letter as they searched for it on the keyboard and then saw it printed on the screen. They did not create a published text, of course, but the children had begun to feel that writing was fun.

This example has shown how adults and children can use the computer for communication in writing—doing writing activities that are enjoyable, pragmatic, and educational. Collecting the panoply of machines, attachments, programs, and services I had in my lab takes time, thought, money, and energy. The chapters in this book discuss why such efforts may be worthwhile and how to carry them out.

Writing and Computers

Children like to write together on the computer.

Demystifying the Writing Process

I

- "I can't think of what to say."
- "I don't know how to get started."
- "My thoughts are faster than my hand, so I forget what I wanted to write."
- "I can't find my mistakes. If I had known something was wrong, I wouldn't have written it."
- "I hate to recopy."
- "Why do I have to write?"

Although they may seem hackneyed, these comments by writers are not empty complaints. They reflect important factors involved in the writing process. Writing is a complex interplay of social, physical, and cognitive factors, as these comments suggest. Some writing difficulties have to do with physical factors, such as forming words on the page and the tedium of recopying. Others have to do with cognitive processes that writers often do not know they can control, such as making efficient use of their memory, attention, and problem-solving abilities. The most troubling questions—"I can't think of what to say" and "Why do I have to write?"—involve social issues about the importance of literacy and the ways in which we introduce it to our students. With experience, writers overcome these difficulties as they discover reasons to write and as they learn composing and revising strategies.

A teacher recently said to me, "I have a computer and a word-processing program, but I don't think I'm using them to the fullest advantage. What do I do with these things to help students improve their writing?" After talking with this teacher for a while, I realized that she expected a piece of software to be a lesson, rather than a writing tool. Either she didn't have a theory of writing or she had such a theory but hadn't made it explicit. All teachers who give writing assignments can benefit from thinking about the complex processes that lead to students' complaints. Even simple explanations of how people create and improve texts can help teachers turn the writing process into a learning process. The three chapters in this section present some writing theory that teachers can use to help their students develop writing skills and discover the joy of writing. These insights into the various processes involved in writing provide a framework for using computers and other tools to simplify and enhance written expression. The information is drawn from both cognitive science research and writing research, but it all relates to the practice and play of writing.

Writing Is a Social Process 1

Contrary to many people's expectations, the computer can be used to stimulate written communication. The computer can serve as a communication channel that is faster and more flexible than the post office. People who write using computers often feel compelled to write with other people. One reason for this may be that the computer is still a novelty in many settings, and since it is an expensive tool, people usually have to share it. More likely, however, the computer is used as a communication channel because of its capacities. It provides a writing environment in which the written correspondences among people are as natural as the connections among the electrons that make the computer work. The computer also reduces some of the physical barriers of collaborative writing.

This chapter addresses the social functions of writing; recounts the common beliefs—both myths and realities—about the appropriateness of computers for language learning; discusses the possible negative social effects of certain computer applications; and reviews the computer capacities and applications that can improve the teaching of writing as a communication activity.

COMMUNICATION AND CONTROL

A person sitting alone talking looks odd; yet this is often what writers do—they talk to themselves. In conversation, the listener asks questions, makes comments, smiles, or grimaces. The listener's reactions, though not always pleasant, guide the speaker. The writer has to do all this alone, however, pretending not to know what is said in the text to be able to evaluate whether it is clear, complete, and interesting. Writers have to learn to imagine their readers. They have to understand the interests, problems, and joys readers will find in their writing. Writers even have to learn to grimace at their own texts, but it is much more difficult to say "Ugh, that's horrible" about one's own writing than about someone else's.

3

Many teachers act as consultants in classrooms that have computers.

Because writing is seldom taught in the context of communication, student writers are often not aware of the many functions of writing in the world. A major problem in writing instruction is that it is done as an exercise—an end in itself. Teachers give topics, and, after studying models of "beautiful logical arguments," students write essays. Then the teachers grade or correct the essays, which takes away the students' sense of having nurtured their texts. Thus, the difficult activity of creating a text is more abstract than it need be, because it is stripped of the supports of communication. Although the written text is a work that must eventually stand on its own—clearly and completely expressing an idea—the process of creating it involves having something to say, someone to say it to, and the knowledge of how to say it.

In many writing classes, teachers give lectures about writing, leaving little opportunity for students to write or share their texts. The result of such writing classes without interaction is writing that doesn't speak. Writing instructors in an Ivy League university expository writing program, for example, lament the lack of voice—or strong personal style—in students' writing. One instructor noted that some students seem overtrained because they've been taught in high school to write like pompous windbags to impress the teacher. This teacher noted that their writing sounds like a committee or a machine turned it out. Another instructor complained that students come in knowing how to write prose in a mechanical way and the voice that speaks in the text is a dead voice, a voice full of received ideas. The voice dies when writing has lost its relation to speaking.

When students write to communicate, they find the activity easier than when they write for the sake of writing. Although writing can be the creation of a work of art and the stimulator of clear thinking, most students discover the joys of writing when they use text to communicate—to others as well as to themselves. The best way to help others learn how to write is to build text creation carefully on communication, so beginning writing—at any age—should be based on communication, such as writing a letter, persuading someone to do something, reading a text aloud, or writing with another person.

When composing letters, which requires imagining a reader, writers have a relatively easy time expressing themselves, because the writing experience is more social than it is when they write an essay. The potential reader is a listener and a reference point for the letter writer. As a teacher, I have found that when students write only for the teacher who will grade the paper, the writing tends to be stilted. Setting writing in a wider communication context can help students express themselves more naturally, even when they are writing formal essays. One way of widening the context is for teachers to read students' papers as interested participants in the writing process, rather than as judges.

As writers hear a reader's reaction, they can begin to internalize the social process. When they are writing for someone else, students often begin to write for themselves as well. Many people write diaries and notes to themselves. Works of fiction may also be created to entertain the writer. Such writing for oneself involves communication across what is sometimes the longest distance—to oneself; expressing the thoughts helps one see them objectively and, in turn, sharpens one's thinking.

Writers also talk to themselves about the process of creating the text. They think about what they want to write and pose questions to guide themselves. Some writers actually make comments like "I don't know anything about this. I'd better go talk to someone" or "That's what I really want to say. I think I'll start over again." Writers tend to carry on such internal dialogues when they are getting started on a piece or revising it, particularly when they are stuck.

Writing classes in elementary schools have recently begun to encourage a great deal of interaction. Children read their texts to one another, critique them kindly, and revise them—looking and sounding much like professional writers, who ponder and discuss alternative wording. Children who learn early that writing is not simply an exercise gain a sense of power that gives them confidence to write—and write a lot.

The Power of Writing

Writing is a powerful human activity. Great power is in the hands of the person who can write a speech, an essay, or the details of an event. People write well when they have the need, the power, and the support necessary to express themselves. The development of such skills also requires nurturing, training, practice, and encouragement.

Writers who work easily feel purpose, power, and confidence. They often have skills, tools, training, and time. Beginning writers who are confident that they have something to say or that they can find out what they need to know can even overcome some limits of training or development. Writers who don't feel that what they say matters have an additional burden that no skills training can help them overcome.

Some people who want to express themselves in writing but do not may be discouraged because they have no readers; therefore, they have not acquired the strategies that develop from anticipating constructive comments. Another problem for nonwriters is that many published texts reflect the language patterns and concerns of the powerful groups in society—adults, or people with "different" experiences. For this reason, people who do not feel part of the mainstream do not feel compelled to express themselves in writing. Thus, both social and logistical problems trap the thoughts of these potential writers inside them. Moreover, many students who feel powerless have been told that they do not speak good English, so they do not want to see their "bad" writing frozen on a page. Unfortunately, students who could benefit from simply writing and then reading their texts to others are often held back to do exercises on the basics of spelling, grammar, and punctuation before they are encouraged to write. In such cases, the students never master the specifics of grammar because they never have the chance to develop the generals—content and voice.

Helping students identify the ideas they want to communicate is one responsibility of writing teachers. In addition, we can help students who do not normally use standard English by encouraging them to write in their spoken dialect—whether it is black dialect, teenage dialect, or a personal style. As part of the revision process, these students can practice translating from the dialect in the draft to the standard dialect for the finished piece. Such approaches can stimulate students to take control over their writing and thinking processes.

To communicate effectively in writing, people need two types of control: they have to feel that what they say matters to others, whether the others are their family, fellow students, the community, or a professional group; and they need to control their own thought processes. They have to think through their ideas, decide how to express them, transform the ideas into written language, and evaluate the resulting texts. Some teachers are cautious about the use of computers because they feel that a powerful machine could stifle the control that is essential for writers to develop and maintain.

Fears about Computer Control

Common fears about computers are based on both facts and myths. Many of these fears involve the interplay between communication and control. People attribute power and even intelligence to the computer, and many believe that the computer controls people, so it is not a good tool for communication. Since communication requires freedom, creativity, and autonomy, many people believe that a stubborn, quantitative instrument like the computer might inhibit expression. The following passage reflects a common fear about the impact of computers in our society:

> It was our one hundred and ninth year in the computer. He was speaking for all of us. . . . He was a machine. We had allowed him to think, but to do nothing with it. In rage, in frenzy, he has killed us, almost all of us, and still he was trapped. He could not merely be. And so, with the innate loathing that all machines had always held for the weak, soft creatures who had built them, he had sought revenge. And in his paranoia, he had decided to reprieve five of us, for a personal, everlasting punishment that would never serve to diminish his hatred . . . that would merely keep him reminded, amused, proficient at hating man. Immortal, trapped, subject to any torment he could devise for us from the limitless miracles at his command.*

Computers are often portrayed as controlling, dehumanizing, and alienating entities. In fiction, computers have typically played the bad guys: they trap people, spy on them, and envy them. After using a computer a few times, people are usually stunned at its ability to perform tedious tasks quickly, so they attribute great powers, above and beyond speed, to these machines.

One controlling computer feature that many people resent is its demand for precision. Because computers have to be told exactly what to do, people have to interact with them more precisely than they do with other people. Computer users have to do things exactly the way the program requires or it doesn't work. When using a spelling program, for example, the student may have to type y, not YES, to indicate a correct spelling, which is an annoying, arbitrary requirement. In this demand for exact trivial interactions, the computer maintains control. People are easier to communicate with because they can understand that *y* stands for *yes*. Of course, people can learn the computer codes, but they can also put pressure on software designers to write programs that are as flexible as possible. Although the machine imposes certain constraints, programmers can try to predict a variety of possible responses. Nevertheless, no matter how smart the programmers are, they cannot predict all responses a variety of program users may give.

People also fear that as we program computers to do more and more for us, they will make humans superfluous, and that those uniquely human virtues of unpredictability, creativity, and soul will no longer have value in a machine-dominated society.

Thirteen-year-old Jack, who wrote the following piece, expresses another common concern—that computers may alienate people from one another:

*Harlan Ellison, "I Have No Mouth, and I Must Scream," in *Alone Against Tomorrow* (New York: Macmillan, 1971), pp. 25–26.

Computers and Kids

By the year 2001, experts are predicting that adults will not have to leave their home. Their jobs will all be done with computers at home. If the adults want to buy something, they will have to type their order into a computer and a teenager will come with a shopping cart and deliver their order. They will just have to write a check.

I (not the experts) am also predicting that by this time all schools will be eliminated as children (other than maybe prenursery through kindergarten age) will learn everything—math, English, foreign languages, etc. through the computer. Another thing they will learn from a teacher is how to play a musical instrument. There will also be summer camp. And there might even be a course at age 5–6 (or 7) to learn how to use a computer.

But ask yourself: are the courses taught by a teacher named above sufficient enough, even with summer camp for a child to socialize, to make friends, to find a member of the opposite sex with whom to live during his/her adult years? And if you answer no to the last part, do you really think the human race can survive if no one mates after the generation spoken about in this writing?

When Jack learned that one couple fell in love through a computer mail correspondence, later met in person, and married, his fears were not assuaged. "If everyone does everything on the computer, there will be no need to meet," he explained. This student has participated in social interactions around the computer. He still enjoys computer programming, writing with computers, and using a calculator, but he obviously realizes the potential social dangers of a computerized society. Although Jack's writing is immature in some ways, it reveals a genuine concern that people will not feel the impetus to go out if everyone has a computer at home. Since Jack is shy, he may be concerned that he would opt for the computer rather than talking to kids at school. Although he feels awkward, Jack welcomes having to be in social situations so that he can meet people. Another, more socially mature 13-year-old thinks that computers aren't very useful, and she can't understand why some kids get so wrapped up in computing. Her comment reflects an awareness of a potential social problem but less fear than Jack expressed: "I don't understand why everyone gets to wrapped up in computers. They're stupid."

Computers are fascinating and frightening when they seem to speak and write. First-time computer users are often delighted when the computer addresses them in some way—"It called me by my name" or "It talked to me!" They learn quickly that this interaction resulted from a rule in the computer program that said something like "Use the letters that were typed in at the beginning of the session every time you present a prompt"; thus, the computer responds, "Harry, good job!" or "Try again, Harry."

Another common fear is that people will become dependent on computers. When they depend on an expensive machine for adding or writing, people give computers control over their lives. Although prices are decreasing rapidly, computers are expensive—more expensive, certainly, than other tools, like pencils. So if someone becomes dependent on a computer at school but cannot afford a machine to use all the time, such a dependency would limit the person's freedom to act independently. If the computer-dependent skill is adding or writing, this is a significant loss of control. A junior high school teacher expressed concern that her eighth-graders had become fluent writers since using word-processing programs but that they would not be able to use them in the ninth grade because their high school does not have computers, nor do their families. The teacher felt responsible for making her students dependent on a machine that would not be readily available. She felt that returning to pencils and typewriters would turn her students off to writing, which they had enjoyed all year in her class. Since there are not enough available computers to make other tools useless, the solution is to use computers to make points about writing and to encourage the continued use of other tools (as discussed in Part II).

The most extreme dependency problem, which has developed recently, is based on the claim that one must use computers to be literate. Many school systems feel pressured to buy computers because, if they don't, their students won't be "keeping up" with the modern world. The problem is that many administrators and teachers have not had the time to figure out what to do with the computers once they get them. As a result, more money and effort are spent on selecting hardware and software than on helping teachers integrate computers into their curricula.

People also fear computers because reports on their importance have reached epidemic proportions. Current marketing pressure encourages computer use with little discussion about what the uses should be or the effects of computer programs. Such hard selling can instill fear and anger with the subtle message: "This machine is so powerful that we don't even have to tell you what it's for." With the widespread use of computers, some negative images have been replaced by unrealistically positive ones. In the movie *War Games*, for example, the computer is portrayed as a hero for helping deter a war (which it had originally started). Similarly, in commercials, a computer named Adam tells parents that it will save their children from educational doom. Such extreme claims, like the negative ones, are overstated.

The more freedom one wants to maintain in using the computer, the more technical knowledge is necessary. A person with little knowledge of computers can use preprogrammed lessons, games, bank transaction programs, and drills. Word-processing programs, however, require learning more about interacting with a microcomputer—learning the commands and the concepts to understand the parts of the program. Each additional activity, such as using a spelling checker, networking to other microcomputers, or creating an original game, require more savvy. Learning computing skills involves time and persistence but no particular genius, although some people find it easier than others to master the procedural and logical operations required in computer programming.

Fears of computer power are often compounded by many adults' fears that they are too old to understand or master computers. Adults are not used to learning new skills, and their fears of computers have been fed by the popular belief that they are more powerful and complicated than most other tools. Even though people are impressed by computer power, they quickly learn how stupid the machine really is. After a few experiences with inappropriate messages from programs, they learn that the computer cannot make many decisions that would be simple for a person. For example, to recognize a word or a name, a program does not consider a meaning; rather, it looks for sections of code that include the set of numbers representing the patterns of electrical flow that stand for "space," "letters," and "space." Since programs reduce all activities to numbers that represent instructions to the machine, it will be a long time before a computer can think—which is the ultimate control.

Computer scientists are divided in their feelings about computers. Some feel challenged to use the computer's powers of speed, instruction handling, and storage to carry out humanlike activities—solving puzzles, grading essays, and turning up the thermostat in a room that is too cold. These people are excited about the potentials of computer power and enjoy working and playing with it. Others, however, feel that the computer can be harmful because it is easy to misuse.

Computers store large amounts of information that programs collect, sort, and manipulate quickly. Thus, a great deal of information about charge accounts, tax records, and writing can be stored in and retrieved from computerized databanks. The productivity of secretaries who use word processors can be measurd by a program that records the number of keys they press per minute, and students' and teachers' activities can be tracked as they use certain computer instruction programs. People using computers to make mischief control and frustrate other people. Computer powers need not be used in such negative ways, however. The computers do only what they are told.

People have also feared that computers will replace them in the work-place—a fear based on the automation of many clerical jobs. One argument against this fear has been that as the computer takes over repetitive, boring tasks, people are free to do more interesting conceptual work. Philip Kraft, a social scientist, noted, however, that despite the argument that computers take over the drudge work, people's jobs have become less interesting when computers have become involved. Another social scientist, Harley Shaiken, found that when computers were introduced into the cutting industries, guiding the scissors through hundreds of layers of cloth, the workers had less control. Managers were the only people trained to use the computers, so they, not the workers, intervened when there was trouble.

Although Jack, the youngster who wrote "Computers and Kids," believes that computers could teach the major subjects—but not the artistic ones—few teachers who have used computers feel that computers could replace them. Teachers who enjoy guiding their students in a discovery process know that the computer stimulates learning in many ways, but they often find they have to work more, rather than less, when the computer is in the classroom. These teachers who use computers as dynamic textbooks often must appeal to administrators for assistants to help them manage the computers. Such a new emphasis indicates that computers are leading to role changes in the classroom.

Role Changing

As in other workplaces, roles in the classroom have changed when teachers bring in computers. Writing classes with computers tend to be student-centered. Teachers and students use the computer together, as a learning tool for writing and for other activities. Donald Graves and his colleagues have shown that teachers and children can work together productively in writing classes, and recent work with computers has suggested that, as the computer makes the writing process more public for children, they welcome their teachers into the collaborative process. In this way, the teacher who is willing to take some risks in writing at the computer with students has a chance to learn as well. Such teachers are participants in the classroom, rather than directors, as their contributions meld into collective stories. Although children love to perform at the computer keyboard, some teachers are cautious, at first, about writing and computing in public. They may feel that their first drafts do not set the proper example of a teacher's writing, and, since they have little or no experience using computers, they do not want to show the students their lack of skill. However, despite mistakes—which all people make—children do learn from working with their teachers. The children can model subtly on the teachers' writing, and the teachers are reminded by personal experience of what the students are doing. After struggling to learn to use a word-processing program for 2 months, a seventh-grade teacher in one of my classes said: "It was painful, but now I write more. What's more important is that now I know how my kids feel when they're learning something new and difficult. I felt like a kid again."

Teachers find that when they use word-processing programs in their classrooms, they have to give up some control of the class and leave some of the learning and structuring to the children's writing processes as their texts evolve. Children pick up the skills of interacting with the computer more easily than adults do, so if the teacher hasn't spent several months learning and practicing before introducing the computer to the children, the children may soon know more about using the computer than the teacher does.

Teachers who don't find that equalizing process invigorating should spend time mastering their use of the computer before teaching the class.

An open-classroom environment is created when several children are working at one or two computers in one part of the room while others work at their seats. The teacher of such a class must have several lesson plans going at the same time. Students at the computers may be working on an autobiography assignment, while the students at their seats work on vocabulary lessons. One group of students may be reading over their writing and making suggestions for improvements, while another group is revising according to suggestions made the day before. The teacher in such a class is a guide, directing the various activities.

The teacher also often acts as a consultant in the classroom, responding to a request for help, such as, "What do you think about Sandy's opening sentence, Ms. Walter. I like it, but he doesn't." The teacher is also a consultant on rules. When students working at the computer can't settle an argument about where to put commas in a sentence they are writing, the teacher could either tell them where to put the comma or offer a worksheet on using commas in compound sentences. In either case, the teacher is a consultant; his or her knowledge of grammar rules is most valuable when the students request it in the context of their needs as writers.

In computer writing classes, teachers are also called upon to be technicians. They have to know how to diagnose problems and answer questions, such as, "Why has the computer just stopped?" Someone in the classroom has

The computer is a writing instrument that is especially suited to collaboration.

to learn how to determine if the problem is in the hardware—in a disk drive or a chip; if it is a bug in the software; or if it was inadvertently caused by a student who pressed the reset key. The knowledge required to deal with such problems comes with experience, and that comes only from using the machine. A teacher can get a useful overview from a manual but must master the machine dynamically—by hands-on experience.

It is ironic that a tool that many have felt would cause alienation can be used instead as a catalyst for changing the classroom from a teacher-centered room with lectures to a student-centered room with a great deal of writing going on. In such a setting, children and teachers work together; they share tools, and they harness the power of the machine to their own ends.

ATTITUDES ABOUT COMPUTERS AND LANGUAGE LEARNING

Some teachers have objected to bringing computers into language education because they feel that computers, creativity, and writing are antithetical. They believe that, like the typewriter, the computer serves only prescribed, mechanistic purposes, as illustrated by the following passage from George Bernard Shaw's *Candida*:

> Prosperine: You've been meddling with my typewriter, Mr. Marchbanks.
> Marchbanks: I'm very sorry, Miss Garnett. I only tried to make it write. I assure you I didn't touch the keys. I only turned the wheel.
> Prosperine: Oh, now I understand. I suppose you thought it was a sort of barrel-organ. Nothing to do but turn the handle, and it would write a beautiful love letter for you straight off, eh?
> Marchbanks: I suppose a machine could be made to write love letters. They're all the same, aren't they?

Many humanists believe that interacting with machines stifles creativity. They feel that since language reflects thought, it is not reducible to specific sets of instructions, so computers could not be useful in any significant way for language activities. Even if computers could be made smarter, many people believe that machines should not do human activities such as writing.

Joseph Weizenbaum, a computer scientist, believes that computers are harmful because they focus learners only on forms, not on meanings, which are the essence of thought and learning. As an example of meaningless forms, Weizenbaum cites programs that guide children to write poems by putting together words following syntactic rules but ignoring meaning constraints. According to Weizenbaum, exercises that ignore meaning may lead to the view that meaning can be ignored beyond the school walls. Although form must be related to meaning in a poem—and the computer cannot analyze contents—some software developers have used the computer to guide the learning of structures, because such patterns as the underlying syntactic structures of sentences have their own meaning. Also, when teachers are creating lessons to help students transfer general principles from one activity to another, highlighting common structural features seems to be worthwhile. When discussing paragraph development, for example, some teachers focus students' attention on relationships between topic sentences, which appear as first sentences, and the supporting details that follow. Although the content of the paragraph is most important, focusing on paragraph structure as well provides students with techniques to use in developing and evaluating their texts.

Language and Drills

Much of the skepticism about the use of computers for language development arises from parents' and teachers' perceptions of the software available on the market. When asked, "Do you have any software to improve writing?" many publishers present grammar and spelling drill programs under the headings: "Writing," "Reading," and "Language Arts." These drills are often sold because they are relatively easy and inexpensive to produce, rather than because they help students learn to write.

Such programmed learning, or **computer-aided instruction (CAI)**, is an obvious use of the computer. The computer workbook presents exercises one by one and gives immediate feedback on the right and wrong answers. It can direct, or **branch**, students to additional exercises for troublesome material. CAI also includes **tutorials**, which present formulas for punctuation rules, examples, and explanations when students give wrong answers in the practice sessions. Most teachers who use such drills augment them with writing and less structured language arts activities. Few of these writing teachers fear that such tutorials could replace them, because writing is too complex to be taught or learned in prescribed steps.

Comprehensive tutorial and drill programs in language arts curricula are often packaged as **computer-managed instruction (CMI)** systems, which can keep track of students' answers, and weight their scores according to how many tries it took them to get a right answer. These programs can also keep track of accumulated results on exercises and tests. Such systems have been attractive to teachers who believe that language learning involves building a repertoire of skills and knowledge, such as spelling and punctuation rules. Comprehensive programs build on established curricula that include the various skills that presumably make up the ability to write. The fifth-grade segment in one large program, for example, includes drills on words with vowel diphthongs, compound words, and punctuating compound sentences.

A student must do well on one unit before going on to the next. Teachers who use such an approach might welcome the help of the computer in presenting, grading, and recording all work, but many find such programs too restrictive. They feel that large, managed systems confine the students to a learning process that does not foster writing development and that the management value of the computer is not worth the expense or the maintenance problems. The teacher should be able to change the order of lessons for a particular child, passing over a section that is frustrating or does not seem necessary.

A big selling point for using computers in education has been the interactiveness of computer programs. In drills and tutorials, however, the computer does the talking, while the students express themselves only in a limited way by pressing number or letter codes for a small set of available responses. Pressing number keys may be a useful way to signal concept knowledge, but students need practice in expressing themselves in writing. The ability to make correct choices on multiple-choice drills on subject–verb agreement is not the same as the ability to write well. In fact, many students who succeed on subject–verb agreement drills have trouble with subject–verb agreement in their writing. Good mechanics tend to come with clear, mature writing, but good writing comes only with practice. Spelling and grammar drills may be useful in specific situations, but only when presented in the context of expressive writing activities.

Despite a general aversion to computers and a specific aversion to drill and practice, many language teachers are excited about the potential of CAI in the language class. Since children often have the most trouble mastering the skills that are the most boring for teachers to repeat, teachers look for tutorial and drill programs on spelling and grammar. Also, since teachers are expected to show that their students have improved in concrete ways, they seek exercises on measurable skills. When they see the available programs, however, they are often disappointed. Typical complaints are that there are mistakes in the program instructions, that the drill becomes boring, and that the screen and the computer graphics are difficult for children to read, especially learning-disabled children. Teachers often find that the programs do little more than printed workbooks but cost much more. In addition, although language drills may help students improve their scores on drill-type tests, research on writing has suggested that grammar drills do not help people write better.

Teachers who have feared controlling influences from the computer do not welcome programs that are merely more expensive versions of work-books. Drill software *is* controlling—not necessarily intentionally, but because the easiest pieces to program are those that require simple responses, such as pressing number keys that represent answers. Real writing is messy and interesting, and it is not predictable by numbers representing pre-programmed answers.

Language professionals—teachers, curriculum coordinators, and re-searchers—have expressed three general attitudes toward the computer.

Some would destroy all computers if they could. Since they can't or don't want to waste their time in such an effort, they simply do not use computers in their teaching or writing. They often argue that computers have nothing to do with art, especially writing, and that students should not be forced to use computers simply because they are the educational fad of the day. Although it is well meaning, this approach pits creativity against technology. Spontaneous, playful activities—such as drawing and writing poetry—are contrasted to dull, workaday technological activities. Such an anticomputer view may widen the educational gap between children whose families have computers at home and those whose families do not. Many students are affected by computers despite their teachers' attempts to protect them. For example, youngsters from poor communities who don't go to college often get jobs doing data entry or coding on computers. Computers also keep track of their debts, traffic violations, and bank accounts. Those who were never exposed to creative uses of computers may feel helpless in the face of computer power, while those who have used a computer for writing, programming, or graphics understand the limits as well as the power of the machine.

A second attitude is that the computer can be useful but that teachers, software developers, and researchers should be responsible for ensuring that computer-aided instruction is as humanistic as possible. According to this view, learners should be in control of CAI programs by selecting program options, content, or pacing. For example, the children and teachers could type in the words for a spelling drill program, enter their names so that the program can address them personally, or practice identifying mistakes in verb phrases before dealing with noun phrases.

The problem with this approach is that CAI is inherently controlling, so attempts to alter it are largely cosmetic. Computer programs work by exact steps, and they respond only to specific input. Thus, when programs are drilling or teaching, they do not leave room for spontaneity. No matter how many options a learner has in using a drill program, the program maintains control. In a program designed to teach spelling, for example, teachers or students can enter their own list of words for practice. They can enter numbers to determine the order of word presentation, and they can alter the speed of word presentation. Nevertheless, the program structures the process and routes students through a maze of exercises, and they spend their time pressing the keys that stand for answers rather than writing. As the program decides whether the student is right or wrong, it takes authority over the learning process. Students should be apprised of writing standards, but, to develop writing skills, they also need time to compose and revise actively. Programmed activities may offer practice in making judgments about correctness, but the students must develop control over the process.

Programmed lessons, even when they are individualized, do not help students write, because writing does not build incrementally from specific steps. Whether intentionally or not, CAI is rooted in a behaviorist theory of learning, which recommends drills with small increments, so that the learner's progress through an exercise is reinforced by small successes. Success is an encouragement to learning, but writers need the particular success of communicating to readers or the success of making their own discoveries. The most popular activities in writing classes are those that stimulate children to write a lot—to experiment with ideas and wording. Such experimentation involves some failure, but it is failure—and sometimes messiness—that leads to growth. In such a context, grammar, spelling, paragraph organization, and style evolve from discussions of students' papers. Prepared packages do not leave the flexibility necessary for developing lessons in the context of the students' writing.

Some learning activities—such as learning multiplication tables or Chinese characters—do require memorizing. Students might want to learn such information in a drill format, but rote mastery of information is only a small part of learning and understanding. We also need process knowledge, which helps us acquire and use facts. We need knowledge of how to use information to solve problems, to understand a text, or to make a prediction. Programmed drills and practice may be appropriate for building knowledge or for passing certain objective tests, but learning to write involves using information in creative ways. Personalizing drills may not be enough; the time and effort would be better spent in developing activities that use computers and other tools to help stimulate writing production.

The Tools Approach

The third approach of language professionals is to use the computer as a tool for writing. This means not only using the computer in much the same way as we use pencils and typewriters, but also exploiting its interactiveness and its other unique capacities. People who support this approach generally feel that, if it is used, CAI should be a minor support—for example, to help children learn punctuation when they ask for help as they write. Advocates of the tools approach believe that the computer can be a powerful communication asset in education as well as in the professional world. They feel that the computer gives writers more control over their writing, since it offers a communication channel as well as physical and cognitive aids. The tools approach also assumes that writers use a variety of programs—word-processing programs and others. By selecting from a set of powerful computer tools, writers take added control over the writing process.

The tools model of computing in education is based on a cognitive-developmental approach to learning. According to this view, writers learn to write by writing—by creating texts, listening to others' reactions to their writing, and revising. Thus, rather than learning by reacting, as in the CAI model, writers learn by doing. Psychologists refer to the ability to understand and control one's own thinking as "executive" capacity. Since writers' stories, essays, and notes are externalized thoughts, they are taking creative control of their thinking as they write and revise. Flexible and responsive writing instruments can aid in this activity.

Recently, software publishers have presented word-processing programs as educational tools, but many teachers are not aware of how to use them for writing instruction. One reason for this is that word processors have mistakenly been described as fancy typewriters. Another problem may be that the word-processing program is so flexible a tool that teachers do not see its pedagogical value. Later chapters in this book offer guidelines for using these flexible tools as instructional aids.

Teachers also resist using word-processing programs because so few computers are available to them. For this reason, and because we do not have conclusive research indicating that using a word-processing program increases writing quality, computers should be used in conjunction with the more plentiful tools: pencils, paper, and dictionaries. Even if word processing were found to be related to better scores on writing tests, the studies would probably show that such improvement takes longer than a school term. We have seen, however, that writers who use word-processing programs enjoy using them because they feel they can work more freely, and many writers feel that such free expression leads to good writing. Finally, word-processing programs and other communications software offer writers more supports than traditional tools do, although traditional tools still have value.

PUBLIC WRITING, COLLABORATING, AND NETWORKING

The traditional writing setting—with traditional instruments—is usually a lonely one. Only one person can hold a pencil and only one person at a time can compose comfortably on a piece of paper lying flat on a table. Two people can collaborate by discussing ideas for a text or by writing different sections, but the composing act is individual, and the separate pieces have to be jointed by cutting and pasting or recopying.

The traditional writing setting is also quiet, except for the sound of the typewriter keys and the crumpling of rejected pages. Although the term *voice* in writing is an abstraction from the word *voice* in "spoken voice," the richest, most natural writer's voice is the one that rings with speech. Young writers should have a sense of talking with their writing if they are to find their voice. Teachers and researchers have noted that when a computer is used as a communication instrument in a classroom, the children spontaneously share their writing—both the problems and the successes. The following scene from a writing class that uses computers illustrates the collaborative, public nature of writing on a computer:

Cathy was writing the personal statement for her college application. Pretending that she was talking to a long-lost aunt, she wrote quickly about what was important in her life. She did not worry about mistakes, because she knew she would be able to correct them fairly easily with the word-processing commands. Several classmates at a table near her computer were attracted by the speed and noise of her typing, so they came over to read the statement. One boy said, "They like to hear about lots of activities. Tell them more about all the stuff you've been doing in student government and the antinuclear movement." Another girl thought the tone was too informal: "Organize it around themes and use anecdotes from your life to hit home some points. But don't chat." Cathy's classmates also enjoyed catching her spelling mistakes.

Working in such a collaborative environment helps students learn some of the purposes, forms, strategies, and powers of writing.

Public Writing

As the example of Cathy and her classmates illustrates, writing on a computer is more public than the traditional writing environment—and more noisy, in a good sense of the word. Although any writing environment can be designed to include discussion and sharing, the classroom with computers may be most appropriate for interaction. Student writers usually have to share the computer; twenty students may share one or two computers in a classroom. Writers who share equipment in labs may be sitting in front of individual computer screens, but each person's text is in full view of a neighbor or passerby. The shared tool, which displays the text upright, invites group reading as well as group writing.

The students who use the computer near the classroom door in one junior high school have an especially large readership. A student who was writing a mystery story intentionally left it at a climax just before the end of class each day to keep the passersby in suspense. He often incorporated his classmates' comments the next day, but he had trouble finishing the story, because he enjoyed watching his readers keep up to date with his drama as they filed out of class.

Often, students read someone else's work while they are waiting to use the computer. Waiting in line to use the computer is not the best use of one's time, of course, but those moments of transition when one student turns the computer over to another student can lead to sharing ideas for writing. When computers are new to the classroom, the comments mostly involve advice on how to use the machine, but discussion eventually turns to the content and style of the text.

Although writers can get useful feedback when they work in public places on an upright screen, some find it disturbing to expose their writing to the world before they are ready—a discomfort that is more common among adults than among children. In most cases, however, a computer-sharing group can agree on rules of etiquette and specific procedures for making comments, so the students also have a chance to discuss their preferences for the writing environment. Such shared writing activities help writers learn about voice and their reader's needs.

Networking

The communication capacities of the computer provide a social context for writing. A brief sociology of computer systems will illustrate these capacities. There are two types of computer systems—time-sharing systems and stand-alone systems. **Time-sharing** systems, which are like communities—consist of **mainframes** or **minicomputers** that have large memories and various resources. The time-sharing community is made up of individual **terminals**, each of which has some resources—a keyboard, a display screen, and a small amount of temporary memory. The terminals connect to the central computer via cables or telephone lines. The individuals in the time-sharing community share processing time, programs, storage space, and resources like the printer.

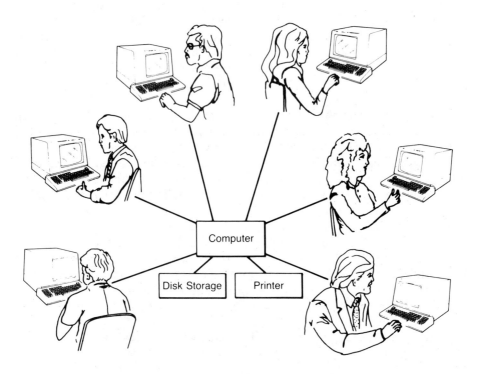

A time-sharing computer system is like a community.

Work sessions on a time-sharing system begin in the public programs—the operating system or system-managing program, messages, and other shared programs. The individual user of the time-sharing system starts with communication—reading messages from the managing program, answering or sending personal messages, checking the list of people working on the computer at the same time, and perhaps engaging in a chat. Since the storage areas and programs on time-sharing systems are shared, communications among people using the individual terminals occur spontaneously.

In contrast, the stand-alone microcomputer system is designed to be self-sufficient and self-monitored. The computer, display screen monitor, printer, and programs usually reside in one place and are used by one person at a time. A person beginning a work session on a microcomputer communicates with the computer but not with other people, unless the micro is networked—that is, connected by a shared component or communications firmware and software through the telephone lines (as illustrated in the Introduction and discussed more fully in Chapters 8 and 12). Writers can also share programs and storage by sharing the diskettes they use on the microcomputer.

Time-sharing systems were once the only available computer setups, but stand-alone microcomputers have taken over because they cost less. Although many colleges have time-sharing systems, most elementary and secondary schools have micros. Micros have been the most popular systems in schools, but a trend back toward time-sharing systems is beginning. One of the major suggestions in this book is that schools with microcomputers should invest in networking capacities, even if this means buying fewer computers, because the social benefits of communication give the networked computer much more educational value, especially for writing instruction.

Electronic Bulletin Boards

Electronic bulletin boards, usually available on time-sharing systems, are postings that all users of the system can read and write. Unlike most files,

A stand-alone computer system is like an individual—independent but capable of joining a community.

which belong to individuals who use the sytem, the electronic bulletin board is shared by everyone on the network. Using the passwords they receive when they subscribe to the network, individuals read public bulletin boards from their terminals or from their micros via phone lines.

Electronic bulletin board messages are often cryptic, but communicating with others via a bulletin board highlights the communication functions of writing. Because the bulletin board is displayed in the same screen space as the writers' texts on the computer, the entire writing environment—the keyboard, the screen, and the computer operations—is associated with general communication.

We might eventually find that mixing prose writing with chatty message writing has a negative effect on the quality of formal texts. Writers who post messages, send mail, and chat on the computer might develop an understanding of the communication functions of writing, but they might have trouble making the texts they write for school or business conform to standards for written text. Student writers can, however, develop the ability to use both formal and informal voices and an understanding of the specific forms and functions of texts.

Electronic Mail

Electronic mail programs offer writers social supports as well as logistical ones, such as automatically setting up the memo form and bringing it to the recipient's **directory**, or individual storage space in the computer. Writers who use time-sharing and networked computers tend to write many communications that they would normally speak. Some people send electronic mail to people in nearby rooms merely to save the time and energy of walking. Some people even use electronic mail to communicate, for fun, to others in the same room, to whom they could talk face-to-face. Such computer communication could have a negative effect if it limited face-to-face communication. Face-to-face interactions should be part of everyone's experience, and some people fear that electronic written communication will replace such direct human interaction. Thus far, however, computer talk has extended communication rather than replacing it. It seems to provide additional communication channels for many people. In her work on computer cultures, sociologist Sherry Turkle reports on **hackers**—computer experts who play as well as work on computers. Many hackers have difficulty relating to other people in face-to-face contact, but they find that electronic mail stimulates their communication as they engage in extended, often personal correspondences that they might otherwise avoid. It seems that people will communicate more in writing, not less. For example, teachers in remote areas of such states as Vermont share lessons and ideas about computing applications via computer networks, especially during the winter, when traveling long distances to meetings is difficult.

It is not necessary or even advisable for all writing in school to be done on the computer, but written communication is likely to be useful in the transition to mature writing as well as for practical communications. Such computer applications have a different value for writers at different developmental levels; these psychological effects are discussed in Chapters 7 through 11.

In addition to the social value of electronic communication, mail programs have logistical value, which is important because easy communication can mean more communication. When a writer uses a computer system and phone lines, a recipient can read and respond to correspondence much faster than when letters are carried physically through the post office. The communication process is speeded up as a computer user reads mail, composes a response, revises it, sends it, and perhaps even receives a response in one sitting.

An executive in a publishing company that develops software but has not yet computerized its internal office communication systems wrote the following memo, which suggests some of the benefits of electronic mail.

TO: Jack
FROM: Loreen
SUBJECT: Electronic Mail
DATE: November 10

I have beside me a copy of your memo on the new technology series. I wrote a response on my wp [word processor]. It took me one hour to plan, write, revise, polish, and get a neatly typed copy of my response to you. If I had done that one year ago before we had the wp, the process would have taken a day because I would have typed two drafts, given one to the secretary to type neatly, edited that, and then she would have had to retype it again.

Now, I'll leave my memo in my "out" basket. It will get into your "in" basket late this afternoon. You'll dictate your response before you leave tonight. Your secretary will type it. You'll edit that hard copy. She'll make corrections. Then the "out" and "in" basket process will take another 1/2 day, and then I will send on the copies of both our memos to Wilma, which will take another 1/2 day.

If our word processors were networked and we could use electronic mail programs that run through modems and phone lines, we would cut out at least three steps and one day. Just think of all the new memos I could write you in that time. And how much editing the secretary could get done.

Mail programs also handle other logistical tasks for writers. For example, they set up the framework for a memo or letter as the writer fills in each piece of information:

```
TO:
SUBJECT:
CC:
MESSAGE:
```

Mail programs on microcomputers can fill in the writer's name automatically if each program disk has a password system, and a mail program on a time-saving system with an internal clock and date record can fill in the time and date automatically:

```
TO: JJONES
FROM: CDAIUTE
DATE: 6 January 1984
MESSAGE:
```

The message, of course, is left to the writer.

One drawback of using mail programs for writing activities is that they usually do not include word-processing capacities. A writer using a mail program can make changes only with the delete key, which means deleting all the last words written to get back to the previous sentence where the change has to be made. Most programs offer a special command for inserting a text written with a word-processing program on the same system into the mail format. For example, in the mail program on one minicomputer, the writer who has filled in the "To:" and "From:" portions of a memo can press CTRL INSERT and type in the name of the text file created with the word processor on the system. When the writer gives the **SEND** command by pressing the ESC key, the text is sent with the memo heading.

There are few mail programs for microcomputers because not all micros are networked, although the number of people networking their micros is rapidly increasing. Microcomputer users can share programs, texts, and messages by sharing the diskettes on which their files are stored. A **diskette** is a 3½-, 5¼-, or 8-inch plastic square that stores programs and texts in separate sections called **files**. The easiest way to set up an electronic mail system on micros is to set up mail diskettes that have a word-processing program and files set aside in individuals' names. Thus, Colette.mail would be my mail file, with messages added from the people who share the disk. When I read my mail, I can decide to erase, copy, or save the messages. Such a system does not provide confidentiality, of course, so the participants have to agree not to read or change anyone else's mail.

Electronic mail correspondences have been started in several settings to help children learn the value and fun of writing. For example, long-distance computer communication was set up so that children in classrooms in Southern California could share their experiences with children in Alaskan villages. In the most technologically simple form, the children fill a micro diskette with messages, stories, and news items and send the diskette to the other school via the post office; the children at the other school return a revised and expanded diskette. After such an exchange, the children see responses to their stories and note changes made in them by their distant peers. Classrooms with access to The Source, Compuserv, or other networking facilities don't have to wait for the mails, but they have the extra chores of setting up, maintaining, and paying for the computer communications.

Computer Conferencing

Computer conferencing systems allow several people at different locations to participate in written discussions at any time. Computer conference files are named according to topic, and the participants can join the conference at their convenience—day or night. Conferences on time-sharing systems have the advantage of providing programs that automatically sign, time-stamp, and send a user's entry to all or a specified subset of the other participants.

Sharing conference files on diskettes has the same value as corresponding on networks, but there are fewer automatic functions. Also, if several participants are writing and reading at the same, they have to work on copies of the master conference diskette, and, after making their contributions, they have to copy their entries onto the master. Such a system makes changing prior entries or inserting new material difficult, because only the most recent copy of a file is saved. Nevertheless, computer conferences on diskettes can be interesting arenas for airing and sharing ideas in writing.

The original reason for developing computer conferences was to provide a constant, flexible, and fast channel for discussion. The computer conference can be a tool for consolidating and transmitting ideas in writing at a time when the writer feels most communicative, most excited, or most confused. The computer conference was first developed to reduce the lag time between scientific discoveries and their presentation at professional conferences. Since publication of a discovery in a scientific journal often appears as much as two years after the discovery is made, the journals serve more to acknowledge ideas than as active interchanges between researchers. One of the first computer conferences was a system called Electronic Information Exchange System (EIES), developed at the New Jersey Institute of Technology to help researchers keep up with recent developments in their fields.

At in-person conferences, individuals' on-the-spot comments depend as much on such factors as assertiveness and political clout as on the value of each person's contribution. Some of these social considerations may be bypassed in anonymous computer conferencing networks. Writing ability may, however, replace social prowess as a determiner of success in a computer conference, so computer conferencing may increase the importance of writing in school settings as well as in scientific forums.

Using EIES, a group of sociologists convened a computer conference on the effects of computer conferencing. For one month, the participants kept notes on their thinking and research as they debated with one another in the public files. The participants wrote when they wanted to; they had the time to think carefully and prepare their responses. The following is a segment of two participants' contributions to this computer conference on computer conferences:

C 72 CC 194 (MURRY TUROFF—HUMOR)

My intuition leads me to feel that humor is a key element in prompting group cohesion on systems of this sort. I think in other communication forms, we take it very much for granted and are not aware that we have to look carefully to determine its actual degree of necessity for any group communication process. As opposed to a face-to-face meeting, humor gets documented in systems of this sort, and in practically every system that has ever been built there have been specific conferences set up to collect humor and conventional folklore. There are two types of reactions that this produces that lead to difficulties. 1. That Congress might make hay out of government funds being used to support people having fun in such a manner. 2. That work is not supposed to be fun.

My concern really comes down to the following two items: 1. Systems of this sort appear to raise issues we have never really viewed as significant for study, and I believe that the role of humor in the group process is one that deserves considerably more attention than it has received. 2. The ability of the computer to process means that there are a host of auxiliary services and structures that can be incorporated in a communication environment to foster the use of humor and other tension relaxation methods (games, e.g., bridge; producing funny remarks by having the computer modify a human's comment, etc.)

C72 CC209 ROBERT BEZILLA (ROBERT, 213) 4/20/77 11:15 AM

(In reference to C 72 CC 194—Turoff—Humor) I can't suggest any experiments on the use of humor in CC, but the following areas of use by humor may be of help to anyone who is working on the problem.

1. Humor as an assessment tool   A. As a means of assessing the intelligence, sophistication of a new acquaintance in a socially acceptable way.   B. As a means of assessing group membership, i.e., does the new acquaintance understand the in-humor of the group. 2. Humor as a socializing mechanism   A. Previous suggestions about its use as an "icebreaker."   B. Previous suggestions about its use as a means of creating multi-stranded relationships. NOTE: Both, however, may be closely related to

the assessment function. 3. Rhetoric—the use of satire, irony, sarcasm, etc. to underscore, vivify, call attention to the point one is making.*

The first entry illustrates the value of writing for clarifying ideas. Turoff expresses a few ideas and then sums them up clearly and concisely. If he then wanted to write a paper, he would already have a few concise sentences with which to begin it. In this way, the computer conference provides an environment for expression; later, the writer can make an electronic copy of good sections from a conference to use in a paper.

Besides being able to work good segments of conferences into texts in a word-processing program without having to retype them, participants can collect and store the computer conference entries in a central place and consult them at any time. This would be very difficult to do on paper. Thus, as a communication event, computer conferencing lies somewhere between talking and writing letters. It has the immediacy of talking but the permanent record and sometimes the consolidation of writing. Although face-to-face conferences have a social value that the computer environment does not, computer conferencing may provide a communication opportunity for people who would not otherwise have such in-depth discussions and for those who are developing writing skills.

Collaborative Writing

The following scene is typical of writing classes that use computer word-processing programs. Three children are clustered around the computer. First, Adam helps Alex learn to use the word-processing program as Michael looks on. All three boys then progress from discussing the word-processing operations to collaborating on a history assignment. Together, they develop a piece about the Civil War—each boy adding details and arguing about whether the war did or did not help America. They expand the text as they relate through it. Sometimes, they respond to one another by changing the text, rather than by talking. The collective work emerges with no handwriting differences to identify individual writers. The children even change one another's sentences slightly, so that few sentences remain that were written by an individual author. The voice is not as unified as if it were written by one author, but all of the children have learned something about collecting details for a piece, using text for arguing, and anticipating a reader.

The computer's ability to copy and to incorporate the writers' changes automatically simplifies the logistics of collaborative writing. Since collaborative writing is easier on a computer than it is with pen or typewriter, the

*R.S. Hiltz and M. Turoff, *The Network Nation: Human Communication via Computer* (Reading, Mass.: Addison-Wesley, 1978), p. 84.

computer can be used as a catalyst for shared writing. The ease of electronic copying could, of course, lead to some undesirable sharing, but teachers can address the issue head on, by specifying when it is all right to copy others' files and when it is not.

Two writers who collaborated on an article about family life kept notes in one computer file that each could copy onto her own diskette and then incorporate into individual pieces. Each writer composed a paper with a different focus—one on children's views of the family and the other on parents' views. After reading both papers, one of the writers made an outline for a comprehensive piece. She marked sections of each person's printed text and noted where they fit in the outline. The computer allowed her to copy each section into a master diskette with the outline. A new text—composed of parts of the two separate texts—was ready in about ten minutes. The two writers then sat together at the computer, reading the text, smoothing out the phrasing, adding transitions between sections, and rethinking the conclusion. The ease of making changes made it possible to work on the piece separately and then join it later. In this way, writers communicate via writing. They can anticipate the audience of a text as their peers become active readers before their eyes—readers who not only read but actually change the text.

Writers can also create texts together from different terminals. On a time-sharing system, they can use a **link** program that allows them to work in the same computer space at the same time. Since the cursor is the only point for entering text into the computer, however, each writer must wait until the other has written a response and has relinquished control of the cursor. This is similar to waiting one's turn in conversation. The CHAT program mentioned in the Introduction is an example of such a link program.

Several years ago, computer scientist Ted Nelson introduced the concept of "hypertext"—text that is created, read, and added to by many authors. In a short time, a hypertext can be started in New York; sent to Chicago, where it is expanded; sent on to St. Louis, where it is rearranged; and returned to New York, where it is again expanded. In the future, hypertext will be augmented not only by many writers but also by various modes of communication, such as graphics. Hypertext may one day become the most common form of writing. Meanwhile, creating hypertext is a useful instructional technique.

SUMMARY

This chapter has discussed common fears about computers and the relative appropriateness of these fears, especially as they relate to the use of computers for developing language skills. Computers do not by nature stifle communication. This chapter has offered specific suggestions on how the computer can be used to enhance communication, which is central to the writing process. Using the computer as a communication machine has helped many writers feel increased control over the writing process. Writers also gain control of their writing by being able to use a powerful machine to carry out massive, tedious editing tasks quickly and efficiently. When the computer takes over some of the tedious tasks, such as erasing or moving paragraphs and recopying, writers are freer to concentrate on the logic, organization, and clarity of their writing. In these activities, writers are using their particularly human potential for thinking and expression, rather than focusing on the mechanics of incorporating changes and recopying. The next chapter discusses such physical factors in more detail.

Writing Is a
Physical Process

2

For many years, learning to write meant learning penmanship and trying to write essays. We learned to form letters and then, almost immediately, it seemed, we learned to grapple with the structures of argumentative essays. Writing was physical—then metaphysical. Although writing involves the mind, the heart, and the environment, the physical factors of writing are the most obvious. These physical factors affect the beginner's enjoyment of writing, and they are often oversimplified or taken for granted, so it is important to consider the impact of the physical aspects of writing on thinking.

This chapter will discuss the important manual activities involved in using word-processing programs and will illustrate what writers have discovered about the physical pros and cons of using the computer as a writing instrument. The discussion of the benefits and drawbacks of using a word processor may seem contradictory, because this complex tool has myriad effects. As we progress through discussions of writing theory and computer use in later chapters, however, any contradictions can be resolved with increased information about creative applications of computer tools for writing instruction.

THINKING FINGERS

Our early encounters with writing are physical—4- and 5-year-olds in literate cultures often decorate their drawings with the letter symbols they see around them. In school, children learn to form capital letters in one-inch cages of solid lines and lowercase letters within dotted lines. They carefully draw their names, copy from books, and sometimes "write" images for the sounds they hear. As writers mature, however, they want their thoughts to pour effortlessly through their fingers. The physical act of writing isn't very popular. Although a goal in early writing is to form letters correctly and neatly, writers soon want to be able to work quickly as well. They want their hands to move as quickly as their thoughts. Writers who can speak their ideas—at an average talking speed of about 180 words per minute—to secretaries, who then transcribe the words into written pages, have the quickest means of getting their ideas on paper. Many people can type much faster than they can write by hand, so typists also have a fast means of writing—if, of course, they can think of what to say.

Recently, as computers have become writing tools, writers and teachers have refocused their attention on writing as a physical process, and many of their initial impressions are favorable. They have found that computers can simplify the physical process of writing, making it more efficient and more fun. Many writers are particularly excited about being able to revise texts endlessly by giving commands to the computer rather than by recopying.

People have also reported drawbacks of computer writing. Some writers find that the computer can be crankier than other writing instruments. Adult writers also complain that learning to use a computer is difficult at first. Sometimes, writers who have been successful using pens, pencils, or typewriters resist experimenting with the new instrument; some even associate a particular pen with their creative thinking. The majority of writers, however, feel that the effort involved in mastering the computer as a writing instrument is worthwhile, because it eventually saves them time and energy.

Using a Keyboard

Writers can use a computer most efficiently by touch-typing. This frees them to look at their notes, the text, or the ceiling as they think. Even children want to be able to type without looking at the keys. They like to watch the words appear on the screen, and they feel liberated when they can get their ideas out quickly.

Touch-typing involves positioning the hands over the center row of keys—the home row—and striking each key with a specific finger. This process makes looking at the keys unnecessary. Many people who are not trained in touch-typing—including children, programmers, and journalists—are fast hunt-and-peck typists. They look at the keyboard, but they are so familiar with it that they can type very quickly. Nevertheless, the criss-cross movements they make to strike keys usually take more time than touch-typing would. When hunt-and-peck typists have to refer to notes, they lose time or lose their place, looking back and forth from the notes to the keyboard.

Typing, rather than forming letters with a pen or pencil, speeds up some writers' work and makes writing more pleasurable for those who would avoid it because it is slow or it hurts their hands. In particular, young children who have not yet mastered handwriting find pressing keys easier than forming letters.

Writing on a computer can also be much easier than handwriting for the physically or perceptually handicapped. Allen Purvis, an experienced researcher and writing teacher at the University of Illinois, found that a word-processing system was helpful to an extremely bright high school boy who had underdeveloped physical abilities. Even though the boy was mentally capable of writing good English themes, he had never handed one in until he was able to use a word-processing system to type it and make corrections easily.

Writers who are already good typists when they begin word processing find that using the computer gives them more writing power and more time. Since these writers are comfortable typing, the computer presents little additional burden. Some make changes directly on the keyboard as they read from the screen. Others note changes as they reread and evaluate the printed copy of the text. Even the writers who mark revisions on hard copy find that entering revision commands on the keyboard is more efficient than re-typing.

Many nontypists who learn about computer capacities become motivated to learn to type. Although traditional typing did not interest them, they want to learn to type so that they can use the computer. Once writers see that the writing process can be more dynamic with the computer, they decide to make the effort of learning to type. It seems that writing is most interesting and fun when it is fast—as it can be when one types on the computer.

Sometimes, however, typing is a drawback. Molly, a teenage girl, was using the computer to write a short story for English class. As she typed, she consciously practiced the touch method, positioning her hands on the home row and looking only at the screen or at her notes. She proceeded to write her opening scenes slowly and methodically but suddenly yelled to a classmate, "Give me a pencil and paper!" She then wrote feverishly, in a scrawl that no one else could understand, ignoring the lines on the paper. As Molly later explained, "The story was writing itself, and I didn't want to lose the idea that popped into my head." Her typing skills did not give her enough speed to capture the idea. She later typed the story on the computer because she knew she would have to revise it and would not want to recopy. Most writers eventually learn to type quickly, but they must also consider ways of integrating the computer with their other writing tools while they are learning to type. In a study of 11- and 12-year-old writers, I found that the students could write more words by hand in 15 minutes than they could with the computer, even after using it for 6 months. This suggests that those who have experience with one writing instrument need some time to become as fluent with the new computer instrument.

In addition to pressing letter keys to form words, writers using computers have to type commands. Text and commands are usually typed on the same keyboard, as word-processing programs transform one functional keyboard into two. When writers press the CTRL and ESC keys in conjunction with letters, the keyboard changes from a standard word keyboard to a command keyboard. Using the keyboard for giving commands as well as for creating text is an added burden for beginners, because they have to learn several meanings for each key. Also, using word-processing systems involves learning command names and pressing sequences of keys to move around in the text and to make changes. (Difficulties with specific commands are discussed in Chapter 12.) Fortunately, the branch of psychology known as human factors research has focused on the effects of keyboard, screen, and program design on writers. The results of such research—coupled with writers' complaints about specific programs—have led to the development of increasingly improved systems.

DYNAMIC TEXT AND WORD PROCESSING

Starting a writing session on a computer involves more steps than starting with pen and paper or a typewriter. When you write in a notebook, you simply open the cover, turn to the first blank page, pick up your pen or pencil—and you're ready to start. When you use a typewriter, you put in a sheet of paper, turn on the machine if it's electric, and begin to write. You might also have to change a typewriter ribbon or clean the keys.

Preparing to write on a computer is not as time-consuming as preparing papyrus and a reed, but it does take time. Writers who use microcomputers must first prepare diskettes to hold copies of their texts. Before data can be stored, the diskettes have to be formatted, which involves running a new diskette through a **formatting** program that prepares the diskette for holding information. One diskette holds many pages of text, however, so writers don't have to go through the formatting step every time they work. Instead of opening a notebook cover to begin writing, the computer writer puts diskettes into a **disk drive**, a boxlike device that transfers information from the diskette to the computer memory. The disk drive reads information in much the same way as tape recorders do.

The process of getting the text into the computer and on the **monitor** screen is like wending your way through a building to get to your classroom or office. On the way, you go through several types of public rooms before you get to your own space: you walk through an entrance way or lobby, check in at the main office to pick up mail or materials you need for the day, and then walk through a public corridor past other rooms to your classroom. During this journey, you use a variety of speech "codes"—one for talking to the principal, one for acquaintances, and one for good friends. Similarly, to reach your writing space in the word processor, you go through several other programs, each with its own system of command codes. The commands are typically short, English-like words or sequences of keystrokes that tell the computer what to do. For example, pressing the CTRL key and D at the same time is a command to erase the character above the cursor on the screen. The hundreds of word-processing systems have many unique command codes, but the basic list of word-processing functions that these commands name is fairly small.

Like an office switchboard system, the **operating system** program manages the communications from the writer to the many other programs and a variety of hardware operations on the computer. In most cases, the operating system greets the writer who has just turned on the machine and presents a list of available activities, such as editing or printing a document. For example, a writer using the popular operating system DOS (disk operating system) is greeted by the symbols A>, which indicate that the system is ready to direct the writer to the word-processing program. The operating system also includes commands for getting to all the other programs, such as mail programs, games, programming languages, and data stored on disk.

With most word-processing programs, the writer begins by typing a few letters that represent the program name. After typing the program name, such as Textchew (a program name I made up to illustrate this process), the writer sees a list, or menu, of word-processing options:

```
Welcome to Textchew

Selections:

C-Create a file
E-Edit a file
F-Format a file
P-Print a file
L-List the files on disk
D-Delete a file
R-Rename a file
X-Edit menu

Type one: E,F,P,C,D,R,X
```

Typing E to edit a file is like walking into one's own classroom, because this command brings the writer into the word-processing program where most of the work is done. The writer can then begin to type, using the computer keyboard like a typewriter keyboard. The words appear on the computer screen and also go into a temporary memory called a **buffer**, until

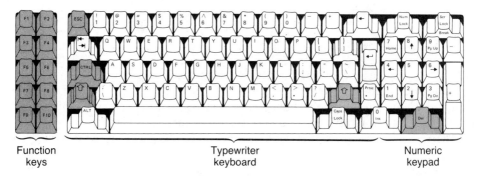

| Function keys | Typewriter keyboard | Numeric keypad |

The computer keyboard can change functions as the writer presses special keys.

the writer turns off the machine or gives a command to transfer and save the text on a diskette. In some programs, the buffer saves the text automatically, thus serving as a backup copy. The buffer copy corresponds roughly to carbon copies.

The writer can make changes in a text while writing. The editing commands for most word-processing programs on microcomputers involve sequences of keystrokes. Just as the SHIFT key on the typewriter changes the letter keys from lowercase to uppercase, special keys on the computer keyboard turn letter keys into commands. For example, pressing the CTRL key and a letter key at the same time sends a command to the word processor, as in the previously mentioned CTRL-D sequence, which is often the command to erase or delete the character above the cursor. The ESC key, usually located on the left side of the keyboard, is also often part of a command sequence. Some computers, like the IBM PC, have additional **programmed function keys**—keys that are devoted to frequently used commands, such as moving a screenful of text up (PgUp) or down (PgDn) or deleting text (Del).

Creating and Editing Text

Working on the computer differs most from working on a typewriter when the writer starts making changes. To make a change while writing on the typewriter, the writer has to backspace, use correction tape or correction fluid, and then restrike the key. In contrast, the writer using a word processor uses the **delete key**, which erases one character to the left of the cursor—the letter the writer typed last. Most microcomputer keyboards have a delete key, but it isn't exactly the same on all machines, nor does it function in exactly the same way in all word-processing programs. Some machines, for example, have back-arrow keys for deleting the character to the left of the cursor. In whatever form it appears, writers use the delete key frequently to correct typing and spelling mistakes and to change their choice of words as they create texts. For example, a writer might type in the following text:

The text appears
on the screen as
the writer types it.

If, after typing the period, the writer decides that "it" isn't necessary, he or she can press the delete key three times to erase the period, the *t*, and the *i*, in that order, and then type in a new period. This simple correction would have been quite cumbersome with correction fluid on a typed page.

Writers who use computers can also arrange to get a printed copy of their texts—hard copy—through a printer connected to the computer. Some writers feel that they can evaluate their texts by reading them from the computer screen, but many prefer to consider changes while reading their text drafts on paper. Like many other writers, I need to see my text on paper to get a sense of the complete piece as readers will see it. Although most word-processing programs have **scrolling** features, which display the text in consecutive screens forward or backward, the programs do not allow the writer to scan several pages at a time. I can spot problems in my text more easily on paper, perhaps because the words seem more stable than when they appear as light on the screen. Some writers like to save printouts of successive versions of their texts to make sure that they haven't revised the life out of certain sections. Saving back versions on paper may be more economical than saving each version on disk, which can be expensive at about five dollars a disk. A question for the future, of course, is whether readers and writers will still want hard copies of their texts when computers are more readily available, are easier to read, and have multipage displays—all advancements that are likely to occur.

Electronic Cutting and Pasting

An obvious advantage of word processing is that the electronic recopying capacity helps many writers compose more freely because making changes no longer requires time-consuming recopying or retyping. Children like to take advantage of the ability to make word-by-word changes, and many adults enjoy using the word-processing capacities to erase, add, and rearrange large sections of text.

Some writers save all the editing until they have written a full draft on a word processor. These writers benefit from the word-processing commands for deleting, adding, and moving sections when they revise a draft.

My twelfth-grade English teacher made elegant use of a physical metaphor for the solution to high school students' writing. "Cut," she would write in the margins of my papers. At that time, "cut" meant cross out, draw arrows, and recopy. When I later began to type, it meant cutting my papers into sections, throwing some away, and rearranging others. Word-processing programs, however, include commands for cutting and moving sections of text. Many writing teachers believe that reducing the burdens of manual cutting, pasting, and recopying will encourage students to act more like experienced writers, who revise extensively. With a word-processing program, the writer indicates the section to cut or to move, and the program carries out the command and then realigns the text, with the words in the new order.

Using Perfect Writer, for example, a writer who wants to erase six sentences in the middle of a text uses the arrow key to move the cursor to the beginning of the section to be deleted and presses the command to "set the mark"—the ESC key and the space bar. The mark is usually invisible to the writer, but the program stores the mark so that it knows where to start chopping. The writer then moves the cursor to the other end of the section and presses the "erase section" command—CTRL-W.

One advantage of electronic erasing is that it is not permanent. Text on paper that is crossed out or painted with correction fluid is no longer visible or usable. In contrast, erasing text on the computer is like putting it in a valise—the buffer. The text can be taken out of the valise and reinserted in a new location in the text. The writer in our example can reinsert the six sentences in their original place if he or she decides to do this before the buffer has been devoted to a new section. If the writer decided to move the six sentences rather than simply deleting them, he or she would move the cursor to the point in the text where the sentences should go and then give the "get back" command—CTRL-Y in Perfect Writer.

This process of moving text sections by erasing and then reinserting them—using the **block move**—disturbs many beginning word processor users until they have tried it a few times and have proof that the section really returns from the buffer. Then the block move becomes a feature that many writers feel they could not do without.

The block move command particularly helps me at the first stage of revising my writing. For example, I wrote the first draft of this book quickly on a word processor. In revising, I moved parts of the original Chapter 7 to Chapter 1, merged the original Chapters 2 and 3 into a new Chapter 2, and rearranged and edited other chapters. I read through the text, outlined what was there, made a new outline, and then moved large sections. Once I had decided what to do, the process was like moving building blocks—easy, neat, and fast. It is especially beneficial that the revised text remains clearly printed, even immediately after the change is made. Writers who use traditional tools have to consider the revised version through cross-out marks and arrows.

The block move command is useful for a quick reorganization of the overall text, but the writer also has to know when to focus on smaller sections of text. After I reorganized the first draft of this book with block moves, I had to reorganize and polish sentences and correct word usage, punctuation, and spelling. At that point, I had to stay away from the computer and its capacities for fast changes. Instead, I had to read each paragraph and sentence slowly, making sure it served a clear purpose and that it connected to the rest of the text. The computer presents an almost irresistible temptation to move quickly, but a writer often has to work slowly. By carefully reading a text printed out on paper or displayed on a screen, the writer can evaluate what is written, consider changes, and make them only when reasonably sure that they will improve the text.

Many writers make major changes first and then do their polishing with editing commands. For example, a fiction writer who was using a word processor to compose a preface for a friend's collection of poems first wrote a three-page draft. As soon as she printed it out, she noticed two unnecessary sentences and one paragraph that would work better in a different place. By pressing a few keys, she reorganized the piece. Then, as she looked over the second printout, she noticed minor errors and began the process again. She devoted the time she would have spent retyping to rereading the text aloud— first slowly, then quickly, and finally backwards—to detect any possible problems of clarity, flow, and mechanics.

Using a computer, a writer can try out two different organizations of ideas without recopying the text or cutting and pasting. By experimenting with alternative organizations or paragraphs, a writer might discover a new idea or a new relationship between the ideas already expressed. Thus, reorganizing can be a conceptual aid to writers as they develop their texts. Trying to make all changes in one or two retypings can inhibit this process.

Freed from the task of recopying, the writer can nurture a text through several stages of development. For example, Eugenia, a lawyer, was writing up a brief that included a statement of her position on a case, possible rebuttals, and citations of prior cases on the issue. In preparing the brief, she followed a method used by many report writers in school, business, law, and other professions. After reading, thinking, and talking about the case, Eugenia outlined the major points of her argument. She created a text on the computer, including a list of the major points, which she reordered several times with the sentence-move commands on her word processor. She then wrote out the argument for the point she felt was the strongest. She decided to present this point last, but she wrote it out first and then inserted the other points as she completed them. As her legal assistants found the exact citations for relevant court cases, she transferred the necessary facts from the citations into the appropriate places in her text. The document grew in stages, and she was always able to consider it from clearly typed and formatted pages. When the document was almost complete, Eugenia decided to move the last point to the beginning because it was the strongest opener. The word processor provided this writer with the tools necessary for building a text around an initial set of notes.

Many writers' plans emerge from their drafts. For example, an advertising copywriter quickly wrote a promotional piece for a trip to West Africa. He wrote freely, drawing on his impressions from films and photographs. His draft captured the atmosphere of the country, but when he reread the piece, he decided that only two catchy phrases and some related descriptions were worth keeping. He moved these sections to a new file, rearranged them, and edited them. As his colleagues read the piece, they offered him suggestions for polishing it. Finally, he added the commands that would format the copy to fit around the graphics and photographs to be used in the ad.

Occasionally, I hear of experienced writers with good planning skills, good handwriting, and sharp scissors who do not believe that electronic cutting and pasting offers any added benefits over manual cutting and pasting. Some argue that with manual cutting and pasting, all the sections are visible at once, which makes the process easier. Writers who prefer manual cutting and pasting to the electronic version are usually those whose reorganizations involve clearly defined sections that only require one revision pass. Electronic cutting and pasting allows the writer the luxury of making a series of revisions and then editing fine points in various passes, rather than making all changes at once.

Despite the wonders of electronic recopying, some writers feel that they have to recopy their texts to be able to evaluate them closely. A prize-winning nonfiction writer, for example, has found that he cannot use a word processor because the electronic recopying capacity takes over a step that he considers essential to his writing process. He identifies problems in a piece as he retypes it. The close contact with each idea, sentence, and word gives him the time to notice problems he might otherwise overlook. Sometimes this close contact stimulates him to throw away an entire draft; then, when he rewrites, he has a sharper focus and better phrasing. Clearly, this writer could retype his pieces on a word processor, simply ignoring the prior draft that is available for revision by word-processing command. Rather than investing in a computer only to use it as a typewriter or taking computer time from others in the newsroom who appreciate the capacities, the writer has chosen to stick with his traditional tools—the typewriter, pencil, and paper.

Research on the effects of using computers for writing suggests that recopying may have value, even though it seems to be an empty task. Preliminary research at Columbia University Teachers College and at the Harvard Graduate School of Education suggests that some writers who use word processors tend to edit first drafts closely when they use the computer, but they rewrite and reformulate texts more extensively when they recopy with pen or typewriter. With the computer, they make small changes, but with the pen, they tend to elaborate and add. Like the nonfiction writer mentioned earlier, such writers make more substantive improvements in texts when their writing instruments require that they recopy. When they don't have to face each word by reforming it, these writers may have trouble reading their writing critically. Not enough research has yet been done to confirm or explain these findings, but the existing research suggests, as one would expect, that writers have to read their texts carefully and critically, regardless of the instrument they use. One of the challenges that writing teachers face is finding interesting ways to get their students to read their own writing. Chapter 6 suggests some methods. Another message from these early research findings is that writers need the capacities of different instruments at different points in the writing process.

In summary, once most writers have mastered the mechanics of typing and of using a word-processing program, they find that they can write faster on the computer because they worry less about mistakes and retyping. They also find that not having to recopy gives them more time to go over their pieces or to write more. Professional writers also appreciate the faster turnover time from composing to seeing a text on paper. Writers have more time to continue revising and polishing when they have a new draft immediately than when there is a delay of a few days for retyping.

GOOD-LOOKING WRITING

Nine-year-old Robert sits at his desk writing. He clenches a pencil and forms a few dark letters on a sheet of paper: "The cave at the . . . " The next word he writes is "ed" instead of "end," which he had intended, so he crumples up the paper and starts again with a fresh sheet: "The cave at the end of my street is dangerus." He looks at "dangerus" and decides that it is probably wrong. He crumples up the paper again and, after asking his teacher how to spell *dangerous*, writes on a clean sheet: "The cave at the end of my street is dangerous." Robert makes three more crumpled paper balls before finishing his story. Such scenes are painfully familiar to teachers and parents. Writers, especially young ones, are concerned with the appearance of their texts as well as the content.

The neat appearance of text composed and revised on the computer has helped many writers progress more rapidly than Robert did. Their writing looks good, they can correct mistakes without starting over, and the text typed with a word-processing program looks good even immediately after they have made changes. Typed text is also professional looking and easy to read. Many writers find that typed text is easier to critique and revise. They also enjoy sharing the printouts of their texts with family and friends. The belief that text looks better in print may be culturally conditioned, of course, but print is related to professional writing and wide readership—factors that stimulate writers at any age.

Writers take pride in their writing when it looks good. In the following piece by 10-year-old Freddy, his interest in the appearance of the text is obvious:

> MY NAME IS FREDDY WESTON AND i like to read write and play. I GO TO SCHOOL
> P.S. two four three and i will be going to the sixth grade in sept. I live on a 103 street i

have a little brother and his name is SAMMY Sammy and I fight a lot. WE also have amale cat and his name is tom. TOM AND I play a lot too . I like to read comics books i have 231 comics my friend has 3,831. WE go to a store called WEST SIDE COMICS on 83 street. I like to ride my bike and i like to watch T.V. and i also like to go swimming on a hot day. I like the X-men comics because I like action in my comics. The end.

Freddy's writing problems peek through the neat appearance of this text, but he was so proud of his efforts that he subsequently tried hard to make his

Physical aspects of the writing process can inhibit young children's expression.

writing as good as he thought it looked. He wrote more and revised more
when he used the computer than he ever had with pencil or pen. His use of
uppercase letters for "important words," as he said, also illustrates the
concern children typically have for the appearance of their text. Just as
children enjoy illustrating their stories, they consider type and symbols as
part of the meaning of their texts. Freddy's increased pride in his writing
seemed to transfer to increased self-pride. When he revised this piece, he
began using the uppercase *I* consistently to refer to himself, as he did for
other "important words."

Experienced writers have also found that neatly formatted copy helps
them see problems that are difficult to detect on pages marked for revisions
with scribbles between lines and in the margins. A frequent complaint of
writers who work with typists is that they see the problems only *after* the
typist has finished retyping. One reason is that time away from their texts
gives them the objective distance that makes it easier to read their work
critically. Also, they can focus more on the meaning of the text when they are
not distracted by scribbles, arrows, and inserts in the margins. Writers may
also find it easier to be objective when their words appear in type rather than
in their own handwriting, because the type is less personal. The fact that many
writers are better editors of other people's writing suggests that techniques
for depersonalizing the written page may improve the revising and editing
process.

A fiction writer noted, however, that he does not type his daily journals
because the impersonal look of type distances him from his material. He
writes these journals to discover his deep feelings and ideas, so he tries to
maintain a personal quality in his writing, including the way it looks. He finds
that handwriting, much more than typewriting, highlights connections in the
self.

Some writers' handwriting is beautiful. These gifted writers want to
combine the aesthetic form of the text with aesthetic content. Poetry is the
most obvious genre for merging form and content, but some fiction writers
also like their words to be unique forms, rather than square, typed letters.

Unfortunately, when the text looks good, some writers become overly
concerned with the text's appearance and use the word processor only to
reformat rather than to revise. Sometimes, the writers who spend the most
time fussing with word-processing and formatting commands do not use the
computer to improve their writing. Mr. X, a graduate student who took my
course in computers and writing, alerted me to this surprising but common
problem. I encouraged the students in the course to use the computer to
learn how to revise their writing, and I asked them to hand in at least three
successive versions of a piece they cared about—for example, a paper for a
favorite course, a proposal, or a short story. I wanted to see evidence that they
had condensed, expanded, rearranged, reworked—in short, revised the piece.
Mr. X. handed in four versions of his paper. He had changed layout features,

such as margin size, typeface, heading scheme, and footnoting format, but he had never changed any wording, other than correcting spelling errors. This student had learned to use two automatic formatters, but he had not used the word-processing capacities to improve his writing. He had written a passable first draft, but the content was cryptic and disorganized in contrast to the polished look of the formatted, printed copies.

The neat appearance of word-processed text can fool writers who do not read their writing carefully. Another phenomenon I noticed in graduate courses was that students who composed their dissertations using a computer finished them in about six months, which is much less time than a dissertation used to take. One student was shocked at first that his adviser made him do a complete rewrite before giving the thesis to his other readers, but he later agreed: "My adviser was absolutely right. The writing was really a mess. I guess I didn't notice it because the printouts looked so good." A comment by 10-year-old Adam sums up this possible drawback of neat-looking copy: he liked the computer because it "makes my writing look better than it is." Adam recognized that good-looking writing is not necessarily good writing. Writers who use computers do benefit from the neat appearance of the text, which presents the piece clearly, but they also need methods for identifying problems in the neat-looking words.

Some types of word-processed text do not look better than other forms of text. Reading words as lights on a screen can be difficult, because one often has the sensation that the words are moving slightly. I feel more comfortable reading the printed copies of my texts rather than relying on screen reading, and I always identify more problems when the words appear on the printed page. Of course, this may be because I have used paper for much longer than the 5 years I have been using computers. Other writers report that, eventually, they do all their writing "on screen," sometimes not even reading paper copies before they send them out. Children also become comfortable with screen writing quickly.

CONTROLLING TEXT FORMAT

Writers who use word-processing programs have more powerful yet less direct control over the placement of the words in their text. Most word-processing programs include formatting commands for the placement of words on the screen and on the printed copy of the text. Some word-processing systems have keys devoted to formatting functions, such as centering or beginning a new page. More typically, formatting commands are **embedded** in the text. For example, the formatting command .c would appear above lines to be centered and the command @Indent(5 chars) would appear above lines to be indented five characters. To use such commands, the writer runs the text through a text-formatting program, which carries out the embedded commands and then creates another copy of the text in the form specified by the commands. The following examples show the text and embedded commands in Apple Writer and Perfect Writer for the manuscript title page of this book:

Text with Apple Writer Embedded Commands

```
.c
Writing and Computers
.sk 2
.c
by
.sk 2
.c
Colette Daiute
.sk 2
.c
Harvard University
.pg
```

Text with Perfect Writer Embedded Commands

```
@Center(Writing and Computers)
@Blankspace(2 lines)
@Center(by)
@Blankspace(2 lines)
@Center(Colette Daiute)
@Blankspace(2 lines)
@Center(Harvard University)
@Newpage
```

Text formatting commands offer writers the power to make extensive changes in text appearance with little effort: the writer enters .c above a line to be centered, and the program figures out the number of spaces to leave on each side of the line. If the writer edits the line, the program does a new computation. Similarly, programs place lines of text evenly across the page or change margin sizes after brief commands.

Before writers have learned to control formatting commands, however, their texts often come out in strange, unpredictable arrangements. For example, a teacher who was learning to use a word processor commented, "This thing sure is literal," when the entire text she had written was underlined in the printout. She had forgotten to insert the end-underline command at the end of her title. She thought that the program should be able

Nice Noise

Some people concentrate best when they are surrounded by noise. These people can write term papers with rock music blaring into their ears through head phones, and they can do homework in front of a quiz show screaming on the television set. They also prefer doing all their work in the reading room of a large library where others' movements, sneezes, page-turnings, and feet-shufflings add up to a blurred din. A friend of mine who loves noise explained that she concentrates best when she has to turn inward, away from the noise in the room, than when her thoughts fly away to fill the air in a quiet room. I'm different. I don't even like to hear the noise of my typewriter keys as I write.

Nice Noise

Some people concentrate best when they are surrounded by noise. These people can write term papers with rock music blaring into their ears through head phones, and they can do homework in front of a quiz show screaming on the television set. They also prefer doing all their work in the reading room of a large library where others' movements, sneezes, page-turnings, and feet-shufflings add up to a blurred din. A friend of mine who loves noise explained that she concentrates best when she has to turn inward, away from the noise in the room, than when her thoughts fly away to fill the air in a quiet room. I'm different. I don't even like to hear the noise of my typewriter keys as I write.

One brief command can change the layout of a document.

to figure out that it was supposed to stop underlining after the short, centered phrase on the first line of the text; "That was obviously a title," she complained. She was right. Programs could be designed to make some such decisions, or at least to prompt the writer to include the end-underline commands, as they sometimes prompt writers to include close quotation marks after they have typed open quotation marks. Computer programs are literal, however, and people have to use commands to tell them exactly what to do.

Writers using computers have a different kind of physical control over the words on the page than they do with pencils or typewriters. With the computer, the writer tells the program how to arrange words on the screen by giving commands, rather than by placing or forming the letters directly. Positioning words on the computer screen and the computer printout is a less direct and more complex process than positioning them by moving a pencil point or typewriter carriage. For example, in the following text, when the writer deletes the phrase "or even have a hint" from Attempt #1, the line on which it appears in Attempt #2 is shorter than the rest:

Attempt #1

Before I visited Iceland, I did not know or even have a hint
that the country was sitting on volcanoes. The image of Iceland
as a country of fire and ice is a beautiful one, and in this paper
I will discuss its impact on the people who live there.

Attempt #2

Before I visited Iceland, I did not know
that the country was sitting on volcanoes. The image of Iceland
as a country of fire and ice is a beautiful one, and in this paper
I will discuss its impact on the people who live there.

In most systems, closing a gap like the one in the first line of Attempt #2 involves moving up each line of text. There is an invisible symbol at the end of each line of text on the screen, and, to even out the line, the writer using a typical word-processing program has to move the cursor after "know" and press CTRL-D to delete the invisible character. This, however, pulls up the next line, resulting in a new line that is much longer than the others:

Attempt #3

Before I visited Iceland, I did not know that the country was sitting on volcanoes. The

To break the line at an appropriate point, the writer has to press the return key at that point. This enters the invisible end-of-line marker and moves the cursor down to the beginning of the next line. This description is not intended to discourage prospective word processor users; rather, it is meant to alert you to the new physical concerns that the computer adds to your activities and to encourage you to select word-processing programs that have commands for realigning paragraphs. Writers who are using word-processing programs can make their texts look better if they are aware of these features that control the placement of words. Despite a general concern for format, recent research suggests that there are times when writers should ignore the physical appearance of the text.

INVISIBLE WRITING

Dan was writing at a work station in the computer lab. When he left the room to take a coffee break, a practical joker in the lab turned down the contrast on Dan's terminal screen. When Dan returned—with an idea for a good concluding sentence—he sat right down and began to type. He wrote quickly so that he wouldn't forget his idea, but when he looked up, the screen was blank. Because he did not yet trust computers entirely, Dan panicked: "It's eaten my idea!" Then he turned the machine off and on again, rewrote the text, and found that he remembered what he had written. He was surprised that it came out better the second time.

Dan's experience has been explained by research on the role of the physical text in the composing processes. Steven Marcus, of the University of California, and other researchers have explored the importance of text appearance by studying writers' composing processes and final products when they cannot see what they are writing. Where computers were not in common use, the researchers asked writers to compose with empty pens on sheets of paper with carbons and second sheets attached. In computer labs, the researchers turned down the screen contrast, as Dan's friend did. Although it is not conclusive, this small body of research has suggested that writers compose differently when they cannot see their texts than when they can see them. In one small study, I found that adult writers who couldn't see their texts tended to leave out more words than they did when they could see what they were writing. Marcus found that college students believed their writing was better when they couldn't see their texts. His explanation was that the students were pleasantly surprised by the invisible writing task, because they devoted more energy to the overall purpose and focus of the text rather than to the local editing, which they tended to do more when they looked at their writing as they produced it.

Two valuable messages can be drawn from this research on invisible writing. First, it demonstrates that when the major concern is getting ideas out, we can use the computer for invisible writing by turning down the screen contrast. Then, with the contrast turned back on, the stored text is available for scrutiny. The second and more important message from this research is that although the physical features of writing are important, especially in a finished text, writers can benefit by ignoring the cosmetic features of their text in the early stages of creating a document.

WORKING AROUND MACHINE LIMITS

A computer, which offers powerful capacities, is also powerful enough to make a writer's life more difficult. So long as a writer can afford an extra pad of paper, he or she can keep writing, but it's not so simple with a computer. When I was writing the section on invisible writing, the message Out of memory! beeped at me from the bottom right-hand corner of the computer screen. The chapter comprised about thirteen pages in the computer, and that was all the memory buffer could handle. I was able to save that much on disk, but I had to create a new file for the rest of the chapter. This physical interruption broke my flow of thought, so I had to go back and read the first sections to be able to continue smoothly. For several minutes, it felt odd to be writing the end of the chapter in a new workspace on the computer.

This example suggests that one limit of the microcomputer writing environment is that the writer may have to work on texts in small sections, although some word-processing programs allow the writer to work on large texts if the computer has sufficient memory capacity. I have noticed that the chapters about word processing in recent books have been quite short, and I wonder whether the subject matter, modern writing styles, or machine storage limits are responsible for this stylistic turn. As micros are advancing to have increased memory capacity, word processor designers have created programs that accept longer documents, because they are sensitive to the adult writer's needs. Writers who want the flexibility to work on a long text in one file should consider the most up-to-date programs in their price range; the programs really are improving.

A physical limit that will be more difficult to overcome is that computer writers can view only a limited section of text at one time. The standard video screen displays eighty characters across and about twenty-four lines down. The PgUp and PgDn keys on the IBM PC display the prior and subsequent screens of text, and some computers have a multiple-window feature, which displays two or more sections of the same or different texts at the same time. Other than these peeks, writers can't view much of their text until they print it. Older computers, such as the Apple II+, and some portable models display even less text on the screen. Although not seeing the entire text may help writers keep the bigger picture of the text purpose in mind—as the studies on invisible writing suggest—writers have to view their texts when they revise.

Also, seeing only a little of the text may make local details even more prominent. The solution for the writer who wants to view the full text is to work from printouts rather than from the screen when considering revisions. Writers' memories for text may also increase as they hold in mind reduced versions of texts they do not view all at once.

Besides the functional and aesthetic limits imposed by the screen, health factors have also been at issue. People who spend many continuous hours reading from a terminal screen have reported eye strain and other maladies. Doctors have recommended that such people take breaks after every 20 minutes of steady work. This limit also emphasizes the importance of using printouts when possible.

CRASHES

A temporary shutdown of the computer—known as a crash—can be caused by a power surge, by an inadvertent press of the reset key, or by too many users on one time-sharing system. When a crash occurs, files can be lost, because the connection between the terminal, where the work is temporarily stored, and the permanent disk storage is broken.

Eliza is a student who managed to get through high school despite a severe writing block. In college, she tested out of freshman composition, so she never had to write essays, and she managed to write reports for other courses by piecing together notes from research. No one ever mentioned her writing problems because she was bright and her writing was passable. Mostly, she elected courses that did not require writing. After having learned to use the university computer for programming, statistics, and messages, Eliza finally decided one night—in desperation—to use it for writing a paper that was due the next day. She had learned the basic word-processing commands in her programming course, so she progressed well on the paper, writing quickly, making changes, and producing twenty pages in one session. She was admiring her work on the screen when suddenly she froze. The computer had crashed, and all twenty pages were lost. Months passed before Eliza tried to write drafts on the computer again. She learned, however, that she wouldn't be so vulnerable to crashes if she saved her text several times as she worked. If a writer saves a text while working and then stores copies on backup disks or on paper, crashes may wipe out the most recent changes but not the entire file.

Another obvious protection against crashes is to keep up one's hand-writing skills. I have found that my notes—even scribbles on backs of envelopes—have been helpful in reconstructing a text. Electronic recopying, cutting, and pasting, and other benefits of word processing outweigh such problems for many writers, and an awareness of the problems can alert writers to take precautions before the problems ever occur. A writer who uses a word-processing program has to save the text, which means transferring it

Writing done on the computer looks professional.

from the memory in the word-processing program to permanent storage on a formatted diskette. Saving—also referred to as writing a text into a file on disk—is usually a simple procedure, and it can save the writer lots of time and frustration. The writer can give the save command—in Apple Writer, for example, it is CTRL-S—at any time while working on a text. After giving the command, the writer sees [S]ave: at the bottom of the screen and should then type in a name for the file the diskette will store. I give the save command often when I work on a text, so I always have at least the last version on disk if the program crashes. After each writing session, I also make backup copies of a text on diskettes, which I call archives, to protect against any rash revising decisions I may make as well as against crashes.

Knowing how the program behaves can also help writers avoid some of the frustrations of using word-processing systems. Writers should spend several weeks practicing with a new program—trying out all the commands and formatting options—before working on an important text. Saving, making backup copies, and becoming thoroughly familiar with the writing instrument are habits that writers using word-processing programs must acquire to ensure that avoidable glitches don't outweigh the power of electronic writing.

SUMMARY

The purpose of this chapter has been to introduce you to the physical process of writing on the computer. The chapter has also pointed out common disagreements among writers about the value and effects of the computer as a writing instrument. This information—with the discussions that follow— should alert you to potential uses and necessary cautions. The electronic "pad and pencil" have changed the writer's craft, especially the physical aspects. This awareness of the social and manual processes of writing provides insights into the cognitive process discussed in the next chapter.

Writing Is a
Cognitive Process

3

When writer James Thurber was at a party, his wife would often have to break his silence with a request that he "stop writing." This image of a writer "writing" in the din of a social situation—without pen, paper, typewriter, or computer—is not common. People usually think of writers as actively pouring words onto paper. Nevertheless, writers do much of their work in their minds—even at parties. Writing is a cognitive process.

COGNITIVE CAUSES OF WRITING DIFFICULTIES

Inexperienced writers often think that writing is inspired. They wait for a rush of exciting words to flow effortlessly onto the page. Such novice writers have trouble because they want to compose a perfect first sentence—catchy, meaningful, and error-free—on the first try. They believe that as soon as the words are on the page, the inspiration is gone and the writing is finished. They view writing as a one-step process. In contrast, experienced writers know that writing a perfect piece on the first try is almost impossible. Although writers often have special messages to communicate, experience teaches them that the writing process involves more than inspiration. People who write well learn that writing also involves planning, thinking on paper, reworking the externalized thoughts, reading their texts, polishing their sentences—and sometimes even throwing away an entire draft. They find that writing is a complex set of mental and physical activities, including thinking, analyzing, making judgments, feeling, and talking to oneself. Experienced writers know that creating a text takes time.

Many writing teachers encourage their students to be concerned with the end product of writing—its style, quality, and effect. They ask their students to write a paper on a topic, hand it in, and then review it after "mistakes" have been noted and corrections have been made. Unfortunately, this focus on the end product often gives beginners the idea that writers always compose good texts. Also, the focus on correcting mistakes suggests that, when revising a piece, the writer should consider spelling at the same time as logical development. Writers should be concerned with creating clear, well-written pieces, but they also need to develop the patience, confidence, and techniques that allow their writing to evolve.

The emphasis on writing as a static product may have come about, in part, because the traditional writing instruments and surfaces do not allow writers to change the page easily. Thus, writers have a physical stake in producing final products on the first try because revising and even minor editing involve recopying. Since writing as a thinking process involves creating and recreating texts, often several times, the writer has to avoid becoming too attached to the written page. "Writing" in one's mind, as Thurber did at the party, is a good exercise for learning how to write. Beginning writers should practice thinking about their writing topics and interesting ways to say things before they start writing. A writer who is using a computer can learn to appreciate the cognitive nature of writing by creating a draft, erasing it, and reorganizing it to try out several versions. Such an exercise can help free the writer from some manual constraints.

Another reason why people sometimes have trouble writing is that they do not use talking as a guide. Most people love to talk, but they hate to write. They think that writing requires more talent and training than talking does. Rather than drawing on the important cognitive similarities between writing and talking, these people are often paralyzed by the differences between them.

The initial steps of talking and writing are similar; they require the same cognitive processes for finding information, setting goals, and selecting the language for expressing ideas. Writers, like speakers, gather information from their memories, translate their thoughts into language, and use similar linguistic structures. The primary differences between speaking and writing involve the method of production. For example, the mouth is faster than the pen, so speakers do not have to hold their ideas in mind as long as writers do before they can express themselves.

Writers develop strategies that help them use their minds and their knowledge in the most efficient way. Their activity is slower than talking, so they have to be careful not to do too much at once. Also, writers' texts remain for scrutiny by readers, whereas speakers can get away with many errors and inconsistencies because their words fade. Unless they are working with familiar topics and formats, writers engage in difficult mental choreography when they try to decide what to say, translate their ideas into sentences, and form coherent, rhythmic wording all at once. If they try to create perfect texts in one step, they are struggling against their natural cognitive processes—their hands are working against their minds.

As an exercise to remind yourself how complex writing can be, write a two-word phrase that captures the greatest success you have had so far in your life. Take two minutes to think and to write the words.

How did you think of the words? Did you change your mind? What decisions did you have to make? Did you see the words or hear them? Did you see the event they describe? Did you think about the ordering of the words? Did you have to think about how to spell them?

The following is a rough transcript of my search for such a two-word phrase:

> Success. Mmmmm? What's that? Well, maybe it's what made me happiest, proudest. Well, maybe it's being a teacher. No, it was publishing my first article. No, that's not it. I better start over again. When did I feel most successful? Answer immediately and stick with that. I see the scene of the party after my dissertation defense. The people there were friendly and relieved that I had finally finished. That was an accomplishment. I miss seeing my adviser, who was at that party. I wonder if he likes living in Canada. Two words. I'm supposed to think of two words to describe this success. "When I finished my doctorate . . . " That's a clause, not a phrase. "Finishing doctorate."

This exercise shows in small scale what writers go through when they are forming texts and sentences. The mental activities involved in this process were searching memory, making decisions based on the assignment, translating from images and feelings to words, taking new directions, and evaluating the clarity and spelling of the words. I had to search quickly because my time was limited; but my directions were precise, so I had strategies for guiding my search. I knew I had to define *success*, which helped me narrow the search area. I first thought about being a teacher and then about publishing an article, but I decided that these were the wrong paths. I tried again and found some good material when I took a tangent path— thinking about a party and the people who were there. The memory of that happy event led me to the word *doctorate*, which I expanded to "When I finished my doctorate." Finally, according to the exercise instructions, I had to change the clause to a two-word phrase. These are also processes writers use to create texts. They search for information, form their ideas into written expressions, revise these expressions, and edit them.

Several cognitive processes are at work when writers are creating texts. Current cognitive science research, which is devoted to identifying the processes of memory storage and retrieval, problem solving, and problem making, can be applied to the important cognitive activities involved in writing and to the ways in which these activities can affect writing instruction and the use of various writing tools.

In writing, two mental systems control most of the action—the thinking system and the information-processing system. These two systems work with and on the writer's knowledge—a collection of facts, information, and ideas. Drawing an analogy to cooking, the ingredients are the ideas, mixing the ingredients is the information-processing system, and heating the combined ingredients is the thinking system. Recent research has suggested that when writers control their cognitive "cooking" consciously, the writing process becomes easier, and successful writing strategies eventually become automatic.

SEEING WITHOUT
AND WITHIN

In studying the development of thought, Swiss psychologist Jean Piaget and his colleagues have identified several stages in the development of people's ability to perceive and interpret objects and events in their world. At first, children have only one point of view, so they are not even aware that they *are* aware. Their cognitive development involves taking alternative points of view, moving from one internal perspective to other external perspectives. As the distinction sharpens between the egocentric point of view and the perspectives of the outside world, children begin to hold more complex relationships in mind. The ability to take an objective point of view of one's self and one's thinking is a cornerstone of the child's cognitive development. The intellectual activities of analyzing and synthesizing information are built on such objective thinking. Piaget referred to this ability as "decentering," and he related it to the child's language development.

The following example illustrates a key step in this development of cognitive and linguistic knowledge. Eighteen-month-old Melissa was playing a naming game with her mother. Her mother would point to objects or facial features, and Melissa would name them: "ball," "choo-choo," "hay" (hair), and "no" (nose). When her mother would say words, however, Melissa would name a counterpart, such as "down" when her mother said "up" and "Mommy" when her mother said "Daddy." Melissa also played her own game: if her mother tried to get her to say one name, such as "Poppy," Melissa would rattle off an entire list of names: "Poppy, Mommy, Daddy, Meema."

Melissa played this game just before the period when she began making two-word utterances. Such combining and juxtaposing of names and concepts was possible because Melissa was beginning to distinguish herself from the outside world and to distinguish other entities in the world from one another. It all began to come together cognitively as the child began to view people and objects as separate from herself and from one another.

Writing researchers, such as Barry Kroll at the University of Indiana, have explained that writing development specifically relates to this ability to be objective. Writers have to be objective about themselves and their thinking to stimulate and guide their writing. When they are composing, writers guide themselves in finding information and arranging it persuasively. When they are revising, they distance themselves from the thoughts in their writing so that they can determine whether the ideas are expressed clearly enough for others to understand.

Children talk before they ever reflect on what they say. As they learn to evaluate their ideas and see their impact on other people, they benefit from the perspectives others offer about their writing. Comments like "I can't really *see* this dancing frog you write about" or "I don't agree with this" can help children realize that there was something they knew but didn't say or that there was something they didn't know but could learn as they explore an idea by filling out a description or discussion in a writing assignment. As writers learn to carry on internal dialogues about their writing topics, they begin to manage thinking and writing processes more efficiently.

Adults, too, can have trouble being objective about their writing. Although adults might have decentered in relation to some activities, they may need to learn to take alternative perspectives when they are writing. This involves learning and practicing specific strategies for creating and evaluating written language. One reason that some adults have writing difficulties is that they have not yet learned methods of composing and revising. Another reason, however, is that adults, like children, need to distance themselves from their writing so that they can distinguish what the words on the page say from what they had intended them to say. (Adult writing development is discussed in further detail in Chapter 11).

Before starting to write a piece, of course, a writer has to have something to say. Professional writers' usual advice to beginners is, "Write about what you know best." This advice makes sense, because it is obviously easier to express well-known ideas or information more vividly and clearly. Writing teachers often ask their students to write about their experiences so that they can concentrate on bringing out and recombining their existing knowledge, rather than worrying about gathering new information. If asked to write a paper, for example, a student who knows something about circuses from having attended them might choose to write about his or her experiences at the circus—perhaps also making some guesses about the purpose of circuses or creating some ideas for new circus acts and characters. Such exploration strategies help writers discover what they know and what they don't know. By developing a small set of exploratory questions, writers can use their knowledge effectively without limiting the specific content of the information they may collect for a text. Teachers often offer such guidelines for structuring a text without specifying the process of developing it. The following questions, for example, could help the student start the paper about circuses:

1.   What do I know about circuses? I'll write a list of words related to my circus knowledge.
2.   What have I seen at circuses?

3. Can I take what I know to invent a new circus event?
4. What would I like to know about circuses that I don't seem to know?

Such self-guided inquiry helps writers use their thinking power efficiently.

INFORMATION PROCESSING

Information-processing factors such as memory and attention also affect writers' thinking processes. The more able people are to focus on parts of a problem, for example, the more able they are to try out alternative solutions until they identify the right one. The mental activities involved in acquiring information, storing it in memory, and accessing it are difficult to separate from content development.

Although there are several theories of memory, the most developed theory is that knowledge—information and concepts—is stored in one memory space and is combined or transformed in another, more temporary memory space. Cognitive psychologists have found that general knowledge is stored in long-term memory, but it is channeled in and out of speakers' and writers' consciousness through short-term memory. Long-term memory is the storage space for concepts, meanings, and information. Facts and concepts are grouped there in meaningful clusters; for example, the names of specific birds are located together within the general concept "birds and animals." Researchers claim such specifics are stored together because words related to similar meaning categories and events can be remembered more quickly than less related words. Moreover, it seems that we remember general concepts or root words and reform them into sentences when we need them, rather than remembering exact words in exact sentences.

Even though individuals' specific knowledge differs, thinking and information processing seem to adhere to general principles. For a historian, detailed historical facts are organized in complex ways in memory, and a musician has an equally complex mental library of sounds and music terms. They use similar processes for arranging the information into sentences or musical phrases.

As writers and speakers search their memories for information, they organize it and translate it into sentences in a limited memory space. Short-term memory holds a limited number of units—such as digits, pitches, or words—in exact form for only a limited time. Psychologist George Miller and other researchers have found that short-term memory can hold between five and nine random units. Since related items can be stored together, people can remember up to twenty-four words if some of them are related.

To explore this view of short-term memory, read the following items in List A once; then write down as many as you can remember:

List A

dust
alley
seed
knob
soda
dress
book
sorrow
are
elephant

Now read the items in List B quickly, and write down as many as you can remember:

List B

album
guitar
apple
house
pear
door
horn
peach
window

You probably wrote down more words from List B because all the words fits into only three categories: music words, house words, and fruits. The items on List A, however, are more difficult to group. We can remember more words if we group them, because the group label is held in the limited slots in short-term memory, helping us recall or reproduce the related items. The strength of the mental imagery and the order of the items in a list also affect recall, so you might have done better on List A if the terms on that list were more meaningful to you or because that list was first.

Language processing is responsive to short-term memory limits in specific ways. The basic unit that is held in short-term memory is about a six-word clause. After the creation or perception of one such clause, the exact words fade from short-term memory, but the meaning of the clause is stored in long-term memory.

Experience can help people use their short-term memory capacity efficiently. For example, writers who compose the same types of texts frequently have stored outlines in their long-term memory, so they do not have to construct the outlines they write. They can thus devote their short-term memory entirely to collecting ideas and translating them into sentences, rather than using part of it to decide how to organize a piece.

Patterns in first drafts indicate how writers proceed as they struggle against short-term memory constraints. Writers are often side-tracked in their search for ideas, and the first draft is often a record of this search through memory. As a writer stumbles on additional information related to the topic, an evolving text may go off on a tangent.

The following sample essays illustrate tangential patterns that are familiar to most writing teachers and to professional writers as well. In the first essay, a 25-year-old student wrote the sentences as ideas came to her. While writing about an important event in her life, she found a pleasant place in memory and followed her recollections of her family.

Essay 1

The thing I care most about at the present time is graduating with my master's degree in nursing administration in June. My grandmother is 77 years old and is looking forward to the day when one of her twenty-three grandchildren graduates with a master's degree. My grandparents struggled to raise their eight children. They have told many stories about the depression years in the south. My grandmother is a very strong powerful woman, who has maintained and stressed the very importance of family bonds and education. Almost all of my cousins have graduated with baccalaureate degrees in a variety of professions. As a child I remember my grandmother sitting in a chair with a newspaper and all of her grandchildren around her. She would tell us about all different kinds of occupations, sing songs and play games. I never heard her complain of hard times. All she would say is "Everything is alright." She never drank or smoked, believed in physical fitness and good nutrition. Holidays were and still are a joyous occasion for my relatives with a lot of laughing, eating and dancing. Some of my younger cousins dance with grandmother and try to teach her the latest dances. They say, "If Disco Sally can dance so can you, Grandma." We call my grandmother Disco Granny when she starts to dance. My grandmother means the world to me and I love her dearly.

Although her master's degree was the original topic of the piece, the writer shifted focus from this topic to her grandmother. She had time to revise, but she did not notice the detour when she reread her piece, presumably because the same limits that occurred as she composed also restricted her revising activities. To catch such problems, writers often have to search for them specifically as they revise. This writer could have refocused the beginning of the piece to the topic of her grandmother, or she could have tied the piece back to the original statement of purpose.

In the second sample, a 10-year-old boy took a similar detour from his main topic, "a community problem that has affected you," onto a subtopic, "tear gas."

Essay 2

New York has the biggest population of any state in the U.S. It also has the most crime for such a small area of land ("even more the Texas"). Because of crime people in New York City (which has the most crime) have been afraid to go outside, not to mention that they are wasting money on weapons that are supposed to protect them. The weapon sold the most is called "tear gas" which is a chemical which burns the skin and can blind the eyes temporarily and causes much pain. This chemical is sold only by special companies which have a license. Take for instance a runner—a runner need protection probably more then any one citizen. Not like a mother who goes shopping, a runner spends her time outside.

Such detours occur commonly in natural language production—even within individual sentences. The following sentences, for example, show that writers can begin with one construction but forget it and end the sentence with another construction:

1.   We get the Public Service man came to fix the wires outside.
2.   This waste of two intelligent women I know would still be active if this boss never had such policies at work.

The first sentence, which starts off with the subject "we," ends up about the "Public Service man" and his activities. The second sentence starts off with the subject "waste" but ends up with a predicate—"would still be active"—that is based on "intelligent women," the modifier of the grammatical subject "this waste," rather than on the grammatical subject itself.

In the developmental writing studies, my colleagues and I have found that the number of words and clauses before such sentence detours increases with the age of the writer. Sixth-graders might make such a detour about five words into the sentence, whereas most adults would have such a problem only after eight or nine words and several clauses. The paths of these sentences are similar to those in the sample essays, but on a smaller scale.

The more carefully a writer plans, the less likely it is that such detours occur, but writers often have to start writing to discover the topic and the message about that topic. Writing a draft can be like trying to get dressed in a small closet; the mental space available for researching, planning, composing, transcribing, and revising is too small for all the necessary activities.

The sentence and text patterns in the foregoing examples reveal two important facts about the writing process. First, these patterns show that it is difficult, if not impossible, to create perfect sentences and texts on the first try. Cognitive psychologists, linguists, and writers find that such patterns are extremely frequent in early drafts—and they occur in published works as well. On close examination, readers and listeners notice when sentences are ungrammatical and texts are disorganized, but they often do not notice many grammatical and textual problems in the normal course of conversation or reading. They miss a lot because they are constrained by the same memory and attention problems that writers have. These natural cognitive processes allow even the best writers to make mistakes, and even the best writers usually have to revise for the reader's sake and for art's sake. This discussion of errors in writing and talking is intended to show why writers should allow their texts to evolve.

It is important for writers to know that following tangential ideas or making certain grammatical mistakes is natural. Tangents often hold seeds of ideas that become main points of a piece. Thus, writers should compose first drafts as freely as they talk and then take advantage of the permanent record of the printed page for improving the text by deleting tangents or transforming them into main points if they seem to hold the best ideas.

Besides illustrating the difficulty of creating perfect first drafts, the common occurrence of tangents suggests the importance of planning. Experienced writers overcome their natural memory limits by developing plans and techniques for analyzing and evaluating drafts. Because many writing problems occur as writers fit small phrases and clauses together, it is clear that having plans for overall sentence and text structures could keep them on track. Journalists, for example, use set outlines for their news stories, automatically including, first, the major event, followed by the informational details of "who," "what," "when," "where," and "why." They also have a general idea of where to include quotations or counterarguments to a given explanation of the event.

Other writers have similar planning techniques for keeping a reader's attention. A friend of mine gave me a formula for writing speeches: "Start with an anecdote. Lead into your main points for the speech. Give your proof, with pictures. Tell a joke, and conclude with quick review of what you've said." If followed mechanically, such a formula could lead to a flat or disjointed speech, but it also helps a speaker plan, and get more mileage out of limited processing space. Experienced writers don't have better short-term memories than other people do; they just use them more efficiently, so the limits have less impact.

LEARNING

After searching and combining information in their mental libraries, writers often get more information from other sources. The acquisition of such new information is a learning process, involving discovery, problem making, and problem solving.

Consider your personal theory of learning. How do you learn best? Do you review a new topic or skill generally and then investigate the specifics? Or do you try to build your new knowledge incrementally, using rules and self-tests? How do you determine that you have not understood a concept? Do you think that children are born with certain knowledge? Do you think that we pour information into our heads as we would pour water into a glass? Your ideas about learning probably mirror one or another of the major psychological theories.

Two major learning theories of the twentieth century reflect themes about learning that have been expressed throughout history. The big debate has been over whether learning is a copying process, whereby information is given to learners, or a discovery process, whereby learners use specific intellectual capacities that guide their perceptions of the world and thus their learning. In the latter view, learners are involved in an active design process, creating a world in their own minds. If learning is such a creative process, writing is a very important learning activity.

Behavioral-associationist theories, as expressed clearly by renowned psychologist B.F. Skinner, assume that learning is a systematic process of acquiring information. According to Skinner, animals and humans acquire knowledge when they are given positive reinforcement. Positive reinforcement occurs when a stimulus following a response strengthens the occurrence of that response; for example, receiving food is a positive reinforcer of new behaviors in animals. According to Skinner, learning occurs in specific steps. Language courses that require mastery of grammar and usage before allowing students to write are much in the spirit of behaviorism. Although they are not always strictly behaviorist, such curricula are based on the idea that expression skills are built incrementally on word and sentence knowledge. A significant limitation of behaviorism is that its goal is to describe observable human activities. Since much human life—especially thinking and writing—is unobservable, those who are interested in intellectual development need theories that also explore inner mental life.

In contrast to the behaviorist approach, the cognitive-organizational views of learning have focused on such abilities as the organization of memory, problem solving, and the learner's control of thought and language. These theories assume that the human mind is, by nature, patterned for learning. We are born into the world with certain knowledge or predispositions for learning language, reasoning, and other mental skills. One of the most convincing arguments for this view is that, despite the speed and sloppiness of everyday speech, babies learn language in similar ways across the globe.

In this view of learning, the students' goals are extremely important. In their learning research program at Carnegie-Mellon University, Newell and Simon developed a computer model—the General Problem Solver (GPS)—that illustrates the importance of goals in learning. What looked like conditioned responses to Skinner are considered internal goals in the GPS model.

Although the goal-making process is not always conscious, people generally advance their knowledge by creating learning goals and asking questions. Cognitive psychologist Jean Bamberger, at the Massachusetts Institute of Technology, cites a key phrase uttered by her students to greet problems and quirks from the computer: "I wonder why *that* happened." Such a comment sets up a goal that stimulates the students to make guesses about the computer and then gather information to confirm or disconfirm these guesses. Wondering why something happened structures the discovery process and leads students to identify what they do and do not know. They are then able to make and test hypotheses to answer the question "Why did that happen?" This process, initiated by the students' self-inquiry, leads them to come up with possible answers to the question, test out the answers by trying to disprove them, and then decide on the best explanation. Students who go through such a process are more likely to remember and use the information. When teachers stimulate their students to do such self-questioning with a few guidelines, they are helping their students help themselves learn by discovering.

Your personal theories of learning influence the way you help others learn. If you think that getting a general feel for a subject sets a context for more specific learning later, you, as a teacher, would probably favor having students write complete texts in one pass, rather than working up one piece over several weeks by building outlines, creating opening paragraphs, and constructing sentences before actually drafting an essay. Students often feel liberated when they are allowed to write without worrying about correctness or even organization. Seeing that they can fill a page bolsters their confidence, which is necessary for sculpting a text. Any necessary outlining and pruning can be done after a draft has been written. In this way, writing becomes a discovery rather than a copying process. The creation of each text involves students in a learning process—learning what they want to say, what they know about the topic, what they still have to learn, and how to express it so that their readers will enjoy the text and learn from it.

Two images will help bring the computer into this discussion of learning. The first involves a teacher who considers it his or her responsibility to give students knowledge. This teacher believes in step-by-step presentation of information, drills, and memorization. This teacher would have students work on grammar and spelling drills before writing stories or compositions. This teacher would be interested in the computer as a tool for shaping the child's learning and knowledge. In this case, we have an image of the computer with its hands on the student's head. In his article, "Why We Need Teaching Machines," B.F. Skinner argues that we need machines because they can segment and present information in an orderly way, which is necessary because the real world environment is "impoverished" as a source of information.

A second teacher, who feels that he or she is a guide of student explorers, believes that students learn by doing and reflecting—by writing and reading rather than by drilling specific concepts. The image representing this teacher's view of computers shows a student using the computer with one hand but placing the other hand on his or her own head. According to this view, the students enter the classroom with knowledge that makes further learning possible, and they develop their own knowledge while interacting with the environment. In this case, the skillful teacher sets up a learning environment with the appropriate stimulation and tools for students at a specific age. The computer is then a small, manipulatable laboratory for the students' explorations and discoveries.

Some people view the computer as a tool that helps students shape their own learning.

Some people view the computer as a tutor that shapes learning.

OVERCOMING WRITING DIFFICULTIES: A PROCESS APPROACH

A few rare individuals would rather write than talk. For people who cannot talk, writing is the only means of communicating. Even those who find writing to be easy, however, know that it is a complex process that requires much time and energy.

Studies of people who find writing relatively easy have provided insights into the cognitive processes involved in writing and in learning to write. In the last 15 years, researchers such as Janet Emig, Donald Graves, Linda Flower, John Hayes, and others have found that writing is a dynamic, multistep process that involves discovering ideas as we think and even as we write. Because composing is often a discovery process, creating a draft requires careful planning and rewriting as the major points, details, and organization of a piece emerge. According to this view, errors are not considered mistakes to be corrected; rather, they are signposts of the evolving text and the writer's abilities. Researchers have also noted that approaching writing as a discovery process frees us from the feeling that we have to do everything at once and also frees us to experiment.

In process studies of writing, researchers have observed writers as they composed and revised. The researchers noted how quickly writers composed, when they paused and looked at the ceiling, when they crossed out, and when they started over again. These studies have concluded that writing involves the general activities of prewriting, composing, revising, and editing. Prewriting activities include deciding what to say, making notes, and outlining or scripting sentences and themes. Composing involves translating these somewhat developed and organized ideas into a sequential text. The revising process is more difficult to identify because it sometimes occurs simultaneously with the other activities. Revising at any stage involves making changes in ideas, organization, and expression, and editing is the process of refining wording, spelling, usage, and punctuation. By working through these steps, writers learn that writing is as lively and as messy as talking, but that, eventually, they can produce a polished text.

The writing processes are not always ordered or even separable. Sometimes, writers revise sentences in their minds before the sentences ever appear on paper. Sometimes, too, writers make their plans only after they have written first drafts. Nevertheless, creating documents in several stages can take some of the mystery and agony out of the writing process, not only because it reflects the general strategies of good writers, but also because it is consistent with the way the mind works.

The process approach to writing helps writers overcome the two common problems discussed earlier; it can reduce short-term memory overload, and it can help writers reflect on their thoughts and their texts more objectively.

Writers who are aware that writing involves planning, composing, revising, and editing—which cannot be done efficiently all at once—are free to compose and revise in separate steps. Therefore, they can delay final judgments about what they write. When writers feel this freedom as they compose their initial drafts, they usually can write with a vitality that might be stifled by a fear of making errors. Letting a piece evolve requires physical energy, however, because revising requires recopying and the mental gymnastics of being objective about one's own writing.

The process approach structures writing activities so that the writers can receive support from others. When writing is a growth activity, writers allow themselves to experiment, which often involves seeking feedback from others. For example, a child who is using a process approach would have the courage to curl up in a chair next to the teacher's desk and say, "I'll read you what I have. You tell me what you think." In this way, writers gain new insights about their work. Young writers, especially, can learn to take alternative points of view in their texts and consider their texts objectively as they listen to other's reactions to their writing.

INTERACTIVE WRITING INSTRUMENTS

Although it is useful to consider writing in the mind separately from writing with the hand to understand the dimensions and complexity of each activity, the writing instrument itself can affect the cognitive process. The instrument can stifle the mental dynamism of writing, enhance it, or make no difference at all. As inscribed clay tablets dried, the writer in ancient times had to feel that the work was complete. In contrast, a writer who is using a computer tends to feel that the process is ongoing. The computer has several capacities that can stimulate and aid the cognitive process of writing. The computer is the perfect tool for a process approach to writing, because it makes revising and recopying texts physically easy. The computer can also help writers use various strategies for gathering information, organizing it, and translating it into sentences, paragraphs, and extended texts.

Writing on the computer is more interactive than writing with traditional methods. Word-processing programs are dynamic, which pen, paper, and most typewriters are not. In addition to displaying words, as the typewriter does, the computer responds to the writer. Programs interact subtly with the writer by carrying out commands. When a writer gives the command to delete a few words, for example, the words disappear and the cursor blinks, waiting for more text or additional commands. The blinking cursor reminds the writer that the program is waiting to do more, which can stimulate him or her to write more or to revise.

A textbook writer found that he regarded the blinking cursor as an audience, waiting for him to write. He also felt a subtle response as the program dutifuly carried out his commands to delete and reformat. He felt less positive about the undpredictable **error messages**, such as **illegal command** and **can't save disk full**, but they did give him the feeling that someone was reading his work as he composed, and he liked the interaction that they added to the usually lonely writer's craft. He also believed that the interactions helped him find his inner voice, because the responsive writing environment made him feel as though he were talking. Since the interaction was usually subtle, he didn't feel that the program interrupted him or his thoughts.

Other writers have found, however, that, until they got used to the computer, it interfered with the writing act. When they had to think too much about interactions with the computer and word-processing commands, they had little energy for their writing. This suggests that writers should compose familiar material on the computer until they no longer have to think about the commands.

Another way that word-processing programs interact with the writer is that they sometimes respond explicitly to commands. For example, when a writer presses the command sequence to replace a word, two messages appear in the message area at the top or bottom of the screen:

Dear Hope,
I am anxious to recieve your letter.

Replace:recieve
With:receive

In most programs, when the first comment—**Replace:**—appears, the writer types in the word to replace (in this case **recieve**, which is misspelled), presses the escape (ESC) key, sees the **With:** message, and types in the substitution (in this case, **receive**).

Some programs also note when a command has been carried out. For example, after a writer has given the same command by pressing S and typing a short name for the text, the typical responses are **File saved** or **File written.**

Error messages also offer direct feedback. For example, a program may reject a command that includes an extra space, comma, or letter, because the program is written to expect only one form of a command. If the writer types **dire** instead of **dir** to see a list of the texts on disk, for example, a message such as **unrecognized command** might appear, even though the incorrect command is the first four, rather than three, letters of the word *directory*—the meaning of the command. Some programs are written to accept several versions of a command, but many still accept only one. Such unnecessary precision is frustrating to most writers and can be especially difficult for handicapped writers.

These program responses involve writing and word-processing activities, rather than the content of the text, and the value of such interaction with the low-level intelligence of a computer word-processing program is not clear. Some writers feel that the necessary mechanics for using the interactive writing instrument hold their ideas down to a mechanical level. Other writers feel, however, that the communicative nature of the computer response reminds them that they will eventually have readers and helps them liven up their prose.

William Styron's feelings about the blank page suggest the value of a responsive writing instrument:

> I . . . with a pencil between thumb and forefinger confronted the first page of the yellow legal pad, its barrenness baneful to my eye. How simultaneously enfeebling and insulting is an empty page! Devoid of inspiration, I found that nothing would come.*

The computer's blinking cursor and program responses seem to provide some sense of another partcipant—a minimally social environment for writing. This environment certainly does not replace real readers and editors, but it can make the individual steps in writing a little more lively.

SUMMARY

Writers are constrained by natural physical and cognitive processes, so they have trouble composing and revising simultaneously. They also have trouble being both writer and reader at the same time. But, people are smart, and their minds can form ideas faster than their hands can type. Computers are not so smart, but they are very fast. They have photographic short-term memories and enormous long-term memories that store clearly organized information. They also take orders immediately and signal when they are done. Thus, writers can use computers to complement their own capacities and to do some of the drudge work.

The computer also can complement a writer's cognitive activities by serving as an alter ego. An important part of writing is taking an objective point of view; this is necessary for the writer to be able to search for and acquire knowledge on a topic and make sure that the text will be clear to others. Computer programs are objective; as they interact with writers, they can remind the writers of their potential readers.

Writers have to do the hard work of carefully evaluating the text for purpose, clarity, and coherence, but they can share with the computer some

*William Styron, *Sophie's Choice* (New York: Bantam Books, 1980) p. 40.

of the tedious tasks, such as storing information, correcting spelling, recopying, and reformatting the text. Computer programs can also guide writers' memory searches and alert them to possible grammatical and organizational problems.

The computer takes a place among other writing and text production tools.

Computer Tools and the Writing Process

II

In his book *The Computer in Education: Tutor, Tool, Tutee*, Robert Taylor, of Columbia University Teachers College, describes three uses of the computer for education. The computer is a tutor when it runs CAI software, presenting and drilling information. The computer is a tutee when it takes instructions from the people who write programs. It is a tool when it runs progams that serve people as they draw, play music, make calculations, simulate experiences, and write. Thus, the computer is like a toolbox that holds the various tools—the software programs—that run on it. Word-processing programs, prompting programs, simulations, mail programs, spelling checkers, and other software are the tools that can serve writers.

Several researchers have claimed that the computer is an especially useful tool for learning. For example, Seymour Papert, of the Massachusetts Institute of Technology, believes that computer programming involves intellectual activities that improve young programmers' abilities to solve problems. Allen Collins of the consulting firm Bolt, Beranek and Newman, argues that "computers provide tools to make reading and writing tasks that students now perform easier and more rewarding." Teachers have also claimed that the computer offers students significant learning aids. In intellectual activities like writing, which is a complex mix of physical, psychological, and social processes, the computer can become an integral part of the activity.

The effects of the writing instrument on the writer's creative process are similar to those of the artist's tools on the visual or musical creative process. The computer can be phased in and out of the writing process, and it can complement more traditional writing tools—the pencil, typewriter, and tape recorder. Professional writers and editors also use the tools involved with publishing—typesetting, photocomposing, printing, and mass-distribution networks. With the computer, student writers, too, can enjoy some of the outlets available to professional writers. Computer printing and copying programs even offer beginning writers the tools to do their own publishing.

This part presents computer tools and their relationship to the writing process. These tools can help student writers improve their writing as they gather ideas, form their opinions, and share their work with others. These applications draw on the unique capacities of the computer and are intended to help reduce the writing difficulties that often curb students' abilities or interest in writing. Once writing teachers have learned about the range of computer writing tools, they can adapt them to their own teaching styles and to their students' writing styles. Complementing a writing program with computers takes imagination, planning, and a willingness to change.

The following chapters offer an overview of useful tools that will be available in the near future as well as those that you can use immediately. Some are still experimental versions or are expensive, but they are likely to be available on the market in the near future—or to be available at lower prices.

Prewriting 4

"I don't know how to get started." Student writers sometimes have trouble getting started because they don't know what to say. They may not have a pressing reason to write, they may not know enough about a topic, or they may not realize that they actually have some ideas to express. Getting started on a writing task—prewriting—involves gathering information, defining the purpose and scope of the piece, and planning how to present it.

Writers invent various strategies for getting their words on paper or on the computer screen. Some writers do much of their writing, planning, and revising in their heads, and some make notes or outlines. When some writers start translating their ideas and plans into the written word, they focus on phrasing and grammar. Other writers think on paper, writing freely as ideas come to mind and not worrying about sentence form.

Researchers Janet Emig, Lillian Bridwell, and others have described two composing styles: the Mozartian style and the Beethovian style. Mozartians plan extensively, write clearly, and revise sentences as they write them. In contrast, Beethovians write quickly and freely but have to revise extensively. Many writers have a penchant for one of these writing styles, but some use both styles, switching between them according to the writing task. For example, the Mozartian technique of making an outline is more appropriate for writing technical reports than it is for writing a story or preparing a first draft of an essay when the writer has not thought much about the subject.

Most writers compose, revise, and edit, but the time and visibility of each process vary greatly for each writing style. Researchers such as Sondra Perl have found that writers don't work in separate, identifiable stages but that they do progress through a series of processes: planning, composing, and revising. Since a major problem in writing instruction has been the tendency to collapse these processes into one—writing a final paper—it is useful to discuss each of them in detail. These writing activities also serve as useful units for instruction and provide a framework for discussing the uses of computer tools.

DISCOVERING WHAT
YOU KNOW

Writers' main source of information is the knowledge in their own minds, and people often know more than they think they know. The idea that we have to search for knowledge in our own minds may seem odd, but knowledge is stored in complex patterns, so it may not always be easily accessible. Therefore, writers have to learn strategies for retrieving information from their internal libraries. They need guides that they often have to create themselves.

Freewriting

One successful approach to getting started, especially when writers are drawing on their own experiences, opinions, knowledge, and feelings, is to think in writing. In the 1920s, writers used an approach called automatic writing to release ideas and feelings from their unconscious. Automatic writing is stream-of-consciousness writing—writing down thoughts as they come to mind. The following are instructions from André Breton, the surrealist artist who guided others in the automatic writing method:

> Attain the most passive receptive state of mind possible. Forget your genius, your talents, and those of everyone else.... Write quickly with no pre-conceived subject, so quickly that you retain nothing and are not tempted to reread. Continue as long as you please.*

Writing in this way reduces several types of pressures that can block thought processes. When writers do not worry about having great ideas, they do not try to do too much at once. They reduce the burden on their thought processes by not worrying about searching for information, writing it, organizing it clearly, and using correct grammar all at the same time. The surrealist writers thus developed a technique that helped them overcome cognitive limits. It is as though they knew about short-term memory limits, which were not defined until the late 1950s and are still being studied.

Automatic writing was an art form—an end in itself—as much as it was a technique to help experienced writers discover their deepest feelings and knowledge. A current version of automatic writing, which is popular among writing teachers, is called freewriting. Freewriting is intended as the first step in the writing process.

In his books *Writing Without Teachers* and *Writing With Power*, Peter Elbow, a writer and teacher, has argued that writers can discover that they have a lot to say simply by writing for about ten to twenty minutes without stopping. Freewriting helps writers search their knowledge banks, because, as they

*André Breton, quoted in T. Rainer, *The New Diary* (Los Angeles: Tarcher, 1978).

write quickly, they grasp associated ideas and topics. When they are freewriting, writers can gather information without also burdening their short-term memory with the task of editing words.

Freewriting and Word Processing

Word-processing programs are useful tools for freewriting because they make it easier to separate the composing and revising processes. As mentioned earlier, writers tend to work quickly on the computer. Also, the computer seems like an audience to some writers, so freewriting can feel as natural as speaking. Some writers find that the blinking cursor stimulates them to continue writing when they might have stopped had they been using traditional methods. Nick Aversa, a textbook writer and veteran writing teacher, found freewriting on the computer particularly useful:

> If freewriting silences that inner censor who is so instrumental in preventing people from committing their words to paper, then typing on the [computer] terminal is better than [free] writing . . . it is easier to suspend your judgment about what you are writing. My writing has more of a voice, my sentences are more textured, simply because I enjoy the ease with which I can type at the terminal without the encumbrances of keys that get jammed or the fear of making mistakes.*

Freewriting is also a good warmup activity. Beginning a writing session with 10 minutes of freewriting helps writers warm up their hands and the mental channels they use in writing. Freewriting helps writers connect with their inner voice, which is not exactly like the voice they use for speaking. Such a warmup process can also help writers clear their short-term memories to make room for the information they need for the writing task at hand.

Getting ideas out quickly helps writers follow and develop a train of thought and reduces their inhibitions. Writers often have to work quickly and undisturbed to capture, combine, and expand thoughts during their search through memory. Freewriting also helps writers express major points and then move on to discover and express more ideas.

Freewriting techniques are valuable in writing instruction for several reasons. After freewriting, students see that they have ideas and information to express. These techniques also illustrate the complexity of the writing process—a process that cannot be accomplished in one step. Freewriting techniques are most useful for limbering, practicing, and recording. Exploration with the techniques gives teachers and students insights into their own unique writing processes. Writers who use this technique begin by discovering what they have to say and finding their voice. Polishing comes later.

---

*Nick Aversa, quoted in C. Daiute and R.P. Taylor, "Computers and the Improvement of Writing," *Proceedings of the Association of Computing Machinery*, 1981, ACM08979, p. 83.

Invisible writing, which was discussed in Chapter 2, relates to freewriting in its releasing function. When writers work quickly and without reading the text as they proceed, they do not take the time to worry about details they can clean up later. One problem for writers who use freewriting and invisible writing is that, as they discover ideas and wording, they tend to repeat, ramble, and go off on tangents. Texts written quickly usually follow associative developments that later have to be changed to logical developments; they contain grammatical problems that are often caused by omitted words. The text is out, however, and it is better to have to rewrite a text than to agonize over the initial steps of getting in out. Even a less-than-perfect draft is valuable evidence that the writer has something to say. Freewriters have to be prepared to revise, sometimes extensively. Since revising with a word-processing program is efficient and neat, however, writers can shape their freely written texts relatively quickly once they have distinguished the good parts from the bad.

Until a writer is comfortable typing and using word-processing commands, freewriting on the computer may be difficult because the writer worries about typing and about what the machine may do next. Such concern with the operations of the writing instrument can add to the burdens on short-term memory, thus complicating the transition of ideas into written words. Also, some writers feel distant from words that go through a mysterious electronic pathway to appear on an alienating screen. They prefer their embryonic ideas to appear in their own handwriting.

Another possible problem with using a computer for freewriting is that a writer who does not have a machine at home might find the office or the computer room at school too noisy an environment for private thinking and concentrating. Such writers prefer to freewrite in comfortable environments—at the kitchen table, in bed, or under a tree. Today, however, even first-graders are learning how to write on a keyboard, so they are comfortable freewriting on a computer.

PLANNING

Although freewriting is often useful, many writers prefer to plan before they weave their sentences. I always carry a little notebook—a tattered book filled with lists:

1. Lists of phrases that outline the details I want to include in a piece I am writing or planning to write.
2. Lists of points in an argument for a piece.
3. Lists of references to make in the argument.
4. Lists of the steps to take in writing the piece.
5. Lists of new ideas.

Each list evolves as I read it over after I have begun to write a draft or after I have discussed my ideas with someone else. This list making and list rearranging usually occurs on the run, and I'm not always near the computer when I have new ideas for the lists. In fact, the kind of thinking that nurtures plans springs from relaxed and subconscious activity when I am walking, riding, or having lunch—not in a workplace. Therefore, the computer has been least helpful to me when I am starting work on a new piece.

My lists are not like the outlines my fifth-grade teacher said I should make before writing. They are sketchy plans, and they are useful throughout the process of creating a document—beginning, middle, and end. Sometimes, when I am working on a difficult piece, I type one of my lists into the word-processing program as a way of getting started on the text.

Planning is one of the most important processes in writing; researchers have found that it often accounts for more than half of a writer's time. Linda Flower and John Hayes, of Carnegie Mellon University, have gathered information on planning processes by asking student and experienced writers to compose texts aloud, including both the text and their thoughts about the text.

Flower and Hayes have found that writers' goals serve as guides for the creation of texts. Writers decide what to say next by reminding themselves of the purpose of the piece and the kinds of information the reader needs to understand the piece. They reveal their goals by such comments as "I can't say it this way if I'm trying to convince them that writing can be fun." Much of the writing process involves clarifying goals that are often carried out when the writer reworks a text.

Flower and Hayes have distinguished two types of writers' goals: content goals and process goals. Content goals relate to the information in the text, and process goals relate to the act of creating the text. The more experienced the writers, the more elaborate the process goals that appear in the transcipts of their composing sessions. This research suggests that student writers should learn to define, create, and develop writing goals as well as content. Beginners often need guidance from others because they haven't yet developed strategies for talking to themselves about their writing.

Ann Matsuhashi, a researcher at the University of Illinois, has found that writers' pauses are active planning times. By analyzing sentences that follow pauses, Matsuhashi found that the longest pauses precede new paragraphs. New paragraphs include new ideas, so writers spend more time preparing to write about new topics. Similarly, writers pause longer before sentences that state generalizations than before sentences that give details or examples. This also makes sense, because generalizations are new ideas or syntheses of supporting points, but details and examples can follow from generalizations. It takes more effort to get the ball rolling than to keep it moving.

Some software developers have believed that recording writers' inactive time at the keyboard and nudging them with a prompt—such as Keep writing—after a predetermined period of silence would stimulate their search through long-term memory. The Matsuhashi research suggests, however, that interrupting a writer's pause time is likely to interrupt important planning time. A study by Woodruff, Scardamalia, and Bereiter, at the Ontario Institute of Studies in Education, on the effects of such nudging of 8-year-old writers showed that the children did not like the interruptions. The children did not explain their objections, but the research suggests that interrupting the pauses is likely to interrupt the incubation of ideas. Although using computer clock capacities to nudge writers is appealing to some teachers, it is not a good idea. A better use of the computer would be to provide a help key that writers can press when they are stuck; then they could be given guidance in defining or elaborating goals.

Textbook writers and teachers have acknowledged the importance of planning by teaching students to write outlines. However, recent research suggests that outlines, which are plans about the content of the piece, may not be appropriate until the writers have defined and developed process goals. Process goals help them define not only the information they need but also how they plan to go about developing it.

A word-processing program can be a useful tool for developing writing goals when it is used in communicative and collaborative environments like those discussed in Chapter 1. As writers try out their drafts on readers, they can clarify their goals. The word processor can also be useful for activities that illustrate the value of making and rearranging lists. Students can type lists of words and phrases that come to mind on a topic and then use the block move capacity to rearrange the words in related clusters. The automatic insert capacity is then useful for writing a phrase or sentence that states the relationship among the words in the list. Performing such exercises with pencil and paper has proved to be useful in helping writers generate and organize buds of ideas. Doing them on a computer can be more effective, because the computer offers features that help students progress more quickly from disorganized lists of words to developments of concepts.

When making lists on the computer, the writer has to remember formatting issues such as turning off the default **filling function** before obtaining a printout. A filling function arranges all the words in a file in relatively even lines across the page—as prose is supposed to appear. To keep words and phrases in list form, the writer has to use a command that overrides the filling function. In Apple Writer this command is .nf. With some programs, the writer can print the list version of the text without running the formatting program.

FRAMING AND OUTLINING

Some documents have prescribed sections, headings, and even introductory sentences. For example, most letters, memos, reports, proposals, news stories, and certain essays are based at least in part on prescribed formats. In some cases, section headings indicate the form and content of the document, as in the following student evaluation forms from a private school in New York:

Student Report

Student:
Term:
Term Objectives:
Test Scores:
General Comments on Current Work:
Progress over last semester:

In other cases, the structural requirements do not require that headings remain in the text. For example, argumentative essays typically include the statement of a position, arguments to support the position, presentation and critiques of counterarguments, and a conclusion. With the computer, teachers list such categories in a file that students copy and expand. Eventually, these structural headings can be replaced by headings that relate to the content of the piece. In this way, writers use the computer as a conceptual and logistical aid in the process of structuring ideas during prewriting. The teachers' headings give the students a place to start, and because the word-processing program offers flexibility for making changes, the students can work on each section as they obtain the relevant information.

Although writers like to use formatting options for altering margins, paging, and spacing, they often find that entering the formatting commands is tedious. To avoid repeated typing of computer formatting commands, they can store frame files with the commands for document formats they use frequently. The following is an example of a proposal frame with the commands in the Runoff and Rno formatting programs—which are similar to those in Apple Writer—for centering (.c), indenting (.i), and blank line (.s):

.c
Proposal for Additional Equipment
.s 2
RATIONALE:
.i 5
Demonstration of student needs:
.i 5
Demonstration of teacher needs:
.s 2

DESCRIPTION:
.i 5
The Equipment:
.i 5
Prices:
.i 5
Sources:
.s 2
PLAN FOR USE:
.i 5
General Plan:
.i 5
Example of 3 lessons with equipment:

Apple Writer, Perfect Writer, and many other programs for micro-computers include **templates**, or formatted frames, for business letters, but writers have to make their own frames for more specialized documents.

Plans often begin as rough outlines, noting the approach the writer intends to take in a writing task. For example, a committee of teachers planned to write a letter of request for donations to fund a program for teenage parents. The committee decided to encourage people to donate money by using vivid descriptions, comparing the lives of teenage parents and their offspring to the lives of young families in which the parents are over 25 years old. After deciding on the general approach of the letter, the writers included phrases for the major points they would present. They used a word-processing program to note their general approach, to refine it into an outline, and eventually to create the frame for the form letter they would send:

Date
Recipient
Street Address
City State Zip

Dear Recipient:

   1. Case study 1: description of a morning in the life of a teenager's child
   2. Case study 2: description of a morning in the life of an adult's child
   3. Paragraph about the program plan
   4. Request for money
Salutations

The committee later used the mail merge program in Apple Writer to insert the names, addresses, and salutations. The computer provided the capacity to begin with lists that evolved into the final letter.

Outlining helps writers structure and evaluate the information they collect when prewriting. Outlining requires that they check their goals for writing as well as the information they collect. Following an outline can also help a writer get started when writing documents with prescribed structures. Writers should not try to outline, however, until they have thought about the topics or have done some unstructured prewriting.

Formal outlining requires that each topic be divided into at least two subtopics. If there is a Roman numeral I, there must also be a II; point A under a Roman numeral must be followed by point B; and an additional subpoint 1 must be followed by a subpoint 2. Such a rubric ensures that ideas are developed completely, but it does not reflect thought processes, so such strict outlining procedures are most useful after extensive thinking and writing.

A flexible outlining program called ThinkTank is available on the Apple and the IBM PC. When writers have thought through their ideas or have done some prewriting, they can use the ThinkTank program to develop their lists into structured outlines. The program offers automatic numbering options and automatic block moves of text sections with related headings. Thus, writers do not have to take the time to mark sections that are already marked by heading boundaries. Writers using ThinkTank can begin an outline as a simple list—unnumbered and unstructured. As the list evolves, they can use ThinkTank to group related ideas, and the program will create a numbering and formatting scheme. The writers can then insert paragraphs under the headings. The program provides commands that allow the writers to "hide" paragraphs when they are considering only the outline on the screen and then bring the paragraphs back in the context of the outline.

The logistical value of frames and outlines is evident, but their conceptual value is more complex. Students can internalize important document structures as they incorporate the headings in their frames into sentences and texts. Frames also guide students in their memory search, help them include the necessary sections and elements in a document, and remind them to keep to the point. While freewriting brings up the unexpected, writing with outlines ensures that the expected is included. Students are more likely to use frames and outlines if they are available on a diskette than if they have to be copied each time from a book. It is important to note, however, that writers should create their own outlines or adapt predefined forms so that the resulting texts are not artificial or stiff.

PROMPTING

Just as speakers are guided by feedback from listeners, writers can refer to comments or **prompts** about their writing. The most useful prompts are those given by a reader in response to a piece. However, the reader isn't always available, so writers have to find ways to guide their own writing processes. An important part of learning to write is learning to develop texts individually, which means playing both writer and reader.

Prompting as a prewriting aid takes many forms. Teachers sometimes give students checklists to follow when they are planning a piece:

1. Decide on a topic.
2. Write as many words as come to mind on that topic.
3. Group the words into categories of similarity.
4. Write a sentence that relates all the categories.
5. If the sentence expresses or suggests an idea you'd like to write more about, . . .

Teachers also offer lists of questions students can use to guide their prewriting:

1. What am I most interested in today?
2. Why is that interesting to me?
3. Why would someone else find that interesting?
4. What would be a good opening sentence for a story or essay about this topic?

Writers also pose questions to themselves as they write. These question and comment prompts encourage them to make their process goals and content goals explicit.

- What do I know about the topic?
- Where can I get information?
- How should I record it?
- Should I just read until it all clicks, or should I take notes?
- I should try to state my general idea in one sentence.
- What do I really want to say?
- Who is my reader?
- What don't I know that I should find out?

Question prompts make the writing process similar to a conversational experience in which listeners stimulate speakers by requesting clarification. Experiments with 8-year-olds at the Ontario Institute for Studies in Education have shown that after simple encouragement to write more, the children had more to write on a topic, even after they had said they were absolutely finished with a piece. It was as though the suggestion to write more stimulated the search through memory. Prompting also helps relieve burdens on short-term memory, because it provides an explicit reminder of the reader. When writers are reminded by prompting that there will be readers, they do not have to take the mental time and space to remind themselves.

The computer is an ideal prompting instrument. Computer programs typically include comments or prompts for the people who use the programs and special-purpose programs can be written to give writers explicit prompts for prewriting. ELIZA is a classic example of a computer prompting program. Joseph Weizenbaum developed the ELIZA program to illustrate that rather simple programs can appear to ask questions and respond to the answers people give. A person interacts with the ELIZA program as though talking to a psychiatrist, and ELIZA responds with stored phrases to specific keywords, such as *mother*, that the user types. ELIZA's responses appear in uppercase in the following example:

I need some help, that much seems certain
WHAT WOULD IT MEAN TO YOU IF YOU GOT SOME HELP
Perhaps I could learn to get along with my mother
TELL ME MORE ABOUT YOUR FAMILY
My mother takes care of me
WHO ELSE IN YOUR FAMILY TAKES CARE OF YOU
My father
YOUR FATHER
You are like my father in some ways
WHAT RESEMBLANCE DO YOU SEE
You are not very aggressive but I think you don't want me to notice that
WHAT MAKES YOU THINK I AM NOT VERY AGGRESSIVE
You don't argue with me
WHY DO YOU THINK I DON'T ARGUE WITH YOU
You are afraid of me
DOES IT PLEASE YOU THAT I AM AFRAID OF YOU*

Weizenbaum used this program to demonstrate the limits of the computer's apparent consciousness. His program presents prompts automatically in response to specific words and word patterns the writer types into the computer. It does not understand meanings or other abstractions that are not reducible to exact words or patterns of words, and it only responds to correctly spelled keywords. The prompts point to text features and leave the thinking up to the writer.

Writing researchers and software developers, such as Hugh Burns, Allan Collins, Chip Bruce, and Andee Rubin, have used conversational computer prompting like Weizenbaum's to stimulate writers as they compose. Researchers at Bell Laboratories, IBM, and universities have programmed computer analyses to stimulate writers as they revise. The programs present text analyses and, in one case, conversational prompts such as "Write everything you know about the topic" or "Have you given your reader enough details about your point?" Because of computer programming capacities, the words "the topic" and "your point" in such prompts can be replaced by words or phrases that the writer has noted as the topic.

*Joseph Weizenbaum, *Computer Power and Human Reason* (San Francisco: Freeman, 1976), p. 4.

The computer is more efficient for prompting than lists on paper or notecards are, because computer prompts can be presented individually when the writer requests them. Writers can initiate prompting if the program includes commands for requesting help. The prompts can appear one at a time within, under, or above the part of the text in question.

Prompts on the computer can also fill in words related to a writer's specific topics. For example, Burns and Culp created a computer program that guides college students in beginning an essay by providing suggestions intended to help them collect information relevant to the topic. In the following example, the program responses appear in uppercase:

DURING THIS EXPLORATION PROCESS, YOU WILL BE ASKED TO CLARIFY THE PURPOSE OF YOUR PAPER ON FEAR OF DEATH.

SO HOW WOULD YOU BRIEFLY DESCRIBE THE PURPOSE OF YOUR PAPER BY COMPLETING THIS STATEMENT: THE PURPOSE OF THIS PAPER IS TO . . .

examine the fear of death people have, where we get those fears, and how we may reduce those fears.

FINE, WALT, YOU AND I WILL TALK ABOUT OUR PURPOSE. RELAX NOW, WALT, AND ENJOY THIS BRAINSTORMING SESSION.

WHAT OBJECTS DO YOU ASSOCIATE WITH THE FEAR OF DEATH? HOW MIGHT THEY BE INCLUDED IN YOUR THEME?

Fear of the Unknown, cessation of life, fear of causing pain to our loved ones.

THAT'S THE IDEA WALT. GIVE ME SOME MORE INFO NOW.

Pain is another fear causer, knowing we have to die does not relieve the pain/fear of dying.

SUPER, WALT!

ANYTHING ELSE? (YOU CAN ADD MORE INFO, ASK A QUESTION, OR GIVE A COMMAND—WHATEVER YOU WISH.)*

Burns and Culp report that prewriting prompts on the computer stimulate writers' thinking, help them dredge up information they already have about the topic, and become aware of information they need to find out. Walt's writing is hardly a composition or even a first draft, but he has begun to think about his topic in writing, and he has made notes that he can use for additional planning and composing.

*Hugh Burns and George Culp, "Stimulating Invention in English Composition through Computer-Assisted Instruction," *Educational Technology*, August 1980, p. 8.

Prompting programs vary in the amount of specific information they request and the method of presentation. Most prompting programs present questions; the writer responds by typing answers and then signals—by pressing the return key, for example—that he or she is ready to go on to the next question.

Helen Schwartz, of Oakland University in Michigan, developed a program called SEEN with question prompts designed to help college freshmen write character analyses for literature class. The questions in SEEN are intended to help the student writers collect, organize, and synthesize information about literary protagonists. The program presents the following questions (a student's responses to a few questions appear in uppercase letters):

1. Name a character. DOROTHY
2. In what work? WIZARD OF OZ
3. What is your opinion of the character Dorothy in the Wizard of Oz? SPUNKY
4. Argue that Dorothy is spunky by providing the following evidence: What does Dorothy do that shows Dorothy is spunky? What does Dorothy say that shows Dorothy is spunky?
5. How do others react to Dorothy which shows she is spunky?
6. Who is in a situation similar to Dorothy's and how does a comparison of behaviors show that Dorothy is spunky?
7. Is there a 3rd person narrator? What does he say which shows Dorothy is spunky?*

Research on prewriting and planning suggests that writers need the flexibility to move from prompting environments to prewriting environments to composing with a word-processing program if an idea begins to flow, because the writing process cannot be divided into rigidly separate steps. Programs should allow writers easy movement between prompts, notes, and text files in the word-processing program.

While some prompting programs are designed as thought stimulators, others are designed as thought organizers. "The QUILL Publisher," developed at Bolt, Beranek, and Newman, is an example of such a guide; it sets up date, salutation, and body sections of letters. Programs based on the form of a document stimulate writers' thinking because they free the writers to focus on the content of the document, rather than on the superficial aspects that the computer programs can provide.

Other planning programs prompt writers to compose their texts according to the sections they have to include in a specific document. For example, a planning program for a book report might include prompts for a brief summary of the text, an analysis of the plot conflict, character sketches, and the reader's interpretation and opinion of the book. A planner for a lab report might include the following prompts:

*Helen Schwartz, *Teachers' Guide to the SEEN Program*, prepublication version, p. 19.

1. Experimenter
2. Purpose
3. Date
4. Hypothesis
5. Apparatus
6. Method
7. Procedure
8. Results
9. Conclusion
10. Discussion

The planner in the Bolt, Beranek and Newman QUILL program gives the writer the option to fill in his or her own prompt questions:

PLANNER

1. USE—Use a PLANNER to start working on your writing.
2. CREATE—Make a new PLANNER
3. NONE OF THE ABOVE

Type your choice and press RETURN

If the writer types 2, the program gives instructions to type in a one-line introductory message, a short topic idea, and additional topic ideas. The program then stores these prompts and presents them to writers who use the planner. Planners are stored according to keywords, titles, authors, and entry numbers. Someone needing a guide for a report on a work by Shakespeare, for example, might type **book report** while using a diskette that stores planners or might decide to type **Shakespeare** to find an appropriate planner outline.

Woodruff, Scardamalia, and Bereiter, of the Ontario Institute of Studies in Education, have written prompting programs that provide more structure than the programs in SEEN or QUILL. These computer-aided composing programs give specific information on structuring essays. The prompts are intended to guide children in using basic discourse elements in their essays. If a student using the computer-aided composing programs wants help, the program offers a list of nine statements about the structural elements of essays. For example, the list on the screen reads, "When you are writing an argument you can include: 1. a statement of belief, 2. an explanation of your belief . . . " The child can press a button to get more information on any item on the list. The program also presents such questions as "Do you have an opinion on this topic?" and related expansions, such as "Okay, let's tell the reader." These prompts are so specific that they function as an outline, so they may be appropriate for lessons on essay structure.

Researchers who have used such automatic prompting for prewriting report that prompts stimulate writers' thinking and keep them on track with a topic. It is easy to postpone writing when the page is mute, but conversational prompts in an interactive environment such as a computer program urge a reluctant or struggling writer to keep going.

Prompting can wake up words in memory and can help writers synthesize knowledge in new ways, but prompting programs cannot respond to meaning or logical development. Writers must deal with these aspects themselves and with the help of other people. Also, because computer prompting can lead to stilted text, writers using such programs should consider the results to be thought-stimulating activities or notes, rather than first drafts. The developers of QUILL suggest in their manual that the texts writers create with the planner be used as notes for a draft. Since prewriting and planning activities serve only to stimulate a writer's thinking about a topic, the results are rarely presentable as complete texts. In the Burns and Culp example, Walt's writing is hardly a composition, or even a first draft, but he has created notes that he can use for additional composing—or the exercise might have convinced him that he has more thinking and research to do. Even if prompts do not offer specific help on details of the writer's point and argument, they function as springboards for self-questioning.

The main problem with prompting programs is that, at this early stage in the development of computer writing tools, the programs are limited for use on specific machines and with specific word-processing programs. Writers who work with a prompting program have to use a compatible word-processing program, rather than one of their choice. Also, some prompting programs trap the writer's responses in a file that cannot be used easily in any word-processing program. The most useful prompting programs are those that create text files that can be stored on disk and loaded into the writer's favorite word-processing program when he or she is expanding and revising the prompted notes.

Despite the positive anecdotal reports on the value of prompting, little detailed research has been done on its effects. Specific uses of prompting programs and their effects on writers of different ages are discussed in Chapters 7 through 11.

GATHERING INFORMATION FROM OTHER SOURCES

In addition to using material stored in their own minds, writers get information from other people, from libraries, and from their environment. Just as the interchange in conversations helps speakers discover their ideas, communication with other sources can help writers search their own memories. Electronic communication programs such as electronic mail, chat programs, and computer confrences, are computer tools that can help writers think of what to write; they serve as environments for prewriting. As discussed in Chapter 1, electronic communication provides a meaningful writing environment because it helps people use writing to communicate. Students can use electronic communication tools to gather information from others by engaging in computer conferences and computer correspondence.

Students can also use electronic mail for conducting written interviews. Besides interviewing others in their own classroom or school, students can use the outreach capacities of electronic networking to interview those who have identified themselves on a network. The value of such an exercise is that the information exchanged in the conference or interview is already written down for the writer to ponder when considering the topic he or she is going to write about. This writer also has written verbatim quotations for use as references. The capacity to save texts is usually a standard feature in computer conferencing and electronic mail programs. Saving networked conversations, such as those in the CHAT program, requires additional software—usually a program that records and saves in a file every keystroke typed by the participants.

Research

As part of their preparation, writers often do research in printed materials. The research process presents students with several problems—some logistical and some involved in defining the goals of writing and evaluating the completeness of texts. Research in the computer environment can minimize logistical problems when writers know how to control the tools. Setting up and using computer research tools can help students sharpen their ideas for writing as well as the expression of those ideas.

Information Storage and Retrieval

The computer offers extensive, compact, and organized storage space for information. The computer's capacities to store and access information are valuable for writers. Because computer programs can follow detailed instructions quickly, they can serve as writers' fingers, searching through large files for specific information.

Computer databases and database search programs are research tools. Computer **databases** include texts of books and articles, lists of services, or other information the database maker has decided to include. Database search programs provide a link between the researcher and the database by locating and displaying sections of the resource material according to keywords or topics. The database maker decides on the information to include and its organization, which also influences the database searching possibilities. Databases vary along several dimensions: control of information entry, flexibility of database design and update, search procedures, and presentation procedures. Writers can subscribe to commercially available database and search facilities, or they can create their own.

One kind of database that serves writers is the information utility, a type of "read-only" database that has been created by an expert database manager or librarian. Resources such as the New York Times Information Service, the Dow Jones Information Service, The Source, and CompuServe, include news, financial data, services, and other information that may be of interest to a general audience. The number of such general-purpose databases is increasing steadily. Special-purpose databases like Medline, Lexis, and ERIC include publication summaries and other information of interest to people in specific fields.

The cost of a full subscription to such databases is high, but researchers can pay a fee to use them one or two times. For example, it cost me $120 to use DIALOG, a library's search program, on the educational database ERIC for a list of articles on word processing. I was charged a flat fee for using the system and a calibrated rate for the time the search took. The program identified about fifty articles on my topic. The list I received was neither complete nor up-to-date, because it is difficult to keep up with such rapidly advancing fields as computer applications, but it would have taken me a long time to find even these fifty pieces in any other way. The reference lists in the fifty articles then led me to other sources. Database searches on subjects with longer histories yield more satisfying results.

Cost also influences the amount of information stored in a database. Much more information can be stored on a 2-inch section of computer tape than in a 2-inch section of a book, which is one reason why computer storage is so useful. Nevertheless, the storage space is not unlimited, and it can be costly, so database managers have to make careful decisions about what to include. Librarians choose the books to include in their collections, but because of the multiple sources of books, readers can easily collect the information they need. Eventually, readers will be able to do likewise with electronically stored information.

Journalists often consult computer databases. Much of the information they need is available from news services, such as the UPI wires, which they can read on their word processor screens. Journalists who have word processors at their desks can consult the news services by giving a few commands. They can view a list of the latest UPI updates, type in the code of a particular story, view it on the screen, and then switch back to the word-processing program to write notes or begin the story. Of course, journalists still have to consult books and articles for background information that is not included in the computer news database.

Databases are also stored on **videotex and teletext** systems, which subscribers can access through cable TV lines in their homes. Videotex and teletext information is transmitted via broadcast and cable channels. QUBE in the United States and Prestel in Great Britain are the oldest videotex systems. From 1980 to 1983, many new videotex and teletext systems began

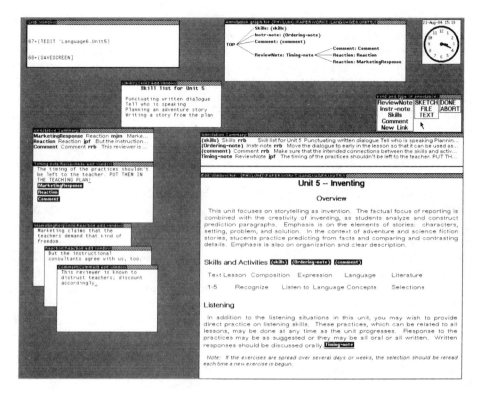

John Seely Brown and Richard Burton at Xerox Palo Alto Research Center are developing flexible tools to enhance the structuring of ideas.

to appear, but several projects have ended because the systems are so costly. Videotex capacities are ahead of their time in some ways. Although the communication channel can be added to existing cable lines, the large companies who can afford the franchises of such systems do not want to begin full-scale operations until they can be sure the information they select will make people "turn on the tube." These systems are under much the same type of pressure as prime-time television productions, because they have entered into the mass-market arena.

Writers can search for information from their homes if they subscribe to a service and have the proper cable attachments, computing attachments, and a keypad for entering commands and responses. A videotex service transmits a limited number of pages over the cable. The information, which might be news, stock quotations, luxury services such as restaurant guides, movie schedules, or games, is changed and updated periodically. The user selects from options on a menu by pressing keys on the number pad. Such limited research services will have more research potential for writers at home when the cost comes down and the available types of information increase. Another limit of these cable information systems is that the user can only select codes that stand for option choices or answers to games and puzzles. When the systems become more sophisticated and large enough to handle input from full keyboards, they will be more useful for people who want to write. The greatest educational value of such tools thus far is that they allow people to read the latest news selectively on their television screens.

On-line database searches, such as DIALOG for ERIC, guide the writer's search for information. Researchers can view sections of text in the computer memory by typing key subject words into the search program. The search program then asks the writer questions aimed at defining the search area. A librarian may assist in attempts to find the exact keywords that will identify all and only the information the researcher wants. Unfortunately, if the researcher spells the keyword incorrectly or gives a synonym, the program does not pick it up. For example, if I search for "word processor," the program doesn't identify "word-processor," "word-processing program," "text editor," or "text-editor." Search programs could be written so that they find synonyms and help the researcher list all possible keywords that relate to his or her topic.

Another problem with database searches is that the organization and keywords in the database reflect the idiosyncratic logic of the database programmer or information coder. For example, the coder may have related the information to a set of keywords that the writer does not have in his or her vocabulary. The researcher must try to think as the database coder did when organizing and categorizing the information. If the coder has thought logically, the system users might not have much difficulty identifying the appropriate search strategy, but there rarely is only one way to organize information.

Databases are currently used in the medical, legal, journalistic, and financial professions. The Medline database is effective because medical information and terms are precise and universal; in contrast, social science databases are more difficult to use because their terms are sometimes vague. Database retrieval systems will probably improve as more research and development is done to define the potentials, the problems, and the users of such research tools.

Doing research from a database is potentially more efficient than gathering information from individual magazines, journals, books, and news sources in different sections of a large library. Using databases, a researcher can find and print information from one location. With a computer terminal, a **modem** to correct the terminal via phone lines, and access to several databases, a researcher can consult more than one database. This gives writers browsing power and direct connection to information without having to run around and collect materials. It would also be useful for the researcher to be able to transfer sections of a database into a personal notes file, but mass copying of databases could lead to problems. Plagiarism would be easy, and a large amount of useless copying would be done—just as people make photocopies of many articles they will never read. Standards and ethics for these issues have yet to be developed within the culture of computer users.

One value of having to tell a computer program exact keywords for research topics is that it helps writers narrow their topics. For example, a psychology student was thinking of writing a term paper about the change in attitudes caused by the Vietnam War. She used the on-line database search program in the university library to obtain a list of articles that included information on the keywords "Vietnam War" and "attitudes." The program searched for articles that included both keywords and suggested that she find another term to help focus her search. She added "patriotism." The program then asked her if there was any type of article that it should ignore. She decided that she did not want articles on attitudes about Vietnamese patriotism during the Vietnam War, which led her to the final choice of her keywords and the general topic of her study—the ways in which American soldiers and their families used newfound patriotism to justify their losses in the war.

Although few schoolchildren have the resources at their fingertips to do a complete report by consulting databases, they can learn about research in a computer environment as part of the writing process. A report-writing exercise on a mini-database can help children learn how to find information, evaluate the information for completeness and relevance to their topic, and take notes in class before they go to the library to seek the information in books. The exploring skills used with databases are not exactly the same as those used in the library, but children can learn about steps in the research process as they sit in groups in front of a computer screen, selecting and refining topics. Moreover, these children will probably be able to use databases as research tools when they grow up.

Writers can set up and search their own databases. Programs that offer writers tools for structuring, entering, and searching their own databases are usually called **database management systems**, but true database management systems are extremely complex and run on large computers. Many of the microcomputer programs that offer templates for setting up and searching databases are called **file management systems**. "Database program" is the more general name used to refer to the various types of programs that offer tools for entering, organizing, and retrieving data. These programs provide writers with electronic notecards.

Database programs vary in the amount of flexibility they allow the writer. Many database programs require that writers structure, name, and leave space for each type of information they will require. Another variable among programs is the amount of flexibility the writer has for restructuring information.

Writers can use database programs on their microcomputers to set up original libraries. The value of the homemade database is that it provides a central location for information. Creating a database requires thinking about the subject and analyzing it as well as gathering information. One reason some writers create cryptic, disorganized texts is that they have not engaged in active collecting, organizing, and thinking about their topics. Setting up a database provides an exercise in such active thinking.

Database programs also allow the writer to categorize and section off information or text after writing it. The Bolt, Beranek and Newman group has included a simple database maker called the Library in their QUILL program. Students enter information into files on the Library diskette, then note keywords for each paragraph. Later, they can type in keywords to find different sections of their own or others' texts that mention the keywords. The files can be searched and printed by topic, author, and titles. In an early version of the QUILL manual, the developers describe how a student can use the Library for research:

> He [Matt] needs information about sharks for an adventure story he's writing. He begins by looking through the keywords in the Library's "Animal Encyclopedia" disk. He finds a list of keywords including "arctic," "cats," "fish," "horses," "whales," etc. "Sharks" does not appear on the list so Matt decides to look at all entries with the keyword "fish." After he chooses this keyword, the titles of four articles about fish are shown on the screen, one of which is called "Denizens of the Deep." He suspects that entry may be about sharks, and so he asks for the article itself to read.*

The process continues until Matt decides that there is no further information and sets up a "shark" file, adding notes to the "Denizens" piece.

Creating a database guides writers in analyzing their subject. Database entries typically include **fields** of specific information on specific lines in each entry. The fields are categories of information that the researcher will later be able to use for retrieving information from the database. For a database on sharks, a researcher would set up fields for names of types of sharks, habitats, markings, and other related topics that become evident as the researcher acquires information. A restriction of a database with rigid field definitions is the number of characters that can fit in each field. The computer needs this structure so that it can know, for example, that habitat fields will appear in characters 20–30 of a given line in the entry. A student creating a shark database with the program dBASE II would fill in information in response to the following prompts:

```
.create
ENTER FILENAME: sharks
ENTER RECORD STRUCTURE
AS FOLLOWS:
   FIELD
   001 Shark types
```

*Bolt, Beranek and Newman, Inc., and the Network, Inc. *QUILL Teacher's Guide*, field test edition, p. 14.

Most programs offer commands for adding and deleting entries and fields, but few offer commands for renaming and reoganizing the fields in an entry. Also, some database programs create files that the writer can revise or merge in the word processor. Further discussion of the use of database creation and searching for writers of different ages appears in Chapters 7 through 11.

Videodiscs

Writing teachers often use visual material for lessons on details in writing point-of-view essays and comparison essays, because photographs and moving pictures include information students can use in their writing exercises. Pictures and films are particularly suited to classroom activities that proceed over time. Teachers and students can select visual springboards for writing that organize the information to be used for a particular exercise. Students can even create their own film essays and stories with inexpensive movie cameras and video equipment. With still or moving pictures, students can compare their impressions, perspectives, and treatments of the visual information in their writing. A picture of one sea shell, for example, can evoke many different ideas and stories for different writers, and several pictures of the same sea shell from different perspectives can help someone examine the shell completely.

Videodiscs provide flexible libraries of visual material that can be used in oral and written discussions. A videodisc looks like a long-playing record, but it is silver-colored, with rainbow hues that appear in the light. The videodisc stores thousands of frames of visual information which are read on a videodisc player that responds to a search program on a computer. Image frames on a videodisc can be identified and displayed in random order, as the viewer types in frame numbers on a computer. This type of image processing is much more flexible than films, which display frames in sequential order. A videodisc can be a valuable visual tool for writing instruction—as photographs and films have been—but the random access capability makes this visual tool more flexible. Students can use the information for research or for creating their own video essays.

A teacher can select a film on videodisc, such as a production of *Hamlet*, which is frequently shown in English classes. As students discuss and write about the film, they can move quickly to scenes they want to examine, compare, and contrast. The students can replay the film in the original order or in novel orders, depending on what they want to look at.

If students make a film that will eventually be transferred to videodisc, they can create segments that they later may view in various orders as an exercise in sequencing of information, exploration of cause-and-effect relationships, and differences in points of view. For example, if they film the same scene from the points of view of different characters, each student can write a piece from the point of view of one of the characters. When the students later compare their writing, they will see the relationship between a character's and a writer's point of view and they can examine specific features of the text, such as organization of information, word choice, and even presentation of facts. Working with film in this way is useful because it gives the students a sharper focus on events and details than they can get when they observe undefined events that they cannot replay later. Writers will have another valuable tool for learning important writing techniques when the cost of making and playing videodiscs decreases. They will be able to illustrate texts with moving pictures, integrate visual and verbal communication, and do research from film archives at their writing desks. Also, when videodisc information equipment can be interfaced with word-processing and database programs, writers will have additional composing and production tools.

NOTE TAKING

Note taking is a memory and organizational aid. Jotting notes stimulates writers' long-term memory search and can help writers collect new information or recombine old information in new ways. Writers' notes might be outlines of material they have read or of their own musings. Notes sometimes trace others' ideas and arguments about a topic, thus guiding writers in learning and reinterpreting ideas. Notes might also include references to books and interviews, exact quotations from sources, or paraphrases. Notes can also be collections of words and phrases that writers jot down as they think. All types of notes help writers plan and focus their attention.

The problem with traditional forms of note taking is that as the notes are transformed into plans, texts, and finished copy, writers have to recopy—or pay someone else to recopy—even the words and paragraphs that do not change. Notecards are efficient, because they can be rearranged as writers decide on the structure of the text, and notes on paper can be cut and pasted. However, these methods are useful only in the rough drafting stage. After that, writers must merge and synthesize their notes from different sources. Cutting and pasting notecards is a messy process, so writers often recopy their notes as they reorganize and recopy them again in subsequent drafts.

The computer can be a flexible notepad. Writers can use a word-processing program to enter notes directly from their sources or from notes they have jotted on paper. With the word-processing program, they can type their notes into one file or several files that can be changed, expanded, or merged as they compose a piece.

The option to divide the computer screen into multiple windows is another feature that writers can use for note taking, although it is not a standard part of all word-processing programs. Some programs for microcomputers offer two windows, and several experimental systems have more than two. The multiple window feature functions in several ways for note

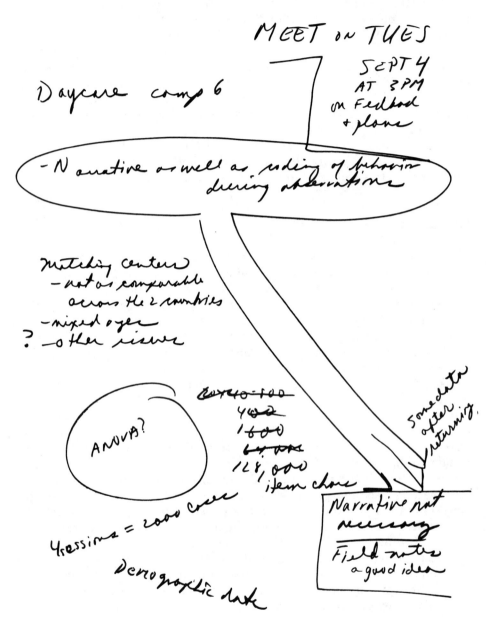

Writers initially express their ideas in a variety of forms.

taking. For example, a writer can enter bibliographic information in the top window in the format required for presentation—such as the Modern Language Association or American Psychological Association style. The notes from each reference can be entered in the bottom window, and each section of notes can be labeled with the number of the bibliography entry of its source.

Once the notes have been coded so that their source can be identified, the bibliography entries can be ordered as required. In this way, the writer has also created a reference list file. After collecting the notes entries, the writer can block move the sections of notes into one or more orders for the final paper.

Bibliography and notes entries can also be entered in database programs. This takes more time than the two-window method, because the information has to be carefully structured, but the writer then is able to identify sections of notes by keyword labels and the bibliography entries are in alphabetical order or in an order related to topics.

Journalists often use word processors for taking notes. As they enter into the computer the notes they took with a pen at a fire, a presidential speech, or while browsing through news service texts on the teletype or video display, they can reorganize the information and craft sentences. They do not have to waste time writing the same pieces of information again and again, and they do not have to worry about losing important pieces of paper. Other writers write the story directly from the computer notepad. The ideal method, of course, is to take notes directly on a small, portable computer. Some portable computers have limited text-viewing capacities, but since scrutinizing notes is not so important as recording them for later use, this limitation might not affect writers negatively. The text files that contain notes taken at a ball game or other event can later be transferred to a word-processing program on a system that has full screen capacities.

One of the most difficult tasks for student researchers is organizing and consolidating the notes they take from the books and encyclopedias they consult when preparing to do a report. Storing their notes in a database helps students begin to organize information as they write it for the first time. After writers have made such databases, they inevitably say, "Now I see a better way I could have done that." After they have worked with the material, they can figure out more categories, better category names, or more interesting relationships among the categories. Such an "Aha!" phenomenon attests to the usefulness of the database-making activity. The writer has been guided in analyzing the subject—which would have been more difficult without the prompting, defining, and refining activities provided by the program.

SUMMARY

Prewriting on the computer is like thinking, because the writer can work quickly and can follow thoughts with few of the constraints imposed by the linear order of writing on paper. The writer can enter lists and notes on the computer as they come to mind and organize them appropriately as the piece evolves. With word-processing capacities, writers can expand their notes and let their texts evolve. Writers can also use computer tools for access to information, coaching, and record keeping as they begin to explore ideas for a piece.

The prewriting session of a writer who had all the tools mentioned in this chapter might look something like this:

Janet sits down at her microcomputer, puts the word processor diskette into the drive and types nonstop for 15 minutes of freewriting. After reading these notes, she labels sections with keywords. She saves the text, and a program groups together all the sections with similar keywords. Once she has written everything she thinks she knows about the topic, she uses a prompting program to wake up sleeping ideas, then sends computer mail to a friend who is writing about a related topic. Together they dial up a computer database to get some facts they both need. They now have several files of notes and an outline, and they feel ready to write their papers.

COMPUTER TOOLS
FOR PREWRITING

The following computer tools discussed in this chapter are particularly useful in the prewriting process:

- Word-processing programs
  —Multiple-window feature
- Outlining programs
- Templates
- Prompting programs
- Electronic communication programs
  —Electronic mail programs
  —Chat programs
  —Computer conference programs
- Database programs
  —Computer databases
  —Information utilities
  —Database search programs
  —Database maker programs
  —Database management systems
- Videotex and teletext
- Videodiscs

Composing   5

"My thoughts are faster than my hand, so I forget what I wanted to say." Composing involves translating ideas, notes, and plans into a structured draft. Some teachers and researchers use the term *composing process* to mean the entire writing process. This chapter deals more specifically with the careful or "composed" process of forming texts—the composing process, which often follows the prewriting process.

Even when writers have done prewriting or planning, composing is not simply transcribing. When they are composing a text, writers are holding facts and goals in mind while crafting sentences, paragraphs, and larger sections. They must attend to the document form as well as to the content. Composing involves several types of creation at one time, even when there is an outline. Sometimes, writers don't notice flaws in an outline until they actually start forming sentences. For example, an outline for a paper on children's written expression might include "drawings," which would be a logical subtopic in such a paper, but the writer might not realize, until he or she has trouble composing a paragraph about drawing, that it isn't related to the rest of the text. Because of the dynamic nature of the writing process, different writers have different plans and paces in composing drafts, and an individual writer has varying success in composing different texts.

Prewriting is like warming up for a race, and composing is like running a race. Writers have an advantage over runners, however, in that their race—the draft—can be rerun; writers can revise. Just as it is important for writers to prewrite with the assumption that other processes will follow, they should also remind themselves that they can revise after they compose. Knowing that revising will follow, writers can compose freely—almost as if they were talking.

One problem many student writers have in composing is that they try to do it too soon. They try to compose a draft before they do any prewriting. Therefore, the planning process is incomplete, resulting in a first draft that is sketchy, poorly organized, or awkwardly phrased. Beethovian writers, as described in Chapter 4, create drafts to discover their ideas, so they are prewriting as they compose. Because they compose texts quickly to discover their ideas, these writers often revise extensively.

Beginning writers have the greatest success composing directly from thought when they write from personal experience. The topic itself provides structure—a narrative, chronological structure—the familiar organization of everyday speech and memory storage. The more abstract the writing task, the more writers tend to perform other writing or talking activities before composing—or, if they are Beethovian, the more they have to revise later.

Study your own composing process and those of your students to determine the most comfortable composing style for each person. After describing your composing process, you could ask older students to describe their own. No research has yet been done to show whether writers' styles change over time, but even young writers have a penchant for one particular composing style. Mozartians don't write until they have done some visible planning. For young children, this planning is usually reflection rather than prewriting, while more mature writers typically make notes when they are planning. In contrast, Beethovians begin to write soon after receiving a topic and write steadily until they have produced a draft.

A teacher who knows how much planning time a student needs can help the student decide when to start composing. A student who is a planner should be given sufficient time before he or she is expected to produce a draft, but a student who plans by drafting should be encouraged to compose quickly and revise later. College students who write well except at exam time may be Mozartians, who have to plan before composing. Their counterpart Beethovians may find it easier to write exams because they can work fast— and most professors make allowances for some mistakes in quickly written exams.

It is also important to have an idea of how much prewriting should precede composing for different types of documents. Highly structured documents provide organizational formats, so writers can focus on creating the document and gathering the information. In contrast, writers must do all the planning—including organizational planning—for fiction, essays, and other types of writing that do not have predetermined structures, so the writers have to spend more time planning.

Another important writing skill is knowing when to recompose a text rather than revise it. A friend gave me advice when I was about to begin revising the first draft of this book. She said she has found that it is sometimes easier to recompose a draft completely than "worry it to death." Sometimes she rewrites the same ideas, and sometimes she changes material during the second composing process. In either case, she has found the new drafts to be "fresher" than overrevised text would have been. When I said that I find it difficult to ignore a draft I have nurtured for months, she added that all the work on prior drafts helps her refine ideas and practice wording and, in short, warms her up for the final composing session—which works the best. This suggests that the writer should be ready to compose at all stages in creating a piece—and to compose again.

WORD PROCESSING AND COMPOSING

The composing process requires flexibility, speed, and structuring ability. The word processor is the main computer tool for composing, because it offers writers flexibility and the potential to work quickly. Word-processing programs free writers from the linearity of the written page as they compose. They can compose a text sequentially, following an outline, or they can insert ideas at any point in a text or in different files that can be merged and rearranged. It is sometimes difficult for writers to free themselves from the linear constraints of composing with traditional tools, because pencils, paper, and typewriters are best suited for composing sentences as they will appear in the text.

A writer who knows how to type can compose quickly on the computer and store the text for later changes. In addition to the automatic insertion and editing commands, word-processing programs have several features that can simplify the writer's task of translating plans into prose. The **word wrap** feature, for example, automatically brings the cursor to the next line when the writer has put about 72 characters on an 80-character-per-line system. In contrast, when using a typewriter, the writer must listen for the margin bell and then press the carriage return key.

The relationship between composing and prewriting activities that precede it can be closer on the computer than with traditional writing tools. The note taking, interviewing, outlining, and freewriting that writers do on the computer can serve either as reference material or as beginnings of drafts. The computer's capacity to work on the same document in stages gives writers the freedom to mesh process and product. Using a word-processing program, writers can compose sections as they come to mind or as they appear in an outline. In addition, they have the freedom to move sections or insert new ones while composing. In this way, writers can compose comfortably in sequential order, as thoughts and wording come to mind, but they can move the cursor quickly to the place where the emerging text fits, type it in, and then continue typing at the place where the next topic to come to mind fits.

Word-processing insert capacities give writers tools for filling in outlines, completing frames, and composing by selecting and expanding sections of freewritten drafts without having to recompose each piece. With pencil and paper or typewriter, creating a draft involves writing it out as if none of it had been produced before. Also, when working with traditional tools, writers are constrained by the sequential ordering of pages. If they think of new material on a topic after they have completed several paragraphs on the topic, they have to write the new paragraph out of place and indicate with an arrow where it should appear when the text is recopied. Such a constraint could influence them to leave out the new information or to write it so that it makes sense elsewhere in the text, rather than with the paragraphs to which it is most closely related.

On a word processor, writers can compose drafts by a building-block technique, collecting good paragraphs and sentences from their notes or freewriting. For example, Doug, a college student, liked to freewrite after he had read each article he had researched for his report on language-learning difficulties. He saved each article summary in a file named for its author. When he was composing his report, Doug viewed these summary files in the top screen of Apple Writer. If he found a good section, he transferred it from the top screen to the bottom. Then he expanded or revised the section and added a transition from the prior section and a transition to the point he planned to make in the next paragraph. He often added paragraphs after transferring notes, because many of his good ideas had not been completely developed.

The two-window feature and buffers provide other valuable composing aids. A writer who learns to manage multiple screens and buffers can compose as ideas come to mind by inserting paragraphs in a logical order, rather than in the order in which they come to mind, which may not be so logical. For example, I had planned to have three sections in a software review I was writing: (1) description of the program, (2) critique of the visual display, and (3) critique of the word processor design. The assignment was straightforward and my ideas were clear, so I decided to compose without writing an outline. I began the description in a file called review.raw, but as I was writing the description, I realized why the visual display of the software was confusing. I gave the Apple Writer two-window command—CTRL Y—moved the cursor to the other window—again, CTRL Y—named a new file, part 2.raw, and typed in the explanation that had come to mind. Then I moved the cursor to the top of this new file and finished the description I had been writing. After saving both files, I decided where the explanation fit best and moved the text from the bottom screen into the top screen.

A writer can also view two parts of the same text in the two windows, which may be necessary because the computer screen holds far less text than can be viewed at once on several sheets of paper. For example, a writer can view the beginning of the text in the top screen and a later section in the bottom screen. Similarly, writers using the two-window feature can refer to an outline in the top screen while composing the text in the bottom screen, or they can move sentences and paragraphs from a notes file displayed in the top screen to the evolving text in the bottom screen.

This building-block approach to creating a draft is more flexible than composing techniques used with traditional tools—unless, of course, the

Writers use windows to merge steps in the composing process.

writer is able to compose mentally. A writer who is able to move a cursor quickly and type a paragraph in a spot where it fits logically is making an on-the-spot and reversible decision about the evolving structure of a piece. Since this decision can be carried out relatively effortlessly by moving the cursor, the writer can focus on content and wording while producing text in a semiorganized way. For example, a teacher who was preparing a student's study plan began with a section on the language arts activities the child needed and then described the social studies curriculum. When the teacher was writing the next section—on science—a few more ideas on language arts activities came to mind. He moved the cursor back to the middle of the language arts section and added a paragraph about a related activity, then returned to complete the science section. As he did this jumping, the program realigned and reformatted the text, leaving it neat at all times. Writers using traditional tools can compose in this way by moving to new sheets of paper when they have new ideas, but it is difficult to insert new sections between two sentences that meet in the middle of a line on the middle of a page. The time it takes to cut apart pieces of paper or to make notes about sections to be added later is time that could distract the writer from new thoughts.

The building-block style of composing is appropriate for expressing the overall scope, organization, and style of a piece. Nevertheless, there are potential problems with such an approach. Drafts composed in this way do not always maintain clear pronoun reference or smooth transitions between paragraphs, so the resulting text may read like a patchwork collection of paragraphs. There may be gaps, repetitions, or both. Sections written at different times may reflect different styles, even though they were composed by one author. Writers who use word-processing capacities to compose in this way must make sure that the sections of text are connected smoothly. After they have built and arranged the sections, they can smooth out transitions between them, rather than spending time recopying the sections.

Finding such problems in word-processed text is easier for some writers, who find that the neat printout clearly reveals sloppy language, transition problems, section imbalances, and inconsistencies, such as uneven paragraph lengths and unbalanced headings. These superficial features that are apparent in print often indicate deeper problems in the text. For example, a paragraph that looks relatively short may not be well developed. Finding a section with four subheadings followed by a section with only one may mean that the longer section should be cut or should include the shorter section. Handwritten or typed drafts are difficult to evaluate in this way because the handwriting or typing is usually messy in the early phases of composing.

FLEXIBLE COMPOSING

Specialized computer programs can help writers to do what I call flexible composing—a process in which writers compose text as they continue planning. Word-processing programs that include planning aids guide writers in this composing technique, which is difficult to do with traditional tools.

One such specialized program, Story Tree, is a word-processing program that accepts text as the writer types, but also prompts the writer to create sections or branches to follow from the first page. The program was designed for writing stories that have several possible continuations or conclusions at major text junctures. At any point, the writer can change content of the branches. When beginning a section of an essay, for example, a writer can tell the program that the text will have three subsections. After the writer has composed one subsection, the program prompts for the next subsections, which are then printed in the order the writer has indicated. Such a program encourages planning.

Writers can use programs with keyword coding options when composing. They can write small sections and store them with keyword markers for topics in the sections. For example, I stored the six preceding paragraphs under the keywords "building-blocks," "printout," and "composing." When I was ready to put the sections together, I printed out sections throughout the book for the different keywords and then decided where each section would best fit. I used the commands for joining or appending files together after I decided on the best ordering of the sections. This kind of rearranging is useful for deciding on the organization of a text or for saving time when the writing is so good that retyping isn't necessary.

INCREMENTAL COMPOSING

Incremental composing involves creating texts in several stages, starting with guides from models and outlines and eventually writing an original piece. Just as sculptors work with molds, writers sometimes compose from structures. These text structures are determined by the document form or by the writer's own outlines. Teachers often use incremental composing techniques, but they do not call them by that name. The computer is a tool that can draw on the valuable activities of incremental composing without requiring some of the more tedious ones, like recopying.

Incremental composing can help student writers learn document forms, try out various styles, and develop original content for their texts. The technique of working from models and outlines was once more commonly used than it is today. Although the currently more popular freewriting approach is valuable for helping writers discover their purpose, content, and voice, structured writing can also be useful when they are learning the conventions of writing.

Composing from a model or outline can also help reduce burdens on memory. When composing, writers should be able to focus on expressing a coherent argument or story. If their composing process involves too much editing, they can get lost in details that are best saved for later steps. As discussed in Chapter 4, even reading the text as one writes it may lead to premature editing of details that might be deleted eventually and that distract the writer from following through on a point. Writers who combine the composing process with the prewriting or revising processes may limit their ability to create ideas. There is just so much an individual can do at one time, and trying to juggle the various composing and revising activities takes a great deal of time.

Using Models

Art students learn much of their technique and style by copying the masters' paintings. Similarly, writing students can benefit from copying the masters' texts. Reproducing well-crafted paragraphs and sentences helps students internalize structural and aesthetic textual features. Forming a beautiful text, even if it is not original, helps a writer gain a sense of what it is like to write. Of course, such writing exercises have to be integrated with original creation, and they should not be done too often. Students can start with models, then personalize them, finally creating original documents of a similar form, style, or purpose—whatever feature made the model an important example.

Writing teachers can also use students' papers as models to illustrate students' writing successes as well as typical problems. Students relate to writing by their peers, so these models serve as a step between the ideal and the real text a student can create.

The computer is a useful tool for an incremental composing process in which students work from models to create original texts. The simplicity of entering text on the computer has already been discussed. In addition, the copying capacities of the computer can save time in incremental composing. For example, if a teacher types a few paragraphs from Carson McCullers's *Ballad of the Sad Café* onto the computer and saves the file as Carson.txt, students can copy Carson.txt onto their own diskettes and work with it in several ways. Copying procedures vary among word-processing systems. In a system with two disk drives and the DOS operating system, the student would put the original disk in drive A and the formatted student disk in drive B and give the command copy A:Carson.txt B:. In a one-drive system, the student would load the original disk, get into the Carson.txt file, replace the original disk with his or her own diskette, and then save the file under the same name on the personal diskette.

The students can then experience McCuller's writing by expanding it. A typical McCullers paragraph makes a general statement about a character and then gives many details. Students can copy the generalization sentences from a few character descriptions, add different examples that could follow from the first sentence, and then write similarly structured paragraphs about someone they know. In this way, a text copy can serve as a springboard for a new piece.

Writers can also work from copies of their own texts. For example, a teacher who was looking for a summer job stored in the computer the self-introduction letter from her job search the previous year. She copied the letter into another text file and read it to remind herself of what she had included. As she read, she updated the information, adding a description of her last summer job, in a publishing company. The summary of her education and teaching activities, described in the second and third paragraphs, remained the same, but her summer job objectives had changed, so she changed the first paragraph. She refocused the first sentence to emphasize her recent experience in publishing, because she was applying for a job in that field. She then added a fourth paragraph about her most recent job as a textbook consultant. After reviewing the letter, she decided to place the paragraph about her most recent job before the paragraphs about her education and teaching qualifications. This change led her to switch the order of sentences in the old paragraphs so that the chronology would progress from present to past, and she changed the transitions between paragraphs accordingly. Finally, she noticed that the old and new paragraphs sounded different. Her new sentences were more tightly constructed, so she recomposed the old paragraphs. She made these changes as they occurred to her while reading a clean draft after each improvement. If she had not been writing on the computer, she would have had to type at least four drafts of the letter—if that task did not discourage her from making so many refinements.

Boilerplates—documents that are used again and again with small but important changes—are also useful in composing. For example, educators, businesspeople, lawyers, and real estate agents, among others, often write letters, plans, or contracts that change only slightly for each occasion. Master copies of such documents can be stored in the computer, and the specific information—such as names, dates, or amounts of money due—can be inserted after the writer calls the boilerplate into the word-processing program. Boilerplate letters save time for educators who frequently correspond with parents. For example, teachers can use a boilerplate permission-request letter, updating the specific information, such as a trip destination, cost, and so on. The computer can make multiple copies of the letter, print it out on a duplicating master for making copies, or print an original for photocopying. In addition, boilerplate letters on the computer can be expanded, so the teacher can insert notes or comments to individual parents without retyping the standard paragraphs.

Word-processing programs such as Apple Writer and Perfect Writer, which are designed for business writers as well as students, provide programs that insert changing information, such as the date of a trip, into boilerplates. These programs also provide features for inserting names and addresses from a database of letter recipients prepared by the writer. Such features, called **document design** programs, can be useful for students as well as teachers.

Writing activities in history, science, and business courses can involve informative and efficient correspondence activities using document design capacities. For example, students could make changes in sample teaching contracts with blanks for amounts and percentages of money, benefits, and other policies. Such an exercise would help students learn about the value and forms of writing in the professional world as well as about their teachers' lives.

Composing from Outlines and Frames

Since outlines on the computer are easy to copy, expand, adapt, and reuse, they are more useful as general-purpose tools than outlines on paper. As computer outlines evolve into texts, the words in the outlines become headings, first sentences of paragraphs, or parts of sentences. Writers can easily delete numbers from outlines as they turn them into prose. Outlines on the computer do not have to be expanded in sequential order, which is a great aid to writers, especially because introductions and summaries are often written after body sections. Although overview paragraphs appear first in many documents to give the reader an idea of what will be covered in the text, many writers prefer to write such sections only after they have composed the body paragraphs and are sure about what the text includes.

My usual procedure for writing research reports illustrates the flexibility of composing from outlines on the computer. After jotting and rearranging notes in several prewriting sessions, I write an outline of the sections typically included in research reports:

```
Project Summary:
Purpose:
Rationale:
Method:
Results:
Interpretation:
Implications:
Conclusion:
```

Then I fill in the parts I have already written, such as the purpose and rationale, which have usually been included in the proposal written before the study. I electronically copy the purpose and rationale sections from the proposal, usually finding that the writing could use some tightening. At that point, I add references to relevant work done between the time of the proposal and the report—sometimes over a year. Then I describe the experimental procedures. This is an easy task, because the steps are exact and ordered. The difficult part of writing the methods section is to include enough details about the experiment so that another researcher could replicate it while leaving out details that don't relate to the following sections. Next, I present the results, followed by the interpretation section, which often is composed several times and then revised. The project summary and conclusion—appearing first and last—are both written last. As such a report evolves, disorganized notes, semiorganized outlines, outline sections, and paragraphs of varying degrees of completion appear together until, eventually, through stages of composing, the entire text conforms to consistent format, style, and precision.

Writers who frequently prepare reports find that the computer saves them time. Elizabeth, a friend who is a sixth-grade teacher, used to go into hibernation every two months when it was student report time. Writing a report for each student took all her free time for a few weeks until she found a more efficient method—on the computer. Preparing detailed student progress reports, rather than merely giving grades, is a good idea, but it is extremely time-consuming, especially since there is little, though sometimes important, change in the children in a 2-month interval. The report format, as shown in outline form in Chapter 4, is always the same, however. It includes specific information such as paper grades, examples of the student's work, and the teacher's observations. It is usually easy to develop the content of the report because the format is prescribed, the purpose is clear, and the audience, though varied, is clear. The reports are read by administrators, parents, and sometimes students, so the wording must be considered carefully. When Elizabeth began using the computer for her reports, the task became more manageable. When her students also began using the computer for their writing, the job became even easier.

Working with the word-processing program on the computer, Elizabeth copied the report outline onto a new diskette and filled in the specifics for each student. After the first report, she copied each student's prior report and made changes in the date, term objectives, ratings, and comments about the student's development. Thus, she had to rewrite only the sections that had changes and type in examples of recent work.

After her students began using the computer, Elizabeth was able to copy exemplary selections of writing from their diskettes to hers. She also kept a record of the comments she made in students' writing files on the computer, so she was able to refer to them and directly copy sections of particularly insightful comments for the comments section of her report. In this way, she had exact records of her observations over time, and she was able to document them by giving copy commands. As in the building-block composing process described earlier, Elizabeth had to expand and smooth out the text after she collected the sections. Including revision time, her computer reports took less time than her old reports—and they included more specific information. Of course, setting all this up and maintaining the computer comments files and copies of the students' writing on disk took time. Elizabeth sometimes had to make notes on students' papers when she did not have access to the computer, so some of her work still came from paper copies. Overall, however, once she had developed a system of working on the computer and keeping track of notes that were not made on the computer, the procedure worked.

The following sample student reports illustrate the value of using the computer for such a task:

STUDENT PROGRESS REPORT

STUDENT: Randy Johnson (Grade 10)
SUBJECT: Composition
TERM: Two—November/December 1983
TERM OBJECTIVE:
   The class practiced planning and composing comparison and contrast essays. We also reviewed punctuation required in complex and compound sentences.

PAPER GRADES:
   By teacher (on a scale of 5)
      3, 3, 4, 3
   By peer raters
      Sarah: 4, 4, 4, 3
      Max: 3, 4, 4, 3

COMMENTS: Randy is one of the strongest writers in the class. Unlike the other students, he prefers expository writing to creative writing. His organizational skills are strong, but he tends to argue passionately rather than rationally. His writing shows evidence that he should consider another point of view, but his examinations are superficial. This essay on communism is an example.

   If communism worked, I wouldn't mind at all. The fact that really bugs me is that there is absolutely no way that communism can work. The reason it can't work is because once you have someone decide how much money each person receives, he has more power than everybody. Also, I, like the Russian people, hate the government. (They never say this because they would be arrested if they did!) They spend millions of dollars on arms while the people are eating stale bread! They do this because they want to take over the world. If they say the U.S. wants to take over the world they're wrong. Because if we had wanted to take-over the world at then end of world war 2, we could have. We had the largest navy in the world. We were unbeatable!!! but we brought the navy home!! We're for freedom. The Russians want to take-over the world. Which is better? Freedom, of course!!!!! So, my dream is to have communism (not the Russian people) stopped. I hope this will happen before a nuclear.

IMPROVEMENTS SINCE LAST TERM:
   Randy used to think he was a great writer and was thus resistant to making improvements. On the contrary, this time he mentioned that some of his points in the "communism" piece were a "little outrageous." He wanted very much to work more on the piece and is doing so now.

STUDENT PROGRESS REPORT

STUDENT: Randy Johnson (Grade 10)
SUBJECT: Composition

TERM: Three—January/February 1984

TERM OBJECTIVE: The class focused on revising. They reworked several pieces composed during term 2.

PAPER GRADES:
 By teacher (on a scale of 5)
  3, 3, 4, 4
 By peer raters
  Sarah: 4, 4, 4, 4
  Max: 3, 4, 4, 4

COMMENTS: Randy has continued to work on his organizational skills but still tends to argue somewhat superficially.

IMPROVEMENTS SINCE LAST TERM:
 Randy has written several good character sketches in which he supports his thesis, so I see some improvement in his use of evidence in writing.

 Also, I have included his revision of the communism piece to show his attempts at being less "outrageous." He removed some exclamation points and a few adjectives to tone down the language and added a few qualifications. He still has to work more on making the piece balanced.

> If communism worked, I wouldn't mind at all. There doesn't seem to be a way that comunism can work. The reason it can't work is because once you have someone decide how much money each person receives, he has more power than everybody. Also, I, like the Russian people, don't like the government. (They don't say this because they would be arrested if they did.) They spend millions of dollars on arms while the people are eating stale bread. They do this because they want to take over the world. If they say the U.S. wants to take over the world they're wrong. Because if we had wanted to take-over the world at then end of world war 2, we could have. We had the largest navy in the world. We were unbeatable, but we brought the navy home. We're usually for freedom. The Russians want to take-over the world. Which is better? Freedom, of course. So, my dream is to have communism (not the Russian people) stopped. I hope this will happen before a nuclear war.

Preparing Lesson Plans and Tests

Allen, a writing teacher whose students were not native English-speakers, kept his lesson plans for specific grammatical concepts stored on diskettes. Before giving the exercises to the students who needed them each semester, he reviewed the worksheets to improve them. He had notes from the previous term indicating parts of the worksheets that had been confusing or that needed expanding. In one case, he reorganized a worksheet on subject/verb agreement to present examples first and then the rules. He reordered the worksheet sections and examples using word-processing block move commands, changed numbering, and smoothed out the wording. He made a copy of the worksheet for each student who needed it and copied a student's paper that included many errors of subject/verb agreement, so that each student could relate the practice to his or her own writing.

Teachers can improve and adapt tests in the same way that they update lesson plans and worksheets. For example, a high school science teacher entered a master list of 250 fill-in, short-answer, and essay questions for the earth sciences and biology finals onto diskettes. Each year, she created term exams with one set of questions and a final exam with different subsets of the term questions by copying examples into new test files and moving each item into the new file using two-window commands. She also recorded statistics on the students' success with each question to help her vary the difficulty of the test items and change items that were too easy, too difficult, or confusing.

Combining Material from Many Sources

Another example illustrates the computer composing processes that can be used by a writer who has to collect information from a variety of reference materials, other writers, and various media. A graphic artist who writes proposals for organizing museum exhibits explained that the computer helped him keep track of many pieces of information and compose a coherent, illustrative plan. He stores one-paragraph biographies of his major collaborators, updating them when necessary and adding them to the resources section for each new proposal. He arranges the biographies in different orders, adding new participants, according to the focus of the proposed exhibit—sometimes the catalog writers are most important, sometimes the display designers, and sometimes the graphic artists. Preparing this resources section takes about half an hour with the computer. He also stores stock paragraphs describing the production process for displays and catalogs and a boilerplate budget, which he adapts and updates for each new proposal. Adding these sections takes another ten minutes once they are prepared. Commercially available software, such as Visicalc, provides a budget form and instructions for automatic updating. The resulting text files can be attached to other files created in the same computer.

Rationale sections and descriptions take most of the proposal-writing time because they are different for each situation. Since this artist is a concept creator, he keeps a diskette log each day, with notes for exhibit ideas and a database of information that he thinks he might use someday. He continually updates this "concept library," using the word-processing program, as he refines and adds notes and quotations from his daily reading. When he writes a proposal, he collects information and references from the concept library. He depends on an architect collaborator to supply sample floor plans illustrating possible layouts for the exhibit. Since the architect uses a drawing program on the Apple, the graphic artist chose the Apple as his computer so that he can insert the floor plan files into his proposal files.

COMPUTER COMPOSING AND WRITING QUALITY

Writers who comment on the effects of computers on society have noted that writing done on the computer tends to be sloppier than writing done with traditional tools. The few studies of writing quality have shown that writing on the computer is sometimes rated lower than writing done by the same people with traditional tools. This research is not conclusive, because none of the studies have been done after the writers have become as comfortable with the computer as they are with pen or typewriter. Researchers would have to examine many types of writing done by the same people using various tools over a long period of time to discover whether computer writing is sloppier writing. If it does tend to be sloppy, there are some good reasons. First, the speed and flexibility of the computer for composing makes writing on the computer more like talking—which is both good and bad. As discussed in Chapter 1, when writing is more like talking, students often find the activity to be more natural and more meaningful. However, writing that is more like talking is also likely to be sloppy. Spoken sentences often are loosely constructed, and there tend to be more grammatical errors in speech. Although no formal statistics have been gathered, texts written on computers seem to include many phrases such as "kind of" and "sort of," and direct remarks to the reader. Computer drafts tend to have more spelling errors and syntax errors caused by omitted and repeated words.

Many of the uncorrected errors in computer texts are similar to spoken errors, as shown in the following examples:

1. The next time someone leaves a computer terminal on with screen flashing "in use", I am going to suggest that he or she pay a quarter per second that the abandoned terminal sits "in use" and other people wait.
2. As he was getting loose, he hurt his foot as he was getting loose.
3. My friend wanted to buy a pink sweater but I convinced her out of it.

Sentences have more gaps—omitted words—as in sentence 1, written by a graduate student. Other common errors are repetitions—as in sentence 2, written by a 7-year-old; overlapping sentences—as in sentence 3, written by a high school student; and spelling mistakes, which are often due to typing problems.

Like the tangent texts and sentences discussed in Chapter 3, these sentences seem to be the result of many activities competing at high speeds for space in the writers' minds. Such errors may occur relatively frequently on the computer because computer writers tend to compose quickly. The computer responds to a lighter touch than the typewriter and makes correction easier. There may also be more mistakes because many people who use computers are typing for the first time.

Writers composing on the computer make some errors that are unique to the word-processing environment. The following passage, written by a graduate student, reflects one of the problems of being able to change words and use editing commands to delete lines of text:

> For the field study, my partner and I decided to visit the
> schools in the area that have computers. Only two years ago, it
> was easy to decide where to go because there was only one school
> using computers. Now we have to visit schools to decide which
> schools it to visit. So, our fieldwork involves developing
> criteria for deciding on the stage of implementation and and
> sophistication of a school computer program.

The writer intended to change the second-to-the-last sentence from "which schools are worth it to visit" to "which schools to visit." She used the delete to the end of the line command, with the cursor positioned after "schools." Because the writer thinks in phrases—rather than in computer lines, as the computer does—she may have assumed subconsciously that the "it" was deleted with "are worth," but it was not; the computer had no way of knowing that "it" was part of the phrase to be deleted. Similarly, she typed "and" at the end of one line and at the beginning of the next. Because this writer was able to make changes quickly as she composed but didn't take enough time to check all her changes, her text had a new kind of flaw—line-delete tails.

The ability to correct errors with a word processor often remains only potential, because many writers stop after they compose. All the word-processing commands in the world won't help if writers do not read, critique, and improve their texts.

SUMMARY

Writers who compose with computers can be guided by prompts, outlines, and models. The dynamic capacities of word-processing programs provide flexibility in the composing process.

COMPUTER TOOLS
FOR COMPOSING

The following computer tools discussed in this chapter are particularly useful in the composing process:

- Word-processing programs
  —Word wrap
  —Two-window feature
  —Formatting
- Prompting programs
- Outlining programs
- Models
- Boilerplates
- Frames
- Document design programs
- Graphics editors
- Database files

Revising and Editing

6

"My paper is done. Well, almost done. I have to read it over to check it." It's not easy for a writer to know when a text is complete. Even experienced writers may need editors to help make final decisions, and most experienced writers find that they have to revise even their most carefully composed pieces. Moreover, after revising a piece and sending it off for publication, a writer often works on it again—sharpening some phrases, deleting a few sentences, fixing some typos, or adding a few commas. Time, distance, and feedback help writers engage in this process of transforming drafts into polished texts.

Revising is difficult, however, because writers know what they intended to say. To predict what might confuse a reader, they have to be objective about their texts and their thinking. Writers also use the rules of standard English and strategies for persuading, arguing, or storytelling in the process of deciding whether or not a text is ready to go.

Lucy Calkins, a researcher and teacher at Columbia University Teachers College, has identified three revising styles in children, which also apply to adult writers: "random drafters," who write new papers on a topic without looking at earlier drafts; "refiners," who make changes in spelling, punctuation, or phrasing; and "interactive revisers," who use the revising process as a way to identify good ideas and sentences in their drafts. The writers who find seeds of good ideas during this process rework their papers; reorganize them; add explanations, examples, and illustrations; and delete warmups and false starts. Such writers read their papers critically, react to them, and make changes; they revise as creatively as they compose, allowing their ideas and their texts to continue developing.

Besides having difficulty viewing their own writing objectively, beginning writers are often reluctant to revise their texts because, with each discovery of an improvement, they make more work for themselves—and the additional work is often tedious. Each time they decide to make an improvement, they pay the price of incorporating the change into the text—recopying. Each change also presents the danger of creating new errors. For example, when recopying a piece, the writer might leave out a word or sentence. Any new "errors" in a revision are often signs of the growth of the text to a more elaborate or refined piece of writing. Of course, it is sometimes difficult to convince students to take risks when they know we expect them to hand in a perfect text eventually.

Another difficulty with revising is finding one's own errors. Recent studies of various types of human errors suggest that errors are natural and systematic. Writing errors, in particular, seem to be caused by automatic psychological processes. Just as memory and attention constraints allow errors to slip out, these constraints sometimes prevent writers from identifying their mistakes. Therefore, writers benefit from tools that help them focus their attention on individual text features. When they are reviewing their texts, writers are more likely to notice problems of coherence and organization if they are not looking for spelling and punctuation problems at the same time. After they have reworked the text content and organization, they can attend to the smaller features, such as phrasing, spelling, and punctuation.

Another problem that inhibits revising is that many writers are reluctant to add or change words because the resulting text looks messy. They want the text to look good at all times, and marking a page with revisions prevents this.

Despite these difficulties, beginning writers do revise their texts when the writing situation is like speaking and when they get feedback. When they are guided by such prompts as "Your reader may not understand what you mean here," writers not only can evaluate their sentences, but they also sometimes make improvements suggested by that evaluation. Prompting draws their attention to problems they might otherwise overlook when they skim a text rather than reread it carefully.

Writers have developed several techniques for improving their texts. Some writers outline their first drafts to evaluate overall completeness and structure. Another approach is to ask someone else to read the text and note where it is unclear, which offers the writer a different perspective. Some writers use mechanical methods, such as reading their sentences in reverse order, which focuses their attention on the clarity of each section. Others try to forget what they have written—putting a piece aside for a few weeks so that, when they return to it, they really have to read it because they may have forgotten what they had intended to say. Writers who have to meet deadlines, however, cannot put their pieces aside, so they use outlines and consult editors. Some writers refer to checklists, with questions such as "Will my readers understand the connection of these two sentences?" These strategies help writers focus their attention and help them become more objective about their texts.

Once writers identify potential improvements in their texts, they have logistical chores to attend to. Many writers cut and paste text sections into a new order to make sure the new organization is better before they recopy the text, and more affluent writers pay typists to recopy draft after draft. These activities are time-consuming and costly, however. Such revising techniques also tend to distort the physical writing process, and they do not lead to finished texts as the reader will eventually see them. The cutting and pasting method, for example, requires that different types of changes be made at the same time to avoid recutting. This often leads to a one-step revision process, which is not always sufficient. The cut and pasted text can also become so messy that the writer has trouble reading it.

MICROCOMPUTERS IN THE LANGUAGE ARTS CURRICULUM

Before looking for specific pieces of software, language arts teachers should think about their goals and approaches to teaching language skills. They should review their current activities, texts, and materials and then look to the computer to help in ways that other tools cannot.

Many language arts teachers who are interested in using computers in their classrooms ask the question "What software should I buy?" Although this is a sensible question, it is not the best one to ask first. This ~~simple~~ question suggests an impression about using computers in education. The question focuses on the computer, and it suggests that there may be one piece of software that can meet ~~the~~ teachers' and students' needs.

The computer capacities for carrying out instructions dynamically and for storing large amounts of data have ~~made it~~ *been used*
~~possible~~ to ~~create~~ *develop* practical and educational tools. These tools
that are most appropriate for language arts instruction are
~~include~~ word-processing programs, electronic mail programs, data base programs, prompting programs, spelling and style checkers, tutorials, and drill. *Language arts teachers can integrate these software tools into the curriculum to demonstrate dynamic writing processes such as revising and to simplify certain physical aspects of writing that burden young writers.*

Many writers mark changes in printouts of texts they have composed on the computer.

In contrast, revising on the computer can easily be done in stages, because the writer does not have to recopy the entire text after each change. Having a neat copy after each successive revision helps the writer focus on additional problems without interference from revision marks. Writers who use computers also report that when each version of a text is neatly typed, they can be more objective than when their handwriting personalizes the text or revision notes distract their attention.

WORD PROCESSING
AND REVISING

The biggest expectation teachers have had of the computer is that it will simplify the revising process. As discussed in Chapter 2, the delete, insert, and move commands allow writers to prune, expand, and rearrange text without having to recopy. Other word-processing features also can be revision aids.

For example, writers can use word processors to collect readers' comments—the most powerful guide to revising. Eleven-year-old Monica wrote the following short autobiography on the computer and sent it to 11-year-old Allen via computer mail. Allen commented (in capital letters) and sent the piece back to her:

> Hi, my name is Monica. NICE NAME. I am a girl. I'm sort of plump and my face, I think, is pretty. I like to write and draw SO DO I. I have a brother and a sister. My mother and father aren't divorced. My sister was born to my mother, but she YOUR SISTER? was married to another man. So, I don't look like my sister even if I'm supposed to. My brother was born when I was, but he still doesn't look like anybody)SMALL "E") Except me. Oh, I forgot to tell you. I also like to read I DO TOO, WHAT DO YOU LIKE TO READ?. My name is African and it means good luck. My brother's name means bravery. My sign is Capricorn SO IS MINE, my sister's sign is also Capricorn and my brother's sign is Scorpio, my mother's sign is Aquarius, and my father's is Leo INTERESTED IN ZODIAC, EH? I'm 11 years old. I use to have a boyfriend, but he moved away TOO BAD. I'm heartbroken! I'm going to get married anyway, but it is still sad. I hope I see JosephYOU NEED A COMMA HERE that's his name someday. THE END (BYE-BYE!!!!!!!!)()

Monica evaluated Allen's comments in the context of her writing and made the appropriate changes without having to shift between pieces of paper. Monica laughed at some of the comments and responded to others by making changes. She added details about what she likes to read, deleted some of the references to astrological signs, changed the capital *E* in "Except" to lowercase, and added the phrase beginning with "except" to the prior sentence. Monica did not want to "just get rid of Allen's comments," however, so she moved them to the bottom of the screen.

Automatic insert and recopy features let readers make comments directly in a text they're reading, rather than scribbling in margins. Being able to write comments in the text saves the readers' time and also gives them the flexibility to use the word-processing commands to edit their comments, since even readers make mistakes and change their minds. I have often appreciated being able to change comments I have made in students' papers.

Teachers and other reviewers can make good use of such a commenting process. They can make comments in the bottom screen while viewing the text on the top screen; they can save the comments in individual student's comments files, which both the teacher and the student can print and copy; or they can write the comments at the end of the text file. The only problem with the two-window method of commenting is that it is difficult to clearly refer to the text in question. The commenter can copy example sentences into the other half of the screen but has to be careful not to delete them from the original text. Copying across screens involves deleting the section and moving it to the buffer, getting it back into the original, and then moving to the other screen and getting it back again. This process can be so fast that the reviewer sometimes forgets to reinsert a section from the buffer. The commonly available two-window programs that split the screen horizontally are useful for commenting, but a vertically split screen would be more appropriate for text comments, because the commenter could make notes next to the words in question.

Collaborating writers can make their changes directly in text files and send them back and forth for revision. This way of working requires trust and agreement about changes, because the backup versions are written over in the computer memory. There is no prior version to check unless each writer has made a printout or backup copy before revising or unless the system has saved the last version of text automatically—as some programs do. Most microcomputer systems do not make such backups by default, because they quickly fill up disk space. Writers who decide that backup copies would be valuable can save each version of an evolving text on a backup disk before making the next revision.

A writer can prepare a file with a list of revising guidelines phrased as comments or questions and can consult this list when revising as a reminder of problems to look for. Teachers can help students create their own personalized lists of "demons." The process of creating such lists can be as useful as referring to the lists. Students can make revision checklists with traditional tools, but updating them and selectively using subsets are easier with a word-processing program.

Several word-processing commands are particularly useful in the revising process. The **search (find)** command allows writers to locate specific words in the text. After the writer gives the find command, the cursor moves to the first occurrence of the specified word. A writer using Apple Writer adjusts the direction arrow on the data line so that it points toward the word or phrase to find. This usually means moving the cursor to the beginning of the text and setting the arrow in the forward direction. When the writer presses CTRL-F in Apple Writer, the program responds with the prompt [F]ind:. When the cursor has moved to (found) the specified word, the writer then types in the desired change and presses the return key to continue searching.

The find command is also useful for locating misused words. Writers often use words that are considered inappropriate in formal text, even when they are aware of grammar and usage rules. Student writers, for example, typically misuse *affect* and *effect*. They can use the find command to bring the cursor directly to these words, so that they can check that each occurrence is spelled correctly. The cursor is then in place for the writer to use in making necessary changes.

The find command also serves writers trying to identify more complex problems. Some words signal problems in clarity and organization. Many writers, for example, use *this* to mark the placement of ideas as they compose quickly. When they are revising, they can search for *this* and the related *that*, *these*, and *those*, to make sure that each occurrence of such pronouns makes a clear reference to prior text. An unclear *this* is often a signal that revision beyond a one-word change is required.

The find command also offers a mechanical aid in revising. Writers who note their changes on a paper copy must then enter those changes into the computer file. They can use the find command to move the cursor to the points where each successive change is to be made. Since many words appear in more than one place in the text, the writer using this method can avoid repeated searching by selecting an unusual word in the vicinity of the change. For example, if I wanted to make a change in this paragraph, I might search for the word *mechanical* because I am fairly sure that it does not occur often in the text before this point.

Writers often know that they have written a particular section but cannot remember exactly where it is. For example, I knew I had written a section on files in the first draft of this text, but I couldn't remember where it was. I used the find command and discovered that I had not explained what files are until Chapter 7. When I rewrote Chapter 1, I moved the section on files there. I then edited the files section to conform to the surrounding text. I also used the find command to search for each computer term to make sure that it was defined when first mentioned.

The search process can also indicate that a word is used too many times. In revising this text, for example, I found that I had used the vague word *aspect* frequently, even though I had tried not to use it at all when I was composing. I used the find command to locate every occurrence of *aspect* and then either replaced it with a more specific word or rephrased the sentence in which it appeared.

The **replace** command changes each instance of a word or phrase to another word or phrase. Like the find command, it begins operating at the position the cursor is in when the command is given. To replace in Apple

Writer, the writer presses Y after typing in the word to replace and then types in the word to replace it. The following examples show a section of text in which the replace command was used to change each occurrence of *Rick* to *Timmy*:

Original Text

Cousin Rick's wedding was, like all weddings, unusual. People who hadn't talked to one another in years were hugging. The brother who had blown his toe off in a fireworks accident looked like an angel with his hands folded in prayer. The best man mentioned the deep love of the newlyweds, Rick and Mary, who had met just two months before this day. Everyone felt warm and close. Rick's sister Sara took family portraits of close and distant relatives in all combinations. The event closed with a song by Mathew, and everyone danced. It would be nice if life were unusual.

Revised Text with Replacement

Cousin Timmy's wedding was, like all weddings, unusual. People who hadn't talked to one another in years were hugging. The brother who had blown his toe off in a fireworks accident looked like an angel with his hands folded in prayer. The best man mentioned the deep love of the newlyweds, Timmy and Mary, who had met just two months before this day. Everyone felt warm and close. Timmy's sister Sara took family portraits of close and distant relatives in all combinations. The event closed with a song by Mathew, and everyone danced. It would be nice if life were unusual.

Writers can use the replace command to tidy up their spelling or usage—for example, changing all occurrences of consistent misspellings. Another use of the replace command is to refine word choices that were made during composing, when the writer was thinking more about content then about precise word choice. For example, many adults still use the masculine pronouns *he* or *his* to refer to a person of unspecified gender, as in "The writer thinks he knows his business." The current preference is to use plurals, which are genderless—as in "Writers think they know their business"—or compromise forms, such as *s/he* or *he or she*. All instances of *he* could be changed to one or another of these alternatives with the replace command.

In some cases, writers use the incremental replace command, which stops before each occurrence of the word and gives the writer the option to change it or not. Such a replace procedure is appropriate when the word to be replaced is not consistently interchangeable with just one other word. For example, incremental replacing is best for replacing vague words, such as *aspect*, because the vagueness is often a signal that the entire sentence, rather than just the one word, is problematic. When *all* occurrences of a word are to be changed to another specific word, a single **global** replace can be used to make the change throughout the text.

In their first attempts at using the replace command, many writers make a classic error—and, as a result, learn a lot about computers. A writer who uses a command such as replace "he" with "s/he" could wind up with text that reads "Ts/he problem with ts/he country today is that ts/heory is replacing s/healing." The computer does not know that "he" is a word unless the command indicates that it has a space before and after it, so the command should have been replace "space he space" with "space s/he space". Even if the writers took this precaution, however, the program might miss occurrences of "he" at the beginnings or ends of lines, because they would not have spaces before or after them. For this reason, replacing such common initial and final letter sequences as "he" is best done with incremental replace commands.

The word processor can make deleting relatively painless, because writers who hate to part with their words can delete them across screen windows into files some irreverently call garbage files and some affectionately call treasure files. More freewheeling writers can use the block deletes, which leave no cross-out or gaps. Block move and section delete commands are extremely useful to writers who know how to use them.

So far, one of the biggest surprises about the effects of word processing on the writing process has been that the availability of such features as the block move does not necessarily lead to text reorganizations. Many writers do use the block move to try alternative organizations and to move sections into better orders, but research findings suggest that simply having the capacity to rearrange texts easily has not greatly increased students' willingness to revise. Beginning writers have to learn the reasons and strategies for revising before they can make significant use of the available commands.

Student writers may not make much use of block move commands for revising because they have not seen them in action. Teachers who believe that the automatic cutting and pasting capacity might improve their sturdents' revising skills could create sample lessons from students' papers that need rearranging. By using block moves to rearrange several texts, the students learn about the function of the command as well as its logistical power.

One problem with revising on the computer is that, because changes are relatively easy to make with word-processing programs, some writers never consider a piece to be finished. Rereading a text on the computer screen "one more time" can lead the writer to more changes. Similarly, while reading a printout, a critical writer can always see another change to make. Such writers, who always find "one more improvement" to make, often welcome deadlines as the only impetus to stop revising and editing. Nevertheless, the change capacities offered by word-processing programs are powerful tools for student writers who need encouragement and help with the important process of revising.

TEXT-ANALYSIS AND
PROMPTING PROGRAMS

Writers sometimes help themselves revise their work by analyzing their sentences and texts. Some writers outline their drafts to find structural problems, and they might analyze sentences that are long or awkward. The computer offers capacities for such analysis with **text-analysis programs**, which are written to do objective analyses of such features as word frequencies and sentence lengths. These tools can help writers focus their attention on text coherence, word use, and conciseness.

Researchers have adapted the analytic capacities of the computer to develop programs that guide writers when they read their texts and stimulate revising. The Writer's Workbench programs are text-analysis programs originally developed at Bell Laboratories for writers of technical and scientific reports, but the programs have also been used extensively by students at Colorado State University. The STYLE and DICTION programs check for such features as repeated words, unnecessary words, usage errors, and readability; and SUGGEST offers information for improvements. After completing a text analysis, these programs offer the writer a list on the screen or a printout of text features they have identified. The following text analysis is output from the STYLE program, run on an essay entitled "Children":

```
Children


readability grades:
     (Kincaid) 10.5 (auto) 11.7 (Coleman-Liau 9.7)
     Flesch 8.8 (61.6)
sentence info:
     no. sent 43 no words 1009
     av.sent leng 23.5 av word leng 4.54
     no questions 0 no. imperative 0
     no. content words 574 56.9% av leng 5.85
     short sent (18) 40% (17) long sent (33) 19% (8)
     longest sent 48 wds at sent 21; shortest sent 11 wds at sent 5
sentence types:
     simple 35% (15) complex 37% (16)
     compound 7% (3) compound-complex 21% (9)
word usage:
     verb types as % of total verbs
     to be 18% (21) aux 25% (30) inf 28% (33)
     passives as % of total
     prep 10.8% (109) conj 3.2% (32) adv 5.3% (53)
     noun 26.2% (264) adj 14.1% (142) pron 5.8% (59)
     nominalizations 1% (12)
```

sentence beginnings:
    subject opener: noun (4) pron (3) pos (0) adj (10) art (12) tot 67%
    prep 14% (6) adv 2% (1)
    verb 0% (0) subj-conj 16% (7) conj 0% (0)
    expletives 0% (0)*

Text-analysis programs offer specific, quantitative information that can lead writers to make significant revisions. Writers who know that varied sentence structure can improve the flow of their writing can use the sentence type information noted in the Writer's Workbench example to guide their decisions about the form of each sentence. Similarly, writers who know that a plethora of auxiliary verbs and passive constructions are signs of wordy texts benefit from the word usage information. They can use such program notes to indicate where they should condense sentences by rewording passive sentences into active ones and by deleting auxiliary verbs whenever possible.

Quantitative text analyses do not always seem related to the act of writing. Beginning writers need more explicit information about problems in their texts, because they may not know the significance of the numbers for their writing. For example, young writers don't know what to do with a sentence that has a high percentage of prepositions; such information is useless to them. By about eighth grade, however, some students know that they should vary the types of sentences they use, so the sentence type information could be useful to them when their teachers help them relate the terms *compound*, *complex*, and so forth, to the sentences they have written. When quantitative analyses are related to qualitative text features and writing strategies, they provide writers with objective views of the wording of their texts. Such analyses also draw students into the exact wording of the text because they are attention-focusing devices.

The Writer's Workbench programs run on mainframes or minicomputers with the UNIX operating system. Grammatik for the TRS-80 microcomputer and Homer for the Apple computer are similar programs, but neither program originally offered word-processing commands in the context of the analysis, which means that the writer using them cannot switch immediately from checking texts to incorporating changes. The writer can use a word-processing program on the text before and after it runs through the automatic analysis program but such rigid boundaries between the various writing processes limit the flexibility of the tool and thus the writer's methods of working.

Complex programs on large computers can analyze or parse sentences, although the parses are not correct all the time. To parse sentences, the computer programs have to include detailed information about specific words. For example, a program can parse a sequence of words if it knows the

*From K. Kiefer and C. Smith, "Textual Analysis with Computers: Tests of Bell Laboratories' Computer Software," *Research in the Teaching of English* 17 (October 1983): 203.

part of speech of each word, but the part-of-speech assignments first have to be entered into the program. Recording the part-of-speech assignments of all the words that might be used in texts takes time and storage space. The program must also include rules about the likely orderings of words or specific parts of speech, so that it can make guesses. For example, since *Dance* can be either a noun or a verb, the program would be told that if *dance* follows an article, such as *the* or *a*, it is probably a noun. The computer can build and store such guesses as it considers each word in a sentence.

The EPISTLE program, developed at T.J. Watson Research Center, does grammar and style checking in texts entered into a large IBM computer. The system is designed as a computer package to help office workers improve their business letters. Epistle works from a general language-processing system, which is a parser that identifies the syntactic structures of English sentences. Such complex analyses require large computers and extensive research/development efforts.

Once the writer has put a letter on the IBM system, he or she can select style, grammar checking, and spelling options. The problem sequences appear enclosed in blocks on the screen, color-coded according to the type of problem. Above the color-highlighted problem section is an identification of the error—for example, **Structure is not parallel. "Neither Mr. Jones or Mr. Walters"**. The writer using this system can then request additional information, such as correction options and grammar rules related to the problem. Errors appear in the context of the text, but the writer cannot immediately switch to the word-processing program to make changes without losing the Epistle notes from the screen. The writer has to take notes from the screen, which is not the most efficient use of his or her time and thought power. The program offers information that can help the writer evaluate sentences more objectively, but these analyses are not related to larger text structures or to the writing process. Epistle is being further developed and tested to extend its interactions with the writer about prewriting and about units larger than the sentence. In this experimental stage, the Epistle system promises to be useful, because it offers more reliable feedback on sentence structures than systems that base their feedback on identifications of individual words, word patterns, and statistics, rather than on parsing rules.

Computer programs that "mark papers" note specific words that might be mistakes or that might relate to problems in the content and form of the text. Although Epistle notes syntax problems, others identify only superficial text features, such as spelling, punctuation problems, and some words, like transitionals, that are related to text organization. The programs cannot always indicate that a particular word is absolutely wrong, nor can they identify the logic, organization, or even grammatical problems that people can spot. Since the programs have to be told exactly what to do, they can identify *recieve*, for example, as a misspelled word, but they cannot make notes such as "the meaning of this sentence is not clear" in response to semantic or logical problems in the text. As in the ELIZA program and Walt's computer composition guide, the computer can present only general questions that would apply to a variety of texts. Computer programs cannot even identify spelling mistakes with 100 percent accuracy. The incorrectness and occasional inappropriateness of computer text analyses distract some writers and give young writers a distorted sense of the feedback they would get from real readers. Nevertheless, researchers and teachers have observed that, since the computer is not always "right," the student who uses text analysis programs gains a new kind of control over the text and the revising process. As the automatic analysis draws the writer's attention to text features, the writer maintains control by rereading the text carefully and making decisions about how it sounds.

Although quantitative analyses can help writers focus on text structure, the writers also need the text-analysis features to be more explicitly related to qualities of good writing and to strategies for creating it. Some programs present prompts that suggest strategies writers can use to guide their internal dialogues about their writing processes and texts. Such prompting programs for revising do not offer as much quantitative information as text-analysis programs do. Rather, they present questions that guide writers in making qualitative judgments for improving their texts, and they leave the revision decisions up to the writers.

Prompting and analysis programs can stimulate writers to think about their writing when the commands and analyses are related explicitly to the writing process. With this point in mind, I designed a program called CATCH that offers writers prompting along with analyses to guide their revising. At any time during or after composing a text, the writer can give a command to see the list of CATCH features. The program presents comments, questions, and a few pattern analyses related to the completeness, clarity, organization, sentence structure, conciseness, and punctuation of the text on which the writer is working. Some of the features present question prompts, such as **Does this paragraph include details that help the reader see, hear, feel, or smell what you're talking about?** Other features identify words and phrases that might include problems. For example, if the writer selects the **empty word** option, the program identifies unnecessary words, such as "sort of," and "well." As these words are highlighted on the computer screen, a prompt appears at the bottom of the screen: **The highlighted words may not be necessary. Do you need to make changes?** The writer can then make changes immediately if he or she wishes. Writers using CATCH are in control of all evaluations and changes. They are also aware that the program may identify words that are empty in some contexts, such as "well" in "Well, I will begin with my childhood," but not in others, such as "My first memories are of throwing pennies into a well."

The CATCH prompts vary in form, function, scope, and relation to the writing process. Some focus on the purpose and content of the piece; others focus on form. Some of the features present questions about important text qualities writers tend to look for as they revise, while others offer specific information about words, phrases, and sentences. For example, the **point** option presents the writer with the prompt **Does this paragraph have a clear focus?** Such prompts are intended to stimulate the writer to focus on the organizational, semantic, and logical features of text that even state-of-the-art computer programs cannot understand. Moreover, the writer can easily change the prompts to make them clearer, more personal, or more elaborate.

CATCH also works within the word-processing program the writer uses to create the text. Writers control the prompting by choosing the features in the order they want, choosing when they want to use them, and choosing what they say. The prompts appear one at a time in the context of a first draft. In this way, the writer's attention is more likely to be focused on one problem at a time, which reduces some of the information-processing burden on the writer. Because we have not completed the research on the effects of CATCH on students' writing processes, it is not yet available on the market. Research findings on the effects of text-analysis and prompting programs differ according to the writer's development and ability; the various findings are discussed in Chapters 7 through 11.

EDITING

Once a text is complete and well organized, the writer can begin to polish it. Some writers pay attention to such details as spelling and punctuation as they compose. Those who feel compelled to edit early in the writing process say they do so because mistakes distract them as they read the text for meaning. It makes sense, however, to encourage students to postpone the editing process so that they do not get bogged down in details that may tire them out and that may eventually be cut.

Spelling Checker Programs

Spelling checker programs compare all the words in a text to words in a dictionary list in the program. Words that do not match or words that are not in the dictionary are identified as possible misspellings. For example, such a program would recognize that *sucess* is misspelled. For a word like *receive*, some programs would note the correct spelling and perhaps even insert the correction into the text automatically. To make a correction suggestion, the program must include a record of mistakes and their corrections. For example, a program would keep track of spellings similar to *receive* that writers have corrected, such as *recieve*, *recive*, *receiv*, and *reciev*, and store them as possible misspellings of *receive*. If the program finds these words in a text, it suggests *receive* as a correction.

A spelling checker guides the writer in identifying and correcting spelling mistakes.

Writers using spelling checker programs should be aware that the programs are not conclusive evidence of correct spelling, because misspelled words in one context might be correct in another. For example, *the* is often typed instead of *they*, but because *the* is in the dictionary, it would not be noted as an error. Similarly, no occurrence of *to*, *too*, or *two* would be identified as an error—even, for example, *to* in "I would like to go, to." A program would have to do fairly complex linguistic analyses to catch such an error. When the Epistle spelling checker program is working, however, it will be able to identify the misuse of *to* for *too* more accurately than existing systems can because it not only will compare words in a text to words in a dictionary, but it will also back up this list checking with grammatical analyses showing that *too* meaning *also*, rather than *to* in the verb infinitive, is probably required.

Another problem with spelling checkers is that many words that are spelled correctly are not in the program dictionary, and are thus identified as possible misspellings. For example, proper names and slang terms are not included in most listings. Some spelling programs do offer writers the option to insert proper names, slang terms, and even invented words into the dictionary. If a name, for example, is noted as a misspelling once, it can be inserted into the dictionary and will not be identified as an error again. The potential problem with such a feature is that a word might be entered incorrectly into the dictionary—often referred to as the augmented word list. Since the computer does not know the difference, it will accept anything the writer or programmer tells it.

Finally, in attempts to improve the completeness and efficiency of spelling checkers, designers have written programs that will accept dictionary words with specified suffixes, such as *-ing*, *-ed*, and *-tion*. This is an excellent option when the words in question are constant words such as *sing*, but a program that does not discriminate between verbs and other words by part-of-speech assignments might also accept a typing mistake like *aned* in the sentence "The wind aned the surf are hypnotizing in the Caribbean," assuming that it was the word *an* with the suffix *-ed*.

Some of these problems can lead to language discovery for students. For example, figuring out how the program is working to accept such a spelling as *aned* could be educational. With a little knowledge about how spelling programs work, students could figure out that *aned* was accepted because the program allowed certain suffixes on the end of any word. Also, writers using spelling checkers have to look over their texts for words the program might have missed. After much of the work has been done by the spelling checker, the writer can scan the text for words the program missed, such as *to*, *too*, and *two*, or *off* and *of*. When writers note words they think the spelling checker missed, they can first determine whether there is a word spelled the same way. If there is not, they can try to determine the rules the spelling program used to find the word acceptable.

Some programs also offer writers personalized spelling checkers, in which students can enter words they typically misspell and the correct spellings. The exercise of creating such program lists is likely to be as beneficial as using the program.

When they are designed well and used properly, spelling checkers can have pedagogical value. For example, a 10-year-old repeatedly misspelled *poem* as *peom*. When the program identified the misspelled word in the first line of the child's text, the child had to ask a classmate the correct spelling because he could not find it in the dictionary. He typed in the corrected form. The next time the program identified the misspelled word, the child thought for a moment and then typed in the correction. The corrected version of the text was stored in the computer for later use. The third time the misspelling appeared, the program asked the child if the change should be included in the spelling correction list—the list of corrections related to specific words. The child said yes, so the next time *peom* appeared, the program guessed *poem*. The first two times, the child had to tell the program whether or not to change the spelling. The last time, the program simply made the correction. That time, the child smiled and said, "I think I know how to spell *poem* now."

Sensible Speller is a popular spelling checker for microcomputers. The program documentation alerts the writer to its limitations—for example, that it does not identify homonym mistakes. After searching through the text, the program notes the number of words it doesn't find in its dictionary—the suspect words. The writer can then view each suspect word at the top of the screen in the context of the line in which it appears and then can change or accept the word.

Some programs can also check for certain types of punctuation mistakes, such as unpaired quotation marks or parentheses. Most other punctuation depends on meaning and syntax, so simple list checking is not sufficient for finding errors.

On-line Dictionaries and Thesauruses

Several publishers, researchers, and computer companies are developing on-line dictionaries and on-line thesauruses. Writers working on a system with an on-line dictionary can type the word they want to look up, and the dictionary search program displays an entry—part of speech, meanings, and sample sentences—on the screen. When I worked for a computer company, I tried such a program. I used the find command to locate words I was interested in, and I was able to use the same command to move quickly to the "see also" words often given in definitions. Having a dictionary like the Webster's Ninth Collegiate on-line takes up so much space that the usual individual space allotment on a mainframe has to be extended just for holding the dictionary. As storage space on microcomputers increases, however, such a tool will be available to writers with spelling checkers.

An on-line thesaurus does not take as much space as a complete dictionary, so this tool may be more readily available in the near future. The Houghton Mifflin research division has developed an on-line thesaurus that writers can consult on word use. This research tool works in much the same way as a thesaurus in book form. The user types a word into the computer and then indicates the desired word relative—synonym, antonym, and so forth.

At Princeton University, psycholinguist George Miller is developing a dictionary and thesaurus program that conducts word searches in much the same way as human memory searches work. A writer who thinks of a word for a text but does not think it is just right can ask to see on the screen words with similar meanings, similar initial or final consonants, or opposite meanings. Writers can use the word that first comes to mind when they are composing, then check the thesaurus for a better word when they are editing.

On-line Style and Grammar Manuals

A writer who is revising and editing on a computer should be able to consult writing and grammar manuals on-line. Although manuals and handbooks are not the best tools for learning to write, they can be valuable to writers when they are checking that the form and expression of their texts are standard—if the writing task requires standard English. Word-processing systems that offer spelling and style checking could also offer manuals, but this feature has not yet been considered a worthwhile use of the precious memory space on the micro. As with other tools, on-line handbooks will probably be added as microcomputer memory increases. The EPISTLE system includes a guide that writers can consult when the style program tells them they have a sentence with a grammatical problem. Viewing grammar rules in isolation has not been a successful writing instruction technique, but reading them in the context of one's own writing is a good way to make sense of the rules.

Formatting Aids and the Editing Process

Manipulations of the text form during the editing process can lead writers to discoveries about important details that they missed when they were focusing on other features during the revision process. Programs with complete formatting features, for example, include commands that tell the program to number, print in boldface, or highlight in some other way the headings or other lines that the writer has noted with a command. A microcomputer word-processing program called Homeword includes a leveling option, which is a useful feature, although it was named and carried out in a somewhat cumbersome way in the first version of the program. Before each heading, the writer indicates its level or importance; for example, major headings would be level one, subheadings under that would be level two, and so on. Once the levels are indicated, the writer can tell the program how to mark each level— for example, level one with numbers, level two with capital letters, level three with filled-in circles, or bullets. The program then adds the numbers and other symbols in order. If this is done during the editing stage, it serves as an outlining exercise for checking the balance and completeness of the sections in the text. While making decisions about leveling, the writer is thinking about sections, adding section headings, and making the structure of the text explicit. Such a postoutlining process can help a writer discover that a text has two sections that really should be combined or that, according to the numbering scheme, some of the sections should be reordered.

An indexing feature can help a writer make the terminology in a text consistent. Writers are usually responsible for creating indexes of terms with the page numbers on which they appear, so that readers can find the pages about topics that interest them. Indexing can be as useful for writers when they are polishing their texts as it is for readers looking for specific topics. I asked a university student to prepare an index of terms in a psychology term paper she had written. When she thought the paper was completed, she read through the text and underlined each term she thought should be included in the index. While doing this, she noted that her use of terms for major concepts in the paper was not consistent; she had used several different terms—"cognitive self-monitoring," "self-monitoring," "self-evaluation," and "metacognition"—to mean thinking about one's own thoughts and behavior. She also noticed that other technical terms sometimes appeared as singular, sometimes as plural. She decided that it was important to make the terms consistent, but she had trouble deciding whether she should change verbs to nouns—for example, "thinking" to "thought—because nouns seemed more appropriate for an index. This question highlighted the difference between indexes and words in text. This student had learned to use verbs as much as possible in her sentences to help her avoid cumbersome sentences, such as "The thoughts of young children learning to read are seldom thoughts that are self-reflections." After the indexing exercise engaged the student in analyzing the important words in her text, her editing process expanded. Rather than linking two big noun phrases, she turned the two noun phrases into verb phrases: "Young beginning readers seldom think about themselves."

Preparing an index made this student think about her sentences in a new way. Her teacher had alerted her to the problem of having too many nouns together in single phrases, but she had not examined her text for that problem until the concrete exercise of indexing led her to that inquiry. After she had smoothed out the phrasing, the student entered the indexing instructions into the Perfect Writer program on the IBM PC by inserting @Index in front of each word she wanted to index. As it noted the first occurrence of an @Index word, the program listed the term and the page on which it appeared on the last page of the text; then it added the page numbers of subsequent occurrences of each term. Upon examining the index, the student made one other check. She looked at the first occurrence of each term in the text to make sure that the term was defined. It's not surprising that she had to move definitions to earlier points in the text two times. Only word-processing programs with sophisticated formatting features offer indexing features like that in Perfect Writer, but this is another option that should be increasingly available in low-cost programs.

Grammar and Writing Instruction Programs

Writing research has shown that grammar drills do not improve written expression skills. Exercises such as labeling parts of speech, identifying subject/verb agreement errors, or diagramming sentences do not seem to make someone a better writer. People who write well often do well on grammar exercises, but doing the exercises does not help someone write.

In the past ten years, such methods of teaching grammar have often been replaced by more active sentence construction exercises, such as sentence combining. Sentence combining provides students with practice in building short, simple sentences on a topic into a variety of sentence structures, using correct phrasing, agreement, reference, and punctuation. Research on sentence combining suggests that such exercises relate to improved writing, but it is not clear that sentence combining helps students learn how to evaluate and revise their own writing. Moreover, the permanence of any positive effects of sentence combining in writing development has not been clearly established in the research. Such exercises stimulate students to write more complex sentences, but these sentences are not always well constructed. The leaders of the sentence combining movement do not encourage sentence analysis, claiming that sentence combining experience eventually leads to an intuitive sense of grammatical correctness. Such an intuitive learning process may occur for those who write and read extensively from a very young age, but most students need more explicit instruction to complement their writing development.

A model that many teachers feel is the most direct way of helping students improve their writing involves discussing grammar and practicing identification of problems in the context of a complete story, essay, or report. A grammar lesson on pronoun reference, for example, would be introduced in the context of pronoun reference problems in students' papers. Students would discuss the problem in context, make corrections, and then perhaps do prepared exercises, also in the context of writing. A student who consistently writes run-on sentences could do a **tutorial** lesson on punctuating compound sentences. Such a lesson could involve presentation of the rules and practice in putting punctuation into prepared compound sentences, but then the student should again practice identifying and punctuating compound sentences in his or her own writing or in writing done by classmates.

Rather than buying expensive computer tutorial programs for grammar instruction, a writing teacher who is interested in the tools approach could collect a library of exercises, activities, games, and drills on important grammar, writing, punctuation, and spelling practices to supplement writing activities. Many workbook exercises are sufficient, but microcomputer courseware and activity programs may be worthwhile additions to classrooms that already have computers, because the students could go through the process of doing an exercise and getting results on it immediately. If the classroom is short on computers, however, the teacher has to decide whether composing and revising are more valuable uses of the limited resources than brushing up on rules. If the workbook is adequate and the teacher or another student can provide feedback on a grammar exercise, the computer time could be better spent on writing. As will be discussed later, however, the final decision depends on the age of the student and the specific circumstance of the writing activity. There may be a time, for example, when one student should recopy a piece rather than using the computer and another student who needs a drill on run-on sentences might benefit more from using the interactive instrument.

COMPUTER TOOLS FOR REVISING AND EDITING

The following computer tools are particularly useful in the revising and editing processes:

Revising

- Word-processing programs
  —Insert, delete, and recopy capacities
  —Find, replace, block move, and delete commands
  —Two window option
- Comments files
- Text-analysis programs
- Prompted revision programs

Editing

- Word-processing programs
- Spelling checkers
- On-line dictionaries
- On-line thesauruses
- On-line style and grammar manuals
- Formatting features
  —Postoutlining
  —Indexing
- Tutorials
- Drills

PART II SUMMARY

The computer writing tools presented in the chapters in Part II can help writers overcome physical difficulties. When they are integrated with the writing process, these tools also serve writers in their conceptual work. As always, the teacher's understanding of the students is key in the actual implementation of learning and production tools like those mentioned here. The next part of the book offers information and suggestions that teachers can use in making finer discriminations about when, how, and why to turn the computer on for writing instruction—and when to leave it off.

Children and adults enjoy different applications of computers.

Writers of Different Ages

Mara, a sixth-grader who had never used a computer before, approached the machine confidently. She remembered all the commands as soon as she learned them and rarely checked with her teacher. She did not take notes during the instruction session, nor did she seem to care about the logic behind the command sequences or the technical workings of the computer. She liked receiving messages from the program—even error messages like illegal command. Mara did not ask about specific editing commands, presumably because she had not had much writing experience. For example, she had never had experience cutting and pasting sections of a first draft, so she wasn't excited about the block move command.

The first time Mara asked for a new command was after five sessions on the machine. She and her classmates were about forty lines into a story about a medieval knight who was trapped in his suit of armor. Mara wanted to move the cursor to the first line of the text to change the protagonist's eye color. She carefully used the command to move the cursor up line by line. After giving the command about fifteen times, she yelled, "There must be an easier way to do this!" Like Mara, many kids seem to view the computer as a servant and tool that eliminates the main problem they have in writing: it hurts their hands.

Children have theories about the computer—as they do about writing and the world—but they do not use these theories consciously to make sense of new information. Cindy, for example, laughed when the word-processing program gave her the message Can't save, disk full when she tried to save her text. She did not really know what "save" or "disk full" meant, except that if she didn't save her story, it would not appear on the computer the next day. When she saw the message, she said to her tutor in a matter-of-fact way, "It said the disk's full. What do I do?" She pressed the sequence of keys her tutor told her to press and then returned to what she had been doing. She did not seem to care about the reasons for the computer requirements.

Adele, a 37-year-old teacher who is studying for her doctorate in medieval studies, approached the computer reluctantly. She described herself as an antimachine person—a humanist by profession—and she was afraid. After learning each word-processing command, she asked why it had been designed that way. She gave each command hesitatingly, checking with the instructor and with her notes before giving it. She touched the keys as though they were hot. As soon as she realized the basic capacity of the word-processing program, however, she began asking questions like, "Can it move paragraphs around?" "Why aren't the command names mnemonic?" "Can I have a copy on paper?" Even though she had taken copious notes, she wanted to use a word-processing tutor for a few weeks. By the end of one month, Adele felt reasonably comfortable working on her own and using a wide range of editing and formatting commands.

Although most children approach the computer with confidence and delight, many adults are cautious. Adults like Adele fear that they will not be able to master the new technology. When they first use a word-processing program, many adults feel they have lost control over the writing process and their texts. Word processors do take control over the text in ways that seem strange. For example, the writer can't see the whole text at one time. Also, erasing a section of text to move it is counterintuitive, and adults tend to be nervous about losing text until they have seen the get back command work more than a few times.

Larry expressed a typical attitude of writing teachers and other professionals who have not used computers before learning word processing:

> I believe that I have a certain resistance to a new tool that could possibly be of great benefit to me. I fight the whole concept, often "tooth and nail," that this computer might actually improve my writing.

Another teacher expressed more apprehension but a similar appreciation for the benefits of the computer as a writing instrument:

> I fear the computer! I am using it with much trepidation. But I see its benefits and will continue to struggle along with hope!

At first, adults tend to be in awe of the machine. If something goes wrong, they think it is their fault. After a few sessions, however, most adults find that the computer is not a mysterious superbrain. They learn that the computer is powerful, but limited, so they have to deal with it on specific, idiosyncratic terms. As one writer put it:

> This is the sixth time on the computer and I spent 50% of my time on actual production, while the other 50% is spent trying to get myself out of trouble.

Often, I think there are better ways of editing than I have discovered. I'm noticing that it isn't always me who makes mistakes; sometimes it's the computer that is not responding quickly enough, and I figure I've keyed-in incorrectly.

Professional writers are often resistant to using the new tool because they have developed methods that have worked for them for many years, and they do not feel they need a new tool. The prospect of introducing a strange new tool for a familiar activity is downright repulsive to some experienced writers. A journalist at a large newspaper reported that many of his colleagues had trouble getting used to writing with a word-processing system but that most had been won over because it helped them meet deadlines. Also, the more experience a writer has had with other machines—such as typewriters and dictaphones—the easier it is for them to get used to the peculiarities of the word processor.

Children assume that they can master the mechanics of using the keyboard and programs. They sling around such technical lingo as "global replace" and "mode" as though they were experts. They follow instructions and take control of the machine without worrying about what they do not know. Ten-year-old Carl's attitude illustrates children's characteristic confidence in handling the computer:

> There was terrible confusion with the computer that I was using to write my storie with. When this happened, a very nasty man came over and decided to take over. My personal feelings were that I wished he had never come to help me. Also, he acted like Pamela and I couldn't do it are self. I do hope it doesn't do it ever again. When I first learned how to do a globle replace, I wasn't so thrilled with it. As time pasted, I began to enjoy it much more. However, I am still a little weak with the command of the write-over mode. but as time goes by, I will learn how to do that also.

Children also remember commands after they have used them once. Two weeks after 12-year-old Bernard wrote a story using the basic commands of a word-processing program, he returned to the computer lab at school without notes, sat down at the computer terminal, called his story up on the screen, read it, and began editing. He did not ask a single question. Even 7-year-olds remember the commands.

In contrast, adults do not seem to remember the commands they learned in the first word-processing session. They often feel compelled to check with the instructor before they press any keys. Moreover, many buy manuals even though they can view the documentation on the screen. They seem to feel more comfortable with the hard copy of the manual, which they can study over their morning coffee.

In addition to manuals, adults often request formal tutoring. Although university user rooms are buzzing oral cultures in which computer information is shared, many adults are hesitant to "bother" other writers in public user rooms. In contrast, children request information readily, and they spontaneously offer one another advice. This difference could, of course, have to do with the fact that adults use the computer for extended individual pieces of writing, and they often have strict deadlines. Children write solo pieces, too, but they are much more willing to perform for each other as they write collaborative stories, plays, and newsletters.

Mature writers eventually use a large set of efficient commands, such as block moves, search, and replace commands. Adolescents and adults also use the commands for moving the cursor backward or forward, by sentence and by paragraph as well as by character. Children, however, tend to use the character key predominantly. They enjoy watching the blinking cursor dance across the screen, so they slow up a process that could be faster. Even after being shown how to move the cursor and how to erase by units larger than individual characters, children prefer to use the character-by-character arrows to move the cursor and the delete key for erasing. For example, even after Mara learned the commands for moving the cursor backward and forward by paragraphs and how to move it to the beginning or end of a file when she wanted to change the knight's eye color, she preferred to crawl through the text line by line. Adults take this approach at first to keep track of the cursor, but they adopt the more efficient commands once they see that they work.

These differences in the range and types of commands children and adults use parallel their linguistic and writing experiences. When children revise, for example, they mostly make spelling and punctuation changes on individual words; but adults tend to move, add, and erase entire sentences and paragraphs.

After initial training and practice, most adults want to bypass aids, such as menus that appear on the screen to guide them when learning command names. They prefer to use the screen for text, rather than cluttering up the limited screen space with menus. After they become familiar with a word-processing system, moreover, many adult writers dream up commands to help them with their particular revising styles.

Children are especially concerned with the aesthetic qualities of their text. From the start, they fuss, spacing letters carefully on the screen. They seem to be creating a visual whole—a design as well as a text. They might play with the repeat key, for example, to add three lines of exclamation points after a particularly exciting part of a story. Children are also proud that their writing looks neat and professional. The clear, "grown-up"-looking text seems to motivate young children to write more. Adults are more likely to postpone tidying up the text appearance until they have resolved issues about text content.

Theories about the development of human memory suggest reasons why children learn seemingly isolated pieces of information more quickly than adults and why adults master more information. Adults and children have the same limited memory space for channeling information between the outside world and their long-term libraries of knowledge, but adults use their knowledge to help them acquire new information more efficiently than children do. Adults use short-term memory more efficiently because they have ways of relating knowledge and experience. They fit clusters of information, rather than isolated pieces of information, into limited memory slots. This explains why Cindy simply asked what to do when the program said Can't save, disk full and remembered the comands. An adult who encounters such a message would try to find out what saving is, what a disk is, and why the program can't save when a disk is full. Such theorizing may interfere with initial learning of the specific command, but it eventually helps the computer user remember a complex set of commands and figure out solutions to problems with the program.

Children may also use fewer commands because they do not have much prior knowledge or experience to which they can relate the new word-processing activities. For example, they do not ask for block move commands because they have not spent hours cutting, pasting, and retyping. This relative lack of prior experience allows children to learn certain activities quickly, because they follow directions. They attend to specific commands, not the command logic. Similarly, their ability to commit commands to memory instantly may relate to the lack of interference from explanations. Because of children's matter-of-fact approach, however, they do not master large amounts of information at once. Just as adults use their knowledge of syntax and text structure to ease the burdens on short-term memory storage in understanding and creating sentences, they use prior knowledge of the writing process to organize new information about word processing. Their resistance to learning isolated commands reflects their need to relate new information to prior information. So what seems to hold adults back initially actually helps them master a new skill more completely. For example, Adele felt that if she understood the design and naming schemes of the program, she would be better able to remember individual commands. Such knowledge might not be necessary for learning the commands, but it could be crucial for acquiring an extended list of commands.

These approaches to the computer reflect factors in writing development. As writers mature, their concerns progress from the physical and concrete to the conceptual and abstract. Just as young children prefer commands that work on a small scale—and just as they are concerned with the appearance of their texts—their early writing development involves mastering the relationships between sounds, letter shapes, silence, and punctuation. Children who have mastered these relationships become concerned with writing as communication and, eventually, with the differences between formal writing and speech. Older writers use writing to demonstrate what they know, so they become more analytical about their ideas.

Although it is difficult to identify absolute stages, the writing process reflects developmental milestones that can help teachers decide how to guide students in their growth as writers. The various approaches to the computer show that people change the ways in which they relate information to their needs as they mature. Writers' use of computer capacities corresponds to their changing physical and cognitive needs. Writing development generally lags behind speaking abilities, so the speed and interactiveness of the computer can be used to help younger writers make the difficult transition from speech to writing. Automatic recopying and printout features help children overcome some physical limits they have when writing. Finally, the interactive capacities of the computer can be useful for fostering the development of self-awareness, which is so important in evaluating one's own writing.

The computer is less useful to children when the program design, the machine design, or the training method is complicated. The technology can also be a drawback if it is not integrated with other writing and drawing tools as the child learns to write. At this early stage in the use of computers for writing, researchers, parents, and teachers must be sensitive to the problems presented by the new technology as well as to the best ways to exploit its capacities. The five chapters in this part of the book discuss the important features of writing development and the ways in which the computer can be used to help writers of different ages, from age 4 upward.

Very Young Writers 7

Seven-year-old Frankie laughed so deeply that he didn't make any noise. "I can't stand this. It's too funny. I can't stand it," he kept saying as he read a few lines of a story that another boy had begun and had sent to Frankie via computer mail. Frankie was supposed to continue the story. "Who wrote this? I have to meet this person. I can't stand it. It's too funny." The story began as follows:

> One day 30 years 3 weeks 2 days and 22 minutes ago there was a bird who lived in a jar of TEDDIE'S PEANUT BUTTER in the supermarket. The bird was happy in his jar of TEDDIE'S PEANUT BUTTER.

The story didn't seem terribly funny to the teachers in the room, who had given the other boy the assignment: "Write a story about a bird that lived in a kid's lunchbox." The mystery of who had started the story was intriguing, we admitted, but why was Frankie so tickled? As he continued to laugh and say he couldn't stand how funny the whole thing was, we gave in. It was simple—everything is new when you're young, so anything can be funny and interesting. In this spirit, we studied very early writing development.

The theories of Jean Piaget, other developmental psychologists, and researchers studying language development suggest that children's perceptual, linguistic, and intellectual abilities are not just miniature versions of adults' abilities. From this perspective, one views children's behavior in terms of what they can do rather than what they can't do. Little research has been done to determine the effects of using computers at the formative stages in writing, but developmental theories and preliminary observations of children's interactions with computers suggest applications and effects. This chapter discusses the major concerns of young writers and the applications of computers that address these concerns. The computer keyboard, simple feedback, flexibility for making changes, and patience are particularly useful features for young writers.

SOUNDS AND SHAPES

A major job for children who are becoming literate is learning to relate sounds and meanings to written symbols—words, sentences, and punctuation. Motor development lags behind cognitive skills. Thus, although children as young as 3 cannot read or write, they can use letter blocks to form what they hear as words. Based on their developing knowledge of the relationship between sounds and symbols, they might spell the word *kite* with blocks *k* and *t*. They do this because the *k* represents the syllable sound *ke*.

Six-year-old Lauren stared at the computer screen, watching every flicker of the cursor and the words. She giggled every now and then as she made letters disappear. Like Frankie, Lauren was totally involved in what she saw, and she was having fun. The rest of the world could have disappeared and she wouldn't have noticed.

Young children immerse themselves in new activities as they test their implicit theories about the world and the activities of humans in it. More specifically, children from 4 to 7 learn that shapes called letters correspond to sounds they hear. As Lauren wrote on the computer, she was acting, as children do, as a little linguist. She unconsciously tested her theories about spelling, punctuation, and word formation. She carefully selected keys to press and looked at each letter on the screen, although she did not seem to read it. Lauren was using letters and words to tell about her birthday party, but the process seemed as important as the content:

I had a party. I had a red balloon movie. We had cookie and cake.

As Lauren began to type "cookie," she said: "Mmm. Starts with *c*. Where's *c*?" Her hand hovered over the keyboard as she searched for the key marked *c*. "*C*. Okay, now *oo*, cooookies: Ha! Now, *Ka*. Is that *c* again?" Her teacher shook her head no. "Oh, I know! I know! I know! It's the other *Ka, K*." The program waited a long time for Lauren to make this important decision about which *ka* to use. Lauren's oral revising shows how children test their emerging knowledge about the relationship between sounds and symbols. She learned that two different letters stand for the same sound. She was excited when she used two letter shapes for *Ka* in both "cookie" and "cake."

Children know how they want their words to look. They focus on details as they learn letter shapes. Lauren also showed a typical concern for aesthetic factors on the page and the screen. Similarly, Frankie's mystery collaborator typed some words in capitals and always ended his stories with THE END, centered below the text. This early concern for text appearance suggests that children think writing is a lot like drawing.

Researcher Ann Dyson believes that children's early writing evolves from drawing rather than from speech. For her dissertation at the University of Georgia, Dyson looked at evidence that traditionally has not been called

Writing emerges in children's drawings.

writing. Freeing herself from looking at texts, Dyson found that nursery school children begin to write in their drawings. As children learn to make letter shapes, they make them part of their drawings. Thus, a child's first letters and words are not confined within lines. Dyson also found that the letters and words complement pictures more often than they describe them, as captions do. For example, one young boy's drawing of Superman showed an *S* on his shirt and other places on his clothing. In another picture, the sky is filled with *B*'s that look like birds. As children get older, they use pictures to complement their texts.

Graphics tablets offer children a way to draw on the computer. A graphics tablet, such as the Koalapad, is a flat, platelike device that attaches to the computer. The child draws letter shapes on the pad, which records and translates the drawings into the computer memory and onto the screen. In this way, the child controls the initial placement of letters, which can be difficult to do when first using a word-processing program. Children can make drawings with a graphics tablet and then alter or decorate their drawings with letters, typing them on the keyboard or drawing them on the pad, whichever they find most comfortable.

Software developers have tried to use the computer to help children practice naming and selecting letters. When using a typical alphabet program, the child presses a letter key and the program presents words starting with that letter. Graphics and voice sometimes accompany the programs. One value of such programs is that they can offer the child endless opportunities to repeat naming sequences. Such repeating seems like play to young children. The programs also offer novel examples of each letter with new words and pictures. Children's Computer Workshop developed a program that presents letters marching across the screen. As the letters join in a parade, the child is supposed to type a word they could form. Robert Taylor, at Columbia University Teachers College, wrote a program that marches a child's name across the screen in big letters. The most recent research has shown that very young children can practice the sound/letter correspondences directly by writing.

Some researchers feel that children should write even before they read as a way of testing their theories about language and as a way of learning that ideas can take concrete form. Such an approach suggests that young children should be encouraged to write freely. They should not even be corrected when they misspell, because they might learn to mistrust their theories about the language. In terms of their language development, they are not "wrong" about spellings.

As children make frequent use of letters in drawings, they can try to write their names and other words. The keyboard is useful at this point in that the children can get their ideas out by pressing letter keys rather than by forming letters. Manipulating clearly formed letters helps children master sound and meaning relationships. Using a keyboard helps children engage in the

Children draw and handwrite on the computer, where they can edit images as they edit texts.

conceptual activities of writing before they have the fine motor coordination for handwriting. In this way, the keyboard acts as a set of letter blocks. Of course, the letter shapes must appear on the screen clearly and large enough for young children to read.

Children as young as 6 can learn the positions of keys on the keyboard and easily use it to type sentences. One particularly motivated 6-year-old marched up to his teacher after a weekend of playing with his dad's typewriter, held his index fingers high, like victory standards, and typed Now is the time for every good boy to kum to the ad of is country with those two fingers. Not

Pressing a key can be easier than forming a letter.

bad, considering that he could barely write or spell. Children this young can type, but they work slowly.

Typically, children use a refined hunt-and-peck method. Terry Rosegrant, a researcher at the University of Arizona who studies 4- and 5-year-olds as they write on the computer, has observed that young children develop a unique system for using the keyboard: they divide the keyboard into quarters for their letter search and immediately move their dominant hand to the appropriate quarter of the keyboard for the letter they want to use; then, after limiting the keyboard size in this way, they search along the rows for the letter.

The computer can make writing one's first words and stories easier, but the personal mark of handwriting may be an important factor in learning to write. Children who see their writing only in uniform Roman block letters may not relate as closely to them as they would to handwritten letters. In contrast to the view that the relationship between mind and symbols is most important, educators like Maria Montessori have said that children should follow a specific procedure for developing writing muscles. It would follow from this theory that bypassing the handwriting step blocks later writing development because all processes build on specific physical actions. Similarly, Piagetian psychologist Vihn Bangh has claimed that physically forming letters helps children develop mental images of letters and words and that such mental images are necessary for developing the ability to make linguistic abstractions such as naming. Certainly, the circular motions involved in forming script letters are crucial to fine motor development, but it is not clear that learning to form letters must involve this practice primarily. It may be that children who learn sound/symbol correspondences on a keyboard can learn to handwrite well so long as they have had some practice in making circular forms. Clearly, children should handwrite as well as type when they are young so that they develop both skills. The graphics tablet allows children to form letters with a stylus and see the letters appear on the screen. Using the computer in this way provides the opportunity to handwrite and make changes later or to merge the letters with drawings or other text.

Another consideration related to this issue of handwriting versus typing by young writers is the method of instruction. Computer graphics programs offer tools with which children can practice forming letters and correcting them by changing only the incorrect part of a letter as they are learning the letter shape. They should eventually form the correctly shaped letter in one motion, but being able to improve a shape by making minor changes can save some time and effort when the children are confirming the match between their image of a letter and their ability to produce it.

It is also important to think about methods of typing instruction. We would not want to put young children through the rigorous touch-typing lessons by which older students learn to type. Methods that help children place their hands on the keyboard and find the keys may be sufficient. Children's individual readiness and penchants for pressing keys or forming letters also affect their mastery of writing.

Before too long, young writers will have the option of speaking into a computer that will transcribe their oral stories to written ones. This will mean that, in addition to thinking about handwriting versus typing, we will have to think about talkwriting versus the silent writing we do with our existing tools.

The computer also comes in handy as the child decides to make changes in texts. Remember the saga of the little boy who crumpled up several sheets of paper because he kept making mistakes in the first sentence of his story.

My name is Alison my
Teacher name is Mrs.-
Croak. ~~don~~ One ~~~~ Sunday
Mrs. Croak got very stan
g I got very scard.
She said don't move.
In a very - very spooky
way.
BOOW.~~~~she said.
I ran as fast as
enything. The End

Young writers struggle to form letters.

Children using the computer can change individual words without having to start over. Reducing the burden of recopying without sacrificing the clear, neat appearance of the text can help young writers develop their skills more easily and more enjoyably. Clear, neat writing is valuable to young writers, who hate to work on a messy page. The neat computer page not only helps young writers read their work, but it also seems to increase their pride in it. Some teachers feel that the neatly typed text stimulates their students' interest in writing and in creating error-free copy.

Speech synthesis programs, like the Texas Instruments' Speak and Spell, also offer practice with sound and letter matching. These programs pronounce words as the children type them. One version says only words that are on the 500-word list in the program. If the child types I like friends, the machine says "I like *bleep*," because "friends" is not in the dictionary. If the child types I like computers, the program repeats exactly what was typed, but if he or she types I like compters, the child hears "I like *bleep*" again, because "compters," a misspelling of "computers," is not on the list. A later version of the synthesis program says words by putting together the basic sound units, or phonemes. This program says "friends" and "computers" by analyzing the parts of the words. So, it also would sound out words like "compters," which are not even English words.

In simple speech synthesis programs, a bleep noting that the program doesn't recognize a word could help the child notice the spelling or typing mistake "compters," but a bleep for "friends" is misleading, because it suggests to the child that there is something wrong with the word rather than with the speech program, which simply does not know "friends." This could confuse the young speller. Therefore, it is best to use speech synthesis programs that sound out words rather than those that read from a set list.

The Talking Screen Textwriter is a word-processing program with speech synthesis capacities that reads children's text to them by letter, word, line, or screen as they type or after they have finished typing. The writer gives a command indicating the units the program should read. The program also reads the word-processing commands on the screen menus if the writer so requests. Because it is designed to accept spontaneous text, this program can piece together words from lists of roots, prefixes, and suffixes, but it does not know all the rules for sound/letter combinations in particular contexts, such as the silent *k* in *knowledge*, the silent *p* in *pneumonia*, or blending rules. Such a program can be a useful tool for 6- and 7-year-olds who are beginning to check their writing to see if the letters they have written match the ones they think they have written. Teachers often tell children to read their papers aloud to find mistakes. When they do this, children are often surprised that the page does not say what they had intended it to say. Even when they do read their papers aloud, children often read what they want them to say, not what is actually on the page. For example, Lauren read "cookies" and did not notice that the page said "cookie." If she had typed this short piece using a speech synthesis program, she would probably have recognized the difference between what was on the page and what she thought she had written. In short, the mistake would have been easier to notice if she hadn't been doing two relatively new activities at once—reading and evaluating. One can also see from this example that some children find talking and writing easier than reading. Lauren recomposed her sentence; she didn't really read it. When the computer pronounces the words, it takes care of some of the child's physical chores. The computer should not substitute, however, for human readers who can understand and respond to many dimensions in the child's text. Of course, speech synthesis doesn't help children when it reads their incorrect but phonetically accurate spellings, such as "burd."

Some teachers are concerned that the poor sound quality of most speech synthesis programs on the market may confuse children who are just learning to analyze sounds and letters. Some programs make mistakes such as pronouncing "k-now" instead of "no" when someone types k n o w. Children learn language despite the extremely sloppy nature of adult speech, however, so if computers do not sound natural, it is partly because they are too neat; they clip words. This is a feature that may actually help children at the early stages of translating sounds to letters and words. If a p at the end of a word sounds the same as a p at the beginning, a child may find it easy to distinguish its shape from b. Thus, in early sound/letter learning, the abstract sound of the word may be more useful than the natural one of the unique p sound in different contexts. Children who are learning English as a foreign language, however, should always hear it as it is spoken—naturally and sloppily. Although native English-speaking children would probably not mispronounce words they often hear spoken correctly, nonnative speakers might imitate the computer pronunciations. Although the inexpensive early speech synthesizers do not have natural-sounding speech, more expensive products, such as DECTalk, have good sound quality. The cost of the high-quality synthesizers is likely to decrease in the near future.

Word games can also serve as instructional support for young writers. For example, exercises on homophones are useful at this stage. Such programs present the alternative spellings for words that have the same sounds, such as *two*, *too*, and *to*. The advantage of having such exercises on the computer is that the program can offer the child feedback on answers to questions and fill-ins. Computers that simulate speech also offer the capacity to present oral and visual sounds and letters simultaneously. Such programs should be written to show a spelling such as *two* in a sentence, such as Two boys went fishing, and perhaps a picture. Then Tom wanted to go could appear, followed by Tom wanted to go, too, accompanied by sound and graphics. If the homophones are presented in interesting and fun contexts, children might learn some of the basic differences between the sound and sight spellings.

Word games can help children build their sight vocabularies, because most games usually offer them the option to try endlessly until they type the correct word. Young children enjoy repetition, and they build theories as they test alternatives each time the program tells them to try again. The programs should show children the words they type and help them focus on contrasts between the correct spellings and their own. One graphics program, for example, presents the letters a child types, such as the letters in his name, in large type on the screen. In more complex programs, the child can press a key to change the sizes of letters—to examine them or to play with them.

Spell Diver, a program developed by Tom Snyder Productions, helps 6- and 7-year-old children with spelling and vocabulary development in a game context. In Spell Diver, the child uses a joystick to control a picture of a diver, whose objective is to identify enormous letters underwater by clearing away "letter moss" obscuring the shapes. After clearing away enough moss to see parts of letters, the child solves the mystery by identifying the letters and the word. Game points add up as the child makes successful guesses, keeps air in the compression tanks, and avoids being bitten by a "flipper nipper." This program is a good exploration of the computer graphics capacity, calculation capacity, interactiveness, and flexibility of input for building literacy abilities.

VOCABULARY BUILDING

Young children see new words as treasures. They can use the computer to store each new treasure and gradually build collective databases. For example, children can write new words into a file using spellings they feel are correct, and they can eventually correct any misspellings and share their individual word files with one another. Such word lists can be stored on the computer as an emerging database of their own personal vocabularies. The young writers can expand these databases with related words, sentences, definitions, and pictures. This is also good practice in note taking.

Such a process is easier on the computer than on paper, because the children do not have to keep track of many little pieces of paper, they do not have to recopy, and they can easily update the files or eventually merge them with others' files. In addition, they can use the computer word files for storing new words they learn in social studies and science. For example, a class can develop an entry on heroes and heroines, which is an initial concept in a New York City curriculum manual. Each child can add to the definition—a meaning, an example, a story, a description. This collective database then serves all the students as material for reports or projects. By building such databases, children can learn early that writing is a process of discovery, research, and creating meanings and interpretations. They learn about the processes of reformulating and refining as they decide how to collect and arrange their individual treasures into a class database.

Building a customized word database is easier with a word-processing program than with traditional tools. The children can keep a file for each word, using the word as the first entry into the file. Then, with the list of the word files on their individual diskettes, the children can decide to write a piece related to one of the words. To do this, they bring the single-word file into the word-processing program and, after discussing the word with friends and with the teacher, add definitions, examples, or even a brief story. First- and second-graders can use programs like the QUILL Library for creating word-treasure databases. With such a program, each child can copy or add to a file on heroes and heroines, for example, and as the children expand and refine the hero file, they can store it under additional keywords for topics that come up in the definition. They might find that heroes are associated with important historical events. The name of a historical event could then be added to *hero* as a keyword, the children can begin building an entry for the event, and *hero* will then be cross-referenced to the historical event.

Children can post printouts of their emerging group or individual word treasures on the bulletin board, and they can illustrate these entries with hand drawings or computer drawings. Computer programming languages like Logo are designed for young children to use for drawing. A child draws a picture in Logo by giving instructions to a little triangle, or turtle, on the screen. The child can tell the turtle to move forward or backward a certain number of steps or to make left and right turns of specified angles. As the turtle moves, its pen, which can be in drawing position or not, leaves lines on the screen. A basic Logo program to draw a box is only seven lines long:

```
FD 100
RT 90
FD 100
RT 90
FD 100
RT 90
FD 100
```

Such computer drawings can appear in the two colors of the monochrome screen or in a variety of colors if a color monitor is available. In a more advanced version of Logo, Sprite Logo, young programmers define shapes and move them on the screen in different combinations, colors, velocities, and directions. Children can also illustrate their database entries on the computer with drawing programs, or **graphics editors**, that allow children to make and change images without programming. Children can use crayons to add color to black-and-white printouts of their graphics, until **color plotter** printers become less expensive and thus available in schools.

Interactions with the computer motivate children to be precise about spelling, because the computer does not respond to words unless they are spelled exactly as the program expects them to be. For example, if a child using Logo spells *pen np*, the turtle will not do what the child wants it to do. Thus, children must figure out the correct way to write the word. This may be valuable when the spelling problems are simple enough that the children can figure out the corrections. Such activities should not be done, however, until the youngsters have had the chance to practice writing freely, tolerating mistakes. Having to stop to correct every error could block young writers. Children are ready to learn standard spelling after they have explored spelling by their own intuitions.

The main value of having children illustrate their writing is that they like to do it. Since the visual abilities of very young writers are more developed than their literary abilities, drawing may allow them to capture more information about the features and ideas associated with their word treasures. As they discuss their writing and their illustrations, they may be able to express additional information in words that they originally expressed only in the pictures. The word processor allows them this flexibility. Such text and graphic expandability is important for an activity like keeping a word database, which should constantly change and grow with the child's observations and knowledge.

SENTENCE BUILDING

As children become comfortable writing words, they can begin to write sentences and texts. Word-processing programs offer them a fast way to begin stringing words into sentences. When children write on the computer, they can write more, because the physical burdens are not so great as when they work with pencil. Researcher Terry Rosegrant has observed 4-year-olds writing several screensful of text, and 6- and 7-year-olds in my laboratory have repeatedly been able to write longer stories when they use the computer. Children may be able to write individual words with a pencil, but they become discouraged when they have to form all the letters of all the words in a sentence they want to express. The neat appearance of computer text helps young children read their own texts and the texts of their peers, whose handwriting might not look the same as theirs.

Although the computer displays the youngsters' words neatly, arranging text on the screen and page can sometimes be difficult, because the child's plan conflicts with the plan of the word-processing and formatting programs. For example, 6-year-old Pammie typed the following sentence onto the screen in this arrangement:

> I like the smell of the ocean and
> the sound of the waves on the beach.

When she erased "the smell of the ocean and," she spent a great deal of time trying to rearrange the remaining words using the space bar, but she finally gave up and retyped the sentence in the following format:

I like
the sound of the waves on the beach.

Arranging words on the screen and page should be easy, or children will spend a lot of time moving individual words or retyping them. Some designers have put joysticks or a **mouse** on systems for children, because these attachments also involve pointing via an arrow on the screen. However, a **light pen** attachment or touch-sensitive screens that allow children to touch the words on the screen to indicate their placement could prove to be most appropriate for children.

Sometimes, after children have fussed with the arrangement of words on the screen, as Pammie did, the words look different when the program prints the text. Typical default formatting features in many programs would take Pammie's words and print them in paragraph form:

I like the sound of the waves on the beach.

Since young children are frustrated by such layout changes, a program that leaves a text the way the writer places it on the screen is better for a young child than one that offers unexpected options, even if they are useful. Teachers of young children should select a program that has on-screen editing and no default filling function, or one that is easy to turn off. Screen-based programs on computers with programmed function keys offer writers the option to press a key to center the text, but such word-processing setups are relatively expensive.

Another major concern when children start writing sentences is that they should be free to compose without too much concern for correctness. The more children write, the more comfortable they become, and, eventually, their texts become more readable to others. Of course, reading texts to others is also useful—but again as a discovery rather than as a demonstration of mastery.

As children begin to write sentences, they learn about the relationship between silence and symbols. As they translate speech sounds into writing, they learn basic spelling, vocabulary, punctuation, and sentence structure. The more they write, the more they practice creating written symbols from thought, eventually decreasing the necessity to translate through actual speech sounds.

The more fluently and clearly children compose, the more they begin to control sentence formation by using capital letters and punctuation. Seven-year-old Daniel wrote the following two stories—the first in pencil and the second on the computer:

Story #1

One day there was a teacher whose name was David and one day he was teaching math and all of a sudden he turned into a monster. So we asked a person who Knew about monsters. and he said we had to Kill David. So we went and put poison in his food and he died and he turned into a ghost.

Story #2

Once there was a banana; it was not a ordinary banana, it was a rotten banana. And this rotten banana started to shake, and it opened and a chicken came out. And the banana said "Oh, what a nice chicken that came out of me. I said "But chickens don't come out of bananas". The banana replied "Of course they do, you silly thing". Then I noticed that the banana had come to life.

THE END

Daniel's story in pencil had 62 words and three sentences—about 21 words per sentence. The story he wrote with the word-processing program included 74 words, with about 12 words per sentence.

Daniel said it was easier to write on the computer. His handwriting was a mixture of script and print, and he did not seem to have control over capital letters or punctuation; he used little punctuation in the handwritten story. When his text was clearly typed on the computer, he was better able to control capitalization and punctuation, as evidence by the higher number of periods and capital letters. Being able to write quickly on the computer and see his words clearly seemed to give Daniel more control. In contrast, Frankie has neat handwriting and good control of capitals and punctuation when he works in pencil. He also works well at a slow pace, apparently planning before each sentence and rereading every few sentences after he writes them. The computer had a less dramatic impact on Frankie's punctuation and capitalization, although he also usually wrote more words when he used the computer.

To be valuable as a tool for increasing children's writing fluency, word-processing programs must be easy for them to use. Word-processing programs for children from 4 to 8 should not have multiple-keystroke commands. Young children can work well with control key command sequences, but, as could be expected, single-key commands are the easiest for them to use. Moreover, command keys should be labeled so that the children can learn to use a word-processing program quickly. Young children remember the command keys even if they are not labeled, but they become impatient with the explanations many adults feel compelled to give when telling children the commands. Daniel, for example, looked over the labeled editing keys on the keyboard to figure out "how this thing works," rather than listening to his tutor's explanations. Children also like learning the commands from a big, colorful chart with command names written over a drawing of the keyboard. Daniel had a chart for the editing commands on the **numeric keypad** that was used on the system he learned.

W ord-processing programs for young children's use should present brief, action-oriented instructions and error messages. The messages should use simple vocabulary at the child's reading level. Rather than simply describing the problem—like **Can't save, disk full**—error messages should give the children instructions on what they can do to solve the problem. To warn a writer when disk space is low and the text will not be saved, for example, the program could present a message like **Erase one blank line**. A message like **This will make the file fit in the program** could be added for the benefit of older children, who begin to request explanations.

Another important factor in word-processing design for children is case limit. Some older and smaller computers provide only uppercase letters on the screen or on the printout. Children who are just learning the differences in function between capital and small letters should have both uppercase and lowercase letters available for their writing. Similarly, such keyboard commands as ESC-C for "capitalize this word" are useful for children who are beginning to be sensitive to capitalization rules. In most programs, the writer has to erase a lowercase letter and insert a capital or write over the lowercase letter.

Managing files should also be easy for children to do themselves, so that they can print, copy, and erase their own files as well as create them. Most young children do not create more than five pages of text in one story, so they do not need programs with a large memory space for text, as adults do. Nor do children spontaneously use sophisticated commands, such as block move commands or find and replace. They certainly could experiment with these commands to learn their importance, but other activities—such as writing a lot—are more crucial for very young writers. No single program has all the appropriate features for young writers, so these writers, their teachers, and their parents must select programs with the most important features— control of the words on the screen, availability of both capitals and lowercase letters, easy and limited command sequences, and clear, large letters.

STIMULATING CHILDREN'S WRITING

Sid likes to write and illustrate stories. He proudly displays the pile of books he has written to anyone who is interested. His father helps him separate the text into different pages, and then Sid draws pictures to bring his words even more to life. The illustrations surround the text, and each book has a cover illustrated with crayon, sometimes glitter, and pencil drawings on construction paper. Although tactile experiences on the computer are not so varied as those Sid uses for his books, the computer does provide capacities for writing in stimulating contexts.

Teachers can use computer mail to send children first sentences for stories, and having the children write round-robin stories in the computer is particularly effective. For round-robin stories, one child begins a story and sends it to another child. After adding to the story, the second child sends it back to the first child to continue it. The child who is not writing at the time can draw pictures to go along with the story. Although children may have to try this a few times to get the idea, they enjoy writing stories together. The effects on their texts of such collaborative activities will be discussed later.

Visual contexts also stimulate young children to write. Children who work with Logo use words to create programs, and they can add brief stories to accompany their graphics. They are stimulated to write after doing some programming because they are creating pictures by using words—the words of the programming language.

Sid told me that he had used a computer for writing before he came to my lab. "We do Logo," he said proudly. "Did you also write on the computer?" I asked him. "That's what Logo does," he insisted. "You write the program to draw pictures." He obviously viewed this programming activity as "writing" pictures, rather than drawing them.

As mentioned earlier, in Logo, the words of the program are instructions to the turtle, which follows the children's instructions and draws a picture. It could be that the children identify with the turtle and feel that they are directly drawing the picture. They also recognize that they are "writing" a picture. Children often write stories spontaneously in the Logo environment, presumably because they have used the words of the programming language to give drawing instructions. This text-to-picture process apparently occurs so readily because the computer provides a varied medium for expression. The computer is different from traditional media, because the children's writing turns into pictures and because writing can become an integral part of the pictures. Using print commands, the children can add text to their pictures. Moreover, the pictures are dynamic; they can move and change as the program runs.

Videodisc technology provides moving pictures of drawings or real scenes that teachers can present to children for early writing stimulation. The value of the videodisc is that the children can select, stop, and arrange scenes on command. The videodiscs can be punctuated with real-life scenes, with graphics such as cartoon characters to represent the characters. Such a whimsical distillation of the real scenes could stimulate children's imaginations for story writing. Don Nix at IBM's T.J. Watson Research Center has written the authoring language Handy for teachers to use in reading instruction. Handy provides commands for teachers to use in setting up lessons using computer graphics and films on a videodisc in an integrated system. The computer gives the student oral instructions from a speech synthesis apparatus, shows text on the screen, and presents visual contexts with films and graphics. Nix developed this experimental system for teachers to use in creating realistic contexts for lessons on making inferences in reading. For example, in a lesson on inference building, the teacher showed a short clip of an argument during a tennis match and a short clip of the film *Dracula*. The computer screen and the speech system asked the children, "Who was angry?" If the children did not get the answer right, the program showed the film again and froze it on the face of the angry person in the context of the action. Although such integrated systems are not yet available, they will be within several years. They have potential for stimulating both early writing activities and reading. For example, after analyzing the anger scenes, the children could switch into the word-processing program on this system of the future and write about times when they were angry.

The visual context is an important support for children's writing for several reasons. First, children are used to seeing words in the context of pictures in storybooks. Also, much of the text read to young children is dialogue, and pictures set the scene for this dialogue. Written words become extensions of the pictures as children learn that the words have special symbolic meanings. Children first use pictures as reference points for text and eventually learn that text stands on its own. At about age 5, children can fill in text under pictures in a book. Such text characteristically depends on the pictures—for example, "They found a bottle. It had a message." The setting, participants, and other details necessary for understanding the text are supplied in the picture. As children get older, they begin to write captions that stand alone, such as "The two boys found a bottle on the beach. The bottle had a message in it."

Writing from imagination as well as from visual stimuli in the world around them is important for young children as they learn to create scenes and translate inner scenes and events into words. Even single, concrete words like *boat*, *snowball*, and *baby* can grow into stories at the hand of a 6- or 7-year-old. Such word stimuli can be presented on pieces of paper, but if a prompting program is available, the words can be written as prompts that the young writers can request to see when they are ready to begin a new story. Young writers should also be allowed to enter their own list of interesting words into a prompting program that will later suggest the words for them to use in a story.

Computer programs can serve as textual stimulators of activities. A program called Storymaker, developed at Bolt, Beranek and Newman, presents pieces of stories for young writers to construct. When they select story parts in this Storymaker program, children are creating stories without physically writing. One goal of the program is to help children learn how sections of text connect. Children who have worked with Storymaker have also been inspired to initiate original computer stories.

As discussed in the introduction to this book, computer simulations also stimulate young writers. The children using the Search simulation, developed by Tom Snyder, kept logs of their imagined experiences on the journey and then wrote a story.

DO CHILDREN READ
THEIR WRITING?

Young children do limited reading and revising of their own writing, unless they have received comments from a reader. Usually, 5- to 7-year-olds do not find more than a few spelling errors on their own—and even those errors are usually found just after the children have written and read a word. Children rarely find mistakes when they read their complete pieces, because they have to work too hard at reading to be able to identify problems.

Katie, for example, made changes in her story in response to her tutor's suggestion that she revise. She separated the strings of words by periods and capital letters, and she corrected spellings that her tutor told her to correct. The following is her revised version:

> I was drawing a picture for my teacher and i was happy when she said what a nice drawing of a house. I drew another picture of a flower. The flowers name was rosebud. I like what I have in my garden. There are vegatables and flower. And i pick up the rosebud that fell down and i like to smell the fresh air.

Katie made changes in the text features she was learning about—periods, capitals, and words that don't look the way they sound—but she didn't change much. A protest by 6-year-old Yvon is typical: "I do not care about my mistakes," he said when his teacher told him to correct all the mistakes in his story about a bear chasing a little boy. Yvon wasn't being lazy; he was merely learning to express himself before editing.

Psychological theories suggest that very young children have not developed the necessary objectivity for revising on their own, which involves reading a text, evaluating its clarity, and improving it. This process requires guided self-monitoring strategies that develop spontaneously in later years. Young children may recreate their stories, but too much attention on reworking texts at this age may take time from expression. Thus, such computer tools as text-analysis programs and spelling checkers may not be appropriate for young children; their time is better spent using the word-processing programs to write as much as possible.

Similarly, although first- and second-graders enjoy collaborative writing, weaving a story with another person involves reading or planning aloud together—enjoyable but difficult activities for very young writers. In a pilot experiment at the Harvard Graduate School of Education, we found that stories two young boys wrote individually were more coherent than the stories they wrote together. The stories each boy wrote alone had smooth story lines, but the stories they wrote together had unresolved loose ends and repetitions, and they lacked an overall coherent shape. Although the children tried to weave coherent stories when they worked collaboratively, they had difficulty, because being able to develop a collaborative story involves understanding the other writer's plans. We gave the boys time to plan together, but they might have needed more encouragement and direction on planning the stories together orally before beginning to write. If they had done this planning, they would not have been so dependent on careful reading for maintaining a coherent story.

Compare Story A, which the boys wrote together on the same computer terminal, with Story B, which one of them wrote alone, and with Story C, which they wrote together on different terminals in different rooms:

Story A

There once was a giant who lived in BOSTON in a VERY BIG house on 113 Washington St. One day he had a sore foot and wanted go to to Kendall Sq. He know about the T but he was to big so the little people decided to build huge T. so he went in the huge T and burst it open because it was too small and he fell on the ground and got run over by a truck and threw it and he got arrested and burst open the jail because it was too small. He had to use his left foot because of his sore foot. then he got scrunched into a heavy-duty titanium cell and he was awful squished in it. All the people knowd about the giant who was in the heavy-duty titanium cell. And he bailed out of the jail tha he was in and by that time his foot was better. And the giant's mother put a Band-Aid on his sore foot. And finally all the little people made the biggest T ever and he fit just right and was able to go to Kendall Sq.

Story B

Once upon a time there was a banana who lived ina fruit store. People came to buy bananas to eat. All the other bananas got picked except for that one banana. The banana was not to clean. so he never got picked. then he started to cry because he was getting lonely at night when the fruit man went home. he was very small and all the other bananas laughed at the little banana because of his height. When one day someone took the little banana and boght him. After he bought the banana he but him on a special chair with a blanket ofer him then went to sleep on his place. he dreamed he was a human and he could walt place to place then he woke up and saw he had legs and feet and arms and a head of his own. he saw he could walk place to place and he was happy living in his own room.

Story C

Once upon a time there were two pairs of sneakers that were just new. They were made out of leather. They wished and wished to be albe to walk. They knew that someone would go and buy the pair of sneakers for them to walk. So somebody came in and bought them and they were too small so they threw them away and the garbage truck came and the sneakers knew that they were in trouble so they wished agin to be able to walk. They both saw the garbage truck coming to take the trash out so they tried with all their might and started to run slowly then faster and faster then they decided to go on a vacation. so they went to HONOLULU and went to the beach there and fell in the ocean and got all soggy and disintegrted and that was the end of the sneakers.

The boys collaborated more than developmental theory would suggest. Although the story about the giant in the subway is somewhat scattered, the writers tried to tie in the sore foot, the continuing calamities of the giant, and the little people who felt sorry for him. As each boy added a new section to the collaborative story, he used story elements that the other boy had introduced and occasionally tried to tie up a loose end left earlier in the text. The writers also affected each other. The boy who had written very little on his own wrote much more when he collaborated on stories with a more prolific writer; but the more prolific writer wrote less in the collaborative environment than he had alone.

The stories the boys wrote in the same computer file but on different terminals in different rooms were more coherent than the stories they wrote when they worked in the same room. For example, Story C, which the boys wrote at separate terminals, is more coherent than Story A, which they wrote face-to-face. This probably occurred because they felt more compelled to read the text when they were not sitting at the same terminal. This experiment suggests that collaborating on a story involves carefully reading and considering the partner's contributions and—more important—meshing them with one's own. Very young children benefit from collaborating by reading their stories to one another and asking for comments. Collaboration helps children think about readers as they do when they read their texts to peers for comment.

ACTION IN CHILDREN'S WRITING

Children's stories are action-packed. They focus on characters' actions rather than on character development or the point that the story is illustrating. Children's stories seem to include action for the joy of action. Katie's piece, for example, was supposed to be about her feelings, but she wrote five clauses reporting actions and only two about feelings. She did not develop the action with descriptions or explanations but devoted most of her attention to the narration. Children may have interpretations or morals for the stories they tell and write, but they do not usually note them explicitly.

Children's interest in action is independent of their writing tools. The main way the computer supports this penchant for narrative is by allowing the young children to work faster. The fluency of a child's narrative could be limited if the child had to work slowly—as those just learning to handwrite do. The most consistent difference between young writers' texts written on the computer and their handwritten texts, given similar topics, is that they write more on the computer. As Daniel said: "It's easier to write on the computer."

Other conceptual issues, such as the superficial nature of conflict resolutions in young writers' texts, are also independent of the writing instrument. Their action stories do not really resolve conflicts—the sneakers went to Honolulu and the giant's mother tidied up the story with a Band-Aid. Similarly, in one of Sid's action stories, Joe's mother simply changes her mind to resolve the conflict about the tiger:

JOE'S TIGER

Once upon a time, There lived a boy named Joe.Now, in three days it would be Joe's birthday. He was very escited.When it came, his mother gave him a tiger!He loved the tiger.The tiger got older.And as he got older he got bigger.Soon he got to big for the house.His mother and father said that Joe would have to give it away."To who?," asked Joe."To the zoo," said his mother.And that is what they did.Sadly Joe walked into his room.Then he way an enormous cage.The next day there was a scratching at the door.It was tiger! "can I keep him?," asked Joe. "Yes," said his mother.So he did.THE END

Many children adopt a rather formulaic strategy for storywriting. They use phrases that mark the important story elements—such as establishing the setting with the common "Once upon a time . . . " They also use other beginnings, middles, and ends, but conflict resolutions tend to just happen, rather than being causally integrated into the story. For example, in the collaborative story, the giant simply "bailed out of" the heavy-duty titanium cell. These conflicts are not just superficial; they are whimsical and fun.

However, young writers might learn more about plot development—conflicts and their resolutions—if they wrote several endings for their stories. With a word-processing program, children could make several copies of the beginnings of the stories they have written. The teacher could choose a point in a child's story after the introduction and development of a conflict and ask the child to erase the ending of the story—the part that has or should have some resolution. Without having to recopy the beginning or lose the original ending, the child could try a new ending—and then another. Children could also write alternative endings to their friends' stories, comparing them later. Such an exercise is fun for children who are ready to devise more sophisticated plot resolutions than they originally came up with. If the children try to create too many alternatives, however, the new endings are likely to be as arbitrary and underdeveloped as the original; one or two alternatives should be sufficient to encourage them to devote more thought to plot resolution in their stories.

Teachers, parents, and peers should read children's writing aloud and react to it—stating what they like and, in a kind way, what they don't understand. Providing such general responses to stories is as important as noting details of spelling and punctuation, because it helps young writers build their intuitive senses of voice, audience, and story. Readers can give children written comments in their texts, as described in Chapter 6, but at this point, when reading may be difficult for the young writer, the comments should be brief. Oral feedback should also continue, of course, since many children can understand it better than written comments. Even when they receive feedback, children make changes only in relation to their developmental abilities, so they may ignore suggestions that don't make sense to them. Comments are valuable for building the young writers' sense of readership, however, even if they don't respond to all the comments or respond to them appropriately.

Such feedback from real readers is important before children can use the quantitative analyses provided in computer feedback. Although no research has been done specifically on the effects of spelling and style checkers on young children, research on young writers suggests that it's not a good idea to offer automatic analysis to children who are just learning about the written language. The discussion of spelling checkers in Chapter 6 illustrates the problems of imperfect recognition in spelling checkers. Very young children do not have sufficient experience to know when spelling and style checkers have made mistakes. Therefore, although figuring out why the program is wrong may be a useful exercise for older children, 4- to 8-year-olds would be confused by the incorrect feedback. Similarly, the superficial factors noted in text-analysis programs might force premature revising on children who have not developed their own sense of text. Limited prompting may be helpful, but children who have not done much self-monitoring might become too dependent on the prompting. Even general prompting for composing may be too structured for children who are learning to create and carry out story shapes. Before giving such prompting to young writers who are still figuring out the basic sound/letter correspondences and have not had much practice, it is best to have them write more—creating stories, telling about their lives, writing anything they like. They should be allowed to do this as effortlessly as possible, and the computer provides them with a physically useful writing tool.

FUTURE RESEARCH NEEDS

Future research will have to find the answers to some interesting questions about the impact of computers on early writing development. Because computer writing tools are taking a place in the classroom so quickly, however, research findings will help refine applications, rather than significantly guide them. Meanwhile, teachers have to do the best with the information that is available now.

I have already suggested some appropriate computer applications for young writers, based on prior research on cognitive and writing development. Some of the important questions for researchers to explore are whether young children can integrate a variety of writing tools smoothly without negative effect on their writing, and what effects automatic text analysis and prompting have on children's composing and revising processes, as noted in the discussion earlier in this chapter. Another important question is whether very young children benefit from such communication tools as electronic mail in the same way that older children do. It seems that young children are happy to keep busy writing just for the sake of writing. Correspondence may be less meaningful to youngsters who are still wroking out the mechanics of writing and discovering that their ideas and imaginations can come to life on paper. The little work that has been done on correspondence and collaborative writing suggest that young children should write a lot and share their writing. Communication networks can add experience, but they may not be necessary at this young age.

Another question is whether some types of writing tasks are best done on the computer and others are best done with pencil and paper. Action-filled narrative writing, for example, may be best done on the computer, because it can be done faster with this writing tool; the later-developing descriptive writing may be best done by hand, because it requires slow consideration of detail and creation of verbal pictures.

Teachers can keep up with research reports over the next few years in the journals of the National Council of Teachers, and meanwhile, these questions may guide their own in-class observations and discussions with colleagues.

SUMMARY

The years from age 4 to about age 8 are discovery years for young writers. They discover that sounds can stand for objects—pictures and symbols for people, places, events, and ideas. Children's writing is full of variety—as their writing tools should be.

This chapter has described computer writing tools that are appropriate for very young writers and has suggested applications of these tools for writing development. It is important that these tools be used in harmony with traditional tools—pencils, crayons, construction paper, picture books—which are as new as computers to children who are writing and drawing for the first time.

The physical abilities necessary for writing often keep young children from expressing themselves in writing as well as they might. The computer tools and applications discussed in this chapter can help very young writers compose more fluently than they could with pencils and pens. The approaches to writing instruction with computer tools discussed here can also aid young writers' conceptual development.

COMPUTER TOOLS FOR VERY YOUNG WRITERS

The following computer tools are especially useful for young writers in the 4- to 8-year-old age range:

- Word processing programs
  —On-screen formatting
  —Clear, large letters
- Graphics editors
- Graphics programs
- Speech synthesis programs
- Simulations
- Alphabet programs
- Spelling games
- Filing programs for creating databases
- Light pens
- Joysticks

Nine- to Thirteen-Year-Old *8*
Writers

It's 3:00 on a hot summer afternoon in New York City. Three 11-year old children have been in a large, ugly room for about two hours. They are writing—one a story, one a letter, one a poem. The children break the silence with comments to each other: "How do you spell *celery*?" "You have to say more." "You need a comma here." Two other children enter. One of them rubs perspiration off her brow, looks at an imaginary wristwatch, and says, "Sorry Charlie, your time's up." She is anxious for her turn to write at the computer.

This scene shows children's social concerns in action. The social awareness that grows during the years from ages 9 through 13 affects writing development in many ways. Children in that age range ask one another questions about writing, and they offer help to one another. Their writing, in turn, their need and ability to reach out beyond their own points of view. As children look outward during these years, they also begin to look inward. They begin to react to others' comments about their writing and to reflect on their own thoughts and writing. In contrast to younger writers, who consider writing to be fun for its own sake, these children write for more practical reasons—to communicate, to inform, and to entertain. Like the writing of their younger counterparts, the writing done by these children shows that they are still learning about differences between speaking and writing. During the upper elementary and middle school years, children's writing increases in complexity, abstraction, and explicitness. The children learn to make generalizations, and they develop a written voice, especially when they are encouraged to be themselves by feedback from their peers.

Youngsters like to help each other.

PHYSICAL CONCERNS

Some of the most common complaints expressed by 9- to 13-year-olds are that writing is slow and that it hurts their hands. At this age, children begin to revise their writing, but they feel held back by the physical chores of recopying. Unlike younger children, early adolescents want results fast. They become discouraged if it takes too long to translate their ideas into text. They want their ideas to appear as quickly as they come to mind. These children do not want to be critical about their writing, but this may be because they hate the slow, sometimes painful process of recopying more than they rejoice in improving a paper. When they do not have to recopy, they do not mind correcting mistakes so much.

Children say that writing on the computer is easier than writing with pencils or pens. Teachers and researchers who have observed preadolescent writers using computers say that they write more and that they stay with writing tasks longer than when they use traditional tools. The experimental research to date has not, however, confirmed the observation that pre-adolescents write more when they work on the computer or that the quality of their writing is better.

My studies of thirty-four seventh-graders and eight fourth- through sixth-graders indicated that the children wrote more words with a pen in a 15-minute period than they did on the computer. In a 40-minute revising period, however, the children added significant numbers of words to their drafts when they worked on the computer, as they did when they revised in pen. Children may write less when they are composing on the computer until they become as comfortable typing as they are handwriting and as comfortable moving a cursor via commands as they are moving a pencil. Our studies showed that although the children seemed to be comfortable writing on the computer, they did not write as much in time-controlled situations on the computer, even after 6 months of using the computer at least once a week. Some of the writing time on the computer was also spent using editing commands to make local changes, but these changes were mostly corrections of spelling, typos, and word choice. The children made more significant changes when they revised the text a few days after composing it and after they have received guidelines for revising.

Ratings of the overall quality—holistic ratings—of texts preadolescents have written on computers have been comparable to or lower than ratings of texts on similar topics written by the same children with pen or pencil. These quality scores correlate significantly, however, with the number of words in the children's texts, so they are a reflection of the amount written rather than primarily of the clarity, coherence, or correctness of the text. Since it appears from these early studies that the more children write, the better their writing appears to English teachers, we should provide means that stimulate children to write often and extensively.

Even when the instrument is the one the child has always used, writing improvement takes a long time; improvement while using different instruments may be even more difficult to show. Although researchers such as Nancy Sommers at Rutgers University and Lillian Bridwell at the University of Minnesota have found that revising activity is related to better writing, we do not have clear evidence that stimulating young students' revising leads directly to improvements in their writing quality. Moreover, research on cognitive development done by Jonas Langer at the University of California, Susan Carey at the Massachusetts Institute of Technology, and others, has shown that before children develop more mature thinking strategies, their behavior often seems to be worse for a time. Such developmental lags occur just before the biggest growth spurts. The message here is not that the computer can't help, but that it can't produce writing miracles.

Many theorists believe that if children enjoy writing, their skills will eventually improve. Therefore, even if it takes time to learn to write with the computer, this may not be as important as the fact that the children *feel* that the task is easier. Most children report that they prefer writing on the computer because it is more fun and because they don't have to recopy when they revise. In fact, preliminary results indicate that children come back to texts they have written on a computer and add to them repeatedly. Although analyses show that these additions do not always improve the development or coherence of the text, the important factor may simply be that the children are writing more than they had before.

Children's resistance to recopying suggests that it is an empty task. Eliminating the recopying stage has certainly helped experienced writers, who know how to revise even if they don't have to recopy. We found in our studies, however, that the revisions the children made when they had to recopy were as meaningful as or more meaningful than those they made on the computer. Children who do not have particularly sophisticated revising strategies make significant changes in texts when they recopy because the recopying task engages them in rereading the text and thus helps them see where improvements can be made. Some, but not all, of these studies indicate, however, that at the end of an experimental year during which children use computers for writing, they write more than they had at the beginning of the year.

Of course, the computer is especially useful for writers who know how to type. Since 9- to 13-year-old children are stimulated to write when they can work quickly, touch-typing is an important skill for them to practice. It helps their hands keep up with their minds as much as possible. Although younger children seem to benefit from hunt-and-peck typing as practice in letter recognition, children over 8 benefit from learning the positions of keys on a keyboard by memory and touch. Moreover, after using a keyboard for writing, children present neater texts when they use pen or pencil on paper. We worked with a 10-year-old whose handwriting improved dramatically during the month she learned to type on a microcomputer. She switched from a very messy, tight cursive writing to clear printing, using both uppercase and lowercase letters. She preferred the representation of her ideas in type on the computer, however, because she couldn't make her own printed letters look as neat. Children who stop using script after working on a computer could be encouraged to handwrite poems and other texts, for example one teacher whose students write extensively on the computer introduced a weekly calligraphy workshop so that the students could learn to appreciate words formed by hand as well as those formed on a machine.

Because of physical concerns, word-processing programs for young adolescents should include several features that are not so important for younger children. Word-processing programs for preadolescents should be easy to use—but more to help the children work quickly than because of conceptual difficulties. Like younger children, children at about age 10 may waste time positioning their words if the word-processing programs they use do not allow them easy control over the words on screen. Therefore, it is worthwhile for them to learn to use formatting commands, which give them precise control over layout features. For example, when writing on the screen, some young writers use the space bar to place the title of a text on what seems like the middle of the screen, and they enter an extra return to add space between lines. They are then disturbed when the printed page does not correspond to the screen pages. To avoid frustration, children at this age should learn screen editing functions and formatting commands for centering and making lists.

If the more expensive systems with keys devoted to formatting commands are not available, embedded commands, like those in Apple Writer, are easy for children to control. The Apple Writer embedded formatting commands are visible, which helps the children control them, and they are short—usually a dot with one or two letters, such as .cj, the command for centering the next line of text. Simple incremental exercises suffice to teach children to use these commands. For example, students can write a short text with a heading—using a centering command for the heading and a blankspace command between the heading and the text. After they run the text through the formatter and print out both the original and the formatted text, they can compare the two. The teacher should also point out that the program evens out lines, so that the children don't spend their time doing this. The children can try out one or two new formatting commands in each subsequent exercise. The main problem with embedded commands is that the writers have to run the text through the formatting program before getting a printed copy.

A word-processing program for use by these children should allow for 80 columns across the screen. Programs with 40-column limits seem to give them a distorted sense of the amount of text they have produced. At this age, quantity of expression is important, so the children should not be held back by viewing only small sections of text on the screen. Another concern in selecting a word-processing program is assuring the safety of the text. These children appreciate the effort they put into producing text—and they want results—so they can be devastated by machine crashes. As protection against this, the systems they use should automatically save texts or make backup copies, or they should have a reasonably easy-to-use system for retrieval from buffers.

WRITING FOR A REASON

Early adolescents write best when they have a reason to write. Writing for its own sake is not so exciting for them as it is for younger children. Unfortunately, much writing in school is prescribed. Ten-year old Allen expressed the problem well:

I like writing because you get to create something. Usually, when you're writing on your own, you get to create something that you make up, and not something you—that somebody makes you make up. So that what you're making up is up to you, and so you're having fun doing it, and not the—cause if somebody else makes you make it up, that, that's like forcing food down somebody's throat.

Like many people, Allen finds writing on command difficult but writing from the soul exciting. The complaint "I don't know how to get started" noted earlier, however, relates to this uncertainty about the purpose of writing. Writing in school is often done in response to assignments related to the curriculum. For example, children are supposed to learn the formats for different types of essays. A typical curriculum requires that students write a narrative, a compare and contrast essay, and an argument. Sometimes, required essays are categorized according to a description of the text function, such as persuasive writing and descriptive writing. Students often write such essays as responses to literature or as expressions of their opinions on current issues.

Educator James Britton and his research group in Great Britain analyzed writing according to its transactional and expressive functions: a transactional piece, such as a complaint letter, has a practical purpose; expressive writing relates more closely to the writer's personal needs—as Allen said, "writing on your own, you get to create something that you make up." When writing assignments are constructed to meet external demands, they are more difficult to create, and they are often stilted. The alternative—allowing children to write when the mood and topic strike them—is not realistic within a school context. Teachers cannot just wait for students to want to write, because some children would never take the initiative. The most successful writing teachers provide situations in which children want to write or at least feel they have something to say.

Teachers influenced by research at the Writing Process Laboratory in New Hampshire and the National Writing Projects have begun to devote writing instruction time to activities that help students express themselves in writing. The research has shown that when students write about topics they have chosen, their writing is better—clearer, more well developed, and even more grammatically correct. Writing about one's own interests and concerns is a meaningful and rewarding activity. This method also helps students discover that they have a lot to say.

The research has shown, moreover, that the process approach to writing helps children learn the necessary strategies for developing texts through several drafts. Since children between 9 and 13 are in a transition from mostly egocentric perceptions to more objective points of view, they respond well to others' comments about their writing. They need and appreciate support from others. Studies on the process approach have shown that when children comment on one another's work, their planning and revising strategies develop significantly. The collaborative and communicative writing environments available on the computer are especially useful to young adolescents, who benefit from interactive writing.

Early adolescents work together spontaneously, so writing exercises that build on this penchant have a high likelihood of success. This is a time when feedback on their writing can help children express themselves and reach out to their readers. Interactive writing activities also help youngsters develop their personal writing voice, as they recognize how their own writing differs from that of their collaborators. Researchers at Bolt, Beranek and Newman have observed that when children work in pairs on the computer, they whet one another's imaginations, point out problems, and suggest improvements in texts they create or review together. Such collaboration is developmentally sound, because it helps children make the difficult transition from talking to writing. The necessary leaps in this transition are learning the conventions of written language, such as punctuation, and evaluating one's writing to make sure it is clear, which involves a point of view other than one's own. It is no accident that middle school teachers in all areas of the country have developed similar computer applications. Many of these applications have centered on interactive writing—writing in groups and sharing single-authored pieces with peers as well as with teachers.

COMPUTER ENVIRONMENTS FOR INTERACTIVE WRITING

Computer environments such as electronic mail, and CHAT programs can be used for communicative writing activities, so they often increase children's motivation to write. When they are communicating in writing on the computer, children are likely to write about topics that interest them. Even if they're corresponding about assigned topics that relate to course work, they write with interest and authority. These communicative and collaborative writing activities are valuable, because they provide social reasons for writing and because they offer models the children can internalize as they learn to work autonomously.

Electronic Mail

Children who have electronic mail capacities in school make it a habit to read and write messages each day. The topics of the messages range from personal to subject-related. With electronic mail, children seek advice, give advice, and entertain each other. The written dialogue offers children an opportunity to socialize in a way that may be appealing because it is more private than talking. In these private written conversations, youngsters can "talk" more seriously than they might in the classroom setting. Also, the physical ease of writing on the computer and the brevity of the turnaround time on message exchanges combine with this "safe" feeling of writing versus talking. The child who is communicating in a private setting has the chance to try out ideas, explanations, and jokes. The young writer can be bold when preparing a message. At this age, when children care what their peers think, they also consider the effects of their writing on their readers, so they begin to review their texts and to revise. Because corresponding is also fun, the letter interchanges tend to build excitement about writing, as the children wonder how others will react to their writing and what their friends will say next. These factors make electronic mail quite popular—more popular than traditional mail because of the computer-specific features of ease and speed.

Two schools in a large city share a minicomputer with the DECMail program. The schools are several blocks apart, but the youngsters engage in extensive electronic conversation. The terminals are in the computer laboratories of the schools, which the students use outside the regular curriculum by signing up for computer time. The English teachers feel that such a capacity has sparked interest in writing—at least, about personal subjects. It is not clear whether the writing development that occurs in this setting transfers to academic writing.

James Levin and his colleagues at the University of California at San Diego have studied the electronic communication between classes in suburban Southern California and rural Alaska. Levin has found that the children have a rich cultural exchange in their correspondence and long-distance collaborative writing that would be difficult for them to experience via paper correspondence and textbooks. Because the children in the two settings have such different lifestyles, their writing must be clear and detailed to be understood. The correspondence was originally begun by sending text files through the phone lines, but the phone connections were not always reliable, so the children began mailing diskettes with a variety of texts and messages on them. With each turnaround, the message diskettes evolved, as the children made comments, additions, and changes on stories, news pieces, biographies, and messages. Levin felt that the children would not have engaged in such rich communicative writing without the word-processing program.

In the young writers' workshop I organized, children used the electronic mail system as a channel for sending autobiographies to each other. The children enjoyed this activity, and we found that revising patterns in the autobiography activity differed in interesting ways from those in the texts the children did not share via electronic mail. Although the autobiography exchange was their first assignment on the computer, the children made a relatively high number of corrections on these texts, compared to their other writing on the computer. This desire to improve their writing could be attributed to the audience of peers and, of course, the important subject matter. In this activity, the young writers had an audience and thus felt a purpose. Each child received specific comments from a reader—including useful information about the content as well as the mechanics of the piece.

Children can exchange electronic copies of their files for such a commenting exercise. The electronic copies are easy to make, and exchanging copies preserves the originals in case of crashes, overzealous deleting, or other changes the original writers dispute. Children can also use the two-window feature for commenting on one another's texts. As described in Chapter 6, with this feature, the text appears in the top window, and the commenter writes notes in the bottom window. The material in the bottom window could be the end of the text file or, more safely, a separate comments file.

An eighth-grader who wrote to a group of graduate students in CHAT on The Source became involved in an analysis of the style and content of the older students' comments in the interchange. Now this student tries to engage someone else using The Source in an on-line written discussion every day. He likes trying to figure out something about the people by what they say rather than by asking them specific questions. In this way, he is sharpening both his reading and his writing skills. With the resources in place, such an exercise might be a useful regular activity during part of a homeroom or English class. The CHAT activities could be related to course work—for example, asking a variety of people what they thought about a particular book, movie, or current event. The students could also interview people, in writing, about their lives or their home states. Such communicative activities provide children with meaningful environments in which to develop their writing.

Collaborative Writing

Children in the 9- to 13-year-old range compose willingly together. For example, a sixth-grade class wrote group stories. One student began the story, choosing the topic, the setting—everything about it. It was her story. Then the other students added one sentence each. As the story progressed, more students became involved and committed to it. They had heated discussions about certain choices. Although they let the student controlling the keyboard make certain decisions, a person who was adding a specific sentence was not free to be independent and arbitrary, because the children wanted consistency and direction. The logistical superiority of working collaboratively on the computer over collaborating by traditional methods has been discussed earlier. This activity has special value for early adolescents who are particularly ready and willing to collaborate—more so than younger children. At this age, children can read their collaborative texts critically enough to identify the problems of coherence that can occur when several authors weave a tale, and they also benefit from group planning activities. These children learn about voice, audience, and even grammar when they work together. As "backseat writers," they suddenly develop high standards of spelling and punctuation. Finding errors is easier when they are looking over the shoulder of the writer pressing the keys, who is involved in several activities that distract him or her from evaluating the text.

A collaborative writing exercise that is popular on the computer is a class or school newspaper—a writing activity that has many advantages both on and off the computer. Teachers in Florida, California, New York, and Connecticut have found newspaper writing to be an excellent computer activity for children in middle school because the newspaper has a real purpose and audience. The students know that teachers, parents, administrators, and other children will read it, so there are political as well as stylistic reasons to consider the content and form of pieces carefully. Newspaper work encourages planning, because the parts of the paper, as well as most of the pieces, are structured. Newspapers also include less-structured feature stories, which allow children to experiment with style and format.

The newspaper activity on the computer is also popular because it is a team effort and it uses publication tools. Without a computer, the physical activities of writing a newspaper are much more cumbersome. Professional-looking layouts do not require much time if the children use a formatting program to set headings, columns, and other spacing. Another physical plus is that the final copy can be reproduced in quantity if the school has a printer. With traditional methods of reproducing newspaper copies, such as mimeographing or photocopying, someone—usually the teacher—has to type the final draft. With the computer, the children can be in charge of the entire production process, from writing specifications and stories to copy editing and layout. The computer offers capacities for correcting all mistakes, even minutes before the paper comes out. When children write on the computer, this capacity to consider the piece at different times for different purposes, to act on suggestions for improvements, and to print a new, clean copy each time is invaluable for creating a sense of writing as a discovery, building, and refining process.

Critiquing and revising skills flower as the children play editor and author. The children discover important points about focus, clarity, and mechanics as they work together toward a common writing goal. In fact, teachers have found that their students are more critical editors than the teachers themselves would be in many instances, and the pieces really do improve. Children also become sensitive to considerations of completeness and clarity, even though they do not use the English teacher's rhetoric. In the newspaper exercise, students begin to demand that pieces stand on their own; the who, what, when, where, and why have to be clear. Students also begin to notice inconsistencies in sentence style, which they express by such comments as "The sentence sounds babyish." Specific linguistic concerns are highlighted in such exercises—pronoun reference as well as theme and logical development. Writing a public piece that has a model in the world—such as a newspaper—also helps students make the crucial leap from writing that is dependent of context to writing that can stand on its own.

The computer is also an excellent medium for writing plays, especially collaborative ones. The students develop characters as they write the dialogue. The writers act out roles as they write them, perhaps because the writing instrument and the setting are public. One student can write stage directions when necessary. If some children want to develop their characters and lines before they start interacting with the other characters, monologues can be electronically cut and pasted on the computer to form dialogues. Similarly, the insert capacities of the word-processing program make it possible to add set directions and other notes after writing the dialogue. The children can also use different windows to develop the characters and lines separately. With these techniques, the play-writing experience takes on some of the rehearsal qualities of plays in production.

Since interactive writing is so important to young adolescents, the computer is most useful when the design, hardware, and software configurations are selected with communication in mind. The best environment for electronic mail and collaborative writing is a time-sharing or networked system, because such systems are designed to be used by many people. See Chapters 1 and 12 for discussions of the appropriate computer setups for communication via computer.

BEGINNING FORMAL WRITING

In grades four through eight, students begin to do formal writing that is not based only on personal experience, as the narratives of younger children are. Children from 9 to 13 still write narratives, but their school work also often includes reports and opinion papers. Teachers begin discussing format and form in the middle grades, so the children have to learn how to plan. Their future growth as writers depends on being able to express ideas clearly and precisely, so children in middle school also begin to revise. In the middle grades, teachers should help their students learn the purposes, forms, and strategies of formal writing. Teachers can ease the transition to formal writing by building it on personal, imaginative writing.

Formats

Children in middle school learn to write papers with set formats, such as book reports, formal letters, and news stories. It is important to learn formats because writing, like formal speaking, must be clearly and efficiently organized. Although connections to speech are important in writing, especially in the prewriting process, speech might be loosely and associatively structured, but a good text is spare and sculpted. In addition, as discussed in Chapter 4, text structures serve as comprehension and memory aids for writers and for their readers.

The value of teaching formats is that children can internalize the basic ones as they use them repeatedly for different texts. For example, many children begin to include titles, summaries, and opinions automatically in book reports after they have followed a form a few times. Formats also can serve as guides to thinking. A category heading can help a writer recall certain facts about a book or character. Also, a question heading such as "How was the character different at the end of the book?" might stimulate a young writer to think about character development. Prompting programs like the QUILL Planner can be set up with such headings and questions.

One problem with requiring children to use formats for abstract rather than personal pieces is that they sometimes do not develop the content within the structure well. When writers first learn forms, they follow them rigidly. Although the words in the outline help stimulate the writers' search for content, an outline could keep them from following the tangential ideas that could lead to discoveries of new ideas. Thus, writing tools and exercises dealing with formats should be flexible—offering structure yet leaving room for breaking the structure. These exercises and tools should also provide students with strategies for getting back on track when they are ready.

The computer can be a storage closet for the structures that middle schoolers, like older writers, need. Programs and frame files can store the who, what, when, where, and why format for a news story, for example, and the child can fill in the various parts as the ideas come to mind. Teachers should emphasize with middle school children that they can use these frames flexibly, as discussed in Chapter 5—entering ideas anywhere in the outline, in any order, as the ideas are born. Such a procedure helps children learn formats and composing strategies for working within formats in such a way that content remains their major focus.

Early adolescents must often write reports. Therefore, they begin doing elementary research using encyclopedias and library references. They learn to use card catalogs, but they do not usually use the indexes of references to articles on various topics in periodicals. Computer databases can be useful for developing these research skills. When they connect to a database such as UPI, for example, children can view a list of current stories on many topics, give commands to read a particular story, and take notes—all in one sitting. They can learn the value of research before they become discouraged by long searches through the library stacks, only to discover that a book they want has been signed out.

Filer programs like the QUILL Library are useful tools for learning report writing. Children can create a database of information they get from other databases, books, or other sources. Several children working on the same topic can add to the same file, or children creating separate files can use the same topic keywords to index the information. Then, when they are looking through the database, they can type in topic keywords to read all the files on a specific topic. Open and flexible notes like these are more likely to be written in the children's own styles than to be copied from books, and they are likely to be expanded upon as different children with different perspectives work on creating the database.

A sixth-grade class described by teacher Peter Wolinsky was writing reports on Greece. Each child selected a part of Greek culture on which to do research and write a report. The children wrote entries on database diskettes and used a variety of keywords. The teacher also entered information. Wolinsky found that the exercise was so valuable for learning research skills that the school administrators became committed to finding a way to use such research and writing tools. Setting up a database can be time-consuming, especially when there is only one computer in the classroom, because children who are just learning to do research do not produce much information quickly. Since the children become personally involved in the research as they write in their own words in individual or group databases, they can identify—and reject—an entry that sounds like it came from an encyclopedia.

After building databases as an active research task, the students can use report frames or outlines that they or their teachers have created. The teachers can enter a list of general headings for subjects that could be covered in the report and, from that, the children can work together to build a more detailed framework that they can follow when composing. The following is such a framework, created for reports on Greece:

INTRODUCTION: Where is Greece? How long ago did civilization begin there?

FOCUS: Name the period of Greece and the specific part of Greek culture that you are reporting on. Why did this interest you most?

PERIOD: Briefly describe the time you chose. Mention briefly the years, the leaders, and the government. What is a good word that would describe the period? Why?

THE MAIN TOPIC: Describe the part of culture you chose. Make a statement about it: _____ was very _____ in Greece during the _____ period. For example, clothing was very unisex in Greece during the ancient period.

Revising

Children's concern for precision and correctness is related to their concern for text form. Children often begin to revise their writing as Karen did in the following piece. When they are working on their own, they make mostly word-level changes, but occasionally they reorganize their texts as well.

Karen made four versions of her autobiography; the talky tone was typical of her writing on the computer.

Karen's Log

July 8 HELLO, MAY NAME IS KAREN JANE HARRISS. My nicknames are karey, Kar, Janie, and Morris. I have brown hair, brown eyes, and a tanish complexion. My hair is crinkly and curly and looks best wet most of the times. I love to look fashionable and sloppy. I love sports, music, dance, acting, and singing. I hate shoes, school, people who have more eyelashes than me, and spinach and flab. I also hate snots I also love tuna, pizza and food.

UNTIL NEXT TIME

GOOD\BYE!!!!!!!!!!!!!!!!!!!

July 9 HELLO, MY NAME IS KAREN JANE HARRISS. My nicknames are Karey, Kar, Janie, and Morris. I have brown hair, brown eyes, and tannish complexion. My hair is crinkly and curly and looks best wet. I love to look fashionable and sloppy. I love sports, music, dance actingtuna fish casserole and clothes. I hate flab, snobs, school and celery.

UNTIL NEXT TIME GOOD\BYE!!!!!!!!!!!!!!!!!!!!!!

July 15 HELLO MY NAME IS KAREN JANE HARRISS. My nicknames are Karey, Kar, Janie, and Morris. I have brown hair, brown eyes, and tannish complexion. My hair is crinkly and curly and looks best wet. I love to look fashionable and sloppy. I love sports, music, dance, acting, tuna fish casserole and clothes. I hate flab, snobs, school, shoes, and celery. I was born in 1970. I am a terible fisher although I like to fish.

UNTIL NEXT TIME

GOOD\BYE!!!!!!!!!!!!!!!!!!!!!!

July 16 HELLO MY NAME IS KAREN JANE HARRISS. My nicknames are Karey, Kar, Janie, and Morris. I have brown hair, brown eyes, and tannish complexion. My hair is crinkly and curly and looks best wet. I love sports, music, dance, acting, tuna fish casserole and clothes. I hate flab, snobs, school, shoes, and celery. I was born in 1970. I am a terrible fisher although I like to fish.

UNTIL NEXT TIME

GOOD\BYE!!!!!!!!!!!!!!!!!!!!!!

In her revisions, Karen deleted some words and a complete sentence that included what seemed to be a contradiction—"fashionable and sloppy"— because she realized she would have to explain that. She revised her list of likes and dislikes, and she added the last sentence on July 15 because another child asked her whether she fishes for the tuna she likes so much. She also paid close attention to formatting features, like the blank line between "UNTIL NEXT TIME" and "GOOD/BYE." Most of Karen's writing has a snappy rhythm, which she improved as she revised. Her first set of changes shaped the meaning and rhythm, but she also worked on spelling and punctuation.

When young adolescents begin to revise more than just individual words, they occasionally reorganize their texts by moving sections. Kids have an easier time with word-processing move procedures that have few steps. With the proper instruction, children at this age can use word-processing programs, like Apple Writer and Perfect Writer, that offer them important features like easy block move commands and the two-window feature. Although children can use these commands for reorganization, the trick is getting them to notice when such changes are necessary. One of the most effective ways to encourage children to revise is to have them do collaborative activities, like those described in the preceding section, and some analysis activities, like those described in the next section.

Young adolescents seem particularly prone to spelling mistakes, especially when they type. At this age, the misspellings are likely to be mistakes in words they know as well as guesses on words they have never written. They may make a large number of spelling errors at this age because they are learning to control complex and abstract writing activities, such as making generalizations and organizing material. Therefore, they shift their focus from sentence and word-level concerns because they cannot do everything at once. At this point, they benefit from suggestions to postpone revising until they have gotten their ideas down and to postpone editing until they have revised the organization of the text. Karen's revisions reflect such an ordering of concerns, but she did so without the guidance that many children require.

At this age, when children begin to make many changes in their texts, the word-processing program they use should involve as few keystrokes as possible and should not require mode switching—separate instructions for creating and editing text—because it is physically and conceptually cumbersome. Mode-switching systems require an additional step between writing text and changing it, such as pressing CTRL-I before adding a word or letter in a sentence. In such a system, the writer has to press a command sequence to get into the **edit mode** before making changes. Then, while in the edit mode, the writer can only erase or move words, not add them. The programs that give writers the most freedom are those that assume that when the writers press letter keys without pressing the CTRL key at the same time, they are adding words, and when they press the CTRL key before a letter, they are giving a command. Mode switching is also conceptually cumbersome, because it requires that the writer remember two sets of commands for the two modes.

The following paper, by Alex, illustrates a 10-year-old child's typical concern for correct spelling and wording. Alex did not always make the necessary corrections, but he tried. The misspelled words and phrasing infelicities are italicized here to highlight them.

Alex's Paper

About twenty percent of New York City's population is made up of *comiters*. People are just going crazy over violence *doon* to *inocent* bystanders. For example, the movie "Escape from New York" is based on *whatsome one* thinks New York City is going to be like in nineteen-ninety-seven. Violence *not only is in is not only* in New York City. For example, "Atlanta *Gorgia*" over twenty-five children have been *disapearing thare* and it has been going on for more *thean* a year and police still do not know who is responsible for the twenty-five deaths. Violence is *swepeping* the nation from New York to *Californea* Now violence is just the result of mean *misstreatment*, not giving them spending money, etc. When somebody *comites* a crime it is a shame.

Alex's Revision

About twenty percent of New York City's population is made up of *commiters*. People are just going crazy over violence *done* to *inocent* bystanders. For example, the movie "Escape from New York" is based on *what someone* thinks New York City is going to be like in nineteen-ninety-seven. Violence *is not only* in New York City. For example, "Atlanta *Georgia*" over twenty-five children have been *disappearing there* and it has been going on for more *than* a year and police still do not know who is responsible for the twenty-five deaths. Violence is *swepping* the nation from New York to *California* Now violence is just the result of mean *misstreatment*, not giving them spending money, etc. When somebody *comites* a crime it is a shame.

Alex corrected many of the spelling errors, but he missed some; and one correction resulted in a new error. Children seem to polish their texts more when they use the computer, but this has not been conclusively documented. Karen did more of such revising than she had before using the computer—whether she was writing on the computer or not—and other children at this age make similar changes. Alex, however, made more local changes, such as trying to correct his spelling.

To help children learn to edit, spelling checker programs can be used for spelling lessons, rather than as a final check on spelling, as adults might use them. The spelling checker can help children identify their spelling mistakes, but—more important—it encourages them to try out alternative spellings. For example, when the spelling checker says, "This word isn't in my dictionary," the child might consider other ways the word might be spelled and check the alternative in the dictionary. If the word is there, all is well; if it isn't, the child can try another alternative.

If spelling checkers are used at this age, it is important that the teacher offer suggestions on how to use them. Use of the spelling checker should be coordinated with activities on using the dictionary. Like Alex, most children at this age make good phonetic guesses about English spellings, but they simply don't know the correct—often counterintuitive—spellings. Also, the program makes some mistakes when noting possible misspellings, so children have to learn how to use it critically. This means checking suggested spellings in the dictionary and noting differences, for example, between proper nouns and common nouns.

Also, if the spelling checker does not identify any problems, the children have to be aware that this doesn't necessarily mean the text does not include misspellings. Only a person can check the spellings of homonyms, like *to*, *too*, and *two*. After running a text through a spelling checker, the children should check the spellings of commonly misspelled homonyms and other words the program might miss or pick up incorrectly. For example, they can use a search command in the word processor to identify all occurrences of *to*, the most common spelling of the three forms, and check in each instance whether they mean *too*. The teacher can provide a list of homonyms and common misspellings for the children to use in this lesson. Such a process might become tedious if it were done for every text, but it is a good spelling lesson because it can be done in the context of each child's own writing.

COLLABORATION WITH ONESELF

Current theories about writing instruction have made the important contribution of bringing communication back into writing, but students must still learn to write on their own. We have to help our students make the transition from speech to writing, which involves being able to compose and revise autonomously as well as with others. This is a process not of isolation but, rather, of communication with oneself. Children between 9 and 13 should begin to create dialogue internally.

Traditional writing curricula assumed that children were able to write and correct their own papers if they were given a good topic and if mistakes were pointed out. There was too little emphasis on conversational supports for writing. According to more current theories, however, teachers are providing strategies for the writing process, but many are not providing sufficient strategies for working independently—and writers eventually work on their own, for both practical and cognitive reasons. Just as children must develop the judgment for thinking and acting independently on a variety of issues, they should be able to express themselves independently in writing.

Researchers and teachers have used the computer to study and to foster self-monitoring in writing—particularly for children in the middle school years. Some children spontaneously develop strategies for monitoring their thinking processes. Studies on cognitive self-monitoring (sometimes referred to as metacognition) done by University of Illinois researcher Ann Brown and others have shown that children and adults who are aware of their mental strategies remember better, read better, and write better than those who do not manage their mental lives strategically. For example, children who decide to imagine pictures for words they have to remember are more successful at recall—even though the pictures are additional items to remember—than children who do not use such a strategy. Although people's awareness of their own thinking strategies develops throughout life as they master new activities, the middle school years are especially important years for this development.

Training on self-monitoring, which psychologist Ann Brown has found to be helpful to many children, typically involves offering children prompts to guide their learning activities. Poor readers, for example, benefit from such prompts as "What does the writer want me to believe as I read these facts?" Preliminary studies suggest that similar self-reflective prompts also help young writers improve their composing and revising strategies. Carl Bereiter, Marlene Scardamalia, and their colleagues at the Ontario Institute of Education (OISE) have done numerous studies on the value of prompting for writing development. The researchers have found, for example, that simply telling 8- to 13-year-old writers to ask themselves questions after each paragraph—such as "Will my reader understand what I mean here?"— stimulated the children to review and improve their sentences.

Guided self-monitoring helps early adolescents for several reasons. First, it draws on conversation, which helps set the social context for writing. Second, it reminds children to take alternative points of view. Third, prompting helps children manage their mental activities efficiently, usually by encouraging them to focus on one text feature at a time. Finally, it offers children standards—not only spelling and grammar rules, but also standards of writing behavior, strategies for deciding on goals to guide their writing, and strategies for evaluating their texts.

Because the computer can be programmed to present prompts as the child requests them, much of the research on self-monitoring in writing has been done on the computer. The OISE researchers wrote several prompting programs for middle school children to use while composing. One program, for example, guides students in selecting structural elements for opinion essays by means of conversational prompts and suggestions about essay structure. The program presented questions—for example, **Do you have an** opinion on this topic?—one at a time, and the children responded by pressing Y for yes or N for no. If a child pressed Y, the program presented the prompt Okay, let's tell the reader, and the child typed in his or her opinion. Prompts also suggest composing strategies, such as State why you believe the opposite, as well as identifying particular sections of an essay, such as Statement of belief.

Although the children in the OISE study reported that the program was helpful, they did not write more developed essays than they had written with pencil and paper. One might expect that such prompts would focus the children's attention on the purpose of the piece and a balanced treatment of the issue. The researchers reported, however, that use of the prompts did not significantly change the children's writing strategies. Prompts may be most valuable as prewriting exercises rather than as composing exercises. Finally, the prompts may have most value when children use them several times for making notes and then just think about them in subsequent writing activities.

The program might have taught children something about what to include in opinion essays, but the children did not integrate the instructions or express them well while the questions were on the screen. Such explicit instructions may have a better effect *after* the children have used them a few times and are left to their own, better informed prompts, using some of the writing ideas they have learned from the prompts.

The students who used my revision prompting program CATCH over a 5-month period made more meaningful revisions on their final writing samples at the end of the school year than the students did who used only a word processing program. The CATCH program—described in Chapter 6—provides conversational prompts like Can your reader see, hear or feel what you have described? to stimulate writers' conversations with themselves about their writing. The program suggests a general strategy of self-monitoring and specific aspects of text about which to ask questions when revising: completeness, clarity, organization, sentence structure, coherence, and punctuation. The students who used the program made significantly more meaningful revisions than those who did not, but they made these improvements when they didn't use the computer prompting more than when they did. The prompting program provided what the simple word processor did not—new ideas about why revising is important and how to do it—as well as the physical features of editing commands and automatic recopying.

The message from these studies is clear. Word processing offers children physical aids in writing, but they must learn how to revise to make the best use of these tools. The other important message from these studies is that computer prompting can be an interesting, interactive instructional tool because it provides a model for inner dialogue—which writers must develop. Like any instructional aid, however, students should not use prompting all the time. They can get ideas from the prompting program but then incorporate these strategies on their own. Children also benefit from returning to the same prompting programs several times, because they can adopt only so much from it at one period in their development. For example, one 9-year-old subject who was not quite ready to do explicit self-monitoring said, "When you don't want to really look hard at your work, you can just use CATCH to review it with you. I'd rather have someone correct my work. It just says 'Do you need to make changes?' I'm not supposed to know." In contrast, a 12-year-old's comment suggested that he was sensitive to prompting and ready to use it: "The 'long sentences' feature helps me find run-ons and even some other problems because it makes me read my sentence. But, some others, like 'guide words,' don't. We found, in fact, that a year after making this statement, this student began using the guide words feature, which highlights transitional phrases.

These studies suggest that prompting programs could provide useful exercises on paragraph elements, which are typically given in middle school. They could also be used as a follow-up to examining models of well-developed paragraphs that include topic sentences and supporting details in the form of examples, anecdotes, and facts. After using a prompting program once or twice to practice writing paragraphs, the children should then write their paragraphs without prompting.

Analysis of the different revising patterns in my subjects' texts suggests that there are developmental periods during which children can benefit most from a prompting program. Case studies of two students in the project will illustrate how prompting helps different children in different ways. Janie, who was 11½ years old at the time of the experiment, and Randy, who was 13½, responded very differently to computer prompting. Although Randy was ranked as a better writer (the best of eight) than Janie (sixth of eight), they performed equally well on a sentence memory task, indicating equal overall language-processing ability. Janie revised more when CATCH guided her, but Randy revised much more when he did not have prompting. In addition, Janie made more meaningful revisions (addition of clarifying information) than superficial revisions (punctuation) when she used CATCH, whereas Randy revised more and more meaningfully without external prompting. Janie was obviously ready to learn more about how to revise. She benefited from being shown the self-questioning strategies and the features to look for, but then she became dependent on the prompting, at least for a short time. Randy—a stronger writer—revised more when he used his own strategies, which might have been better or more relevant to his texts than the strategies displayed by the computer. Randy learned new strategies from CATCH, but then he needed to work without the computer guide, because something about it limited him. As a writer, Randy was more mature than Janie, so he learned something from the program but did not need it all the time. After responding to the prompting for a while, his autonomous self-monitoring actually surpassed the computer prompting. Janie, too, may eventually transfer the conferencing strategies suggested by the computer to her spontaneous revising. As noted earlier, Randy did not feel that the guide words feature was helpful. However, during the next phase in his writing development, he began to use transitionals to guide his reader through the discourse structure of his text. At that point, he found the guide words feature useful.

These preliminary studies suggest that some children revise more when the computer talks to them, but others do better on their own. Some children, like Randy, learn additional revising strategies from the computer, but they use them to the greatest advantage when they talk to themselves. Researchers Arthur Applebee and Judith Langer at Stanford University have also noted that explicit training in writing strategies serves as "scaffolding" that is useful during growth stages but can be taken away later because it is no longer needed.

Although the findings are not yet conclusive, research on the effects of prompting and experience with it provide several suggestions for teachers. Computer prompting—especially for revising—can be helpful as an instructional aid for children in middle school. Children use prompts as guidelines for the self-monitoring strategies they are developing. Thus, computer tools such as prompting programs could be available for occasional use, to illustrate self-monitoring strategies in action. After these tools show children how self-monitoring can work, however, the children should try it on their own.

LINGUISTIC CALCULATORS

In the 1960s, teachers and parents feared that children would not learn arithmetic if they used calculators at too early an age. If they could get the answers by pushing buttons, the argument went, they would not develop an understanding of arithmetic concepts. After much debate, it became common practice to allow children to use calculators as time-saving devices only after they had learned the basic concepts—and perhaps even the multiplication tables—by heart.

Today, we face a similar issue about linguistic calculators—spelling checkers, text-analysis programs, and prompting programs. Although these automatic language tools are much less precise than arithmetic calculators, the question arises whether children who use such tools will become dependent on them.

In this chapter, I have presented applications of these automatic writing tools that are consistent with the mathematics teachers' solutions to the calculator issue—suggesting that the tools be used only when they are appropriate in writing instruction. In some cases, they offer possibilities that were not feasible with traditional tools; in other cases, electronic lessons are more efficient than their paper-and-pencil or lecture counterparts. These tools should not draw the children's attention only to the mechanical concerns of text. Quantitative programs, like the Writers' Workbench, might be appropriate for older writers, but they focus the young writer's attention too much on minute, formal features. Also, programs that present analyses but do not provide prompts do not offer the conversational support necessary for self-monitoring. Finally, it should be noted that computer analyses and prompting are intended to complement conversations about texts with real readers, not to replace them.

Another question relates to the quality of electronic writing-analysis programs. "If these programs sometimes know less than a child, how will they help the child?" A related question is "Will the low-level language analysis capacity hold children back?" Spelling checkers, text analysis programs, and prompters do not work the way humans do although they mimic natural language. Helen Schwartz, of Oakland University in Michigan, has offered a metaphor for such programs. According to Schwartz, writers' aids are like training wheels. As training wheels help children learn how to ride bicycles by giving them support for balancing, prompting programs help them learn how to write by giving them supports for focusing their attention and asking themselves questions. Having training wheels is not enough for learning how to ride a bike; children also need a sense of balance, the strength to pedal, a place to go, and practice. Likewise, young writers need more than computer tools for learning how to write. The programs can guide them, but they have to think about what to say and how to say it.

INTRODUCING PREADOLESCENTS TO ELECTRONIC WRITING TOOLS

For children of this age who have not used computers before, it is useful to have a brief discussion about handling the machine and to give the children a list of dos and don'ts. They should learn how to handle diskettes, insert them into the disk drives, and turn on the machine. Children of this age might want to experiment with the machine repairs they have seen the teacher trying, such as opening up the computer and pressing down chips to ground them more securely. It's best to tell the children that they shouldn't try such things.

Just as children in middle school respond well to socialized writing, they work well together while learning how to use a word-processing program. Group discovery activities have proved successful in many settings. For example, children learn how to use a word-processing program by making revisions in a prepared text. The children work in groups of three or four around the computer, with one child sitting in front of the keyboard and pressing the keys. Another child reads the instructions from a worksheet noting the commands to use to make each of the changes noted in the prepared text, and the others watch the screen to make sure that the child typing the instructions makes the appropriate moves. In addition to instruction sheets, the children refer to a list of commands. As the children progress through the exercise, they change roles. Once they have gone through such an exercise, they can immediately create texts together, referring to the list of commands when they want to make changes.

A follow-up step to this lesson is for the children to load the word-processing program and, as a group, write a few paragraphs. As they write, they can refer to the list of commands for making changes. Surprisingly, they won't have to refer to the list very often. After composing a text, they can try to find a section that is out of place—for extra practice with the block move command—or they can replace a frequently occurring noun in the text with another noun that might change the meaning of the paragraph in an interesting way. Teachers can develop similar activities to help the children learn how use other computer tools, such as spelling checkers and database programs.

Children also show one another in an unstructured way how to use commands they need. If the child-teachers are too experienced, however, they sometimes progress too quickly for a novice and miss some of the important basics—unless they are particularly gifted budding teachers who remember what it was like before they knew how to use the program. A one-on-one tutorial session between a teacher and a child is also a supportive way to teach word-processing, because the tutor can give the child appropriate commands as he or she needs them for original writing. Tutorials that come with programs are sometimes helpful, but the best way for preadolescent children to learn to write is to use the tools for actual communicative and creative writing. If they are working on their own, a program with menus and on-screen prompts can guide them in learning to use the word-processing program. Eventually, they can bypass the menus or progress to a program that doesn't have them. With the proper guidance, children can learn to use any type of word-processing program.

WRITING AND PLAY

Almost all reports on children's use of computers for writing include such statements as, "Children think writing on the computer is fun." Although there is ample anecdotal evidence that children like to write on the computer, no one has found out why. Some researchers have suggested that the novelty of writing with a computer, which children also use for playing games, turns what used to be an unpopular activity into fun. Many researchers have mentioned that children appreciate the physical ease of computer writing. It could be that they enjoy expressing themselves but that the tedium involved in writing usually negates the fun. Thus, when some of the physical burden is removed, the fun can resume. As discussed earlier, writing on the computer is lively, and the more lively something is, the more fun it is.

Researcher Tom Malone, of the Massachusetts Institute of Technology, did a study of the features that make games motivating. Malone found that people enjoy games that are challenging, unpredictable, and responsive. Writing on the computer may be fun for the same reasons. For example, mastering the word-processing system is a challenge, and the prize—learning how to write on the computer—provides a great sense of accomplishment. Also, the text looks good and can easily be shared with others. In addition, it's fun for children to feel smarter than something that pretends to be smart— and they learn quickly that computers are only machines that carry out people's instructions. For example, children enjoy telling the computer "You're pretty dumb" when it tells them that their own name may be misspelled.

Another appeal the computer has for young writers is that they like to push buttons. At first, the children delight in the buttons, and this attracts them to writing and editing. The fascination with key pressing and the graphic images on the screen also leads them to play with writing. For example, one student discovered that if she pressed the repeat key as she pressed a symbol key, such as the exclamation point or asterisk, she could repeat the symbol many, many times. This fascination fades after a while, of course, but a concern with decorating text can grow into a concern for text form.

The interactive features that make the computer useful for sharing writing also make it fun to work with. Children enjoy receiving messages and feedback on their writing. Also, unpredictable events can occur when writing on the computer. These events introduce an element of surprise, which can be fun. For example, if someone links to your work space, his or her words appear on the screen with yours. Such messages become surprise additions to the writing process and to the text. Children find such occasional, unpredictable occurrences as error messages from the program to be fun.

Students invent games with some of the computer features. For example, 13-year-old Randy made a game out of a feature in a text-analysis program that identifies sentences that are longer than the average in a given text. As the program computations appeared on the screen, Randy wrote down the average sentence length and the length of each sentence. He then played a numbers game, cutting long sentences down to be closer to the average. He did this several times until no sentence was more than four words longer than the average—the cut-off point. In the process of the game, Randy also corrected a few run-on sentences and spelling mistakes, because playing with the words drew his attention to details. Such play suggests that computers are fun for children because they receive reactions to their activities. There is a potential drawback to the playful possibilities of computer writing, however.

Children might spend too much time on features of the writing tool that have little to do with writing—concentrating too much on pressing keys and tricking the program.

To keep children's computer use in perspective, consider the case of 11-year-old Martha, who had been using computers for a few years. Martha was very impressed with notebooks, because no one in her class had one. She asked her computer lab teacher to buy her a notebook, because she thought it would be fun to carry one around with her and make notes whenever she wanted. She then used the notebook whenever she worked at the computer, sometimes even copying texts from the screen.

SUMMARY

Nine- to thirteen-year-olds can develop their expressive skills if they have reasons to write and the appropriate tools. This chapter has suggested ways to use computer tools to help children grow as writers during these important formative years.

COMPUTER TOOLS FOR NINE- TO THIRTEEN-YEAR OLD WRITERS

The following computer tools are particularly appropriate for preadolescent writers:

- Word-processing programs
  —Basic commands
  —80-column screen
  —Uppercase and lowercase letters
  —Very easy block moves
  —Two-window feature
  —Formatting commands on screen
- Typing programs
- Networked or time-sharing system
- Mail programs
- Linking program, such as CHAT, for real-time communications
- Filing programs for creating databases
- Spelling checkers
- Prompting for prewriting
- General frames and outlines
- Prompting for revising
- Analyses in conversational contexts

Adolescent Writers   *9*

When they use the computer for writing, adolescents behave like adults—and like children. They approach the computer confidently, yet they know that it is a complex machine. They do not like to participate in activities they are not good at, so they take a serious approach to word processing. Like adults, they want the programs to make sense, but they also want quick results. The following report by a teacher who worked with a 14-year-old girl using a computer for the first time illustrates adolescents' concern for results:

> Paula frequently mentioned that she would rather write out her assignment in pen. This occurred at the beginning when she was typing her assignment by hunting and pecking keys and when progress was slow. She had completed only one of her handwritten pages in two hours. . . . The requests to return to pen started disappearing as her typing improved and she learned the [text] editing commands.

Paula's emphasis on finishing her report rather than fooling around with the writing machine relates to her desire to turn in an error-free paper. She was writing a history report in which she was making formal references to research sources. Her teacher had told the students that the form of the paper was as important as its content, so Paula was anxious to do, as she said, a "super job," and learning to use the word-processing program was holding her back from her immediate goal.

Similarly, adults have found that when they are learning to use a word-processing program, they become anxious if they are writing something that requires a great deal of thought. Learning the mechanics of the writing system requires mental energy that the writer needs for creating the text. Since younger children don't put as much conscious effort into learning the mechanics of word-processing, and since they expend less energy in planning, they feel comfortable writing a story or some other interesting piece as they learn to use the word processor. Teenagers and adults, however, need more time to get used to the machine.

The range in individual differences among students is accentuated in high school as some students prepare for college and others do not. High school students begin doing writing that formally presents them to employers, to colleges, and to audiences other than family, school, and friends. Thus, they are concerned with form and style as well as content in their writing. In high school, students become aware that their writing will reflect on them outside the school setting as well as within it; there is heavy emphasis on correctness and form, especially for college-bound students.

Because of the concern with the formats and mechanics of writing, rhetorical and grammatical problems are tolerated less in teenagers' writing than in the writing of younger students. The students and their teachers are aware that college entrance tests and college programs are based on the assumption that, by the twelfth grade, students have been taught to write formal essays in clear, standard English. The assumption for non-college-bound students is that they have learned enough about writing to function as citizens, which means at least being able to write a persuasive business letter in standard English. There is a gap, however, between expectations about high school students' writing and what they actually achieve. Some high schools provide many writing experiences across the curriculum, but others do not make many writing demands on students. Although the amount of practice the students have varies, the students and teachers are concerned with written form as well as content. It is difficult to make writing instruction in high school exciting, so it is often side-stepped for activities that students find more relevant. A major challenge for high school writing teachers is to make writing interesting as they help their students learn forms and formats.

This chapter suggests ways of using the computer to aid in the difficult job of teaching writing in high school. The applications are based on the assumption that one of the main goals in a high school writing curriculum is to provide instruction and practice in formal writing. The computer can help make writing interesting because of its interactive capacities—among people and between the writer and the writing instrument. It can also be useful because it is an efficient tool for practice. Sophisticated writing tools that offer ease of expression, guidelines on form, revising aids, and formal presentation tools, can help high school students integrate writing with their other learning activities.

ESSAY FORMS

The following papers by a 14-year-old in the tenth grade and a 17-year-old in the twelfth grade illustrate the adolescent's typical concern with form, synthesis of facts and ideas, and sounding smart. The papers also show how high school students, though concerned, often fail to express themselves perfectly in writing:

Fourteen-Year-Old's Essay

Vandalism

A community problem that has affected me directly is vandalism in the public schools. Many times I have been denied the use of equipment essential to the project I have been working on because it was ruined or broken by vandals and the schools do not want to see it happen again. Because of this I have had to find another place that has suitable materials to meet my needs or if I could not find these materials (micro film, overhead projectors, recording devices, etc.) I would have to do without and make the best of what is available to me but many times what is available to me does not suffice for what I was denied use of. Because it is harder to get access to these materials I respect the machine more and try to handle it well, without ruining or breaking any part of it. But other people do not seem to look at the situation this way, most feel that once they have used it, it does not make any difference to them if the next person who wants to use it cannot because they broke it. It seems that these people do not realize that their parents are paying for the materials anyway through town taxes.

The 14-year-old's paper sounds formal and sometimes stilted. This student hopes to go to college, so he takes English classes that stress academic writing. This student author attempted to use a sober, intelligent tone—even acknowledging the vandals' point of view. He included necessary essay elements—such as the topic sentence, "A community problem that has affected me directly is vandalism in the public schools"—but the essay is one paragraph, and the writer did not introduce new topic sentences in an organized way.

Seventeen-Year-Old's Essay

Goodbye West Woods

A community problem is directly affecting me now. I live a few blocks away from West Junior High School, in Addison. In back of the school there are trees and swamp land. Known to everyone in my neighborhood as the "West Woods. There are many things the woods are used for. Small children play in them,—older kids climb the trees. Teachers often use the woods for English and Science projects, which provide nature. During sunny days, while the school year is in session, many students go out to the woods, just to hang out. Whether the reasons I have listed seem practical or not, the West Woods are indeed appreciated by the people in my community. Especially the young teenagers who use the trails to ride their motorcycles. But now, the West Woods are being cut down. Way back in October when I was walking through the trails one day, I saw men sawing down big, beautiful trees by the hundreds. It made me sick. But then they stopped for a while. Now, they're starting to cut down the woods again. (or should I say finishing?) An office building is supposed to be built there. Do not we have enough buildings in our community as it is? Addison is already the only town in the state with the most shopping centers in it. With the Garden, the Center, Addison Mall, and the Maybrook Mall, all of Marble County depends on Addison for their clothes and furniture needs. Another thing wrong with cutting down the woods to build another office building is the fact that it is right next to the school. I think this would disturb the children. And, even worse, the new building is directly behind people's houses. I mean, how would you like to go out for swim on a beautiful day, in your own pool, and having executives and secretaries smiling and waving at you? No privacy at all is to be expected if this building is built. My third and final reason for not building this new office building, is that the beauty of nature, our woods, would be destroyed.

The tone of this paper by the non-college-bound 17-year-old is not so formal. The sentence patterns are simpler, and some sentences are incomplete. A high school teacher pointed out that this writer also attempted to use essay conventions, but she was not consistent. The sentence beginning "My third and final reason..." illustrates her attempt to highlight the organization of the paper with transitionals—a technique taught in writing classes and style guides. She had given several reasons earlier in the paper, but they were not marked with a consistent set of transitions.

Sometimes, such a concern for form overpowers the concern for content development; therefore, much writing by high school students is insufficiently developed. Students who are pushing themselves to achieve may write generalizations with stilted sentence patterns, and other students cling to the narrative forms they used successfully in lower grades.

There are practical reasons why adolescents learn to write, but the act of writing can also foster certain types of development. Analytic writing, for example, serves adolescents' development in several ways. According to Piaget, a milestone in human development is the transition from concrete to formal operations, which can occur in adolescence. Formal thinkers are able to be analytical—seeing an idea clearly from several points of view. While a child might notice the action and candy at a parade, a teenager might focus more on the various reasons why people march in parades when they could be relaxing on the sidelines or why certain observers are wearing silly clothes. Essay writing involves such mental gymnastics. Evidence of such thinking in "Goodbye West Woods" and "Vandalism" is the analysis of arguments against tearing down the woods and the slightly less mature analysis of various attitudes about school property. When students learn to control the development and refinement of their analyses and arguments, writing can actually become a method to support cognitive development.

A common writing activity in high school is the compare-and-contrast essay. In such an essay, the writer explicitly considers similarities and differences of two objects, events, or ideas. Considering the similarities and differences between communism and capitalism, for example, focuses attention on the critical features of each. Citing examples, such as the United States and the USSR, brings up further twists. Comparing and contrasting also involves taking several points of view. Writers who construct such essays are developing skills they can eventually use to write more complex argumentative essays.

The computer can help students in their analytic writing in several ways. To overcome the stilted quality that often creeps into such writing, the students can engage in ongoing computer conferences—either in real-time networks or on shared diskettes. What matters most for high school students is being able to write a lot and to write freely, so that they can find a voice that is comfortable dealing with academic or abstract topics—which might be quite different from the topics they discuss with friends.

One problem for students is that they consider essay writing an exercise. They find it difficult to imagine actual situations in which they would need to write a compare-and-contrast essay or an argumentative essay. Setting up communication channels for high school students can help them relate essay forms to real communication goals. Similarly, teachers can suggest writing activities that require comparison and argumentation to carry out writing goals—such as comparison of two Olympic skaters' styles to represent differences between two countries.

The networking environments that younger children so enjoy can offer high school students contexts in which to try out essay techniques. Computer conferences serve as ongoing forums for discussion of certain issues—current events, social issues, educational issues, and high school students benefit from sharing ideas for their essays and reports via electronic mail and computer conference files. They participate in such written conferences—as a regular part of the writing curriculum—on schoolwide or national networks. The broader the network and the more diverse the participants, the more the students must learn to write clearly and persuasively; they can't rely on their readers' common knowledge, as they can with readers who know them and their environment well.

Microcomputer diskettes can be set aside in a classroom or computer lab for ongoing written debates on topics students are thinking about for their essays—such as school or social policies. For example, two diskettes can be devoted to a debate on an issue of interest to teenagers—such as whether parental permission should be required for teenagers to buy birth control devices. The teacher should provide a diskette with the word-processing program on it. The word-processing program is a tool for writing quickly, which they want to do when they are arguing, and it offers them capacities for adding, merging, and editing files. After making two diskette copies of the word-processing program, the teacher can set up two files—one beginning with a statement for the issue, the other beginning with a statement against it. Students can then add to the arguments with which they agree. They can be required to read and add to the written debate a few times a week. Two students can be assigned to organize the files once a week, so that like topics can be discussed together and so that the argument begins to take on a persuasive structure. They should also keep backup copies of the originals. As the argument files increase to the limit of the file space that fits in memory, the students can use two-window and block move features in the word-processing program to break up the files into topical sections. Printouts of the files can be posted at the end of each week, and the teacher can develop exercises for practicing various structuring techniques. Individuals or groups of students can then make copies of the files, revise the texts, and compare their results.

Programs like Superfile, which allow writers to separate text files according to keywords, are also useful in such exercises. For example, *trust, free choice,*

High school students are often asked to debate—especially in writing argumentative essays.

independence, and *economic issues* might be keywords for different sections of a written debate on pro-free-choice birth control. After the keywords have been entered, a student can type a keyword into the program and the program will display or print out the sections of text relating to that keyword. Students can obtain the same effect by reading printouts and using various symbols to note the placement of important keywords. The following sample exercises could help students learn how to structure their computer conference files:

1. In groups of four, print out and read the two files on birth control freedom. In the margins, use two- or three-word phrases to describe the content of each paragraph or section. Then write a brief outline for a reorganization of the texts so that the pros and cons of each aspect of the argument are grouped together. Using the word-processing program, move each section into a new file for the merged essay according to your outline. Print out your new file and make sure that the essay is coherent. What are the two points of view expressed? What are the major topics addressed with pros and cons?

2. Print out and read the two files on birth control freedom. Select the one you think has the best material, and decide how you could make it even more convincing. You may use material from the other piece if you feel you have to address the other point of view. After making the necessary changes with the word-processing program, decide how to smooth out the wording and make the piece more grammatically correct.

3. Print out and read the two files on birth control freedom. Select the one you think has the weakest arguments, and decide how you could improve it. You may use material from the other piece if you think it would help. After making the necessary changes with the word-processing program, decide how to smooth out the wording and make the piece more grammatically correct.

Students can circulate their finished pieces and discuss them. Also, if the issue is a current one, the students might want to try to publish their pieces in the school or town newspaper.

Besides using the computer communication capacities to structure their ideas, students can also engage in essay-building exercises on the computer. The building-block composing style described in Chapter 5 is useful, for example, when they are preparing to write compare-and-contrast essays. Writers can list similarities in one file and differences in another, developing the essay first around similarities and then around differences, or they can regroup the similarities and differences according to categories.

Moving sections of text and trying out several alternative organizations of the ideas is relatively fast with the word processor, which can help students synthesize their ideas. For example, one student wrote an essay in which he grouped all the similarities between Russia and the United States and then grouped the differences. After finding that he had noted many more differences than similarities, he looked through an article about Soviet youth and found more similarities, but the emphasis was still on differences. Because he had to repeat himself too much when he organized the essay around the similarities and differences, his teacher suggested that he organize it around the cultural aspects he was comparing and contrasting. He wrote a list of these cultural categories in the word processor and then block moved sentences or parts of sentences to each section—school life, dating, music, and future plans—listing similarities first, then differences. The file he created in this way became his outline.

Students can also use computer conferencing, mail, and chatting systems to do written interviews for research. In this way, they learn to analyze audience needs for background, definitions, contexts, facts, and examples. For example, the student who wrote the essay on vandalism could have developed his arguments better and practiced expressing them more clearly in a computer conference about vandalism. He could have collected arguments by both vandals and nonvandals. The writer who was upset about the destruction of the West Woods developed her point of view better than the younger student had, but she did not mention or try to defeat opposing points of view. She could have benefited from written discussions of the issue by reading, collecting, and synthesizing opposing arguments into her essay.

TERM PAPERS

A major step in the adolescent's writing experience is preparing a term paper. Although not all high school writing curricula include term paper assignments, most colleges assume that students have had some written research experience. Conceptual and physical difficulties abound in writing a term paper, and many people remember the task with horror. To write a term paper, the student must identify a worthwhile thesis or argument, do research, take notes, prepare a bibliography and footnotes, and present the paper formally. Also, a term paper assignment is often the students' first typing experience.

A major problem is beginning—defining a relevant question for research. This becomes a problem, in part, because the students do not have prewriting strategies. They have not had experience in writing to find out what they think and then stating their interest in the form of a researchable question. Students might think of research topics, but it's difficult to start researching a topic when it is expressed broadly in a word or phrase, like *pollution*. The student who has gone so far as to decide on pollution as a topic is on the right track, but it would be easier to do research on the topic if he or she began with a statement, such as "Pollution is bad," to stimulate thinking. Developing a topic idea into a statement that might make someone angry—such as "Pollution is the fault of the corporations" or "Pollution is everyone's fault"—is a useful exercise for beginning research with a goal. The research can then be devoted to supporting or arguing against the statement. Research is also a process of answering questions, so students find it easier to do the necessary research if they start with interesting questions. The next problem is making sure that the questions are at least partially answerable from information they can find in books, articles, interviews, simple observations, or experiments. Although the first goal is to create an interesting topic sentence, the process of discovering this sentence can involve quite a bit of writing, erasing, moving words around, and rewriting. This process of developing topics into statements or questions can be faster and thus more productive if the student uses a word-processing program.

Once the students have found the focus for their term papers, they are confronted by a major conceptual problem related to the logistics of researching and note taking. They search for books and articles with relevant information and take notes from each source, often forgetting, however, to write down the bibliographic information or postponing it until a later stage, when they will have to spend time finding the sources again. As they prepare their papers, they might accumulate as many as twenty pages of notes from seven books. Then they must group notes on related issues and begin to write the paper. What often results, however, is a term paper made up of lists of summaries organized according to sources. The reason this occurs is related to the reason students have trouble deciding on the focus of the term paper— they lack the background necessary for identifying the purpose of the research and the motivating focus. It is difficult for them to analyze, categorize, and synthesize the chronological information they have collected into a form that is thematically related to their term paper topic. This problem of conceptual analysis is not an easy one to overcome. Guiding students to identify research questions that relate to compelling ideas is often effective; brainstorming and corresponding with other students can add importance to their ideas. In discussions with students, we often find that, intellectually, their interests range beyond what they label as such. The task, then, is to help them recognize these interest areas, which can often be done by means of written exchanges with other students. Daily or weekly electronic mail correspondence among students and teachers are useful for identifying the students' areas of interest.

In one high school that has a minicomputer and many types of micro-computers, the librarian, the history teacher, and the English teacher coordinate the term paper assignment required of all tenth-graders. The history teacher helps the students identify questions or debate issues as motivations for the term paper; the librarian discusses methods for finding relevant information; and the English teacher discusses organization of ideas, bibliography formats, and footnoting conventions. The teachers also co-

High school students have to synthesize information and ideas from many sources.

ordinate the students' use of the computers. The students use the New York Times Information Service on-line database as well as books written about the period of history they are studying; they are discouraged from using encyclopedias. Each student makes a copy of a bibliography entry form in a text file, so they all have a guide for proper form and punctuation. They use this frame in the word-processing program as they insert specific information for each source they use. A procedure for block moves across windows is convenient at this stage. The student can load the master bibliography frame in the top window, block delete it, and then put it back in the other window. This can be done as many times as there are bibliography entries. The student then inserts the specific information for each reference into the appropriate positions by deleting the descriptive words and typing the specific reference information in their place. The following are sample bibliography frames for two types of references—books and journal articles:

Book

Author's last name, First initial. <u>Book Title</u>. City of publication, State: Publisher. Publication date, page numbers used.

Journal Article

Author's last name, First initial. Publication date. "Article Title," <u>Journal Name, Volume number,</u> Issue, pages of article.

When they insert specific information, the students follow the capitalization scheme in the frame and leave the punctuation and format as they are. Each time they add a new bibliography entry, they make an electronic copy of the frame and fill in the appropriate information. Groups of students prepare similar frames for title pages, report outlines, and editing checklists.

Students narrow their term paper topics in consultation with the librarian and the history teacher. In history class, they discuss the contents of their databases and focus their points of view, asking, for example, "How would I have viewed this event?" In English class, they work through all the steps required for preparing the paper on the computer. Each student consults the format files and makes copies of frames for title pages, outlines, reference forms, and checklists. They then use these frames to start building their own papers. All three teachers enter comments in each student's emerging term paper files.

The students use the word-processing programs on the micros to write notes from each source, so sections of each student's evolving notes file are arranged according to the reference books and the order in which the writer used them. When they are ready to write the paper, they use search commands to find the sections on related topics and move them together.

Students also use database programs for recording bibliography entries and brief notes. For example, the PFS:File program can be used to design, structure, and organize a database of information on research sources and topics. Using this tool has both logistical and conceptual value. Once a student has read about a research subject in several books, he or she can design a database that includes the bibliographic data on the relevant sources and notes on information found in them. The program's main menu shows the range of activities available:

PFS:FILE FUNCTION MENU

1 DESIGN FILE   4 SEARCH/UPDATE
2 ADD   5 PRINT
3 COPY   6 REMOVE

SELECTION NUMBER:
FILE NAME:

The student selects the design file menu to begin creating the database:

DESIGN FILE MENU

1 CREATE FILE
2 CHANGE DESIGN

SELECTION NUMBER:

The student then specifies the categories and space allotments for the items that should appear in each database entry. At the teacher's suggestion, the student leaves room for about one sentence under each note category, so the notes will include only what the student considers the most important information. The following is a sample database entry frame for a report on using videodisc technology for games:

REFERENCE TITLE:
AUTHOR:
CITY OF PUBLICATION:
PUBLISHER:
DATE OF PUBLICATION:
NUMBER OF PAGES:

NOTES:
MAJOR FOCUS OF BOOK:

VIDEODISC FEATURE #1:

VIDEODISC FEATURE #2:

VIDEODISC FEATURE #3:

ADVANTAGE #1:

ADVANTAGE #2:

ADVANTAGE #3:

DISADVANTAGE #1:

DISADVANTAGE #2:

DISADVANTAGE #3:

After completing all the entries, the student searches and prints out, first, all the features, then the advantages, and finally the disadvantages. With the notes grouped by category, the student then makes a rough outline and begins to write the paper. The most difficult part of this process is deciding on the categories for the qualitative information. This requires some prior knowledge of the subject domain and general groups of relevant facts. Students precede database-making activities with brainstorming sessions in which they note the topics that came up in their reading. Such sessions can be valuable because, if the students realize they don't have enough information for a database of notes, they know they have to go back to their references.

Students who are writing term papers on similar topics can create general outlines together. For example, several students reporting on advances in electronic technology wrote the following general outline:

1. What are the "new" technologies?
2. How are they different from the "old" ones?
3. What impact will these changes have on (one of the following)
   a. politics
   b. education
   c. social life
4. My thesis—what I think the result will be
5. Evidence from a prior historical development
6. Case studies and reasons
7. Conclusions

Each student in the group copies this general outline onto a personal diskette. One student fills in point 4 with "Young people are taking the creative lead in technological developments because they use computers before they have to understand them." The student types in two or three case studies—for example, Steve Jobs, the young creator of Apple Computers. As the students enter their case studies, they note similarities among the case studies that they use as generalizations to support their theses. As the generalizations occur to them, they move to the "evidence" section by means of the search command and write in the points they later expand.

At this point, the ThinkTank program, described in Chapter 4, can be useful for developing, organizing, and refining the ideas further. Students type the general outline into the major Think Tank slots and then fill in their specifics in full sentences and paragraphs that they are ready to write. For example, one student had read a lot about Steve Jobs because she had followed his interest in sponsoring rock concerts, so she was able to write a few paragraphs about him. When it comes time to reorganize sections of the outline, the outlining program helps in reorganizing all the text under each category with a heading line as the writer gives commands. The program is designed so that headings and sections can be moved with brief commands, thereby simplifying the outline reorganization process.

Such a research project is active, and the group work, question defining, note taking, and outlining are heuristics that help the students guide their thinking about a subject. Making thinking active by giving it reference points in the outside world can stimulate and organize the required mental activities. Following such a term paper development method doesn't solve all the conceptual difficulties in doing and presenting research, but it can help students whose conceptual activities have been hindered by physical limitations. With such a method, the process of beginning to consolidate and synthesize ideas is physically easier because it does not involve recopying or cutting and pasting. Determining whether this increased physical ease leads to increased conceptual clarity is a task that remains for researchers.

Fourteen-year-old Paula was writing her first major term paper on the computer for a teacher who stressed form in the assignment. The students were to present six to eight double-spaced pages with footnotes. Also, they were to express a topic sentence at the beginning of each paragraph and underline it. Although Paula had been reluctant to use a new tool for an assignment that was important, she eventually found that the computer was particularly useful. She found that, on the computer, filling pages was easy, and a program did the double-spacing automatically. When she was about to underline her topic sentences, she discovered that several were the second sentence in the paragraph, rather than the first. The move command allowed her to bring the topic sentences to the beginning of each paragraph easily. As she did that, she noticed that some of her sentences were awkward because she had tried to pack too much information into them, so she reworded two sentences several times, making additional small improvements. Paula's teacher noted, however, that the final versions of these sentences were not clearly better, other than punctuation and type corrections—possibly because of Paula's rigid adherence to the topic sentence rule.

PROMPTING

Prompting programs have a different value for high school students than they do for junior high schoolers. Even though prompting is intended to enhance the general self-monitoring skills of younger children, it may have more value for older students. By the time students are in high school, they have probably learned to choreograph their mental activities in the areas in which they excell—sports strategy, dancing, math, influencing their friends, and so on. The value of composition prompting programs for those students is to help them learn specific strategies for writing.

Prompting programs such as Burns's computer-assisted prewriting programs can be useful to high school students, as can programs that prompt writers according to the organizational structures of particular types of essays. As discussed earlier, teachers can create frames for specific essays on the computer, or they can adapt tools, like the QUILL Planner, that were developed for younger children. The QUILL developers have reported that, in some schools, teachers have not used the Planner much with the third-through sixth-graders for whom it was developed. This suggests that such structured composing is more appropriate for high school students than for upper elementary and junior high students. Teenagers still write unbalanced or stilted essays, so some instruction on essay form might be helpful after they have become generally acquainted with the purposes of such essays and have had practice writing them without guidelines. The information gleaned from working a few times with prompts from a program designed to guide the structure of an opinion essay would have been useful for a student like the author of the "West Woods" piece, who needed help organizing the points in the text. Such exercises become active and personal lessons on essay forms, because the prompting program applies to the students' writing rather than to an abstract example.

STYLE

Along with correctness and form, style is a major concern for adolescent writers. Students often experiment by imitating the styles of the writers they study in literature class, and some teachers encourage their students to practice using various types of sentence and prose styles. With the computer, students can easily create alternative versions of a text, allowing them to practice controlling their writing style. The students write a text in one style, then make a copy of it and change such features as sentence length, paragraph form, and word use. As they compare their alternative pieces and also contrast them to works by noted authors, they refine their understanding of style.

Adolescents advance linguistically by using compound and complex modifiers and predicates. As a result, problems with misplaced modifiers and parallel structure are common in their writing. As we saw in the "Vandalism" and "Goodbye West Woods" essays, teenagers often write complex sentences that they cannot always control. As sentence complexity increases, so does the incidence of sentence fragments; complex clauses might seem to be sentences because they are so long—for example, "Known to everyone in my neighborhood as the 'West Woods.'" For this reason, automatic text-analysis programs can be useful to high school students. Automatic identification of empty or vague words and very long sentences can draw their attention to just the sentences that need reworking. Since high school students are experimenting with expressing complex ideas, they have to learn how to untangle awkward, complex sentences. Because correcting these sentence problems often requires that they rework an entire sentence, simple suggestions by a computer program to substitute another word or phrase may be inadequate. Therefore, when programs like the Writer's Workbench or Homer note certain problems with word patterns, teachers should encourage the students to look for solutions beyond the word—in the complete sentence and paragraph.

An equally common problem is the lack of sentence variety in many students' papers, resulting from repeated simple sentences, in the subject, verb, object form, with a few transitions between them. If students and teachers work together, with printouts from text analysis programs, they can relate the program counts of complex versus compound and simple sentences to the meaning and rhythmic flow of the paragraph.

Another approach to the problem of lack of sentence variety is to present model paragraphs with repetitious sentence forms and instruct students to combine or rewrite sentences in different syntactic patterns. When these sample paragraphs are on the computer, the students can focus on making the changes rather than copying the piece. Students also compare their individual solutions to the sentence-combining exercise or work on them together, either face-to-face or at different terminals, so that they may be more sharply critical of one another's sentences.

Teachers also demonstrate grammatical and writing concepts in simple paragraphs written by students in the class—to make the lesson more interesting than it would be with paragraphs from a textbook. If the students' paragraphs are on diskettes, the teacher can rework them slightly to highlight examples of major points, and the students can use the word-processing program to focus on changes that need to be made. Students can then use the two-window feature to compare improved paragraphs by different students.

Teachers also help students increase the variety of sentence structures in their papers by making specific notes on their papers, suggesting places where they could recombine or reform phrases and clauses. As noted earlier, the mail programs and word-processing programs can be used for comment writing. Written conferencing about style and mechanics may be welcomed by high school students, who do not like to show their weaknesses in class.

One of the first uses of computers in the humanities was to do **concordances**—counts of specific words and the contexts in which these words occur—for stylistic analyses of important authors' works. Literary analysts used concordances to support their discussions about a particular author's style. For example, a concordance was prepared on the uses of *black* in Shakespeare's "Othello." Quantitative analyses of sentence length, like those in the Writer's Workbench, were also used to identify consistent features of writers' styles. These analyses showed that some great writers wrote very short sentences, but equally great writers wrote very long ones. Used creatively and integrated with other information, these quantitative analyses can be clues to important stylistic features. Of course, style is not only a question of numbers, but if students discuss such analyses in relation to qualitative aspects of the texts, they might develop insights about how the analyses can help them with their writing.

Full parsers, such as EPISTLE, or analysis programs with prompting can support students in controlling their stylistic presentation of sentences. One section of CATCH, for example, identifies guide words, or transitions, such as *but*, *however*, *so*, and *then*, and presents the message: Do the highlighted words guide your reader in understanding the meaning and structure of your paragraph? When there are relatively few guide words, the message is You may need to add guide words to show the relationships between ideas. Such analysis and prompting alerts students to sentence and paragraph forms that might need to be connected.

Students in high school are mature enough to use spelling checkers on their own. Unlike younger students, they have probably developed the basic English spelling concepts and need help mostly in identifying typos and words they do not yet know how to spell. Students with severe spelling problems, however, should be guided in their use of the spelling checker so that they become acquainted with its idiosyncrasies. The methods described in Chapter 8 for junior high school students would be equally appropriate for high school students who have severe spelling problems.

IGNORING FORM

Freewriting is important for adolescents. After they have focused on form, style, presentation, and sounding smart, teenagers benefit from composing freely to recapture their natural voice. Although younger children write quickly on the computer to learn to use varied structures and to learn that they have something to say, adolescent writers need freedom to unlearn some of the rigid structures and integrate them with a natural voice. Mike Rose, a researcher who studies writing blocks, found that the common characteristic among adolescents with writers' block is that they rigidly follow dicta, such as "Grab your reader," to such an extent that they cannot go beyond writing a series of first sentences, which are crossed out because they do not seem catchy enough. When freewriting on the computer, adolescents are encouraged to use only the parts of their formal training that they have internalized and incorporated with their ideas and other abilities. Being able to compose a piece quickly helps writers keep their ideas flowing and connected. The move command, which the writer can use to pull a precious sentence up to its proper place as an opener is essential. Also, high school students have found that getting rid of deadwood in their papers is easier when they can remove it to a deadwood file, leaving little mess and little trace of wasted effort behind. When they can set aside problematic sections, they can experiment with new wording, and the original text can be reinserted if it turns out to be better than later attempts.

PRACTICAL WRITING

By the time students are in high school, their writing travels beyond the walls of home and school, but, they may have trouble typing and formatting a résumé, college application letter, or job letter so that it looks professional. The professional-looking copy they can produce on the computer now has practical import. Imperfect typing is not of much consequence on the computer, because corrections are easy to make, and the final printout of a corrected computer file does not have to be corrected in pen—as is often necessary even after laboring for hours over a typing job. The formatting capacities of the computer are also particularly useful for laying out résumés, letters of introduction to prospective employers, and college application statements. Students often work together to figure out the appropriate commands for centering, spacing, and indenting a résumé, for example, with the formatting program they have. This may take some time, but a frame with the résumé formatting commands can be stored on a diskette that can then be used by any student who is writing a résumé. As part of their discussions on form, the students also think about content.

The following is a sample frame for a résumé that works in a program I use:

```
@Center(Person's Name)
@Center(Street Address)
@Center(City, State, 02138)
@Blankspace(2 lines)
EDUCATION:
@Indent(Smothers High School)
@Indent(Street & Address)
@Indent(Town, State Zip)
@Blankspace(2 lines)
PART-TIME JOBS:
@Indent(Employer)
@Indent(Address, etc.)
@Blankspace(2 lines)
```

```
INTERESTS:
@Indent(List hobbies, clubs, interests)
@Blankspace(2 lines)
JOB OBJECTIVES:
@Indent(State professional goals)
@Blankspace(2 lines)
REFERENCES:
```

Business letter formats are also appropriate for high school students to use in college and job searches. If the available program has a mail merge system, they can also refine the letter-writing process by typing in a database of names and addresses of the people they are contacting, and letting the mail merge program insert the names, addresses, and headings into copies of the basic letter. Of course, sophisticated-looking letters cannot mask poorly developed content. Ideally, the time saved by using such tools—and their structuring value—will leave more time for the writer to work on the content of the letter.

SUMMARY

Adolescents need a great deal of encouragement and support to continue their intellectual and creative development, and writing can be a stimulating activity for them, because it is reflective and challenging. This chapter has offered suggestions for using computer tools to meet adolescents' unique developmental needs that affect their writing.

COMPUTER TOOLS FOR ADOLESCENT WRITERS

The following computer tools are particularly appropriate for adolescent writers:

- Word-processing program
  - —Basic and advanced commands
  - —Allowance for documents longer than 10 pages
  - —Two-window feature
  - —Full set of formatting commands
- Prompting for essays
- Outlining programs
- Information utilities
- Database programs
- Spelling checkers
- Prompting for revising
- Mail merge programs

Writers in College and Graduate School   *10*

A college computer room is more than just a place where people use computers. It is a lively, informal learning center, where students write papers, write computer programs, and work on statistics in harmony or in disharmony—depending on the time of year. The computer room is alive with learning; it's rare to see someone "goofing off" there. Near the beginning of a term, a person peeking into the computer lab would see students helping one another learn to use the computer hardware and software. Even more typically, one would see the resident "computer person" leaning over the shoulder of a newcomer, suggesting the command keys to press, and other students sitting in front of terminals together working on history or statistics projects. At midsemester, the people in the computer room seem to be working more on their own. They are concentrating on what they are doing on the computer, rather than on the computer itself. Unfortunately, a visit at the end of the term would be less pleasant—impending deadlines seem to make the students anxious, hasty, and sometimes competitive.

No matter how rich a school is, there are never enough terminals or microcomputers to serve everyone who has to finish a final paper, take-home exam, or program. One college newspaper reported at the end of the fall term that a young woman had gone to the computer center at 2:00 in the morning because that was the only time a micro and printer were available. She was so rushed trying to polish and print out her term paper before morning that, bleary-eyed, she pressed a fatal sequence of command keys and lost her twenty-page paper. She had not saved a copy of the original paper on another diskette when she had last worked on the computer. The college reporter recounted this story as a commentary on what happens to people in a computer society; computer rooms can be full of nervous people, especially at the end of a term. However, the story illustrates even more about writers in college. It shows that they work independently as well as together and that they have many pressures that affect their writing. Although college students face pressures no matter what tools they use, the computer adds new complications, and because people tend to share computer tools, these pressures become public. But, the computer also offers college students several capacities that address their needs.

Writers in college share many concerns with adult writers. For example, they have to use facts persuasively to carry out the purpose of their writing. They often write long texts, and—because their writing represents them to the world—the overall form of the presentation seems as important as the content. Nevertheless, the functions of writing in college courses, like those in secondary school, are different from the functions of writing on the job. The major difference is that students have time to practice their writing, while adults on the job are writing to communicate immediately. The computer also helps college students work on long documents and, as it does with students in secondary school, build their writing skills in communication contexts.

The major differences between writing in high school and writing in college are (1) the volume of work, (2) the interdisciplinary nature of assignments, and (3) the amount of independent learning. The computer can help college students in these three areas as follows:

A college computer user room is a lab, workshop, and study.

1. Word-processing programs, information storage and retrieval systems, and spelling checkers help students handle large volumes of work and large documents more efficiently.
2. Computer storage and communication tools help students with inter-disciplinary work.
3. The interactive and writing tools help students work well independently.

College students are expected to write in clear, correct, standard English in several prose forms: essays, letters, and reports. Unfortunately, many people leave secondary school without mastering even the basic writing skills, so basic or remedial writing has become a common course in post-secondary educational programs.

BASIC WRITING SKILLS

The text samples in this section illustrate typical problems in the writing of college students who take basic writing courses. The first paper illustrates problems with the mechanics of written English:

> Not too many people acheve their degree in the these fields so therfor you can say that, in a way they are an abundance of jobs for them, though it they are the jobs least demanded by. As in contrast to the Jobs most demanding it is because as I mentioned before if the quality of knowledge obtained and so forth. In comparing the status the persons with degrees in the least job demand would be highly regarded then to that of a person with the form of a job which was most demanding.*

Besides the mechanical problems, this text marks the place for ideas, rather than expressing them clearly. This is a common problem for students who have not written very much—they have ideas and opinions, but they have trouble developing their ideas in writing. The student who wrote "As in contrast to the Jobs most demanding it is because as I mentioned before if the quality of knowledge obtained and so forth" would not express the idea the same way orally.

Many students have trouble writing as they would speak because most of the writing they have seen is different in form and content from their ways of speaking. A student's written phrasing is often more awkward than his or her spoken phrasing, because writing requires more objective control of language. Writing has to paint complete pictures in words, while speech can draw on the environment and the shared knowledge among people. Another reason students do not write as well as they speak is that obtuse and collapsed sentences like the one in the example sound more like writing to them. A

*M. Shaughnessy, *Errors and Expectations* (New York: Oxford University Press, 1977), p. 46.

basic writing student once told researcher Mina Shaughnessy, who collected the sample essay, "Good writing is writing you can't understand." Since many college students speak nonstandard dialects of English, writing seems foreign to them. Shaughnessy and others have noted that the college students with the most severe writing problems write the most complex and convoluted paragraphs. Students who feel that written language must sound stilted have had language experiences that are different from those assumed by the writers of standard English texts. Students who think good writing is writing you can't understand do not trust their own inner voices or ears.

Students may also feel that writing should sound stilted because their teachers have told them *not* to write the way they talk. This advice is given to help students avoid creating text that relies more on physical context than on linguistic context and explicit statements. Nevertheless, beginning writers could become more comfortable with writing if they could relate it to talking. One hurdle can be overcome by these students if they are encouraged to write drafts as they would talk, giving legitimacy to their dialect—at least in the prewriting process.

Many of the ideas students are asked to write about are ones they do not usually talk about, so the topics are as foreign as the language. Another hurdle for these students can be overcome if they discuss abstract subjects before writing about them. Nevertheless, expressing ideas clearly in writing requires that the students organize and phrase the ideas differently than they do when they speak. Writing also requires certain conventions, such as punctuation, spelling, and concise syntactical forms.

Basic writing courses typically include formal reviews of grammar, punctuation, usage, and paragraph development, which are similar to the topics covered in middle school curricula. Recently, the focus has been on composing and revising long texts, but basic writing courses drill mechanics because the students have not mastered the basics of writing. The value of the computer for such skill development and refining is becoming a hotly debated issue.

Unfortunately, the pressure to use computers could lead to a return to outdated methods of writing instruction. Computer programs designed for individual diagnosis and instruction in the mechanical features of writing, such as punctuation and spelling, are being used in remediation centers, and basic skills teachers have been tempted to use drill and tutorial programs because they offer instruction on just the mechanical features that cause problems in student writing. The research suggests, however, that improvements are best made in the context of one's own writing, rather than by means of isolated drills. Rather than drilling on precise spelling and punctuation, the students should be writing, writing, writing.

In the context of a basic writing course in which students write a lot, read their writing aloud, and discuss it with teachers and fellow students, CAI programs may be used to help students with the mechanics. Drills are more acceptable as complementary exercises for college students than for younger students, because college students do not have as much time to work out problems by writing extensively, as younger students do. Also, adults learn well deductively—from rules—but children learn better inductively—from examples. Adults and children both benefit from examples as well as from explicit statements of principles, but the order of presentation is important. Since stated rules are too abstract for children, they tend to perceive and play with facts and eventually intuit the rules. In contrast, adults use rules as conceptual hooks for the facts and examples that are given to illustrate the rules. Many basic writing teachers work with college students by going over the content, organization, and logical development in their essays and asking the students to revise the essays. Then, if mechanical problems remain, teachers point them out and suggest that the students work on those problems.

Printed worksheets and handbooks state rules for the students and provide exercises for them to practice such mechanics as punctuation, for example, by adding commas, semicolons, and periods to a prepared text. Worksheets are also useful for fill-in-the-blanks exercises. In these cases, however, the teacher or other students have to check the work, evaluate it, and suggest follow-up activities. Computer programs provide more dynamic handbooks and worksheets. If a program is designed well, its presentation of drills may be significantly better than worksheets. The program can immediately tell the student whether specific commas or semicolons are appropriate in the prepared text, because the program can store a correct copy. Similarly, the program can compute the number of errors and suggest further exercises.

Teachers develop and store their own models and boilerplates with a word-processing program. Then, students copy the master text without punctuation, insert punctuation with the word-processing program, compare it to a master with punctuation, and then use the word-processing commands to make changes. With **authoring languages** like SuperPILOT, teachers can design interactive worksheets that compare, compute, and suggest additional practice. An authoring language provides the teacher with a structure, such as a fill-in-the-blanks exercise. With an authoring language, the teacher adds specific sentences, target words, and instructions on features for the program to check and compute automatically. Using the authoring language as a tool, the teacher can write exercises for college students who require complementary drills, but the exercises can be based on sentences and texts written by the students themselves. Once teachers have learned to use the authoring language, they are likely to spend less time preparing and checking students' exercises than they would spend preparing and checking worksheets. This gives them more time for inserting appropriate, up-to-date examples and individual students' sentences, rather than spending their time on checking fill-in answers or typing over worn-out worksheets. More important, teachers have more time to read and discuss students' writing. Some teachers find that they must spend the same amount of time on preparation, but that the dynamic worksheets provided by the computer are better exercises for the students.

College teachers should feel free to suggest that students use spelling checkers. With this tool, students identify typos and sometimes learn the correct spellings of words they have never written before or words they have been writing incorrectly. The teachers should also alert students to check their papers for the kinds of spelling mistakes that spelling checkers miss—such as homonyms in the wrong place, as discussed in Chapter 6.

Text-analysis programs can also be useful as grammar lessons in the context of students' own writing. Basic writing students who use programs like the Writer's Workbench or Homer should discuss the program output with their teachers so that they can relate the quantitative analyses—numbers of prepositions and sentence types—to characteristics of good writing and their own papers. Students who use such programs can also be guided by the output to look up information in grammar and style manuals as a way of developing some independent writing-analysis skills. For example, if students using text-analysis programs need specific information on the use of the semicolon, they can find the information in a style and grammar handbook, either on-line or in print. In the near future, many computer writing systems that offer text analysis will also offer on-line style and grammar manuals, which would be most appropriate for college students. Another common problem among students who write in standard English is that their texts are not well developed. For example:

> This quotation implies about equity in human thoughts and actions. Generally the statement is correct. What varies is how you meet the enemy and his reaction. Sometimes people happen to be in certain situations where they meet their enemies. At those moments they expect the enemy to strike back at them on the basis of their previous disagreements, however, his reaction to you may be considerate and polite.
>
> I personally disagree with the implication of this quote because you can never predict the actions of others even if you are very close with them, especially since they are your enemies.

Teachers can use the computer to help students fill out paragraphs by inserting questions in text files and by suggesting that they use prompting programs, like CATCH, that encourage students to evaluate the completeness of each paragraph.

Often, students in remedial writing classes have trouble because their writing has not been related to communication, and much of their practice and feedback on essays is divorced from discussions of the piece as a whole. Therefore, drill and practice—though an easy and apparently optimal application of the computer—should not be its major use for such students. Students in basic writing classes should also use the computer's capacities for writing in realistic contexts, for freewriting, for reader responses, and for revising—in the ways described in Chapters 4 through 6 and in Chapters 8 and 9. The communications applications described for students in secondary school are also appropriate for college students. The main difference is that college students can be guided to engage in such electronic written dialogues more independently and about different topics.

FRESHMAN COMPOSITION

Freshman English classes usually offer students instruction and practice on essay forms, so that they can demonstrate their general knowledge, their original ideas, and their ability to synthesize information. Freshman writing courses are usually intended to help students develop scholarship, style, and precision in planning, composing, and revising various types of essays. Reviews on grammar, usage, and punctuation tend to be individualized and are based on instructors' comments on the students' papers.

Writing tools for freshmen in composition classes should help them handle large volumes of text, create alternatives, and synthesize what they have learned. In addition, the presentation of papers in freshman composition is important. Professors expect compositions to be neatly typed, and some expect them to include headings, footnotes, and bibliographies. Word-processing and formatting programs can be used productively by freshmen, who are sometimes required to revise compositions as many as four times. The word-processing tools they use should allow them to work on long texts—as long as twenty pages. Sophisticated formatting features and an automatic footnote option would also be appropriate for these students. For example, the Perfect Writer program offers footnote commands that place the notes on the bottom of the page, number the notes consecutively, and format the text on the page above. In Perfect Writer, the writer enters the footnote information directly after the text to which it applies:

@FOOT [Wade, Howard H., @u(Perfect Writer/Speller User's Guide,) 1983, p. 184.]

Like other automatic aids, such a footnote option should be used only by students who are already aware of footnoting conventions. The teacher could use such commands in an introductory lesson on footnotes, but students must know the reasons for using footnotes and the punctuation conventions for footnotes in various formatting styles—such as the Modern Language Association (MLA) and the American Psychological Association (APA) formats. A program that figures out the number of lines for the footnote and the number of lines that can appear on the text section of the page above allows writers to use footnotes freely without worrying about space implications when they are typing a paper. Some students actually try to limit the number of footnotes they use because typing a paper with footnotes is such an arduous task; figuring out the number of footnotes per page and the amount of blank space to leave at the bottom of a text page for the notes costs even accomplished typists considerable time, energy, and retyping.

Although less class time is devoted to the mechanics of writing in freshman composition than in basic writing courses, students and teachers still spend some time reviewing and editing texts for sentence structure, word use, punctuation, and spelling. Automatic style and spelling checkers seem to be appropriate for these students in composition classes.

In a study on the effects of the Writer's Workbench programs, Kate Keifer and Charles Smith at Colorado State University have found: "Textual analysis with computers intrigues college writers and speeds learning of editing skills." In this study, two groups of students in freshman composition courses were randomly selected. One group was a control, and the other group used the Writer's Workbench DICTION, SUGGEST, STYLE, and SPELL programs for 1 hour a week for 13 weeks to determine whether the programs helped these students edit more thoroughly and helped them to edit on their own. Keifer and Smith gave the students a two-part editing task, pre- and posttreatment attitude surveys, and pre- and posttreatment summary and response essay assignments, which were rated according to a holistic scoring procedure. The experimental subjects improved more than the control subjects (15.03 compared to 10.50) on part two of the editing task— revision of errors for simplicity, directness, and clarity—which was taught by DICTION, SUGGEST, and STYLE. The two groups showed similar gains in writing fluency, according to holistic scores on the summary and response essays. The attitude survey showed that the experimental students found the computer programs to be enjoyable, easy, and free from frustration.

This study showed that text-analysis programs can be useful in conveying editing skills, but that students still have to write extensively for the skills to transfer to their own writing. The students who used the Writer's Workbench programs did not score significantly higher than the control subjects on part one of the editing test, which covered material on essay writing. Both groups had discussed essay form in English class, and the Workbench does not cover essay form, so it is not surprising that the groups did not differ in this aspect of writing. The study showed, however, that although analysis programs are appealing to students and help their editing skills, editing skills are not the same as composing and revising skills. This lack of transfer of specific editing skills to writing fluency is not surprising, since the computer feedback in the Workbench is geared to local editing. Class discussions are usually more concerned with style, organization, and logic. Skills at one level do not automatically transfer to skills at another; that is, training on editing may eventually transfer to skills for editing local features of one's text but are not likely to transfer to organizational skills.

Other computer tools are useful in helping students focus on organization and development in their writing. In college composition classes, much of the teachers' work involves student conferences and comments on the students' papers. No computer program can replace a conference about the content, logical development, or affect expressed in a paper. Spelling checkers and text-analysis programs do, however, put some of the responsibility for mechanics into the students' hands. In addition, the computer is a useful tool for commenting on students' writing. Chapters 5 and 6 described techniques for using the word-processing two-window feature for writing comments files for students' papers and inserting comments directly into copies of the text files. With the word processor, the commenter has editing commands that are extremely useful when one is trying to phrase comments precisely and kindly. Comments inserted into the text files help the writer see the impact of the text in a concrete way. For example, a well-placed HUH? can convince a student that the prior sentence really does need more work.

Richard Marius, of the Harvard University Composition Program, is developing an efficient commenting program. With Notewriter, the instructor inserts symbols in the students' text files. When students encounter a symbol in their text files, they press an appropriate key to see the teacher's discussion of the problems or good features at that point in the text. When they have finished reading the comment, the students press a key to return to the text to make a change or to read on to the next comment. Such a commenting procedure offers the student feedback in the context of the text, which remains clear of handwritten marks that could distract the student from reading the text.

PROMPTING AND OUTLINING
FOR THESIS ORGANIZATION

Thesis statements are an important part of college writing. Stating a complex idea in one sentence takes practice, and learning to write an essay that develops the thesis statement by explanation, example, and argumentation requires not only practice but a sharpening of thinking skills. College professors have begun to explore the use of computer prompting tools for developing these skills.

Writing a good thesis statement is a process. SEEN, the prompting program that was developed for use in college literature classes, is an example of an interactive lesson that guides students in this process. SEEN guides the student in answering a set of questions in preparation for writing a character sketch. While writing the answers to SEEN's questions, the student thinks about a character in tasks of increasing difficulty—first naming and describing the character, then analyzing, then interpreting. Prompts such as What is the name of the character? What is the name of the work? and Write one word that describes the character, guide the writer's thinking process. The questions that elicit descriptions, comparisons, and analyses of the character are followed by a final prompt, **Write a sentence that sums up what you have said about this character.** It would have been difficult for the writer to write such a summary sentence without considering the factors brought out by the other questions.

Teachers can use authoring languages or prompting templates like the QUILL Planner to write their own questions. Although they are perhaps only subtly different from a list of questions on paper, questions presented on the screen as the writer requests them seem to be stimulating. My hunch is that this occurs because the program presents the questions one at a time, which captures the writer's attention, and in a conversational format that accepts the writer's answer immediately.

An important point to remember when using prompting programs is that the programs tend to stimulate writers' memory search; thus, the resulting text appears in an associative order, rather than in the logical or thematic order expected in college writing. When writers who use prompting programs go through explicit revising processes, they can benefit greatly from the word-processing capacities for revising.

Since many writers in college compose long, analytic documents, text organization tends to be more of a problem for them than it is for younger students. Complex ideas must be presented in logical orders, rather than the simple chronological orders typical of earlier writing. Writers who like to organize their thoughts before drafting a text can benefit from an outlining program like ThinkTank.

Lillian Bridwell and her colleagues at the University of Minnesota did a study to identify the composing processes of college writers who use word-processing programs. Their research on eight college writers in a business writing course showed that the writers' individual composing styles determined how they used the word-processing program and how much the program affected their writing. The students learned to use the WordStar word-processing program, although the researchers had to prepare their own manuals to guide the students, because the program documentation was not clearly written. The researchers found that the program was adequate for word processing but that it should be augmented with various electronic prewriting, revising, and editing tools to encourage a complete and balanced composing process. These researchers are currently designing a set of templates writers can use to customize commands to their own composing styles.

Bridwell and her colleagues found that the students who tended to plan before drafting their texts—in this case, complex business letters—were the most comfortable using the word-processing program. These writers had good ideas about both the organization and the content of their letters before they used the program. In contrast, the more Beethovian writers, who developed their ideas as they composed, reported that writing on the computer was frustrating. The researchers found another interesting result—the word-processing program revising features did not help the writers who didn't like to revise. Despite the ease of revising and editing, the subjects who reported that they did not like to revise still didn't revise.

This research has offered insights into the power of the computer as a revising instrument. It has reminded us that the writer—not the computer—does the difficult conceptual work. Contrary to reports by many professional writers, the students who revised extensively did not find much solace in the easy block move and automatic recopy commands. This may be because the precursor to using these commands—thinking about how the text should be pruned, expanded, and reorganized—is hard work. Another major difficulty for extensive revisers is that they cannot view the entire text at one time. Working with printouts of successive revisions helps overcome this limit, but one does not want to make a printout after moving each section, so scrolling to view different sections is still necessary. Writers who revise extensively may take longer to adapt to computer writing because they have to alter their strategies; in contrast, planners, who probably never have to make major revisions, use the word-processing program as a more efficient typewriter. These writers found the program most useful when they were refining a text—making improvements in sentences and words—rather than when they were doing major rewriting or reorganization. We have to remember, of course, that within about twenty years, many college students will have learned to write using word-processing programs, so this issue of variations in adapting to new tools in college will be moot—or at least different.

Writers who have to revise extensively may first need guidelines for exploiting the word-processing capacity. For example, the writers in Bridwell's study did not use a two-window feature, which helps in revising. Writers can use this feature to view, rearrange, and rewrite text in ways that are not analogous to methods used with traditional writing tools. For example, a writer who has decided that a text needs major work could be guided to read the text on-line and move the sections and sentences that are good to the other window and into another file. These sections can be inserted into the new file in new orders to improve the organization of the paper. Writers can also make outlines of the text as it is, then outlines of how it should be, and they can then move the sentences from the draft into the outline file, polishing the sentences with the editing features at that point or waiting until the new draft is created. These procedures can be extremely useful and efficient, but it takes time to become comfortable with them. Chapter 6 presents additional revising techniques to use with word-processing programs.

Students who have fulfilled their freshman composition requirements still must write a great deal in college and graduate school. In advanced writing courses and subject-area courses, the students continue to develop as writers, as their assignments and their teachers' comments stretch their abilities.

SCHOLARSHIP

Along with practicing reference forms, writers in college learn the functions of citations. Although students often think that they have to consult books for all the information in their papers, writers in college learn to develop their own ideas and back them up with references to published works in which other writers have presented ideas, research, or predictions. Selecting appropriate quotations is an art, however, and it takes many years of practice, beginning in college and continuing through graduate school and later professional writing. In deciding why to quote as well as how, students can benefit from the following guidelines:

1. Cite the sources of specific information you give.
2. Use direct quotations as succinct, well-said illustrations of points you want to make.
3. You have to make the point yourself.
4. Use quotations as illustrations or supports from an authority.

Thus, one selects quotations not only for what they say but also for who said them. The nuances of referring to other writers in one's text develop as the originality in one's academic writing develops. I often tell my graduate students to present an argument in every paper they write—stating the gist of the argument in four or five sentences, then looking for statements by experts that support each point in the argument. When someone has made a point particularly succinctly, dramatically, or convincingly, they should use a direct quotation. In other cases, they should simply refer to the expert's work.

Writers use computer storage and word-processing tools for developing the art of making citations. When they are doing research, mature students create databases including their references and notes, following a procedure similar to that described in Chapter 9. Advanced writers, however, must have database tools that allow them to enter many pages of notes and to assign keywords and search fields after writing, as well as before.

After one has read extensively on a subject, it is often difficult to remember where the ideas came from. The most fluid research writing often comes when writers write from knowledge acquired from reading but when they do not stop to refer to the books every step of the way. In this way, writers can synthesize the ideas and facts derived from the reading. When their drafts are composed and revised for correct organization, the writers can begin to check facts and references by viewing the text on one half of the screen and their notes database on the other. If the word-processing program allows writers to give search commands to outside files while keeping the text on the screen, they can search for keywords in the database as they come up in the original text. When they find sections of notes on the same topic, the writers decide whether a quotation or a footnote reference to another author is appropriate. If so, they copy the quotation or reference information from the file on one half of the screen to the other half. Such references are equally important in report writing and in original research.

ORIGINAL WRITING

Academics and professionals often use writing to express and explain original ideas. Writing original ideas—whether fiction or nonfiction—requires practice. Original scholarly writing also involves imagination and creativity (not, one hopes, fantasy) and a certain type of precision that can require extensive planning and revising. For example, developing new perspectives on a subject often involves redefining terms or coining new ones. A student writing a thesis named thirty-six types of inferences people make when they are reading. His advisors disagreed with some of the terms he used, so he changed them—some more than once. One concept was especially difficult to name, and he had to change the term eight times before everyone was satisfied. The word processor's automatic replace feature came in handy for this writer. He was developing an entirely new area of research, and rather than spending many hours retyping the text to make terminology changes, he could devote his time to improving his theory and his writing.

Original writing involves creating worlds in words, so writers constantly have to check the clarity of their ideas and expression. Writing text from original thoughts involves extensive conceptualizing, noting of ideas, and refinement. This translation of original ideas into text is apt to take longer than translation of ideas that others have already expressed, so tools that simplify the revising process are especially useful for creative writers.

WRITING IN THE ACADEMIC DISCIPLINES

College students are expected to write essays not only to master discourse forms but also to demonstrate their mastery of material in their courses, such as English literature and political science. Many colleges and universities have recognized that they can best help students improve their writing skills by preparing them for specific writing tasks they will encounter in graduate school or in their professions. Although professional documents include sections in the discourse modes, such as description, persuasion, and argumentation, they also conform to unique characteristic outlines. The storage and interactive capacities of the computer can help students learn and practice writing in report, article, legal, and other formats. Moreover, students can use the computer to learn efficient strategies for gathering information, taking notes, and synthesizing information that eventually goes into the various formats.

An example of an exercise that uses the computer advantage well is a program that helps journalism students learn the basic elements of a news story. A program developed at one school of journalism presents students with a list of facts about an event, and the students use these "story notes" in preparing a piece. Because the computer program knows the facts, it can prompt writers when they have made a factual error in a story—such as a wrong date, a misspelling of a name, or a relatively unimportant fact presented too early in a piece. Since the program stores the story events and facts, it can make these judgments according to specific rules in the program. Of course, no computer program can judge the relevance of a piece of information in a spontaneously written piece, but this program also alerts writers to organizational and stylistic problems.

Such a model could help writers in other disciplines as well. For example, in psychology classes, students often must critique research reports. The teacher could create a mini-database that includes four representative articles on memory research, for example, and a prompting program could guide the students in collecting the relevant information from the articles for a report. If the word-processing program and prompting program are connected, the writers could read prompts, or they could place the article in the top screen and write a notes file in the bottom screen. Finally, an outline or prompts could guide the students in organizing the information according to the format specified by the instructor. Each student would use the outlines and prompts prepared by the instructor in his or her own way. After the students' documents are composed, the writers could consult a text-analysis program for clues to stylistic problems.

Students in specialized writing courses also benefit from access to specialized databases for research in their fields. A science-writing instructor, for example, could ask the librarian to subscribe to Medline so that students can access medical information. College students also create their own extensive databases, which become increasingly important as the quantity of information they have to master increases. For example, a college student could use a sophisticated database management system like dBASE II to organize information and notes for all subjects. Besides storing information in files, these programs offer computing power for sorting and merging the notes according to topics. A student who has made a database of notes, ideas, and readings for art history, for example, would set up a database **field**—a devoted line or part of a line in a file—for the artist's name, another for the name of a specific painting, another for the date of the work, another for the name of the period, and additional fields for other specific information. When the student is studying for an exam or preparing to write a paper, he or she could ask the program to give a list of all the baroque paintings or all the paintings done in 1789. The program can be asked to sort the information or collect sections together in any order.

Several university researchers are developing specialized tools that will be appearing on the market in the next few years. The University of Minnesota Composition Program, for example, is developing computer software to help their upper-division students learn to write documents for science, history, business, and literature courses. The software will work in conjunction with a word-processing system, and writers will be able to use programs that help them go through the various steps in the writing process and create texts in proper forms. Similarly, Valarie Arms, a technical-writing instructor, has modeled a prompting program on the one developed by Burns and Culp to help engineering students at Drexel University with the document that accompanies their senior design project. The program prompts the students to write in the required categories for the project presentation, such as descriptions of the work, the background and context of the work, and the intended user or consumer. Such a program would be useful for students in fashion, architecture, and engineering, who often have to accompany their design work with text.

LEARNING TO USE COMPUTER WRITING TOOLS

For college students, it is more appropriate to talk about "learning to use computer writing tools" than about "introducing computer writing tools," as we did in discussing younger writers, because college students can guide their own learning more than children can—even their learning about computers. Nevertheless, college students still need some guidelines from the writing teacher, because the technical documentation for the applicable computer programs is usually not clear or functional enough for writers. Writers in college also have the support provided by a public user room or computer lab, which is open all night in many schools. Students who have specific writing problems may need special or individualized word-processing instruction.

SUMMARY

College and graduate school students often must do extensive writing. For them, theories of writing and computer tools can become essential to getting the job done. More important, mature students are advancing their knowledge by writing, and many are just beginning to work creatively with ideas and language. Computers can be useful tools to assist these writers in expressing themselves often and well.

COMPUTER TOOLS FOR WRITERS IN COLLEGE AND GRADUATE SCHOOL

The following computer tools are particularly appropriate for writers in college and graduate school:

- Word-processing program
  - —Full set of editing and formatting features
  - —Allowance for documents of at least 20 pages
  - —Footnoting features
- Computer conferencing and electronic mail systems
- Essay prompting
- Outlining programs
- Database programs with fixed formats allowable in some instances
  - —Flexibility to enter multipage sections
  - —Flexibility to redesign and assign keywords after entering text
- General and specific large utility databases, such as Medline
- Spelling checkers
- Prompting for composing
- Text-analysis programs
- On-line style manual
- On-line dictionary and thesaurus

Teachers as Writers 11

Imagine arriving at school one morning and, when you check your computer mail, seeing a message from another writing teacher:

> I finally came up with a good way to teach the use of transitional sentences. It's sort of a game. I wanted to share it with someone. Thought you would like it. Do you have any suggestions? Use it in your class if you think it's good.

A copy of the student instruction sheet for the game/lesson accompanies the message. You think the lesson is good, but you want to change the subject of the sample text from *rivers* to *rebels*, because your class has been reading Hawthorne's *Scarlet Letter*. You separate the lesson plan from the rest of the message and move it into a file called Trans.raw on your diskette. Using the word-processing program, you change rivers to rebels in the sample text and change some wording in a few other places. You print the lesson out on a ditto master, run it off, and have a lesson on transitionals. With your return message, you send your revised copy of the lesson, explaining why you made the changes. You also promise to share some of your exercises.

As this example shows, writing teachers can use computers for their own work—to simplify some of the logistical chores of teaching—and for other professional and personal writing they do.

ADULTS' WRITING DEVELOPMENT

Because adults' abilities vary so greatly, their writing development is not a straightforward process. Recent cognitive developmental research has shown that adults continue to develop intellectual capacities. The formal operations that Piaget described as the most advanced stage in adolescent development occur in relation to specific activities. Adults who have not developed or flexed their mental muscles in specific activities, such as formal reasoning, perform much as children do. Deanna Kuhn and Eric Amsel, at Columbia University Teachers College, did a study in which they asked students in first grade through college and adults in various professions to solve a set of reasoning problems. The researchers presented series of pictures depicting different types of situations and evidence, such as a piece of cloth with a stain on it, a bottle of dark liquid, and a bottle of light liquid. By examining the various combinations of evidence, the subjects were to figure out which bottle contained spot remover. Adults who had not practiced resolving contradictions in reasoning did no better in solving the problems than children did. The conclusion from this study was that the development of

Teachers can use a computer to simplify lesson planning and materials preparation.

formal operations relates to practice in specific areas, such as complex reasoning. Even adults who are competent in one area may have to go through initiation procedures in new skills. The relevance of this research to writing is that it shows that adults can continue the exciting cognitive development we observe in younger students, whether this be in writing, in learning to use computers, or in developing other intellectual capacities. Even the most experienced writers continue to develop their skills and ideas, and writing teachers should also be able to enjoy such growth. Teachers who write on their own or share writing with their students find that their writing and their teaching continue to improve. Learning with one's students can be embarassing, but in the long run, students respect and learn from teachers who set examples for learning processes.

Those who have not written much throughout their school years can master basic skills when they learn to write again as adults. Although their writing initially may display some of the same superficial problems found in children's writing, the problems reflect different levels of cognitive development. Adults' writing may include advanced forms side-by-side with simpler ones. Even poorly written texts by adults tend to include generalizations— points they want to make—although the support for such generalizations may be thin or disorganized. In contrast, children's texts characteristically include details that are not related by generalizations.

Adults who have continued to write since leaving school continue to develop their style, composing strategies, rhetorical techniques, and content. Adults also continue to use analytic tools for relating ideas and facts. They become increasingly able to view situations, ideas, and information in a variety of ways and from a variety of perspectives.

FUNCTIONAL WRITING

Adults usually write for a reason, so they are concerned with the accuracy, persuasiveness, and presentation of their texts. When teachers write for their students, one of their major concerns is clarity. Directions on assignments and tests can affect the students' performance, so they must be clear. Teachers write lesson plans, reports, letters, and proposals as part of their jobs, and, like writers in other professions, they may write business letters, stories, critiques, or textbooks. Such documents serve a variety of explicit and implicit purposes. For example, in business letters, writers give information or instructions. Also, underlying the specific content of documents is subtle information writers convey to make contact with their readers. For example, letters to remind people that they owe money often include subtle warnings in the first notice and more explicit ones in later reminders. Another tactic in some letters with negative content is to use passive sentences that depersonalize the message, such as "It has been decided that your talents would best be utilized elsewhere." Such passive constructions are also prevalent in the writing of school administrators and teachers, especially in teacher evaluations. In contrast, letters that announce a meeting of two parties, such as a first meeting between an employer and a new employee, include phrases that establish rapport: "We look forward to receiving your completed application for our records." These subtle interpersonal messages are often sent via sentence patterns, word choice, and other linguistic devices that may not be immediately apparent.

The constraints of real situations help writers shape the contents and style of their pieces, even if they are not always aware of doing so. For example, many writers in business know that they have to make their points early in a letter, because their readers do not have the time to wade through unnecessarily lengthy documents. Effective business documents present important points early and provide background information for reference. When teachers write instructions for their students, they have to make their points early and briefly, because even though their student/readers have loads of time, they may have limited attention spans.

Since adults often write under the pressure of deadlines, they need different kinds of support from their writing tools than children do. Adults need tools that help them with formal writing, that help them use their time efficiently, and that provide communication channels for functional reasons.

ADULT WRITERS' CONCERNS AND RELEVANT COMPUTER TOOLS

A teacher who also contributes to textbook series writes in her home office 15 minutes away from the school at which she teaches. Going from home to school, she carries a small plastic box instead of a briefcase. In this diskette carrier, she keeps copies of all the specifications, notes, drafts, references, and letters she is working on at the time; she also has copies of all these files at home. She uses one of the available machines at school, and she has her own computer at home. She can read and edit comfortably on the screen, so she does not have to carry paper drafts. Also, she is replacing her filing cabinets with metal shelves that hold diskette boxes. When a piece is finished, she saves only the last version on a diskette, reuses disk space for current work, and gives one paper copy to a secretary, who sends out paper versions to interested readers. This teacher/author sometimes sends her texts to editors over the phone wires if they have their own printers.

Adult writers who want to improve their writing processes or products can benefit from using computer word-processing tools that allow them to write more efficiently and to write more. Many professional writers report that they

Teachers find that computers can enhance their own writing processes.

can write more books in a year if they use a computer, because they do not have to recopy when they revise, and they are no longer held up by the lag time when typists are working on their drafts. Many adults do extensive revising, so they need tools that are suited to experimentation and change.

To produce documents efficiently, adults need frequent access to reliable writing instruments. Those who have limited access to a word-processing system and printer find that they can complete only parts of their writing tasks on the computer, which reduces the efficiency and value of the tools. Even limited access to computer writing tools can give adults new perspectives on writing, but since they often have deadlines, they find such limited access frustrating. Adults who have only limited access to computers and printers tend to plan and compose their texts in pen or on a typewriter at home and then type the near-final versions on the computer. They then benefit from the computer program in the process of refining the text—selecting more appropriate words, sharpening phrasing, and correcting mistakes in punctuation and spelling.

Adults have to adapt their usual composing styles to the new writing instruments, so switching between typewriter procedures and word-processing procedures may be disruptive for a time. When I first started to use the computer, I decided to use it for only one type of writing. Since I had access to the computer at work, I wrote only my work-related reports on it. As I became comfortable with the new tool, I expanded my use, but I still carefully planned the steps I would do on the computer and the steps I would do in pen. Like many adult writers learning to use the computer, I composed in pen and used the computer after deciding on major revisions. Over time, however, I have become more comfortable using the computer in all phases of creating a document.

Limited access to computer writing tools may keep adults away from computer writing until they have made a plan. A teacher who commutes one hour to his school decided to use the computer for commenting on students' papers. He did not have a computer at home, so he could not use the computer to prepare lessons or comment on student papers unless he arrived at school early or stayed late. He had preparation periods, but they were barely long enough for him to maintain the students' disks, which he had to do. Because of traffic problems, adding half an hour on each end of his time at school meant adding three hours on the road. This teacher managed to get an extra prep period so that he could write in the same medium as his students, at least some of the time. Since he could comment on as many papers in one hour on the computer as he could in an evening at home in pen, he decided to use the computer for writing letters to students about their papers.

Some teachers have found that the most appropriate word-processing program and computer for their students is not necessarily the most appropriate for them; they need different software or a different machine. The purchase of adult-appropriate software can be justified in school budgets, because the teacher who uses the computer tools is better able to help the students who use them. Whenever possible, the word-processing program the teacher uses should create files that are compatible with the students' program, so that the teacher can use adult tools but still comment on the students' texts in computer files. Adults need word-processing programs that allow them at least twenty pages of work space and that have both uppercase and lowercase letters; eighty columns, two windows, copy capacities, and formatting. The two-window feature is extremely valuable for commenting on students' papers, and for copying excerpts from students' papers into lesson plans or reports. Letter-quality printers are also important because the teachers often send documents outside the classroom and school context. One problem with using a different program than the students use is having to remember two sets of commands. Once the teacher understands and has used specific programs for a while, however, switching command language codes takes only a few minutes.

Volume and Flexibility

Adults who write at all tend to write frequently. Some writers' incomes depend on the amount they write, and other adults have to write daily on the job. Adults are often overwhelmed by the amount of reading and writing they have to do. As the volume of their writing increases, they have to spend time keeping track of deadlines, specifications, notes, and drafts for each writing job. Sometimes, writers work in several places—at home, in the office, on the bus. They may have their files in the various places or they may keep transportable file copies. Keeping track of all this takes time.

Writers who work in several places should have integrated and compatible writing systems. Since some manufacturers think compatibility is not in their interest, the writers often have to set up an integrated writing system themselves. For example, some of my work is done on a minicomputer, some on a mainframe. I write on one machine at home and another one at school. My students, colleagues, and experimental subjects use a variety of computers and word-processing programs. To maintain the flexibility to write in a variety of settings with a variety of collaborators, I have acquired a variety of conversion programs, communications software, modems, and cables. Such communication tools, which are necessary even for working on one's own files on different machines, are described in Chapter 12. The point here is that writers have to think about how and where they will be working before they decide on the computer tools they will use. File compatibility among microcomputers is becoming more standard, so a text file created in Apple Writer on the Apple computer can be loaded into a word-processing program on the Franklin computer. This is not true between Apple and IBM or between IBM and Commodore, however, unless a conversion program is used. Various word-processing programs may also insert invisible control characters in the text that a program on another machine might not understand or that might have a different meaning in the other program.

Ease of Use

Computer programs for adults should be easy to use, yet they should offer the wide range of features that adult writers need. Problems with the writing instrument hinder adults more than children, largely because adults use more features and expect better performance. Cumbersome menu-driven programs or hidden traps—such as buffers that one can get into easily by mistake—frustrate many adult users. Using a menu-driven word-processing program can be helpful when a teacher is first learning to use the program, because the command procedure and list are always on the screen. The extra keystrokes required with such a system become burdensome, however, once a writer has learned the commands, which can take a few months if the program is complex. The idea of learning with one program that guides the user and switching to another that is less cumbersome once the user doesn't need guiding anymore may not seem viable to some adults. People who have had difficulty getting used to one program are reluctant to switch. Once a writer has learned and understood the basic structure of one word-processing program, however, learning another one is much easier. The value of learning a second one that does not make the writer work through menus is greater working speed, because the command sequences are shorter. Some adults prefer to learn word processing on a program designed for children and then switch to a program that offers them a wider range of capacities.

Other problems with the writing instrument may hinder adults' initial comfort with computer writing. For example, some adults do not want to type. Word processor salespeople report that male business executives still resist using the computer because the activity looks too much like what their secretaries do. Moreover, some people simply do not like to type. They find that sitting up and looking at a console gives them back pains. These writers welcome the movable keyboard, like the one on the IBM PC, because they can place it on their laps and lean back in a chair as they think and type. Some adult writers have difficulty reading the computer screen, and they feel that the screen limits their sense of the text. Also, some writers prefer the calm and tenor of inner speech, and writing with a machine that can work so quickly and publicly makes them feel they have lost the control they had always associated with writing. Some people may be more comfortable when the writing process or parts of it are slow, so that they can focus and reflect on their ideas. Of course, one could decide to work slowly at the computer, but as noted before, the power of the computer tempts one to work quickly. Also, many people prefer to do certain types of thinking, planning, and revising in more comfortable positions, such as lying on a couch. Such writers tend to read and revise their texts on printouts before they sit at the computer to make changes electronically.

Writers must take care not to focus too much on physical features when the computer is involved. A teacher ran into the teachers' room, panting "John, that memo you wrote . . . That memo!! You of all people should be more careful." John, an English teacher, was terribly concerned that he had misrepresented an important fact or made an obviously illogical inference from the facts. John's colleague complained about the embarrassment of handing out such a document to the rest of the staff until, finally, John persuaded him to explain what the problem was: a heading appeared at the bottom of a page and the paragraph under the heading appeared at the top of the next page. A human typist would not commit such a formatting error. To the formatting program, however, the heading was simply the last line that could fit on the page. This was a relatively unimportant formatting problem to John, but it was an embarrassment to his colleague, who was extremely concerned with text appearance. For him, the computer was a nuisance because it created new kinds of problems. As the computer relieves writers of some physical concerns of writing—the text is always neatly typed, updated with revisions, and reformatted—they should concern themselves with the conceptual and functional aspects of writing.

Teachers can adapt computer tools for their own needs. For example, the computer's storage and recopy capacities help teachers in several important tasks. Teachers can store, update, and print lesson plans and tests from diskettes. Also, they can make diskette copies of student papers, which are useful for examples, models, and exercises. When they are looking for texts that illustrate specific good or problematic features of writing, teachers can peruse an archive diskette and copy a relevant text onto the diskette with the new lesson description or instructions. An archive diskette can also be used as described in Chapter 7—to provide examples for student evaluations.

Recording

Teachers spend a lot of time recording information. Writing teachers spend many hours reading and commenting on their students' texts. Using a process approach spreads out the reading of students' papers among student readers as well as the teacher, but the teacher still does a lot of reading because, with this approach, the students write longer texts and more drafts; the teacher is still the major reader. In such settings, however, the teacher comments as much on content and development as on mechanics. Teachers' reading of students' papers also helps them identify lessons that address the students' needs, as evidenced in their writing, and gives the students an active and reactive audience.

Teachers can create databases of records, like rollbooks, in which they can keep attendance records, test scores, and brief comments. Computer databases can be more dynamic and complete. Teachers use a database program not only for recording such brief data as attendance, grades, and student interests, which are easily structured into a database program, but also for maintaining a text file for each student, with copies of comments, text excerpts, and notes. The structured database and text file database of comments are expandable and revisable, which makes them most useful. Teachers who use the word-processing program for writing comments to students make electronic copies of each set of comments, copy them into the student file, and then refer to them when they are considering the students' progress. Such files serve much the same function as student folders, in which students keep all their papers with their teachers' comments. The computer files are records of comments, which can be rearranged and woven into evaluations and reports or examined as the teacher plans class lessons or individualized assignments.

Record Files

Teachers also use the computer to study writing processes—their students' and their own. Unlike humans, who remember what is useful, computers remember everything. The computer can keep track of all the writers' words—the ones they erase as well as the ones they keep. Programs that set up **record files**, logs, or more graphic names like "dribble files" can keep track of all the command keys and letter keys a writer presses during a session with the word-processing program. Some programs can also keep track of the time between commands—the writer's pause time—thus recording some of what occurs in the writer's mind. The following transcript of a writing session shows how the writer, a committee chairperson, refined her word choice while composing:

> I 3 want 7 think 7 hope that all participants will 7 8 come to the next meeting as it will be very important 777777777 9 TI1.

The words appear linearly, as they were written. The numbers indicate commands that were pressed. The writer pressed the shift key (3) and I and then typed want, erased it (7), typed think, changed her mind (7), and settled on hope. Later, she made other changes.

Timing records, which insert the time every 5 seconds, provide information about writers' pauses and insights about their planning processes as well as trouble spots. Such records show, for example, that the writer paused a few seconds before want, think, and hope, but not noticeably between other words in the sentence. Research with such programs has shown that writers pause more before words that require extra decision making—topic sentences as well as word-choice refinements. We can thus see which steps in writing are most complex or give a particular writer the most trouble. A teacher who is interested in such information—and wants to take the time necessary to review it—could discover, for example, that a student who does not pause before paragraphs might benefit from extra work on paragraph structure. The student's text, which lacks clear paragraph statements, is important related evidence, of course. Record files are available on some mainframes and minicomputers. It is not clear, however, whether they will be readily available on microcomputers.

EXPLORATIONS

Home-based Networks

Teachers set up communication channels to share their writing with students and colleagues near and far. Teachers within a school who have networked systems keep announcements, lesson plans, tests, and coordinated assignments up to date. Electronic bulletin boards are used to post personal information—invitations, items for sale—as well as meeting announcements, book and software previews, text and software reviews, and special events. Mail and computer conferencing programs help teachers coordinate and share assignments within and across departments.

In schools that cannot afford a time-sharing system or the attachments necessary for networking micros, the teachers communicate via diskettes that they use and store in a microcomputer in the teachers' room. They consult and update the bulletin board and messages to other faculty members during lunch or prep times. Such a system should offer some privacy, so that even if all files are stored on a single diskette, messages can be read only by an individual or group who knows the password. The teachers decide whether to keep all files open or to set up a directory system in which each person has an individual password for accessing messages and texts.

Outreach Networks

Teachers also might want to have ongoing discussions with colleagues beyond their immediate environment. Teachers would have to subscribe to a communications network and acquire the proper add-ons to the micro in the teachers' room. If the computer in the classroom or lab is networked for students, the teachers can use it at times that are set aside for them. They can contact teachers in different areas of the city, state, or country to exchange ideas about curriculum, computer use, or any topic of mutual interest. Teachers can set up such a network by talking to people with whom they want to communicate and helping them get the necessary equipment, software, and expertise. For example, specific interest groups that are already in place can start a network if someone takes the initiative to guide the setup. Teachers who are interested in networking can also contact local computer user groups and find people in those groups who have the same interests.

PRESENTATION

Adults, especially writing teachers, are often judged by their writing. Unfortunately, the physical appearance of the text is as important as the content and style. Grammar and spelling mistakes are conspicuous in adults' writing, so they are particularly concerned with mechanics, especially spelling, but other functional factors are also important. Style guides like *The Elements of Style* by Strunk and White and *The Art of Readable Writing* by Rudolph Flesch give adults guidelines for improving their writing. They suggest ease of reading as the main criterion of good writing. Readable writing is direct and concise. Therefore, writers should get to the main point in each sentence and paragraph quickly, with as few words as possible. When in doubt about a sentence, a writer can read it aloud and ask, "Was it so long that I stumbled? Did I repeat any words? Does it feel awkward to read?"

Since adult writers are often pressured by deadlines, they must check their texts quickly for content and coherence. In doing this, they tend to read for meaning, which prevents them from focusing on individual sentences and words—even if they try to edit to make sure that all details are correct. Identifying passive sentences, unclear pronouns, and overabundant prepositions in long texts is not easy, however. Such checking requires more attention to detail than people normally give when they are working on conceptual problems. Writers could use the word-processing program to check for passive sentences by searching for instances of the word *by*. Of course, as in the preceding sentence, *by* does not always indicate a passive, but focusing on such words and evaluating sentences one by one can draw a writer's attention to small details of text form.

Stylistic problems in paragraphs and texts can be identified with some mechanical uses of the word-processing program. A writer can make a summary file by moving the first sentence of each paragraph into another file. When the writer reads the summary file, he or she gets a condensed version of the topics and organization of the text. If the condensed text does not seem to cover all the major topics the writer intended to include in the text, he or she should review the organization of the paragraphs and the full text. Text-analysis programs, like the Writer's Workbench and CATCH, offer abstracting options that, upon the writer's request, automatically put first sentences together.

AUTOMATIC STYLE CHECKING

Style and text-analysis programs were originally designed for adults in business settings. Business writers were the original audience, because most early computers were in business environments, and most computer companies have decided that the business market is more profitable than the educational market. Adults who were designing software for other adults included features in the programs that they wanted for themselves and, of course, that were adaptable to computer capacities. Applications of these tools, however, can be geared to educators and students.

Concerns about adults using grammatical calculators like the Writer's Workbench are different from concerns about children's use of such programs. Adults who have not used spelling or style checkers often feel that writers become dependent on them, because the skills they have taken years to develop atrophy. These people might have found that their memory of the multiplication tables was rusty the day the calculator battery went dead. Writers who have used the Writer's Workbench programs realize that they serve mainly to draw writers' attention to possible problems. Like the spelling checker, the style checker can't identify sentence fragments with the same precision with which numeric calculators can multiply.

Style and grammar checkers can be useful for adult writers who have to check their texts quickly. Adults can use these tools with less caution than children require because adults have probably developed the written style and judgment to know when the programs are appropriate and when they are not. To use such programs well, writers have to know what is wrong with using too many prepositions, for example, and how to improve their sentences.

One problem with programs that identify individual words as problems is that they suggest, either implicitly or explicitly, that word or phrase substitutions will suffice for improving the sentence. This is rarely the case with problematic sentences. For example, the following draft sentences need rewriting, not just word substitutions, although a style checker would pick them out because they include too many prepositions or the specific demon *by*:

Draft Sentences

The increase in development of educational software is of questionable value today.

Much of it is still written by programmers with neat ideas rather than by design teams, including teachers and programmers and both their neat ideas and expertise.

The following rewrites are better, but the second sentence needs further revision:

Revised Sentences

Educational software today is not worthwhile.

Its value is limited because programmers rather than teams of teachers and programmers develop it.

Just as writers have composing and text styles that are unmistakably their own, they also tend to have unique problem styles. For example, when I am writing ideas for the first time, I do not focus on form. I build up to the idea in a paragraph. My first-draft paragraphs often include (1) a first sentence that leads from the last paragraph, (2) a few sentences with examples or quotations, (3) the topic sentence of the paragraph, and (4) another perspective on the topic. When I am revising, I have to refocus such paragraphs by moving the topic sentence up or down, working the supporting sentences away from or closer to it, and developing a new paragraph about the perspective added at the end. Such patterns recur because of the interaction between information-processing factors and writers' habits. Those same limits make the patterns difficult to detect, however, so writers benefit from specific methods for identifying them.

In research on adults' use of the Writer's Workbench, Pat Gingrich and her colleagues at Bell Labs found that adults used a relatively limited set of the program options. The adult businesspeople who took a course in which they used the Workbench programs noted that they were most concerned with the organization of their texts. Nevertheless, when they used the Workbench, these writers chose the STYLE and DICTION options, which check for mechanics and word choice, rather than the ABST option, which is intended to help writers identify organizational problems. This feature automatically collects first sentences or last sentences of paragraphs for the writer to examine. The relationship between such abstracting based on form rather than meaning may be too indirect for many people. Also, many writers may not use first or last sentences as organizational markers in the text; or single sentences from each paragraph might not be enough to provide even a brief summary of a text. Such features have helped some writers, like me, get an overall idea of the development line in a long text. However, for the feature to be useful the writer has to (1) practice using it, (2) write very long texts, or (3) have the types of text organization or problems that such a strategy can highlight.

Writers have reported that the STYLE and DICTION features were helpful in guiding local editing. One experienced writing teacher found the vague-word identifier helpful because it made her notice and correct her overuse of the word *aspect*. Another writer found that he had used *moreover* too many times. A third writer found that her sentences needed restructuring, because many of them had too many prepositions.

PROMPTING PROGRAMS

Prompting programs can help teachers give students dynamic instructions for writing tasks. For example, on tests or other writing tasks for which the topic is supplied, the teacher can describe the activity in a way that makes it easier for the students to do well. This is the wording I used in a project description for my students (who are teachers themselves):

1. Get together with three other students who have similar teaching backgrounds.
2. Write a list of typical problems in teaching your subject.
3. Arrange the items on your list in decreasing order of difficulty.
4. Describe the materials and methods commonly used to overcome these difficulties.
5. What were the successes and failures associated with each method?
6. Explain how the computer can or cannot help alleviate these problems.

Each step of such an assignment can be presented in a subsequent item on the QUILL Planner, for example, or on a line in a prepared file on a diskette.

COMPUTER USE AND COMFORTABLE HABITS

Research findings have suggested that the most significant factor in experienced adult writers' use of the computer is their composing styles. After their initial adjustment to this new and somewhat strange tool, adults differ in how well they use the computer and how well they like it.

In a study of eight experienced writers' use of a word-processing program over a period of about two months, Bridwell and her colleagues at the University of Minnesota found that writers who typically plan before composing found the word-processing program more useful than writers who discover their ideas as they write and then have to revise extensively. Writers who compose freely and then revise extensively tend to develop new writing methods that use unique capacities offered by the computer. For example, when he felt himself digressing from his topic, one writer used the move to end of file command, typed in XXX, and entered the digression. He planned to find that section later and move it into an appropriate place in the text. Other writers, however, tend to adapt the machine to their writing habits. Rather than finding new composing methods that use machine capacities, such writers use the machine only as it relates to their tried-and-true writing habits. For example, a writer who does extensive planning might create notes files, write in outlines, and use the move commands when reorganizing the notes. Other writers who do extensive planning might make their notes on paper so that they can include diagrams, trees, and other graphic idea organizers.

Since composing style is related to adults' use of computer writing tools, adult writers can benefit from defining their writing habits. An awareness of composing styles could help you decide how to best use limited computer time and how to develop strategies for adapting the computer tools to your personal writing styles or adapting your styles to the tools when necessary. Being aware of your composing habits could also help you understand why using the computer might be difficult at times. For example, if you have used the computer for freewriting but find it difficult to use when you are revising the unruly text that results from freewriting, it will help you to know that other writers who compose this way have the same trouble. The discussions of composing and revising in Chapters 5 and 6 offer suggestions on how to harness the computer capacities to help you with the difficult task of doing a major revision or a rewrite of a draft. Describing your student's composing styles or asking them to do so could be useful for the same reasons. Describing one's own composing style can help one take more control of the process.

The following exercise should help you describe your composing style. For each item, choose the response that best describes your writing habits:

What types of documents do you write most?
  1. Letters
  2. Reports
  3. Assignments
  4. Proposals
  5. Essays
  6. Stories
  7. Journals
  8. Other _____

How do you plan?
  1. Mentally
  2. By making notes in various forms
  3. By making outlines

How do you compose?
1. Directly from thoughts
2. By transforming outlines
3. By a combination of transforming notes, outlines, and thoughts into text

How much revising do you typically do?
1. Limited
2. Two to four drafts
3. More than four drafts

What type of revising do you do?
1. Considerable rewriting
2. Mostly deleting to prune wordy or repetitive drafts
3. Throwing drafts away
4. Evolving new drafts in stages of revision
5. Mostly adding to expand undeveloped drafts
6. Reorganizing
7. Combinations of the above
8. Little revising; mostly editing

What gives you your best insights for revising?
1. Readers' comments
2. A few days' rest from the piece
3. Revising techniques such as reading the sentences from the end to the beginning
4. Retyping the text
5. Reading the text aloud
6. Outlining the text

Where do you write best? What are your most productive writing hours?

What seems to affect your writing process most?
1. The document type: you compose your assignments in one way and your letters in another.
2. The setting: you can compose well at home at night, but have trouble at school during the day.
3. The subject: you compose in one way about familiar subjects, in another way about unfamiliar subjects.
4. The deadline: you compose in one way when you have time, in another way when you are rushed.

After you have gone through this list, think about how the computer might help you most with your writing. For example, recently I have found that the computer helps me most when I am composing, because I can plan as I write quickly by moving around in the text, adding sections in appropriate orders but as they come to mind. How do you think the computer can best suit your writing style?

LEARNING TO USE
THE COMPUTER

The effects of computer writing tools on the quality of adults' writing will be difficult to determine for a while. In the meantime, it is clear that effective training methods should be developed to help adults become comfortable with the tools if they decide to use them. The introduction of computer tools to adult writers should relate to their composing styles.

One way to help adults become computer users is to teach them about specific uses of the machine in relation to activities they have already mastered. Researchers Carroll, Thomas, and Mack at IBM's T.J.Watson Research Center are studying adults' problem-solving skills. They have found that adults work with complex word-processing systems more efficiently when they are given a metaphor that relates the computer's operations to something they know well. For example, an analogy can be drawn between computer systems and governments. The operating system corresponds to the federal government, and the word-processing program, the spelling checker, and other individual programs are the states.

When training children, an instructor can sit down at the computer with them and tell them the keys to press. A step-by-step, hands-on approach works well from the very start. Adults, however, are more comfortable with a hands-on approach after they have had some introduction to the principles and procedures of word processing. Giving them an overview of the program structure and commands helps. For example, when presenting a new program, the instructor should go through the steps for getting into the program, entering text, doing basic editing, saving the text, and printing it. By using examples, the trainer can identify the typical command structures, such as the use of the CTRL and ESC keys and the relationship between inserting and editing modes. A diagram analogy for the program spaces is useful in this description. For example, in a mode-switching program with menus, writing occurs in one space—the kitchen—editing in another—the den—and command menus are the door between, with a key for moving from one space to the other. Programs that allow the writer to insert or edit at any time, like Apple Writer, are more analogous to writing on paper. It is also important to convince adult writers early that the get back command really does work. It may be necessary to explain buffers as temporary storage spots where erased text is kept in case the writer wants to get it back. When providing introductory overviews, it is important to stress to adults that they need not worry about remembering all the commands and details mentioned as examples in the overview. The overview is intended only to help them get a general idea of the word-processing activity.

After a general introduction and overview, a successful first use of the word-processing program—for adults as well as for children—is to correct a paragraph by following a list of instructions and referring to a list of commands. When adults tackle the task of learning the word-processing system themselves, they tend to create a test document, consulting a command list card that comes with the program documentation or that the instructor has prepared. Such an exercise provides practice with a small but useful set of commands for frequent editing operations. Adults later request more esoteric commands for important revising activities, which they try as they gain confidence. These self-taught users relate commands to something they already know—writing. Novice computer users who try to read the word-processing program manual as a way of becoming acquainted with the program are usually confused and frustrated because the manuals do not relate to the writing process and tend to assume an understanding of programs. These manuals typically present commands without reference to the writing process. However, adults who have used other types of computer programs can work their way through a manual and glean the important information for using a word-processing program, partly because they do know some of the assumed information the manual assumes they know about computers, but, more important, because they have learned what to ignore in the documentation. A computer expert who is not sensitive to teacher-training issues is not the right person to ask for help. Computer experts, like the manuals they write, often are not aware of the best techniques for presenting the necessary information to writers who have not used computers.

Adults with unlimited access to a machine have reported that it takes from about six hours to a few weeks to become comfortable with word-processing instruments—if they are accomplished typists. Adults who must share a machine find that it can take several months to become comfortable with it. Also, people who use mainframe computers often feel less comfortable at first because the wide range of activities available on the system suggests how much they do not know. Devoted word processors or word-processing programs on microcomputers have a small set of programs, so writers can sense the boundaries of their task and do not feel lost in a galaxy of programs. For this reason, it is easier to learn word processing on a small system, even if a writer will eventually be using a mainframe or a minicomputer.

Some companies offer training to those who purchase their word processors. People who buy word-processing programs for micros, however, usually hire an instructor, ask a friend, or slug through it themselves. The following list suggests an order of events for an adult training program. It includes key steps in mastering computer writing tools and a general time frame. A teacher who is comfortable with computers and understands the potentials and problems they present writers could provide such training.

1. *Introduction: How to use computers for writing*
   a. Overview of a word-processing program
   b. Practice in editing a prepared text (see Chapter 12 for a list of the features to cover)
   c. Basic treatment of the hardware

This stage takes about three hours and should include demonstrations, hands-on practice in groups, and guidelines for solo practice of about one hour, with a brief follow-up session with the instructor for questions.

2. *Practice*

The teachers should use the system for their own writing for about six hours to see the value and the problems that arise. Individual help should be available at specific times for answering questions and helping the learners get out of trouble before too much time elapses and frustration makes them give up.

3. *Applications*

A group discussion of philosophy and methods of teaching writing, the writing curriculum, and specific needs should precede the discussion of the computer applications. Teachers should then discuss the relationship between the word-processing program and the type of writing they and their students do. This outline could guide the discussion:
   a. What are our theories of writing?
   b. What do we have to cover in the curriculum?
   c. What are some of the methods we are using now?
   d. How should the computer be used in the classroom? What is its value as a writing tool? What is its value for specific points in writing instruction?
   e. How can the word-processing program be related to the curriculum?
   f. What do we expect the computer to change? These should be conservative.
   g. How will we manage computer use in the classroom? (Chapters 12 and 13 offer suggestions.)
   h. What pitfalls do we have to avoid?

Such a training module could also serve as a model for mastery and integration of other computer writing tools, such as spelling checkers, prompting programs, and database makers.

SUMMARY

Writing teachers who write can guide their students especially well because they share experiences, strategies, and the joys of expression. Writing teachers who share and communicate through the same writing instruments can help themselves and their students make the tools work for them to simplify and enhance the writing process.

COMPUTER TOOLS FOR
ADULT WRITERS

The following computer tools are particularly appropriate for teachers who write:

- Word-processing programs
  —Full set of basic and advanced features
- Letter-quality printers
- Access to all the tools the students use
- Communications tools
- Text-analysis programs and spelling checkers
- Electronic bulletin boards
- Database programs
- Mail merge programs
- Prompting programs
- Authoring languages
- Record files

The computer equipment must serve writer's needs.

Setting Up Computer Writing Environments IV

Last week in my neighborhood stationery store, I saw a man carefully selecting supplies. His rituals gave him away. He bought four yellow, letter-sized, lined pads, a box of blue number two pencils, six snap-on erasers, rubber cement, and an electric pencil sharpener. His bill was $36.40. This man was obviously a writer, whose tools are intimately related to his craft. He reminded me of the way I feel when I buy new notebooks—a habit I have not broken despite my use of computers.

A few days later, a friend called me to announce that she had purchased a computer to use for her personal and professional writing projects. After months of researching home computing equipment, she had bought a microcomputer, a word-processing program, software for connecting to her publisher's computer, a modem for the connection, a printer, a spelling checker, and a game to play on her breaks. Her bill was $3,500. Like the man in the stationery store, she was anxious to begin. She had spent two months selecting the equipment, and now she needed help setting up her writing system. "Picking out the pieces was hard enough," she protested. "I hope this thing isn't as complicated to use."

Preparing for your first computer writing experience, on your own equipment or someone else's, is certainly more complicated and expensive than preparing to write with pencils or typewriters. Later, the process involves flipping a switch, pressing command sequences, and maintaining the equipment and the storage disks. You buy floppy disks rather than pencils and use commands rather than rubber cement. Few writers have totally abandoned pencil and paper for their computer keyboard and screen. Likewise, teachers integrate computer use into their existing curriculum. When they are deciding which computer tools to buy and how to integrate them with traditional tools, teachers should let their goals, the curriculum, and the students' needs guide their decisions. Since computers are usually public writing instruments, the setting in which they are used should be designed so that students can share the resources in a way that most enhances their writing development. The two chapters in this final part of the book offer specific guidelines for selecting computer writing tools and setting up a computer writing environment.

Selecting Computer Writing Tools

12

This book has presented many types of programs and applications for writing on computers: word-processing systems, prompting programs, electronic mail, computer conferencing, databases, automatic text analyses, and spelling checkers. The first question teachers ask is "Which of all these tools should I buy?" Before making purchases, it is important to assess your needs and resources as well as the available software. After reading this book, you probably already have a wish list of the computer tools you would like to use in your classroom or your home study. These applications considerations merge with hardware issues as you begin to make decisions about purchasing computer tools.

The major factors in deciding on computer tools, as discussed in Chapters 7 through 11, are the writers' ages, levels of development, and composing styles. Another consideration in selecting tools is the number of writers who will be sharing them, because the amount of time each writer needs to accomplish certain activities is a major factor in the writing process. Since computing equipment and software are expensive, cost is often the factor that shifts the others around in importance. Tradeoffs are usually made, therefore, between the planned computer writing activities, the number of students, the available access time, and the nature of the computer writing environment.

ASSESSING NEEDS AND RESOURCES

Many teachers begin using computers for instruction in writing and other subjects simply because the computer is there and someone has to do something with it. Also, parents often urge teachers and administrators to bring their children into the "computer age." Of course, some teachers begin to use computers because of the pure desire to try something new. Some educators feel that the computer is a dramatically new tool with yet-unknown potential and that it is important to buy one without preconceived notions of what it should be used for—but few have the luxury of leaving the use of such expensive tools to chance. More important, such attitudes have led to frustration when the computers arrive and no one knows what to do with them. The message of this book is that the most sound motivation for using computers in a writing class is that they offer writers capacities that other instruments do not.

One exercise that teachers find helpful when deciding on how best to use computer writing tools is to identify difficulties in learning to write. With this exercise, teachers can identify such problems as "Students find reorganizing texts to be very difficult"; "Students' academic writing is lifeless"; "It takes my students so long to get out an idea"; "Students have trouble finding exciting reasons to write"; "Written mechanics and development are terrible"; and "I have to spend more time correcting spelling than guiding students in logical development." All of these problems can be addressed by interactions between student writers, their readers, and their teachers, but many of them can also be alleviated by carefully orchestrated lessons, activities, and tools—as noted in earlier chapters of this book. After you note the problems your students typically have in learning to write, you might decide that you can address your students' needs for writing instruction with the computer and you might not—but starting with these considerations can simplify subsequent decisions.

After identifying your students' needs, it would be helpful to note the approaches and materials that you have used to overcome these difficulties. Since difficulties, by definition, are persistent problems, teachers usually have developed a repertoire of lessons designed to address them. For example, teachers often go over papers with the student authors to help them gather ideas for revisions. However, many teachers have found that although the students often seem to be enlightened during the conferences, they do not revise their texts when they work independently. This suggests that students may need more peer feedback and more practice in identifying problems from their own perspective. Students' difficulty with revising may also be attributable to the physical difficulties involved in recopying. In such cases, a teacher might decide that the word processor is a more appropriate tool for revising than a pencil. The computer can also help students work better in areas with which they had no particular difficulty. Young writers who are already doing well may begin to write more frequently, because the computer capacities provide "publishing" tools for printing out texts and sharing them with others. Being able to do something *better* is a good enough rationale for trying something new.

Referring to the earlier chapters in this book, make a list of the computer tools you would like to use, and note some of the purposes you think these tools should serve. As you begin juggling costs and use time, this list will no doubt change, but start with what you think would be ideal. Also note the number of students who would use the tool and the approximate amount of time in a week or term that each student would need to use the tool. When you think about the developmental issues and applications in this way, decisions about hardware and software are much easier than if you start with the question "Which computer should I buy?" Decide on the machine after you have identified specific needs, software, and applications.

You might also want to make a list of the tools and instructional aids you have been using successfully. It is important to remember that crayons, pencils, pens, typewriters, paper, and lessons on paragraph organization are useful for your students. Likewise, worksheets, examples, and books are still important tools on the writer's desk.

To be realistic, it is also necessary to assess your resources. Answering the following questions will help you identify the resources that are available to you:

- Do you already have access to a computer? Which one?
- What is the available software?
- What is the software budget?
- What is your access to the computer? (1) unlimited; (2) somewhat limited; (3) strictly limited
- What is your budget for additional or new hardware and software?
- How much technical knowledge do you have about computer workings? (1) none (2) little; (3) some; (4) extensive
- What is your access to technical assistance? (1) little; (2) some; (3) extensive

If you already have access to computers, you should find out which ones they are. The next step is to identify and evaluate specific programs of the types you want to use and then make sure they would run on your machines. If you still have to buy the computers, identify the pieces of software you want to use and then select a machine on which most of the software runs—if, of course, it is within your budget. Whether or not you still have to buy a machine, you should evaluate the software you plan to use. For example, if you will have two micros and twenty-five students, it might be best to use software that offers examples, such as prompting programs, and software that provides opportunities for collaborative activities, such as electronic mail. Using the computer to give interactive lessons and examples makes it possible for a large number of students to benefit from the computer.

As you find more specific suggestions in this chapter, return to your lists of needs and resources. Your decisions about which computer writing tools to use will undoubtedly change as you learn more about specific systems. Also, because the computer field is developing so rapidly, your plans will change even after you have begun using computers in your classroom.

The following sections provide guidelines for evaluating the major types of computer writing tools mentioned in this book: word-processing systems, spelling checkers, text-analysis programs, prompting programs, typing programs, and database systems.

WORD-PROCESSING SYSTEMS

After using a word-processing program for about a month, 10-year-old Carl told me that the ideal word-processing program would be "a computerized pencil; you push little buttons on the pencil to make all the changes. Then you just set the pencil on the paper and all your words come out." Carl likes the feeling of control he has with a pencil. When he writes with a pencil, the link between his movements and his words is clear. He can see how the pencil works. Carl's dream of a computer pencil reflects a sensitivity to the good and bad features of existing word-processing systems. They have useful automatic capacities for storing and transforming text, but writers who use them cannot control everything that happens to their words all the time.

Design Considerations

Although Carl likes the automatic changing capacity of the computer, he also wants direct control over the instrument. Crossing out by pencil involves putting a line through the rejected words, but writers work less directly on the computer; they give instructions to the program, which in turn gives instructions to the computer. Interaction with the keyboard is direct enough, but the operations that put the text on the screen and make the changes are invisible. The writer can open up the computer to see the flat black processing chips, but they do not move. The movement of electrons is likewise invisible. In many word-processing programs, the commands are codes that require translation of human writing processes to machine operation names. For instance, when moving a paragraph, the word processor user "deletes" the paragraph, moves the cursor to the paragraph's new home, and then "undeletes" it. This process confuses and misleads many writers who are using computers for the first time, because they are confronted with names for operations defined in terms of computer workings rather than in terms of writing processes. For example, beginning word processor users are often confused because they are unaware that this deletion process involves placing the paragraph into a temporary memory buffer and then pulling it out of the buffer into a new text position. All word-processing systems take some time to get used to because their design is constrained by the limits of the specific computer on which they run. Like other computer tools, word-processing programs vary according to three general factors:

1. Power
2. Ease of use
3. Flexibility

No one thinks of these factors when selecting a pencil, because pencils are easy to use and flexible—I used one recently to dig a toothpaste tube cap out of a sink drain. Computer word processors are not as simply flexible, but they have additional power for storing texts and carrying out editing operations. With this power, however, comes intricacy of use, so writers and teachers selecting computer tools have to consider design features seriously.

All word-processing programs offer writers basic editing features that change and reformat text on command, but three factors relating to processing power are important to consider when selecting a system:

1. The amount of text the program can handle at one time.
2. Program speed.
3. The variety and number of extra features, such as multiple windows and formatting commands.

Some word-processing programs only allow writers to work on texts of under ten pages, while others can handle hundreds of pages. Similarly, some programs separate the composing and revising stages and offer a limited set of editing and formatting options because the programs are very basic.

Program design is constrained by the computer. Although computer experts disagree on the details of these issues, the general rule is that the best word-processing programs are designed on machines with relatively more working memory, storage space, and processing speed. In general, good text programs require large and sophisticated processing power, so the more powerful the computer, the better the program—and the higher the cost of both hardware and software. Like automobiles, the most powerful computers cost the most. The most powerful word-processing systems, which offer writers multiple windows, many useful commands, and the possibility to work on long documents, are likely to be on large computers, which are also relatively expensive. Similarly, the programs that run on large computers are usually the most flexible and often the easiest to use because the computer memory allows the programmer to design the program to do much of the procedural work for the writer. The basic computer capacities that differ are working memory and processing speed.

The Computer

Computers differ in the amount of memory they have for carrying out their tasks. Memory is the amount of space available for the word-processing program and the text the writer is working on. The basic unit of computer memory is counted in thousands of bytes of memory (K). The myriad microcomputers on the market vary in the amount of processing space they offer: a 48K microcomputer holds 48,000 bytes, a 64K machine holds 64,000, and so on. The computer memory capacity determines the size of the programs and texts the writer can work on at one time. Good word-processing programs are typically large, and many writers like to work on texts longer than ten pages, so writers need at least a 48K machine, although word processing on 48K machines is still quite rudimentary. Every few years, the amount of memory on the standard microcomputer increases. In four years, the standard microcomputer grew from 16K—processing 16,000 pieces of information—to 64K—processing 64,000. Most machines can be upgraded to include more memory. Extra memory chips or memory extensions, such as a 16K language card, can be added to some microcomputers. For example, an extra 16K card, can be added to the Apple II+. The extra 16K extends the amount of space for writing and running programs. Large computers like mainframes and minicomputers have extensive processing space. The memory on the large computers is described in larger units—megabytes—or 1,000,000 byte units.

Linguistic programs like word processors, text-analysis programs, and database programs, require powerful computers. The more unpredictable the writer's text, the more complex the program has to be. The more linguistic niceties the program offers, such as sentence-delete commands, the larger still the program becomes. Also, writers who want to work quickly require computers with large memories and fast processing. Word-processing programs that run on small machines are limited because there just isn't sufficient space for a complex program to accept letters from the keyboard or carry out editing and other commands fast enough for the writer to work efficiently. All instructions to the computer are expressed in numbers, so computer operations that involve numbers, such as budgeting programs and drills with number-coded answer options, are easy to program on small computers because the application activities match the computer activities. Linguistic interactions, which are not by nature numerical, have to be translated into numbers to run on computers. Although numerical operations, like adding and subtracting, are built in to the computer circuitry, linguistic operations, like identifying words and sentences, have to be translated to numbers. Adding and subtracting are more directly translated into streams of electricity than identifications of words; it takes many more lines of computer code to tell the computer to delete a word than to add two numbers. As programming expertise develops, more complex programs are written into less memory; and as new micros offer increased memory at old prices, computing power increases. The quality of a word-processing program, of course, relates to the writer's age and ability. Six-year-olds need basic word-processing tools that are easy to use more than they need space for large documents, and even young writers need flexibility for sending computer mail which is easiest to do on large time-sharing computers. The main point of this discussion of memory is that writers have to be aware that processing limits determine both the sophistication of the word-processing program and the length of the text the writer can work on. The computer user should check the program documentation to determine the text length limits for the program. A writer who isn't aware of a ten-page limit could lose all ten pages of a text while trying to write the eleventh because the program could crash if it is overtaxed.

Some programs are designed to use available memory efficiently, thus offering the writer the option to work on long texts. In computers that have 128K memories, like the IBM PC, the writer can configure, or customize, the program by running a special program that changes the way the word-processing program handles the available memory. A program can add "virtual memory" with some software tricks. A procedure called swapping sets up a file on the external diskette storage and moves pieces of text from the working memory in the computer to this temporary space, thereby increasing the length of text the writer can work on. This swapping process is a lot like the game of "hot potato." The program throws a section of text out to the disk so that it can grab another. The program keeps track of the chunk of text it moved out, remembers where to go look for it on disk, and remembers that it had brought in one chunk and sent another out to disk. With such swapping, a writer who normally would be able to work on a text of only twenty-five pages can work on sixty pages at once. The program's swapping operations do not interfere with the writer's work other than causing occasional slight delays, and the disk drive makes sounds when sections of text are being sent out to the disk.

Most programs provide ways for writers to join short sections of text before printing, so they can eventually get a complete copy of a long text they had to work on in chunks. In some cases, to move sections across files, the writer has to copy one file, delete from the copy everything that will not be moved, append—or attach—the two files, then move the appended section from the end to the appropriate place in the text. Some programs also offer commands like the @Include command in Perfect Writer. When this command is placed at the end of one file along with the name of another file on the disk, the formatting and printing programs will handle the second file as part of the first, so the pages in all the sections are numbred consecutively and footnotes are kept in order across the sections from different files. The more memory that is available on the micro, the less likely it is that a writer would have to take such circuitous routes. Powerful computers offer the capacity to move sections of text around quickly without having to move these sections between separate files, as one does when working on long pieces on smaller systems. The recent interest in low-cost microcomputers, however, has attracted the imaginations of talented software developers, who have created good writing tools that get the maximum use out of the relatively limited memory in microcomputers.

Programs and text are stored permanently on magnetic disks outside the central processing unit in the computer. Large computers store shared programs and individual users' files on magnetic disks, which are usually

```
┌─────────────────────────────┐
│      Additional Buffer      │
│             for             │
│     Text in Block Move      │
├─────────────────────────────┤
│        Main Buffer          │
│            for              │
│           Text              │
├─────────────────────────────┤
│      Word-processing        │
│         Program             │
│                             │
└─────────────────────────────┘
```

64k Memory

The program the writer is using and the text the writer is creating are held in the computer memory.

housed in a central location, with the computer. The typical microcomputer storage medium is the diskette, which the user can carry. A diskette formatted for the Apple stores about 140K of information, and a double-sided disk for the IBM PC stores about 320K. The disk drive heads transfer the information stored on disk into the computer memory, which can take only as much as the memory capacity. Diskette storage capacity is limited only by the number of diskettes the user has bought. A hard disk, which can extend microcomputer memory, includes from 2 to 15 megabytes—or two to fifteen million bytes of storage.

Processing speed is another factor that distinguishes the various types of computers. Many micros are 8-bit machines, which means that the basic unit of instruction the computer can handle at one time is composed of eight bits—basic units of recognizable change in electrical flow. In these machines, 8 bits make up a byte. Some microcomputers have 16- or 32-bit instruction units. In the 16-bit machine, the instructions are made up of 16 bits. These machines are capable of processing several actions at once because the basic instruction unit is longer. The longer the basic instruction unit, the faster the machine can work. To imagine the difference in speed between 8- and 16-bit processors, think about keeping track of three important activities in your home: watching a child, loading the dishwasher, and checking the oven. An 8-bit processor would have one instruction for each task and would have to do them one at a time; a 16-bit processor could do all three at once. Processing speed is important, because the faster the computer carries out instructions, the faster the writer gets action and responses.

Flexibility is another issue to consider in selecting a machine. I have suggested in this book that teachers mix and match a variety of computer tools for writing instruction. It is important to note, however, that not all programs run on all computers. An obvious question is "Why can't I run programs written for the Apple on the Radio Shack or some other micro?" In some cases, software can run on several machines, but, in general, programs are machine-specific. One reason for this is that each machine has a slightly different version of even the most popular programming languages, like BASIC. But, in the spirit of advancement, this compatibility issue has recently been addressed by TRUEBASIC, which runs the same on all machines.

Hardware and software attachments can also make one micro act like another one. The operating system, rather than the computer, is often the key to what will run on the computer. The operating system acts as a host for the programs and can make minor adjustments for certain machine differences. For example, some programs run on any computer that has the CP/M operating system. UNIX is another popular operating system because some writing software, such as the Writer's Workbench programs, has been written for them. A teacher who wants to use a variety of writing programs has to consider the machine for which each program was written. For example, a program written for the Apple with the CP/M operating system can run on an Atari with CP/M but not on a machine without CP/M.

Since computer tools are developing so quickly, another major consideration when buying a system is the possibility of upgrading it—at least the potential for adding memory and more user access, which usually involves adding networking capacities.

Differences in price usually reflect differences in memory capacity and processing speed. Microcomputers can range thousands of dollars in price. The display screens, printer, disk drives, and storage disks are often separate items at additional cost. Larger computers, such as minicomputers, cost much more, so an institution that is considering buying a mini should have a large initial computing budget. Consulting with a school that has a good setup is an effective way of getting information.

Junior high and high schools should carefully consider the value of writing systems that have communications capacities. Time-sharing systems are appropriate when many people, usually doing a variety of activities, share the computer. Written communications, such as electronic mail, bulletin boards, and collaborative writing are most naturally done on time-sharing systems. These activities are important for young writers, so it is not possible to say that the cost of the computer reflects the writer's age. Although young writers can get by with simple word-processing programs on individual microcomputers, the more expensive capacities of electronic mail and computer conferencing may also be important to give young writers the necessary motivation to write.

Colleges and universities often buy time-sharing systems because they have larger initial computing budgets. Mainframes and minicomputers typically support several programming languages, **statistical packages**, and work-processing programs—all coordinated under one operating system.

Also, although time-sharing systems typically have electronic mail systems and other shared communications services like linking, they do not run much of the educational software designed for microcomputers.

The most typical decision in schools is to purchase microcomputers, which are like tool chests, because they run many types of useful programs. Professional writers and other professionals also buy microcomputers if they want to experiment with programming, graphics, **spreadsheets**, and database management systems, as well as electronic writing. Many schools feel more comfortable starting smaller—dividing the budget among faculty members so that each teacher can make an individual decision—or using their entire budget to buy as many machines as possible. Since communication is so important in writing, it makes sense to put some money aside for the hardware and software necessary for networking. The trend away from big systems to micros, which was prevalent for several years, now seems to be reversing. Schools that have spent lots of money on microcomputers have realized the limits of the machines and the available software, so if they have the resources, they go to time-sharing systems or network their micros.

Teachers and writers who want to use the communication power of time-sharing systems for electronic mail and collaborative writing can network microcomputers. For example, they can turn a microcomputer into a terminal for a mainframe or minicomputer. To do this, they need a **communications card**, providing a connection to the modem, a boxlike device that translates signals to travel through phone lines. Connecting by phone is necessary when the host computer is far from the micro. To turn a microcomputer into a networked terminal, they also need software that pretends the micro is a terminal rather than a stand-alone computer. With the correct communication add-ons and cables, a microcomputer can be connected directly to another computer. When the micro functions as a terminal connected to a mainframe or minicomputer, it uses the increased processing power, storage space, and programs available on the large system. With such a setup, users can work on a university computer from their homes or from any other place where they have a micro and a phone line.

A series of **cards** is inserted into the computer; these cards hold chips and circuitry that serve a variety of functions. The cards have programmed circuits that provide memory, timing and control of the computer operations, or links between the computer, the printer, the modem, and other **peripherals**. When putting together a writing system, the user has to make sure that all the necessary cards are in place.

In addition to the modem, communications software, and firmware, networking from a microcomputer to an information utility or database requires a subscription to the service. These services such as CompuServe, charge initial subscription rates and connect-time rates. Users have passwords that let them onto the computer and provide minimal storage on the system. A budget for networking should include telephone charges. Some of the services offer users local phone numbers that connect them to discount long-distance phone services. If this is not available, they can subscribe directly to the discount phone services.

Micros can also be networked with a hard disk, which is a shared storage capacity. The micro users share software and communications stored on the hard disk. The various participants on the system also have special access privileges, which they prove by using a password, and space on the disk to store their personal files and messages. In this configuration, programs can be transferred to and from diskettes, since one of the networked machines is attached to a disk drive. To do this mixing and matching, a teacher has to make sure that all the pieces are compatible for fitting into one system and connecting to others outside of the local network. The teacher who does not have technical expertise should feel free to consult technicians, computer magazines, and technical books.

When deciding on an information utility like The Source or CompuServe, the user has to consider cost, the type of people in the user community, and use-time schedules as well as the available features. For example, The Source has many users in business because it is the oldest utility; it is more expensive than CompuServe, but access times for CompuServe are only during the evening. Both provide the kinds of services one would want on a communications network: mail, chat, word processing (though not great), news check, and databases on a variety of topics. For classroom use during the day, The Source is adequate, although it would be better if there were a utility for educational use. Administators, teachers, and students can also share subscriptions. There are ways to make such an investment worthwhile, such as linking teachers and administrators throughout a school district.

Many individual writers who have a budget of at least $7,000 buy devoted word processors if their main use of a computer is writing. Although devoted word-processing machines are computers, their use is specialized and is mostly limited to one function. Some word processors serve a variety of purposes and can be upgraded with a communications package and other add-ons. Because they are designed specifically for writing, word processors are easy to use. They have labeled command keys, and the writer does not have to go through extraneous operations, as is necessary when using more flexible systems. One high school writing teacher has devoted her entire computing budget to purchasing one machine. The teacher decided that the ease of use and the professional presentation qualities of a devoted word processor and printer were worth a $7,000 investment. This teacher's class is a small, informal lab, so even though there is only one machine and one printer, the teacher feels that her students have adequate access. The school has many other types of microcomputers, and many of the students have their own computers at home. In contrast, most junior high or high school teachers with that budget would elect to buy as many machines as possible with the money—unfortunately sometimes not leaving enough for software, and almost never leaving enough for communications.

The Printer

Regardless of which computer system you buy, you need a printer to make hard copies of texts. Printers range in quality, speed, and price. One problem with the most inexpensive printers is that the copy is not sharp and clear. **Dot matrix printers** are relatively inexpensive, but the copy they produce is fuzzy-looking—not letter-quality. Dot matrix printed copy is fine as a record, for editing, and for many readers, but most writers would not hand in such copy to publishers. One trick that has been tried to make dot matrix print look clearer is photocopying it, which often blurs the distinction between the small dots. **Letter-quality printers** are more expensive, but they do not leave telltale signs of the computer. Such **impact printers** look like typewriters and use similar ribbons, but the letters are pressed from a **daisywheel**, a circular set of letters that turns to select characters on command from the computer. When considering printers, it is important to check out their speed. Slow machines may print as few as thirty characters per second—about one page in 80 seconds. Faster **bidirectional printers** produce about one and a half double-spaced pages per minute.

Evaluating Word-Processing Systems

Try a few word-processing programs to compare them for ease of use. Ask friends what their favorite word-processing program is and why they like it. Watch them use the program, try it, and then compare it to others. If you have access to a devoted word processor, you do not have to select software, because the hardware and software are one. Mainframes and minicomputers are usually ordered with one or two word-processing programs, so again there isn't much choice of software. If you are going to use a microcomputer, however, you have to choose among an ever-increasing number of word-processing programs.

You should select a word-processing program that you find easy to use. The chapters on writers at different ages (Chapters 7–11) includes lists of word-processing features that are important at each age. Those suggestions could serve as guidelines in your software selection. The resources section at

```
Dot matrix printers and letter quality printers are quite different.  The
dot matrix output is rather rough, because the letters are formed by a
series of dots.  However, a letter quality printer resembles a typewriter,
and its output is very refined.  Compare these two examples.
```

```
Dot matrix printers and letter quality printers are quite different.   The
dot matrix output is rather rough, because the letters are formed by a
series of dots.  However, a letter quality printer resembles a typewriter,
and its output is very refined.  Compare these two examples.
```

Printers vary in price and quality, but even dot matrix print can be clear.

the end of this book includes software that has been used in schools, universities, and research projects. Some of the programs are noted because they are popular, others because they are the best available or because they are representative. Trying a program out more than one time is a good idea. Teaching and observing a student using the program is also a good way to make sure you have chosen an acceptable piece of software. As you try a word-processing program for the first time, use the following questions to guide you:

- How do I create a file?
- How do I move the cursor up, down, forward, backward?
- Can I move the cursor by words, sentences, and paragraphs, or only by lines and characters?
- How do I insert and delete characters, words, lines, sentences, and sections?
- How do I move a section?
- How do I save a file?

When you are trying out a word-processing program, write something that will be easy to compose—such as a letter to a friend. Save the file and make a printout. Read the letter over, and edit it to try out the important commands; for example, (1) delete a word, a few lines, a sentence, and a section; (2) move a section from one spot to another; and (3) try formatting, spacing, centering, paragraphing, and paging. This exercise should give you an idea of how easy the program is to use.

The following list of types of commands can organize your learning so that you know what you are looking for; it can also serve as a checklist of the features a program should have. As you test a word-processing program, put the commands on this chart. Such a chart is also useful when you are switching among several different word-processing programs.

Word-Processing Commands

Filing Commands (Some of these may be in operating system)
- Create a file
- Name a file
- Rename a file
- Print a text
- Edit a text
- Save a file
- Exit a file
- Delete a file
- Copy a file
- See a list of files (also called catalogue or directory)

Pointing in Text
- Does the writer have to refer to line numbers to point in text? (If yes, choose another program; this one's outdated.)
- Can the cursor be moved via commands?

Cursor Move Commands
- Up
  —Line
- Down
  —Line
- Forward
  —Character
  —Word
  —Line
  —Sentence
  —Paragraph
  —Page
  —End of file
- Back
  —Character
  —Word
  —Line
  —Sentence
  —Paragraph
  —Page
  —Beginning of file

Basic Editing Commands
- Insert
  —Character
  —Word
  —Line
  —Sentence
  —Paragraph
  —Page

Automatic insert is the easiest to use; that is, whenever you type, the program enters letters in the text. Commands are recognized when pressed with the control key.
- Delete/erase
  —Character
  —Word
  —Line
  —Sentence
  —Paragraph
  —Page

- Undelete last section (How many of the last deletes can you get back?)
  —Character
  —Word
  —Line
  —Sentence
  —Paragraph
  —Page
- Move
  —Character
  —Word
  —Line
  —Sentence
  —Paragraph
  —Page
- Overwrite
- Search
- Replace
- Copy

Formatting Commands
- Are formatting commands embedded? (What is the code that signals a command—., @, other?)
- Are formatting commands given from a menu?
- What are the commands for
  —Center a line
  —New paragraph
  —Indent
  —New page
  —Number of characters per line
  —Headings

You could do a tutorial on the computer or read the program documentation. If you are not familiar with software documentation, merely browse through the manual at first, because the art of manual-writing has yet to be perfected. One helpful feature in many manuals, however, is a command list or command reference card, which lists only the program functions and commands. Also, do not feel that you have to know everything about the program. It's likely that only the programmers do—and a program may present surprises even to them.

After trying a few word-processing programs, look at the command chart you prepared and compare the programs for important design features: ease of use, user-friendliness, and integration with the writing process.

Managing Files

A word-processing program should give the writer a clear sense of creating, editing, saving, naming, and printing files. When these activities and their names relate to the writing process, they are relatively easy to remember. Some programs are menu-driven, presenting writers with choices at various points in the writing process. Menus are often helpful guides to beginners, but some menus are puzzling, and they become a nuisance to more experienced word processor users.

The following is a sample of a word-processing menu:

```
Type one letter:

e—edit a file
g—get a file
w—write a file
q—quit
```

When confronted with these options, the writer has to know that "edit a file" means to "move to the buffer to input text." If a text was left in the buffer during the last use of the program diskette, that text reappears the next time the program is loaded into the computer memory. If no text was left, the buffer appears empty, and the writer has to know that new text can be inserted there and then saved in a file space he or she will name when saving or "writing" it onto disk. "Get a file" means "edit a file that has already been saved," and "write a file" does not mean to compose or create a text, as one might think. Rather, "write a file" means to store a file or save it on the diskette so that it can be printed or edited later. Faced with such ambiguity, some writers simply press q, for "quit." Even young writers learn these codes eventually, but the first writing sessions can be frustrating because of these seemingly contradictory names and conceptions of the writing process. Another problem with a menu-driven system, even if it is easy to use, is that even though experienced word processor users often do not need the menus, the program does not allow them to bypass the menus. It is wise to select a program with menus that are both easy to understand and easy to bypass.

Another typical problem is that some programs don't ask the writer to name a file until after the text has been typed. Writers who use such programs ofte lose texts, especially when they are first using the program, because the fact that they have written the text gives them a false sense that the computer will store a copy. Even though the writer has typed and edited text, however, the program does not have a permanent copy stored until the file is named and saved. Writers have to remember to give a save or write command to store a copy; the program then prompts for the name. Some systems include an automatic save option, which stores a copy of a text on disk after the writer has been working on it for a specified amount of time.

Since word-processing design is still a relatively new art, many systems are not as easy to use as they should be. Four factors determine the ease of use of a word-processing program:

1. Pointing to text (cursor move processes)
2. Editing commands
3. Menus and modes
4. Formatting
5. Managing memory

Learning to relate to the cursor as the pencil point requires conscious translation for most adults and some children, but since the cursor obviously moves in response to pressing keys on the keyboard, adults and children eventually have no problem thinking of the cursor as a pencil point and eraser. Many command systems involve pressing the CTRL key at the same time as the letter key. When the CTRL key sequence is pressed, the program interprets a letter as a command, rather than as text. Several types of terminals offer devoted keys—word-processing keys or programmed function keys. Some word-processing systems provide peripherals for pointing. Since cursor moving is so important, system designers have experimented with several such devices—such as the mouse, the joystick, and the light pen, described in Chapter 7. Besides pointing to specific places on the screen, these devices often have one or two command buttons for general operations, such as deleting. **Touch-sensitive screens** and panels give the writer the most direct, tactile contact with words.

Although alternative methods of identifying and selecting words on the screen are appealing, the most common command instrument is the keyboard. It may be that keyboard commands are most appropriate for writers who are using the keyboard for typing their texts. A light pen is an obvious parallel to the pencil, but moving one's hands from the keyboard, picking up the light pen to mark a word, then moving the hands back to the keyboard to type in a new section could be very cumbersome. Using editing commands directly on the keyboard seems easiest to integrate smoothly with typing. However, research has suggested that the mouse is also an efficient device.

The way the space bar functions in word processing confuses many writers. Although spaces on the screen are apparently empty, they are represented by characters recorded in the computer; each time a writer presses the space bar, another space is entered, and other words on the line move over. Most people expect the space bar to move the cursor to the next position but not to displace any words that may be there. Another problem many writers have is getting used to the fact that on some machines, a delete command erases the character to the left of the cursor, and on others, a command, typically CTRL-D, erases the character above the line cursor or under the inverse video cursor.

Programs also differ in their user-friendliness—the way they address the user. Few have clear instructions and messages, such as illegal command or out of memory, to help the writer stay out of trouble or get out of trouble.

Commands

Most word-processing programs offer the basic editing and cursor move commands, but programs vary in the advanced commands they offer and the command units. Some programs have commands for word, sentence, and paragraph units as well as character and line units. Many programs offer search, replace, and block moves. More and more are offering multiple windows. These advanced features are appearing on more new programs because writers like them.

A particularly valuable feature in a word-processing program is the capacity to save prior versions of texts, in case revisions do not turn out to be as good as the writers had expected when they were wielding editing commands or in case a power failure cuts off the temporary memory where the text in progress resided. Programs on large systems often store the last version of a text even after the revision is saved, but few microcomputer programs offer this feature.

Command names should be easy to learn and to remember. Each command should involve minimal physical and mental steps, because each extra step imposes additional burdens on the writer. Commands can take the writer's time and attention from important activities. Learning commands for using the computer and specific programs is somewhat like learning a new language. Cognates, or words in the foreign language that sound like words in the native language, are the easiest to learn and remember. Likewise, the word-processing commands that are easiest to learn and remember are those whose names or letter codes relate clearly and unambiguously to the operations they represent. For example, many programs use CTRL-D for character delete, but they use everything from CTRL-B to CTRL-Z for moving the cursor up one line. CTRL-P may mean "move to previous line," which could be considered mnemonic, but it seems that many people think of moving the cursor "up" rather than "to the previous line." As might be expected, single-keystroke labeled commands are the easiest to learn and to use.

Writers can work more quickly and more meaningfully when commands refer to linguistic units like words, sentences, and paragraphs. In systems that offer only commands by character and line, writers have to spend time erasing part of a sentence on one line, then moving to another line to delete the other part of the sentence. Since writers work in word and sentence units, the commands should make these units easy to address.

One common feature in many word-processing programs is mode switching. A writer who is deleting a section and writing new text in its place would have to give mode-switching commands before and after each deletion and insertion. When they are working quickly, many writers find the extra steps involved annoying. At any pace, writers often forget to switch modes before editing, and the editing commands they press then become part of the text. Although mode switching is not necessary, many software developers have chosen to design their programs in this way because such programs are easier to write, require less code, fit into small machines, and they work well with on-screen menu commands.

Formatting

For mature writers, formatting options can be a major factor in deciding which word-processing systems to use. When I talk to writers, I often hear comments like, "To tell you the truth, I chose my word-processing program because it makes setting up formatting options easier than the other programs I have tried." For example, the Apple Writer program, which is popular because of its formatting design, presents a list of default formatting features so that the writer can decide on the formatting for each document just before printing it. Features such as margin size and spacing are clearly presented on a table and are easy to change by editing the numbers. The writer can also enter formatting commands, such as .p, for more local control. Such embedded commands are easy to use, but some require too much typing. The embedded "dot" commands like those in Apple Writer, Runoff (for Digital Equipment products), and other programs are the briefest. These commands are also mnemonic, so they are easy to remember. In addition to the command names, the writer has to learn whether the commands are global or local. Global formatting commands—such as .lm +5, meaning "move the left margin in 5 spaces from the overall margin setting"—apply to all text following the command, until the writer enters a command that undoes it or overrides it—such as .lm –5, meaning "move the left margin back out 5 spaces." Local commands, such as .c for "center," apply to the next line. Remembering which are global and which are local commands is not difficult, because the distinctions are logical. For example, the underline command—@U in Perfect Writer—tells the formatting program to begin underlining, so the writer also has to tell the program where to end the underlining—by entering the close parenthesis after the section to be underlined.

Some writers prefer formatting programs that use full English words for each command, such as @Index, @Footnote, @Center, and @Blankspace, because there's no code to remember. The initial symbol @ tells the program that the next word is a command, rather than a word to be entered in the text. As with menus, full-word commands are helpful when first learning to use a program; later, however, they are not necessary, because people who use the program remember the commands.

Some screen editors have formatting of the "what you see is what you get" variety. Since most microcomputers do not have devoted keys, the programs that run on them do not offer such options. Programmed function keys, which appear on some micros, can be assigned to formatting commands; word processors have on-screen formatting options for paragraph beginnings, new pages, indents, and tabs labeled on keys the writer presses to give the commands. Many word-processing programs use a double carriage return, which looks like an empty line on the screen, as the signal for a new paragraph. Such single-key formatting commands, however, require a sophisticated program and machine. When the formatting is complicated, it is better to see the actual commands than merely to imagine them.

Another formatting issue is whether the program offers the writer the option to view the version of the text that the formatting program has produced before printing it. Seeing the results of the formatting program can save the writer time and paper. By viewing the formatted text on-screen before printing, the writer can catch such problems as headings appearing on the last line of the page. Programs that do not have labels for chapter and section headings cannot distinguish headings from lines of text, so they might put a heading at the end of a page. A program that has formatting labels for headings can follow a rule, such as "Never put a heading on the last line on a page." Writers who do not have such programs can insert a new-page command, such as .pg or @Newpage. Then, when the formatting program runs again, it will start a new page before the heading, as the writer has directed. Checking for such layout problems takes much less time when the writer can view the formatted text on-screen, rather than waiting to check a printout. The program Homeword shows a small sketch of the formatted page in the lower right-hand corner of the screen so that the writer can see the results of commands while entering them.

Another common problem involves the filling command, which places all words on continuous lines of text unless told otherwise. When preparing a list, the writer must enter commands like @Begin(Format) before the list and @End(Format) after it, telling the program to leave the text as a list, rather than filling it as if it were a paragraph. Most formatting programs have such an option, which is also called a "literal" command.

Before using a formatting program, it is a good idea to note the default features. Defaults for margin width, justification, and automatic filling can confuse the unaware writer and add time for going back into the text file to enter commands that override the defaults.

Writers should always work on the original or "raw" version of their text—the one they produced with the formatting commands—not on the formatted version, which the program produced. The formatted version is intended for the printer, not the writer. The formatting program creates a copy of the text with a new suffix. For example, I named the file for this chapter twelve.raw. After I ran the file through the formatting program, the program created a text called **twelve.fin**, which I then ran through the program that sends the formatted text to the printer. When I wanted to make changes, I went back to my **twelve.raw** copy to change the text or the formatting commands. The .fin copy includes invisible control characters that make it nearly impossible to work on. If writers edit the formatted text of the .fin copy, they would confuse the formatting program, which looks for the embedded commands that do not appear in the output version. If I had tried to call **twelve.fin** into the word-processing program, Perfect Writer would have told me that I couldn't edit it, because that file is intended only for the printer.

In summary, the features to look for when considering formatting options are as follows:

1. Integration with the word-processing program.
2. Ease of changing and customizing default options.
3. Brief, yet mnemonic embedded commands.
4. Visibility of commands (invisible control characters can cause trouble).
5. Options for viewing a text before it is printed to check for layout (e.g., to check that pages do not end with section headings).

SPELLING CHECKERS

Spelling checkers compare each work in a text to a list of words in the program. Typically, such lists include about 50,000 words from a dictionary, so proper names and slang are not usually included, but some spelling checker programs offer writers the option to add proper names, slang, or technical terms. Some spelling programs also keep track of common misspellings related to each word and offer guesses on correct spellings of words it catches. As noted in Chapter 6, however, one should not expect that the program can catch all misspellings, because it cannot judge meaning.

Most spelling programs run on text files and present the possibly misspelled words in lists or lines at the bottom of the screen. Spelling programs should present the words they identify in the context of the sentences and paragraphs in which they occur. The context often determines whether or not a word is a mistake, so writers should be able to see at least the sentence in which a possible misspelling occurs. Seeing the word in context, even if the context is only a line, is necessary for making decisions about whether or not to change a spelling. Another value of seeing identified words in context is that it gives the writer an opportunity to read the section and note problems other than spelling. For example, when writers view words that are identified as possible misspellings, they may be encouraged to read the text closely and recognize that the word in question is not even needed. This is a good way to cut unnecessary wording as well as to check spelling.

TEXT-ANALYSIS AND PROMPTING PROGRAMS

As described in Chapters 4 and 6, text-analysis and prompting programs can stimulate writers to compose and can alert them to possible problems in their texts. Because these programs are not sensitive to meaning, teachers and writers have to be fully aware of what the programs can and can't do. As with word processing systems, writers have to decide on the appropriate point in the writing process when such aids are most beneficial. The major guideline for selecting text-analysis and prompting programs is to look for programs that are helpful but humble. The following questions and comments reflect points made in earlier chapters. They can serve as guidelines to consider when selecting specific programs.

General Features

To make sure a program is appropriate find out the following:

- For whom was the program designed (adults, children, what age)?
- What is the best setting for the program (school, business, home)?

These factors can make a difference. For example, programs designed for business use may make automatic corrections, which is not a desirable feature for school use.

When you are trying a text-analysis program, note the following:

- On what does the program focus your attention?
- How will this help your writing or your students' writing?
- What kind of teaching or other support is required with the program?
- Are the manual and the on-screen instructions clear?
- Is the menu easy to read and to use?
- How do you get in and out of the program?
- Is the program integrated with a word-processing program?

Switching from the analysis or prompting program to the word-processing program requires that the writer hold the analyses and comments in mind. This switching could, of course, discourage rash decisions based directly on the program rather than on reflection of the program suggestions—but computer feedback should always be viewed as suggestions. Given this attitude, flexibility, such as being able to work smoothly with various other computer tools, is a priority design feature.

If the analysis program runs through a text and then presents bits of analysis on the screen or printout, writers have an additional burden: they have to figure out the relationship between the analysis and the overall text, such as noting the effects of having too many prepositions in a text.

Does the analysis program warn of possible glitches, such as lines that may be too long for the program to process? One writer using a spelling program lost her text because the lines of text stored in the computer were too long for the program to process. The lines were too long because, in a program that did not have automatic word wrap, the writer had forgotten to press the return key when a line of text appeared on the screen. Text files are stored in units called records, which—although they are like lines of text—do not correspond exactly to the lines of text on a screen. Typically, a new computer record begins after the return key is pressed. In this case, the spelling program stopped running after it processed the first line that was 256 characters—the maximum record length. This caused the program to abort, causing the rest of the file to be erased. This discussion should not be discouraging; rather, it should be taken as evidence that knowledge and practice are power.

It is important to be aware of program features and to try out new programs on test files and copies of existing files. Fortunately, careful program developers try to avoid problems like those mentioned here and, when necessary, note clearly in the documentation all the conditions required for using the program.

Self-Integrity

Does the program do what it promises? If an advertisement says that a text-analysis program "corrects" the writer's grammar, don't believe it. This is a promise no program can keep. Similarly, if an ad says that a word-processing program helps writers correct spelling and grammar, make sure the program offers additional spelling and grammar-checking features. Word processing does make changing text easier, but editing commands should not be confused with additional text-analysis features. Find out the following:

- How many features does the analysis program check?
- What are the features?
- Are they the features you care about?
- Does the program warn of its limitations?

Automatic text-analysis programs identify possible problems, but writers should not consider their checking done after they have used such programs. Moreover, many features of text-analysis and prompting programs are determined by the computer's capacities and the designer's knowledge of the writing process. For example, programs can identify specific words but not organizational and logical problems, so most programs focus on word-level problems, which are very important but are not the only features of good, clear writing. Also, programs do not identify problems with 100 percent accuracy. For example, a program might identify "so," as unnecessary, but it might not mention that it could also be a necessary conjunction.

Is the program humble? In response to a specific composing prompt, the writer has to be aware that the prompt isn't dealing with all that may be involved in the subject. The prompt helps start the writer's search for information and ideas, but prompting programs don't yet offer writers significant help in developing and refining the ideas. The program design and the documentation should make this clear. A program that ends its analysis with an open question like "What else should you consider about this subject?" would be fulfilling this requirement.

What are the claims about the program's ability to improve writing? Little research has been done on the effects of text analysis and prompting. Computer writing programs can be useful, but there is no conclusive evidence that they help all students write better. The little research that has been done suggests that prompting and analysis tools should be used as instructional aids—as discussed earlier in this book—rather than as the other tools student writers always use.

Does the program warn of possible negative effects? In QUILL, for example, the developers suggest that students use the results of the planner as notes, rather than as a first draft. This is a good suggestion, because although planning prompts can help the writer get started on the track of an idea, the path in prewriting exercises is likely to include unbalanced side paths, as shown in the examples in Chapter 4.

Does the program identify keywords, even if they are misspelled? If spelling isn't the focus of the program, it should try to identify various spellings of a word. For example, in a program that checks for vague words, the program should identify "stuf," as well as "stuff."

Does the program suggest single word and phrase substitutions, or does it suggest that rewriting may be necessary? Make sure that program suggestions are correct; sometimes, they are not. Programs that make suggestions for "corrections" often note only simple substitutions, which could distract writers from seeing that rewriting is required. Don't be disappointed by programs that present question prompts without complex analyses or notes of "right" and "wrong." Prompting the writer to reflect while composing and revising is important and potentially more useful than programs that offer too much control.

Ease of Use

Consider the following factors in determining how easy a program is to use:

- How many steps does it take to run the program?
- How many steps does it take to get from the word-processing program to the analysis or prompting program?
- Are the names of parts of the program clear and easy to remember?
- Does each program option name relate to writing?
- What are examples of program labels and commands?

- How does the program tell you that you are or might be wrong?
- Does the program have menus of the various checking options?

Relationship to the Writing Process

The following questions will help you relate a program to your writing instruction needs:

- What view of writing is the program based on?
- Is the program consistent with your view of writing?
- Does the program make clear the relevance of its features to the writing process and product?
- What standard has the designer used in selecting features to identify?
- What view of error does the program exhibit?
- Can you move easily from the analysis program to the word-processing program?
- Has the program been tested in writing classrooms?
- Do the prompts relate analyses and problem features to the context in which they appear?
- If the program focuses mostly on local features, what are ways of working it in with other writing activities you do with students on meaning, logic, and organization?
- Can you or your students adapt the program?
  —Can writers decide on the order of features?
  —Can you bypass steps?
  —Can you change word lists and prompts?

Whenever possible, read about research that has been done on the effects of such programs. This will give you ideas about how best to apply the programs. Also, make sure you have the most up-to-date version of a program. Sometimes, programs are improved, rereleased, or republished shortly after the initial publication. Later versions are likely to be improved on the basis of experiences early users had with them.

TYPING PROGRAMS

Typing programs should use computer capacities in several ways. They can show the keyboard on the screen and indicate key placements when students are learning to type particular letters. The letters can appear on the keyboard to build the typists' memory for key placement. Since the computer can store and compare the typed letters to strings of characters in the program, it can tell students when they have pressed the wrong keys. It can also guide them to the next sequence that they missed. Teachers should be aware that many of the typing programs on the market are games that drill for speed rather than teaching a method of typing.

DATABASE SYSTEMS

Choosing an appropriate database program depends greatly on how the writers will use it. The appropriate uses for writers at different ages suggested in Chapters 7 through 11 are particularly relevant in decisions about which database program to buy. Database management programs vary greatly in the flexibility with which they can search and display specific pieces of information. After thinking about some of the activities you think would be valuable to do with electronic research tools, consider the following points.

At present, most database makers and searchers are not integrated with the word-processing program, but some create files that the writer can call into the word-processing program for editing. Rather than allowing editing, most database programs let the writer "update" fields.

Another limitation of many database programs is that they allow for only a few lines of text in each entry. Programs for student writers to use in research should accept extended text—at least a few pages per entry.

How difficult is it to set up fields? Does the program prompt the writer, as in PFS: File, "What is your item?" It might not be entirely clear what an "item" is, but the teacher can help students identify the various categories of information to put in each entry in the database. Does the program alert the writer to identify field and record limits? What type of sort features does the program offer? What is the text limit in each field? Most programs have fairly limited maximum fields. When the writers will be composing extensive text, it may be better to use a program that simply files texts under keywords, rather than a full database management system.

INTEGRATED PROGRAMS

The ability to switch from a word-processing program to a prompting program to a spelling checker is very useful, so software developers have become sensitive to the value of having a variety of composing and revising tools that work in conjunction with a word-processing program. As discussed throughout this book, writers need the flexibility to shift among various parts of the writing process, and thus they need tools that support this movement. Teachers should evaluate the quality of each part of an integrated system and help their students tailor the system to their needs.

SUMMARY

After assessing their needs for writing instruction tools and determining the available resources, teachers should examine specific machines and programs carefully. This chapter has provided guidelines for evaluating computers, printers, and the major types of software discussed in this book: word-processing systems, spelling checkers, text-analysis and prompting programs, typing programs, and database systems.

Designing Computer Writing Environments *13*

I had spent 6 months planning a computer writing class with a teacher in a junior high school. This was to be one of the first classrooms in which students would have frequent access to microcomputers for writing. I went to the classroom about a week after the eight computers arrived, watched for a few minutes, and my heart sank—the students didn't seem to be excited. They were sitting in front of computers using a word-processing program—a computer tool—not a drill and practice program, but they weren't using the revising resources of the word-processing program. After my initial disappointment, however, the problem became obvious. I knew that the computers had just arrived and that the children needed time to get used to the new writing tool, but another issue seemed more important. The classroom setup didn't support the interactive writing environment we wanted. The environment had to encourage the development of interactive revising. The computer salesman had placed the computers at about six-foot distances around the periphery of the room. This left space for discussion groups to sit in the center, but we also wanted the students at the computers to be able to share texts, ideas, and advice. After we had rearranged the computers in closer proximity to one another, the atmosphere supported communication—in harmony with our tools and lesson plans. Students now wrote their individual assignments, but they also discussed their writing, especially when they were using prompting programs. They were able to ask a neighbor's advice on the effectiveness of a paragraph the program pointed out for reconsideration.

A major part of using computers for writing instruction is designing the type of writing environment that best supports the use of the equipment in relation to the teacher's writing philosophy and the curriculum. The budget, administrative policies, and the writers' ages are also important, as noted in previous chapters. This chapter describes typical computer writing environments and offers suggestions on classroom management issues that are raised when computers enter the classroom.

COMPUTERS IN THE CLASSROOM

Many teachers who use the computer as a tool adopt a modified version of the open-classroom approach. Children take turns using the computer individually or in small groups, while other children in the class work on projects at their seats or in other activity centers. When there are fewer than two machines, teachers often design computer writing activities that exploit the computer capacities for collaboration and communication. As discussed in the chapters on children's writing development, students use the computer to write reports, newspapers, and messages. Although there has been little research to demonstrate the value of collaborative writing, these activities provide more computer access in a communicative context than children get when they use a limited number of machines individually. As small computers become less expensive and more compatible, schools could purchase some to lend out to individuals or groups of students for note taking and brainstorming. Since the viewing capacities on these machines are limited, however, the students should print out their texts and then view them on a larger compatible system when they are revising.

When there are only one or two computers, teachers have to use the limited resources creatively, trying always to develop computer activities that depend on the unique capacities of the machine. The teacher who has only one computer should probably think of it not as a powerful typewriter, but as a learning aid for class demonstration, group activities, and action-oriented writing lessons. Lessons on the computer can always be related to the writing process. If a lesson on the computer exploits its most powerful capacities, the students may not have to use the machine all the time.

One use of a lone computer in a classroom is as a dynamic blackboard. I use a word-processing program and a large projection screen or several monitors linked to the same computer in my lecture classes to make points about the writing process. For example, one day, I asked my students—who were teachers—to list the most persistent problems students have in their subject areas. As they listed their problems, I typed them on the computer keyboard. When we had a list of apparently unrelated problems in different subject areas on the screen, I asked the students to group them under the general categories of process versus content problems, then under subcategories of processes—research, scientific method, calculation—and contents—facts, theories, and so on. I used the word-processing capacities to move lines noting the problems. Reorganizing points written on this dynamic blackboard helped the students reorganize familiar concepts into a new view of the curriculum.

Writing teachers in high school can use a demonstration computer to work with the students on alternative organizations of an essay. Rather than discussing a better organization of points in an argumentative essay, the teacher can use a word-processing program to make changes as the students suggest them. Then, as a group, the students can immediately view the changes on a large screen or on additional monitors.

Another way to use a single computer appropriately is to set it up as a communication center. Students can work alone or in groups in extended written dialogues on the computer, thereby practicing writing in a communicative context with a tool that simplifies physical aspects of revising. Over time, such a use can give students a practical understanding of the functions of writing and the social importance of integrating their knowledge of grammar and spelling conventions gained in lessons. Similarly, the lone computer can serve students well as a publication tool for their class newspaper. Students can rotate use of one or two computers to write their stories, book reports, and essays, but routine writing on computers is done most effectively when many computers are available, in school or at home.

The computer is also a dynamic bulletin board. Students can read announcements and notices on the electronic bulletin board, and they can add to it easily. After a while, the students can be in charge of updating the bulletin board. They can also write and update a variety of databases on academic and extracurricular subjects, leaving the files open for other students to add facts, opinions, interpretations and to use the databases as sources for assignments. Although it might not always be accurate, a student-made "knowledge" disk can be much more meaningful than a factually precise but terse encyclopedia.

A teacher who has four or five microcomputers in a classroom can realistically assign more extended individual writing exercises on the computer, because each student has more time to compose and revise. The open-classroom or writing workshop approach remains appropriate for any number of computers, except perhaps one per student, but it will be a long time before classrooms or even computer labs will have one computer per student. At that time, the work stations may be used for writing practice as much as for student-centered instruction.

When students have computers at home, they can follow up on the computer writing activities they are doing in class, but these activities should always be generalizable to writing, regardless of the instrument. Teachers who work in communities in which parents buy home computers should let the parents know the hardware and software that is available in the school, so that they can buy the same or compatible machines. Since developing their texts takes so much time, students do more and more of their writing at home as they get older. It may sometimes be appropriate for students to bring texts they have begun at home into school on diskettes to complete or to share with others.

COMPUTERS IN THE
WRITING LABORATORY

School administrators often start out by buying one or two computers that reside in a common room or lab. Teachers and students sign up to use the equipment, and there is often a lab coodinator or monitor to keep track of the sign-ups and the software. Additional machines are then added to this room, unless individual teachers or groups of teachers arrange for funding to have computers in their rooms.

At the elementary school level, computer labs serve each child for a limited amount of time. Lab sessions are also usually formal group sessions, because the students need help and supervision. Thus, the computer lab in an elementary school is probably best used for group activities and exercises to make points about prewriting, writing, and revising. If a class uses the lab every day for a few weeks, the teacher can design research report activities on the computer. The students can do brainstorming and note-taking activities on the computers for a few days, then organize their notes and compose a draft. The students can read and critique printouts of their draft reports in their classroom and return to the computer lab to revise and edit. When children develop reports in groups, the process of researching, developing plans, writing, and critiquing is faster than when one child has to do all the work and evaluation. Such group work on the computer can serve as a model for the children to think about when they are doing later reports on their own with the tools they have available. As noted earlier, when children collaborate, the computer is a useful tool because they can merge and transform their notes into texts more easily than when they have to recopy.

Older students visit computer labs on a more individual basis, often using the computer when they think it will be useful for developing papers and reports. If the writing teacher has not introduced the full range of prewriting and revising software aids, the computer center director can give the students an overview of the software tools, so that they can decide whether or not they would like to use a prompting program, an outlining aid, or a spelling checker in addition to a word-processing program.

One problem in university computer centers is that system managers often object to students using terminals or microcomputers for word processing. Their argument is that the "word-processing people" dominate the machines because their activity takes a lot of "real time." However, the computer processing power required for word processing is much less than the time thinking about what to write. This imbalance between time at the terminal and use of computer power often leads computer center directors to limit word processing in favor of statistical work or programming. They also often encourage students to write out their texts or programs before coming to the computer center so that they can use the computer time more efficiently. Writers will not benefit most by using the computer simply

Teachers keep track not only of assignments but also of the instrument the student used for each assignment.

as a fancy typewriter, however. They can use software in all stages of the writing process—for brainstorming as well as revising. Therefore, college writing teachers should try to pave the way for their students to use the computers for researching and writing, which involves convincing computer center directors that writing—like statistics—is not merely typing.

COMPUTER TIME AND MATERIALS MANAGEMENT

When planning a computer writing environment, teachers must consider scheduling and materials. At the beginning of a class session, one teacher asked, "Who hasn't used the computers recently?" and all of the students raised their hands. The class then deliberated about who had been on the computer yesterday, the day before, and so on. After a few weeks of this scenario, the teacher began using a sign-up sheet, noting the dates and activities of each student on the computer. He had eight machines in his writing class and about twenty-four students per class, so each student used a machine at least one full period a week. Although this is a relatively large amount of time considering typical student-use ratios, these students rarely

Teachers have new materials to keep track of in computer writing classes.

completed a writing task in that one period. They were used to freewriting, planning, composing, revising, and editing—often sharing their texts with classmates at least once as the texts were evolving. Since they could work on the computer versions of the texts only once a week, they reviewed and discussed printouts, working with pencils. They would think about extensions and improvements for their pieces and perhaps begin new ones in pencil as well. Then, when they returned to the computer, they had an idea of how to use the word-processing capacities to work further with the texts.

Many writing teachers ask students to keep all their writing—notes, drafts, revisions, pencil copies on paper, and computer printout copies—in a writing folder that stays in the classroom. One way to develop interest in writing is to encourage students to share their writing outside as well as inside the classroom, which means letting papers out. When texts are stored on diskettes and students can easily print out multiple copies, they can share their writing easily. Also, there is always a copy in the classroom if master copies of all the students' texts on diskettes remain in the classroom diskette boxes at all times.

Diskettes provide efficient archiving, but the teacher has to think about how to manage this new material. One way is for each student to keep a diskette with his or her own files in the writing folder. If resources are limited, students can share diskettes, but they have to keep track of which students' work is on each diskette, and they must keep at least one backup at all times because the more people who use a diskette, the more chance there is that a file might be inadvertently erased.

SUMMARY

This brief chapter was intended to whet readers' interest in some of the issues that are raised when computers enter the classroom. Computers are useful tools, but because they are big, expensive, and interactive, their entry into the classroom involves design issues with logistical and pedagogical implications. The discussions in this book might simply have raised your consciousness, rather than outlining exactly what to do about using computers. If you have decided that a computer could help, however, try it—set up a computer with a word-processing program in your classroom, and observe your students as they use it for their writing. I hope this book has alerted you to some interesting possibilities and that it continues to be useful at various stages of the growth of your interactive writing classes.

Afterword: The Future of Writing

THE DEVELOPMENT OF
WRITING TOOLS

This book has described the interrelationships between writers, writing environments, and the instruments that offer people channels for transforming their thoughts into written language. It has discussed early research and applications efforts, which will no doubt develop and reveal additional problems and potentials. Moreover, new research programs will offer insights about the questions we should ask and eventually will provide answers regarding the effects of using computers as interactive writing tools.

The computer has appeared on the scene at a time when researchers with psychological, sociological, pedagogical, and literary backgrounds are studying writing as a dynamic process. At this time, the writing process, more than the finished written product, is the major concern of researchers and teachers, and the computer is a process tool par excellence, for reasons described earlier in this book. This writing instrument is also more interesting in light of the relatively recent grounding of writing research in cognitive psychology, because writing seems to be influenced by the kinds of tools writers use. If the typewriter had just been invented, I think it also would attract attention as a tool that could affect the translation of ideas into written symbols. However, it would seem less interesting because it is not so dynamic. The effects of prior writing technologies like typewriters were probably not studied because, at the time they were invented, research focused on literary analyses of style regardless of the writing method. The effects on our writing will change as developments in hardware and software alter the speed, flexibility, and language-processing power of computers.

COMPUTER HARDWARE
DEVELOPMENT

Computing systems are becoming more powerful, more flexible, and more communicative as they offer more processing space and speed in increasingly smaller and cheaper machines. If artificial intelligence research and software development keep up with these advances, writers will be able to work on long documents with complex composing and revising aids, and they will have communications powers on small portable computers that they can use even while sitting under a tree. Writers who wanted powerful word-processing programs a few years ago had to buy expensive word processors, and writers who want sophisticated text-processing programs today have to use mainframes. In a few years, however, writers will have prompting and text-processing tools that can diagnose some of their writing problems and that they can tailor to their own needs—right on their own little micro-computers.

One advancement in hardware that has yet to be made in a significant way is system compatibility. Ideally, hardware and software should be inter-changeable, so that writers can work on the same texts at home and at the office, even if the equipment is not the same. At present, most software runs on only one machine—or, with forward-looking companies, on one family of machines. Programs and even text files have to be converted for use on different machines. The desire for compatibility is so great, however, that conversion programs are becoming easier to come by.

An increase in compatibility among systems is essential, because no single machine is likely to have all the tools or qualities that writers need. For example, a family might more readily invest in a writing system for the adults' professional needs if the system can also run good games for the children's pleasure, an easy word-processing program for their schoolwork, and communications software for everyone's exploring pleasure. Microcomputer systems enable people to share computing tools, but the companies seem to have decided that compatibility may not be good for business or for design freedom. The public has some power in influencing these compatibility issues. If people buy the hardware that offers them the widest range of use, companies will have to develop compatible systems, rather than unique ones, if they want to compete. Another problem is software piracy; software developers are protecting their rights by merging programs with hardware, in the form of cartridges, and by creating uncopyable code, or copy protecting.

COSTS AND ACCESS

Costs of computing equipment have decreased in the last 10 years. For under $5,000, a writer can now purchase a system with features that would have cost about $10,000 five years ago. Prices continue to go down as the capacities of small machines go up. Nevertheless, prices of individual machines have to go down considerably before all writers can afford them. Electronic writing will not be as inexpensive as typing for a long time, but if people can write on the same machines they use for televisions, telephones, and checkbooks, the initial outlay of money may seem worthwhile. Writers need frequent access to computers if they are going to benefit fully from them, so until computers cost no more than television sets, access to electronic writing tools may be so limited that writing in this society might not change at all.

HUMAN FACTORS

Word-processing programs will evolve with computer hardware in the next few years. Programs will be easier to use, and problems such as cursor movement will be alleviated by hardware solutions, such as devoted command keys and touch-sensitive screens. Research on human factors has already given system developers more information about how to make friendlier, more flexible systems.

Friendlier Systems

People should be able to focus on the activities they do on the computer, rather than on the computer itself. This means that systems will have to become easier to use. Programs have already developed from making sense only to programmers to being user-friendly. System designs will continue to improve so that users will not have to try to think like computers to get them to work.

Programs should include options for changing command names—an easy replacement on computers—so that writers could personalize a word-processing program by assigning command names that they find mnemonic—even the first letters of foreign words if the writers are not native English speakers. Also, people who switch among several systems often get into trouble if CTRL-C means "insert" in one system and "delete" in another. Changeable commands would allow these writers to use the same set of commands on all systems.

Other hardware developments that will make computer writing systems friendlier are on the horizon. One advancement—speech recognition—will make writing more like talking; by actually turning talking into writing. If such systems and printers are inexpensive enough, they will eliminate what is still the greatest hurdle to using computers for many people—the keyboard. Speech recognition or voice typewriters record speech, enter it into a computer, and print it out in English. These systems have been difficult to perfect because translating from sound to symbols involves complex linguistic recognition of words, phrases, meanings, and sentences, which are much more difficult to pin down than individual sound-to-letter correspondences. Simply recognizing where words begin and end is a difficult task.

To imagine how hard this is, think about the last time you heard an unfamiliar foreign language. Did you hear individual words? Recognizing individual words in the steady stream of speech requires knowledge of the sound, grammar, and meaning systems of the language. The most sophisticated computer program knows enough grammar, semantic, and phonological rules to approach 90 percent accuracy in identifying words in a limited database, but such programs will still make such mistakes as "Their homes on the hill" for "There're homes on the hill" or "They are homes on the hill." Perfect recognition is still far off, but imperfect recognition may be good enough to offer writers a valuable new tool. Speech recognition machines will simplify writers' physical chores, but the writers still have to be in charge of the meaning, quality, and precision of their texts. They will have to edit hard copies to correct the programs' misinterpretations of words.

Writers who like to work with pen may soon have another aid that eliminates the need to type—optical scanners, which transfer print into files on the computer. These machines free writers to compose with several tools but still use the computer in the tedious revising process. Such machines are expensive, but they will be very useful during a transition stage, when texts can be entered into the computer for future updating.

More Flexible Systems

Writers can now pull together several resources and adapt others for flexible use of the computer. They can use databases, return to their word-processing programs, take notes, run their texts through analysis programs, return to the texts, make changes, and send them to collaborators. Such use of the computer, however, requires a collection of hardware and software. At present, writers have to switch among a variety of programs, hold information in memory or make several printouts, and tolerate the disk management problems involved in eclectic use of computing tools. Writing systems of the future could integrate these capacities into a compact but flexible system that is, moreover, easy to use.

Dynabook, created by Alan Kay, is an example of a flexible system. Dynabook is a hand-held computer that the user can talk or write into. It enables a large community of users to share resources, and it can also be easily attached to a printer. A flexible system like Dynabook could be effectively adapted for writers if their special needs are taken into consideration. Since a writing system is most useful when it has a large display screen, hand-held systems for writers, which often have small screens, have to be easily connected to larger screens and printers.

A flexible writing system creates separate workspaces on the screen for many different types of researching and writing: visiting databases, scribbling, outlining, composing, revising, graphing, and illustrating. An experimental system called Scholar's Notebook, developed at Xerox Palo Alto Research Center, offers an electronic notecard writing and filing system that allows writers to view cards, menus, and the emerging text on the screen at the same time. The computer research processes described in Chapters 4 and 5, which writers can now do if they use their word-processing programs creatively, will be available in the near future in a coordinated system.

An integrated system for writers should also offer evaluations of the text—analyses of patterns of writing and patterns of mistakes. Added graphics capacities could help writers analyze problem sentences and paragraphs by drawing rough diagrams that indicate major parts of the structures. Writers working in different contexts could use such capacities according to their special needs. Writing systems should also enable writers to run tutorials or brush up on style rules by checking manuals on the computer. Thus, children could learn grammar rules as they relate to problems in the context of their own writing. Since adults know many of the rules but often forget them or ignore them, they could use automatic correction programs for specific errors.

Simple error-analysis programs could be combined with more complex programs that record errors and writers' revisions. A program to help students master problem-solving strategies has been developed by John Seely Brown at Xerox Palo Alto Research Center. The Buggy system makes analyses of users' strategies, answers, and corrections as they solve mathematical word problems. The program makes suggestions on the basis of learners' attempts to match the answers. Since language analysis is not perfect on the computer, writers have to be involved in the process of studying their own texts as the computer program guides them.

Automatic summarizing programs, such as options in the Writer's Workbench, create abstracts by collecting the first sentences of all paragraphs in a text. Such a collection of sentences can be used as a summary if the writer has put the topic sentence first in each paragraph. This superficial form of summarizing helps children see patterns and problems in their own texts. Adults can use such aids as reminders, but they need something more exact for abstracting.

As language analysis and computer memory develop, more meaningful writers' aids can be developed for standard systems. Researchers at Yale University and Columbia University are working on programs that build text summaries based on information stored in the computer and specific rules related to certain situations. For example, the program can summarize texts on a particular topic, such as terrorism, if it has a list of rules that outline events related to the topic. The program stores rules about the topic, such as "Terrorism is often used as a political strategy" and "Terrorism involves a small, visible group that threatens people's lives in a public way." A database on terrorist stories would supply the information for testing the program and adding to the basic list of rules. Researchers and other writers who compose repeatedly on a specific topic could build databases of their own texts and include rules related to their subjects. They could be guided by a program to create their own programs. In this way, they could build a resource for summarizing their pieces. Also, such a tool could let them know when they have not been explicit enough. The systems cannot, of course, develop beyond linguists' and psychologists' progress in outlining exactly how language works.

WILL MACHINES WRITE?

Improvements in semantic recognition make computers look smart. As a result, people have begun to reconsider old science fiction questions about intelligent machines. Some people predict that machines will be able to write someday, but this will not happen for a long time, if ever. Writing teachers, who know how difficult it is to convey writing processes to intelligent students, can appreciate how difficult it is for programmers to tell computers how to write stories or essays. Computers can follow rules, but even cognitive psychologists do not know the exact rules for developing logical, semantically coherent and creative texts. It will thus be a long time before programmers can convey to computers the intricacies of human thought processes.

Writers in business often use computer programs to "personalize" form letters by adding special greetings and information. Such attempts are not usually successful, however, because the letters come out sounding unnaturally friendly and clipped. Moreover, these personalized form letters with an artificially friendly tone are only partially composed by the computer; texts composed entirely by means of programs have many more problems.

Although some artificial intelligence experts predict that computer programs will soon be able to write routine letters, many important problems of automatic language creation remain unsolved. Even if linguists can specify sentence patterns well enough to write rules for computer programs to follow, they cannot tell programs how to use idiomatic expressions and other nonliteral usages, such as "I am blue today." Computer writing would have to be unnaturally literal. Smoothly relating sentences with pronouns and other reference patterns is also very difficult. Linguists have begun to study texts to find systematic rules of text structures, but there are many patterns of text, and they often are not marked by specific words.

Automatically created texts are undoubtedly poorer in quality than most naturally created texts. They may have few errors in individual words, but they have limited style, variation, and coherence. The sentences often are short and choppy, do not have transitions, and include outdated phrases that few people use spontaneously. The difficulty of teaching computers to write is apparent when one recalls that even automatic translation from one language to another has proved to be a great challenge to programmers.

LITERACY

The United States is supposedly suffering a literacy crisis. One reason for this crisis is that many people have begun to feel that they do not have to do much reading or writing to function in society. I was convinced that there might be such a problem when a magazine editor told me: "We had to add more short headings and bullets to your article. You know, magazines are for people who don't read."

Although the telephone and the television have been the compelling media for receiving and giving information orally, communication on computers is largely visual and symbolic. Most communicating on computers is done in writing. The increase in writing that is emerging as computers are used by more and more people may be only coincidentally related to the increasing resurgence of concern and interest in writing.

As the cost of television sets decreased, many families scraped together money to bring this form of entertainment and education into their homes. Similarly, if computing applications become appealing to a large majority of people, computers may also become desirable machines to have at home. If people find it entertaining to read the news on videotex or to write electronic messages to far corners of the earth, they will engage in interactive writing and reading much more than they have with television. In such a world, literacy will be more important and will probably cease to be the problem it is reported to be today.

If electronic written communication tools become readily accessible, affordable, and compatible with systems that handle large amounts of text and offer high-quality printouts, people may be more willing and eager to plop down at a terminal after a hard day at work to write a story, a poem, or a letter to a senator. The possibility of immediate feedback from a reader is so stimulating to children—as well as to adults—that if their writing system is networked to the computers in other people's homes, they may actually find writing to be an adventure—better than a computer game.

CHANGES IN WRITING
SYSTEMS AND QUALITY

Writing systems have evolved from pictographic representations of ideas to symbols that represent sounds. About 5,000 years ago, the Sumarians and the Chinese used pictures to represent objects and ideas. As the content of writing expanded from record keeping to political and religious themes, using pictures became cumbersome. Ideas and concepts were not always directly related to images, and writing systems with one-to-one idea-to-picture correspondences required many symbols. The Sumerians solved this problem by creating written symbols to represent the sounds of the spoken language.

Since languages have a finite set of basic sounds that combine to make up words, writing systems can more easily be made up of symbols to represent sounds, rather than symbols for every idea. Chinese has remained largely pictographic, but modernizations in that language have included more flexibility for representing sounds. Many changes in electronic communication have extended prior developments in the history of writing. Specific developments in hardware and software will influence the development of writing in technologically advanced societies.

Talky Writing

As writing becomes a natural form of communication in computer interactions, it more closely resembles talking. Computer use may change the nature of writing as voice typewriters become standard tools. When writers talk their texts into the computer and receive a printout instantly, the printed text will include characteristic speech patterns. For example, the errors that occur frequently in fast writing, such as substituting *the* for *they* or leaving out small words every now and then, are characteristic of speech errors. In written exchanges on the computer, which writers create quickly and readers skim, such patterns may become more acceptable, just as telegrams are acceptable in their limited context. Voice typewriters will be time-savers, but some writers may prefer to produce their words from a silent inner voice, rather than from a spoken voice, because they prefer the tenor and calm of inner speech.

People write differently on the computer than they do when they are slowed down by the pencil or typewriter, and they may not leave time for their internal sensors to check or rethink what they have said. The lag time in traditional document preparation and mailing gives people more time to consider their pieces. However, quickly written computer mail often includes incomplete ideas and many spelling and grammar mistakes, which the writer often does not confront, because many mail systems do not automatically keep copies. Another drawback of talky writing is that it is loosely constructed. It takes more words to say something in simple sentences that are strung together, and spoken discourse usually comes out in a less deliberately organized way.

Despite the possible decline in writing quality if writing becomes more talky, writing that is more like talking simplifies the composing process for many people. If people feel that they are talking, they do not feel that they have to be perfect on the first try, so writing on the computer has reduced many writing blocks. Texts written on the computer or entered into speech recognition systems are likely to be more fluid and natural. Texts of computer conferences illustrate this talky nature of writing. Like spoken sentences, the sentences in such conferences tend to be compound—two basic sentences connected by "and" or "then"—rather than the complex sentences that are common in writing. Complex sentences are more compact because they include sentences nested within sentences, and they sometimes convey complex ideas better than simple sentences do, but research has shown that they are harder to read.

The public nature of computer writing may make people more concerned about quality, although some may be so concerned about their appearance in writing that they will stay mute. Students at one ivy league university ridicule one another when they make spelling and grammar mistakes on the electronic bulletin board, so some students prepare their notices with a word-processing program before posting them, and some do not write publicly at all for fear that they will not catch their errors. Such peer pressure to write correctly sets up more compelling reasons than instructors' urgings, but a focus on grammar and spelling may not be as useful as a focus on content.

An ironic twist of making writing easier could be that people will prefer to write rather than read. Whereas television and books make people recipients, computers, like telephones, may turn them into expressers. Similarly, notes written on the computer may be more complete than notes on bits of paper, because they can be written faster or because they are part of a written discussion in a computer conference. Communicating regularly in writing via computer networks and being able to correct mistakes easily in quickly typed texts could encourage people to produce more than they read. Some writers may read their texts less on the computer because they find it difficult to read from the screen. Since the difficult process of revising requires that writers reread their texts carefully and slowly, they have to resist the temptation to just keep writing because it is easier and more fun. People may not revise because their texts look so good or because they depend on the superficial judgment of a program's automatic analysis. And even when electronic editing capacities are available, writers may not use them because they don't read their texts.

In summary, if writing on the computer becomes more talky, writing quality may suffer, but talky text may appeal to many readers who like the more casual flow of speech.

Coded Writing

Fast access to stored images may make writing more condensed and pictographic. Many computer interactions are condensed forms of language, and many messages from computer programs are not like natural spoken or written English. Programmers choose reduced forms of messages whenever they can. For example, when I wrote specifications for a word-processing program, I included such prompts as "Are you sure you want to erase this file? If you want to erase it, press y for yes and n for no." The programmer changed this message to Delete file.y/n. Such brief messages may save time for people who are familiar with a system, but they can confuse beginners. When I asked the programmer to write the message in English, he wrote, **Delete file? y/n.** The added question mark did not provide much more information for the reader. Although I was bothered by the unnatural English, children usually understand such condensed messages after they have gotten used to such language. For speed and conciseness, a message such as **list? type number.** may not only be clear to people but may also be preferred.

This tendency to reduce writing could be the result of programmers' using reduced forms of English as their programming languages. For example, the following lines of code in BASIC look like English, but in much reduced form:

```
0500 GOSUB 660
0510 IF X=1 THEN PRINT "HI THERE!"
```

Condensing could also be influenced by the reduced forms of messages on electronic bulletin boards, which include notices, announcements, and trivia. Such notices rarely appear in complete sentences or natural English word order. People who become familiar with the reduced linguistic forms in programming languages may accept them more than nonprogrammers do. Program writing may seem like writing in general to them. In fact, many computer science students have told me that they cannot write well when they use the computer because they feel as though they are programming, and their writing becomes rigid and chopped, like lines of code.

If coded writing becomes more acceptable in computer communications, the gap between writing on the computer and writing with other tools may widen. For example, scholars and humanists who resist using computers may use more varied forms of writing than businesspeople and children who use computers all the time. The gap could also widen between people who use computers extensively for communication or programming and those who use them only for word processing. Programmers may write in reduced forms, while people who do word processing may use extended language forms.

Graphic Writing

Rather than reducing language to smaller word forms, computer writers may eventually begin using images. Graphics, charts, diagrams, and outlines are becoming readily available on computing systems. If graphic communication becomes fast and easy to understand, it could supplement or replace writing for certain purposes. Some computer scientists feel that graphic symbols will replace words because symbols can be more efficient communicators than words in linear order. Iconic systems that transmit information faster than linguistic sequences are being developed. One system offers small pictures of objects—cars, houses, flies—that can be moved around the screen like a cursor. Such reusable pictures, which are also alterable, make it possible to put together pictographic messages.

If producing and understanding symbols becomes even faster than producing words, pictographic writing could become the most efficient form of communication. This would reverse the trend of using symbols to represent words. Of course, such dramatic changes in writing would affect language. A group of psychologists has noted a relationship between language evolution and humans' perceptions. According to researchers, Bever, Carroll, and Hurtig at Columbia University, grammatically correct patterns that are difficult to hear or speak evolve into patterns that are easy to perceive. Several patterns in spoken English are acceptable even though they are ungrammatical—for example, "The recent outbreak of riots are upsetting" and "I enjoyed flying in an airplane that I understand how it works." The incorrect matching of the verb "are" with "riots" rather than "outbreak," which is the subject, would probably not be noticed in speech, even by people who would notice such an error in another context. Similarly, the overlapping of two correct clauses in the second sentence—"I enjoyed flying in an airplane that I understand" and "I understand how it works"—creates a sentence pattern that is not a grammatical pattern in English. Such sentence patterns are used frequently by educated speakers. They also appear in college application essays and even in published pieces. Such errors occur and remain unnoticed for the most part, presumably because people forget the exact form of the beginning of a sentence by the time they speak or write the verb.

Research has suggested that it is difficult to perceive many words strung together loosely because they overburden short-term memory. Therefore, certain types of sloppy sentences are difficult for writers to correct unless they analyze them. It is interesting that the condensed messages that evolve from working on the computer may be easier to perceive than talky ones. Symbols that stand for ideas may be easier for people to understand and to speak.

Writing on the computer may become a form of publishing when people send and share their texts. Publishers may find a way to hook into computer communication channels, and an electronic form of publishing could develop that might answer many of the communication needs of readers and writers. Two types of publishing could flourish with different standards—the quality of text on the computer reflecting new standards while the quality of officially published texts remains traditional. Books published by traditional methods may be more polished, but they might not be as up to date as texts written on the computer.

CONCLUSION

Changes in writing are likely to occur gradually. Many years may pass before we have conclusive answers from research about the effects of computers on writing, because the hardware and software keep changing before research proposals are approved. Nevertheless, writers, teachers, editors, and students who work with computers will notice the changes and will adapt appropriately—albeit slowly. Those with the most experience using computer writing tools will see the changes in writing most clearly, because these new tools are bound to affect the process of writing more than the products.

I hope this book has provided some useful insights about writing, teaching writing, and using computers. I would like to close with a scene that shows what writing could be like in the future.

A 10-year-old boy and a 10-year-old girl are standing in a basement. Their hair is disheveled, and they are wearing dirty, untied sneakers and droopy blue jeans. They turn on a computer and address themselves to a gigantic screen. Their goal is to write an invitation to their friends to come to a Halloween party. As they speak, their words appear on the screen.

> Hey, kids. Come to a secret party. Beware, you'll have to be brave. Ware a costume so no one knows who you are. Because you'll be in trouble. There will be trap doors in the floor and you will go on a hunt to find the ghost that has been haunting our town.

The children then say "Command" and give instructions to the computer to look up the history of Halloween and mysterious occurrences that have been reported on Halloween night in the last twenty years. The stories appear on the screen. "Put that one in our invitation. Go get a picture of a vampire. No, first show us some." They see pictures of vampires from horror magazines, encyclopedias, and history books. They select a picture and give instructions to put it in the invitation. They rework the text many times by giving instructions—sometimes contradictory ones and sometimes instructions that they plan together. The screen reflects one command and then—immediately—the next. When the children finally agree on the wording, they give further instructions: "Go around the block and give a copy of the invitation to all the kids in the class. Be sure to put everyone's name on the letter."

Two children in dirty sneakers had control over a powerful machine. The computer took over the physical activities of writing, and the children expressed themselves as well as they could. The computer also gave them tools for creating a text together relatively easily, which—most importantly—doubled their power as writers, creators, and thinkers. The subject wasn't of great importance, but the collaborative process they used is one of the most interesting ways for writers to work.

Bibliography

Adams, A., and Jones, C. (1984). *Teaching humanities in the micro-electronic age.* Milton Keynes, England: Open University Press.

Applebee, A. (1978). *The child's conception of story.* Chicago: University of Chicago Press.

Applebee, A. N., and Langer, J. A. (1983). "Instructional scaffolding: Reading and writing as natural language activities." *Language Arts*, 60, 168–175.

Bamberger, J., and Schon, D. (1983). "Learning as reflective conversation with materials." *Art Education*, 36:2, 68–73.

Bereiter, C., and Scardamalia, M. (1981). "From conversation to composition: The role of instruction in the developmental process." In R. Glaser (ed.), *Advances in instructional psychology*, Vol. 2. Hillsdale, N.J.: Erlbaum.

Bever, T. G.; Carroll, J. M.; and Hurtig, R. (1976). "Analogy or ungrammatical sequences that are utterable and comprehensible are the origins of new grammars in language acquisition and linguistic evolution." In *An integrated theory of linguistic ability*. New York: Crowell.

Bridwell, L. S.; Johnson, P.; and Brehe, S. (1983). "Computers and composing: Case studies of experienced writers." In A. Matsuhashi (ed.), *Writing in real time: Modelling production processes*. New York: Longman.

Bridwell, L. S.; Sirc, G.; and Brooke, R. (in press). "Revising and computers: Case studies of student writers." In S. Freedman (ed.), *The acquisition of written language: Revision and response*. New York: Ablex.

Britton, J.; Burgess, T.; Martin, N.; McLeod, A.; and Rosen, H. (1975). *The development of writing abilities*. London: Macmillan.

Brown, A. L.; Bransford, J. D.; Ferrara, R. A.; and Campione, J. C. (1983). "Learning, remembering, and understanding." In P.H. Mussen (ed.), *The handbook of child psychology*, Volume 5: J. H. Flavell and E. M. Markman (eds.), *Cognitive Development*. New York: Wiley.

Brown, J. (1983). "Process versus product: A perspective on tools for communal and informal electronic learning." Palo Alto, Calif: Xerox Palo Alto Research Center.

Bruce, B., and Rubin, A. (1983). "Phase II Report for the QUILL Project." Cambridge, Mass.: Bolt, Beranek, and Newman.

Burns, H., and Culp, G. (1980). "Stimulating invention in English composition through computer-assisted instruction." *Educational Technology*, August 5.

Calkins, L. M. (1983). *Lessons from a child: On the teaching and learning of writing.* Exeter, N.H.: Heinemann.

Carey, S. (in press). "Are children fundamentally different kinds of thinkers and learners than adults?" In S. Chipman, J. Segal, and R. Glaser (eds.), *Thinking and Learning Skills*, Vol. 2. Hillsdale, N.J.: Erlbaum.

Coburn, P.; Kelman, P.; Roberts, N.; Snyder, T. F.; Watt, D. H.; and Weiner, C. (1982). *Practical guide to computers in education.* Reading, Mass.: Addison-Wesley.

Collins, A. (1982). "Learning to read and write with personal computers." Cambridge, Mass.: Bolt, Beranek, and Newman.

Collins, A.; Bruce, B.; and Rubin, A. (1982). "Micro-based writing activities for the upper elementary grades." In *Proceedings of the Fourth International Congress and Exposition of the Society for Applied Learning Technology*, Warrenton, Va.

Daiute, C. (1982). "Children and adults write notes to the computer." *Parents League Review*, 16, 138–144.

Daiute, C. (1983). "Writing, creativity and change." *Childhood Education*, March/April, 227–231.

Daiute, C. (1983). "The computer as stylus and audience." *College Composition and Communication*, 34(2), 134–145.

Daiute, C. (1984). "Performance limits on writers." In R. Beach and L. Bridwell (eds.), *New directions in composing research.* New York: Guilford Press, 205–224.

Daiute, C. (1984). "Rewriting, revising, and recopying." Paper presented at the AERA meeting, New Orleans, April.

Daiute, C. (1984). "The state of the art: Technology and writing." Paper presented at the AERA meeting, New Orleans, April.

Daiute, C. (1984). "Can computers stimulate writers' inner dialogues?" In W. Wresch (ed.), *A writer's tool: The computer in composition instruction.* Urbana, Ill.: National Council of Teachers of English.

Daiute, C. (in press). "Do writers talk to themselves?" in S. Freedman (ed.), *The acquisition of written lagnuage: Revision and response.* New York: Ablex.

Daiute, C., and Taylor, R. (1981). "Computers and the improvement of writing." In *Proceedings of the Association of Computing Machinery.* ACM 0–89791–049-4/81. Baltimore, MD.

Dyson, A. (1982). "The emergence of visible language: Interrelationship between drawing and early writing." Doctoral dissertation, University of Georgia, Language Education Department.

Elbow, P. (1975). *Writing without teachers.* New York: Oxford University Press.

Elbow, P. (1981). *Writing with power.* New York: Oxford University Press.

Emig, J. (1977). "Writing as a mode of learning." *College Composition and Communication*, 28(2), 122–128.

Flower, L., and Hayes, J. R. (1981). "A cognitive process theory of writing." *College Composition and Communication*, 32(4), 365–388.

Flower, L., and Hayes, J. R. (1981). "The pregnant pause: An inquiry into the nature of planning." *Research in the Teaching of English*, 15(8), 229–243.

Gelb, I. J. (1963). *A study of writing.* Chicago: University of Chicago Press.

Gingrich, P. (1982). "Writer's workbench: Studies of users." In *29th International*

Technical Communication Conference Proceedings, Bell Laboratories, Piscataway, N.J., May.

Glossbrenner, A. (1983). *The complete handbook of personal computer communications*. New York: St. Martin's Press.

Graves, D. (1983). *Writing: Teachers and children at work*. Exeter, N.H.: Heinemann.

Hiltz, R., and Turoff, M. (1978). *The network nation: Human communication via computer*. Reading, Mass.: Addison-Wesley.

Kiefer, K., and Smith, C. (1984). "Improving student's revising and editing: The Writer's Workbench system at Colorado State University." In W. Wresch (ed.), *A writer's tool: The computer in composition instruction*. Urbana, Ill.: National Council of Teachers of English.

Kraft, P. (1979). "The industrialization of computer programming: From programming to software production." In A. Zimbalist (ed.), *Case studies on the labor process*. New York: Monthly Review Press.

Kroll, B. (1978). "Cognitive egocentrism and the problem of audience awareness in written discourse." *Research in the Teaching of English*, 12(3), 269–281.

Langer, J. (1969). *Theories of development*. New York: Holt, Rinehart & Winston.

Levin, J.; Riel, M.; Rowe, R.; and Boruta, M. (in press). "Muktuk meets Jacuzzi: Computer networks and elementary school writers." In S. Freedman (ed.), *The Acquisition of written language: Revision and response*. New York: Ablex.

Malone, T. (1981). "Toward a theory of intrinsically motivating instruction." *Cognitive Science*, 5:4, 333–369.

Marcus, S., and Blau, S. (1983). "Not seeing is relieving: Invisible writing with computers." *Educational Technology*, April, 12–15.

Matsuhashi, A. (1981). "Pausing and planning: The tempo of written discourse production." *Research in the Teaching of English*, 15, 113–134.

Miller, G. (1956). "The magical number seven, plus or minus two: Some limits on our capacity for processing information." *Psychological Review*, 63, 81–97.

Miller, L.; Heidorn, G.; and Jensen, K. (1981). *Text-critiquing with the EPISTLE system: An author's aid to better syntax*. Paper presented at the National Computer Conference, Chicago.

Nancarrow, P.; Ross, D.; and Bridwell, L. (1983). "Word processors and the writing process: An annotated bibliography." Westport, Conn.: Greenwood Press.

Nelson, T. (1974) *Computer lib*. Chicago: Hugo's Book Service.

Newell, A., and Simon, H. A. (1982). *Human problem solving*. Englewood Cliffs, N.J.: Prentice-Hall.

Nix, D. (in press). "Unhandy guide to HANDY." Technical report. Yorktown Heights, N.Y.: IBM T.J. Watson Research Center.

Norman, D. (1969). *Memory and attention*. New York: Wiley.

Ong, W. J. (1983). *Orality and literacy: The technologizing of the word*. London: Methuen.

Papert, S. (1980). *Mindstorms: Children, computers, and powerful ideas*. New York: Basic Books.

Perl, S. (1979). "The composing process of unskilled college writers." *Research in the Teaching of English*, 13(4), 317–336.

Piaget, J. and Inhelder, B. (1964). *The early growth of logic in the child*. New York: Norton.

Rainer, T. (1978). *The new diary*. Los Angeles: Tarcher.

Rose, M. (1980). Rigid rules, inflexible plans, and the stifling of language: A cognitive analysis of writers' block. *College Composition and Communication*, 31(4), 389–400.

Rosegrant, T. (1984). "Fostering progress in literacy development: technology and social interaction." *Seminars in Speech and Language*, 5(1), 47–57.

Rubin, A. (1982). "The computer confronts language arts: Cans and shoulds for education." In A. C. Wilkinson (ed.), *Classroom computers and cognitive science*. New York: Academic Press.

Scardamalia, M. and Bereiter, C. (in press). "Written composition." In M. Wittrock (ed.), *Handbook of research on teaching*, 3rd ed. New York: Macmillan.

Schank, R., and Abelson, R. (1977). *Scripts, plans, goals and understanding*. Hillsdale, N.J.: Erlbaum.

Schwartz, H. (1980). "Computer aids for individualizing instruction throughout the writing process." Rochester, Mich.: Oakland University.

Schwartz, H. (1984). "SEEN": A tutorial and user network for hypothesis testing." In W. Wresch (ed.), *A writer's tool: The computer in composition instruction*. Urbana, Ill.: National Council of Teachers of English.

Shaughnessy, M. (1977). *Errors and expectations: A guide for the teacher of basic writing*. New York: Oxford University Press.

Sheingold, K.; Kane, J., and Endreweit, M. (1983). "Microcomputer use in schools: Developing a research agenda." *Harvard Educational Review*, 53(4), 412–432.

Skinner, B. F. (1957). *Verbal behavior*. New York: Appleton-Century-Crofts.

Skinner, B. F. (1961). "Why we need teaching machines." *Harvard Educational Review*, 31(4), 376–398.

Sommers, N. (1980). "Revision strategies of student writers and experienced writers." *College Composition and Communications*, 31, 378–388.

Taylor, R. (1980). *The computer in the school: Tutor, tool, tutee*. New York: Teachers College Press.

Turkle, S. (1984). *The second self: Computers and the human spirit*. New York: Simon and Schuster.

Tydeman, J.; Lipinski, H.; Adler, R.; Nyhan, M.; and Zwimpfer, L. (1982). *Teletext and videotex in the United States*. New York: McGraw-Hill.

Weizenbaum, J. (1976). *Computer power and human reason: From judgment to calculation*. San Francisco: Freeman.

Wicklein, R. (1979). *The electronic nightmare*. New York: Viking Press.

Woodruff, E.; Bereiter, C.; and Scardamalia, M. (1981). "On the road to computer-assisted compositions." *Journal of Educational Technology Systems*, 10(2), 133–148.

Wresch, W. (ed.) (1984). *A writer's tool: The computer in composition instruction*. Urbana, Ill.: National Council of Teachers of English.

Zinsser, W. (1983). *Writing with a word processor*. New York: Harper & Row.

Resources

The programs listed here were selected because they are used in schools and because they are good examples of the types of programs discussed in this book.

WORD-PROCESSING PROGRAMS

Name: Apple Writer II
Distributor: Apple Computer, Inc.
   20525 Mariani Ave.
   Cupertino, CA 95014
Computer/Operating System: Apple DOS
Description:

- Cursor movement by character, word, page
- Clear documentation
- Versatile print commands
- Search and replace
- Window feature

Name: Atari Writer
Distributor: Atari dealers
Computer/Operating System: Atari
Description:

- Insert/delete character, line, block
- Search and replace
- Automatic page numbering
- Headers and footers
- "Print preview" to screen

Name: Bank Street Writer
Distributor: Scholastic Publications
                     730 Broadway
                     New York, NY 10003
Computer/Operating System: Apple, Atari
Description:

- Mode switching
- Includes a tutorial
- Cursor movement/delete by character, word, block
- Menu-driven
- Easy to learn
- Classroom-oriented

Name: Final Word
Distributor: Mark of the Unicorn
                     P.O. Box 423
                     Arlington, MA 02174
Computer/Operating System: IBM PC DOS, DEC Rainbow
Description:

- Menu-driven
- Cursor movement/delete forward and backward by character, word, line, sentence, paragraph, block
- Search and replace
- Boilerplates
- Automatic footnoting, indexing
- Window feature
- No mode switching for editing
- "State save" feature to protect against crashes

Name: Homeword
Distributor: Sierra On-Line, Inc.
                     Sierra On-Line Building
                     Coarsegold, CA 93614
Computer/Operating System: Apple, Commodore 64, Atari
Description:

- Icon-driven
- True page visual model
- Optional joystick control
- Audio cassette tutorial
- Mode switching

Name: Leading Edge Word Processor
Distributor: Leading Edge Products
Fortune 1300 Division
21 Highland Circle
Needham Heights, MA 02194
Computer/Operating System: IBM PC
Description:

- Function key controlled
- Window feature

Name: Microsoft Word
Distributor: Microsoft Corporation
10700 Northup Way
Bellevue, WA 98004
Computer/Operating System: IBM PC
Description:

- Multiple windows
- Uses a mouse for cursor movement and commands
- Global search/replace

Name: PeachText
Distributor: Peachtree Software
3445 Peachtree Road NE
Atlanta, GA 30326
Computer/Operating System: CP/M, PC DOS, MS DOS, DEC Rainbow
Description:

- Menu-driven
- Help menus
- On-line thesaurus and basic dictionary
- Cursor movement by character, word

Name: Perfect Writer
Distributor: Perfect Software, Inc.
1400 Shattuck Avenue
Berkeley, CA 94709
Computer/Operating System: PC DOS, CP/M-80
Description:

- Mnemonic commands
- Cursor movement/delete forward and backward by character, word, line, sentence, paragraph, block
- Search and replace

- Boilerplates
- Automatic footnoting, indexing
- Window feature
- No mode switching for editing

Name: PFS:Write
Distributor: Software Publishing Company
1901 Landings Drive
Mountain View, CA 94043
Computer/Operating System: Apple, IBM PC
Description:

- Screen-oriented
- Integrated with spreadsheet and database programs

Name: PIE Writer
Distributor: Hayden Software
600 Suffolk Avenue
Lowell, MA 01853
Computer/Operating System: Apple
Description:

- Cursor movement by character, word, line, top or bottom of screen/text
- Search and replace
- Horizontal and vertical scrolling
- Can look at formatted text before printing (see page breaks)
- Simple dot formatting commands, like WordStar
- Delete or save to buffer feature

Name: Screenwriter II
Distributor: Sierra On-Line, Inc.
Sierra On-Line Building
Coarsegold, CA 93614
Computer/Operating System: Apple II
Description:

- Tutorial
- Global search and replace
- True upper- and lowercase

Name: Select
Distribution: Select Information Systems
919 Sir Francis Drake Boulevard
Kentfield, CA 94904
Computer/Operating System: IBM PC, TRS-80 II, CP/M, DEC Rainbow
Description:

- Screen-oriented
- Mode switching
- Cursor movement by character
- Delete by character, word, sentence, block
- Search and replace
- Tutorial
- Automatic page/line prompter

Name: SuperScripsit
Distributor: Tandy/Radio Shack
1800 One Tandy Center
Fort Worth, TX 76102
Computer/Operating System: TRS-80 Models I, III
Description:

- Status line with page/line numbers
- Cursor movement by character, word, line, paragraph, printed or video page
- Search and replace
- Delete only by character or block
- Mode switching
- Help menus

Name: The Correspondent
Distributor: Southwestern Data Systems
10761 Woodside Avenue, Suite E
P.O. Box 582
Santee, CA 92071
Computer/Operating System: Apple II, IIe
Description:

- Character/line insert and delete
- Block move/copy/delete
- Window feature
- Math functions
- Bidirectional scrolling

Name: Volkswriter Deluxe
Distributor: Lifetree Software, Inc.
               4111 Pacific Street, Suite 315
               Monterey, CA 93940
Computer/Operating System: IBM PC
Description:

- Horizontal and vertical scroll
- Uses as much memory as available
- Programmed keys menu
- Mail merge
- "Write to buffer file" feature

Name: Word Juggler
Distributor: Quark Engineering
               1433 Willimas, #1102
               Denver, CO 80218
Computer/Operating System: Apple IIe
Description:

- Keyboard command overlays
- Deleting by character, word, paragraphs, blocks
- Interface with PFS:File or Quickfile
- Text-oriented

Name: Word Perfect
Distributor: Satellite Software International
               288 West Center Street
               Orem, UT 84057
Computer/Operating System: IBM PC
Description:

- Template overlays for function keys
- Text-oriented
- Mail merge
- Math functions
- Good formatting

Name: Word Vision
Distributor: Bruce & James Program Publishers
               4500 Tuller Road
               Dublin, OH 43107

Computer/Operating System: IBM PC
Description:

- Uses icons for some operations
- Color stick-on labels for function keys

Name: WordStar
Distributor: MicroPro International Corporation
33 San Pablo Avenue
San Raphael, CA 94903
Computer/Operating System: CP/M, PC DOS, Apple DOS
Description:

- Screen-oriented
- Menu-driven
- Cusor movement/delete forward and backward by character, word, line, sentence, paragraph, block
- Sophisticated formatting
- Mail merge option

INTEGRATED PROGRAMS

Name: AppleWorks
Distributor: Apple Computer
20525 Mariani Avenue
Cupertino, CA 95014
Description: Includes word-processing, database, and spreadsheet programs.

Name: QUILL
Distributor: D.C. Heath
125 Spring Street
Lexington, MA 02173
Description: Includes a word-processing program, Mailbag, Library, and Planner.

Name: Writer's Helper
Distributor: CONDUIT
University of Iowa—Oakdale Campus
Iowa City, IA, 52242
Description: Includes The Prewriter, The Word Processor, The Analyzer.

DATABASE PROGRAMS

Name: dBASE II
Distributor: Ashton-Tate
10150 West Jefferson Boulevard
Culver City, CA 90230
Computer/Operating System: IBM PC, CP/M
Description:

- Can be used as a high-level programming language (authoring language)
- Complex database system

Name: DataFax
Distributor: Link Systems
1640 19th Street
Santa Monica, CA 90404
Computer: Apple
Description:

- Free-form data entry
- Keyword searchers (singly or combination)
- Supports wildcards
- Simple screen editor
- Easy to use
- Minimum report generation

Name: Data Perfect
Distributor: LJK Enterprises
P.O. Box 10827
St. Louis, MO 63129
Computer/Operating System: Apple, Atari
Description:

- Includes a report generator
- Utilities generator (sort, merge, re-form data)
- Calculator for data entry

Name: File-Fax
Distributor: TMQ Software
82 Fox Hill Drive
Buffalo Grove, IL 60090

Computer/Operating System: Apple, Atari 800, IBM PC
Description:

- Up to 31 fields
- Unlimited records
- Up to four reports per application
- Business-oriented
- Tight input controls

Name: Information Master
Distributor: High Technology Software Products, Inc.
P.O. Box 60406
1611 N.W. 23rd Street
Oklahoma City, OK 73106
Computer/Operating System: Apple
Description:

- Defines, enters, sorts, searchers, modifies, deletes, selects, and prints (records and reports) commands
- Allows manipulation of files
- Adds new fields, deletes old fields, lengthens and shortens fields, combines and subdivides files and fields, calculates field values, rearranges field locations, reassigns field types, and transfers print formats to other disks

Name: Magic Memory
Distributor: Art-Sci
5547 Satsuma
N. Hollywood, CA 91601
Computer/Operating System: Apple (48K, 2 disk drives)
Description:

- 12,000 records
- Unlimited number of fields
- Menu-driven
- Designed to simulate a telephone address book

Name: Notebook
Distributor: Pro/Tem Software
814 Towlman Drive
Stanford, CA 94305

Computer/Operating System: IBM PC, CP/M
Description:

- Unlimited records
- 20 fields per record, with full screen of text for each field
- Full-screen editor
- Sorts and searches by field

Name: Perfect Filer
Distributor: Perfect Software, Inc.
1400 Shattuck Avenue
Berkeley, CA 94709
Computer/Operating System: CP/M, IBM PC DOS
Description:

- Integrated with Perfect Writer
- Generates reports
- Menu-driven

Name: PFS:File
Distributor: Software Publishing Company
1901 Landings Drive
Mountain View, CA 94043
Computer/Operating System: Apple, IBM PC
Description:

- Menu-driven
- User-defined forms
- Retrieves, updates, and prints sorted information

Name: Quick-Search Librarian
Distributor: Interactive Microwave, Inc.
P.O. Box 771
State College, PA 16081
Computer/Operating System: Apple
Description:

- For technical records and bibliographic information
- Cross-referencing with up to 12 keywords
- 1000 records per disk

Name: Visidex
Distributor: Visi Corp
2895 Zanker Road
San Jose, CA 95134

Computer: Apple
Description:

- Menu-driven
- Editor for free-form data entry
- Keyword or string searches with wildcards
- Can create templates
- 101 suggested applications in the manual

INFORMATION UTILITIES
AND DATABASES

Most information utilities must be accessed through special telephone services, such as Tymnet and Telenet. Each service has different fee schedules, which are explained as part of the sign-up procedures for the information utilities it services.

Name: The Source
Operator: The Source
                1616 Anderson Road
                McLean, VA 22102
                (800)332-3300
Description: Contains databases and services over a wide range of topics, including bulletin boards, electronic mail, shopping, newspapers, public domain software, and computer conferencing.

Name: CompuServe
Operator: H&R Block Company
                5000 Arlington Centre Boulevard
                P.O. Box 20212
                Columbus, OH 43220
Description: Electronic mail, national bulletin board system, CB simulator (real-time, multiple conversations), special interest groups, news and information, business and finance information and services (Dow Jones, etc.), personal computing information and services, electronic banking and shopping, computer conferencing, games, on-line *World Book Encyclopedia*.

Name: ERIC
Distributor: Available on DIALOG, BRS, and ORBIT
Description: Contains the information available in indexes compiled by the Educational Resources Information Center; updated monthly.

Name: DIALOG
Distributor: DIALOG Information Services, Inc.
Marketing Department
3460 Hillview Avenue
Palo Alto, CA 94304
(800)982-5838 (California)
(800)227-1927 (other states and Canada)
Description: A clearinghouse for more than 200 databases, including *Books in Print, Microcomputer Index, International Software Directory, Newsearch, Book Review Index,* and other business, social sciences, chemistry, medicine, technology, engineering, law, government, and education databases.

Name: BRS
Distributor: Bibliographic Retrieval Services
1200 Route 7
Latham, NY 12110
(800)833-4707
Description: Databases include *Academic American Encyclopedia*, ABI/ INFORM (abstracts from 500 journals), MEDLINE or MEDLARS onLINE (indexed articles from over 3,000 international medical journals), and Compendex (3,500 journals and other engineering publications).

Name: ORBIT
Distributor: ORBIT Information Retrieval System
SDC Search Service
2500 Colorado Avenue
Santa Monica, CA 90406
(800)352-6689 (California)
(800)421-7229 (other states and Canada)
Description: 80 databases; those found exclusively in ORBIT include Accountants, APIT (petroleum), COLD (disciplines dealing with Antarctica), MONITOR (index to *Christian Science Monitor*), and SPORT (literature on training, sports medicine, international sports history, etc.).

Name: The Information Bank
Distributor: New York Times Information Service
1719A Route 10
Parsippany, NJ 07054
(201)539-5850
Description: Contains abstracts of all *New York Times* articles from 1974 to present, plus abstracts of articles from a dozen other newspapers and about forty magazines. The Information Bank is one of seven databases available from the New York Times Information Service.

Name: Dow Jones News/Retrieval Service
Distributor: Dow Jones News/Retrieval Service
                   P.O. Box 300
                   Princeton, NJ 08540
                   (609)452-1511 (New Jersey)
                   (800)257-5114 (other states and Canada)
Description: A news and financial database including Dow Jones News
(drawn from *Wall Street Journal*, *Barron's*, and the Dow Jones News Service),
World Report from United Press International, and Wall Street Journal
Highlights Online.

MAIL PROGRAMS

Name: E-Com
Distributor: Electronic Mail Service Co.
                   David Whitney Building
                   1553 Woodward Avenue, Suite 708
                   Detroit, MI 48226
Computer/Operating System: TRS-80 Models I and III

Name: E-Mail
Distributor: Jones-Engineering Associates, Inc.
                   P.O. Box 26134
                   Charlotte, NC 26134
Computer/Operating System: IBM PC

Name: Electronic Messenger

Distributor: BT Enterprises
                   171 Hawkinds Avenue
                   Centerreach, NY 11720
Computer/Operating System: TRS-80 Model I

Name: Micro-Courier
Distributor: Microcom, Inc.
                   1400 A Providence Highway
                   Norwood, MA 02062
Computer/Operating System: Apple, IBM PC
Description:

- Creates and edits messages up to 4,000 characters
- Mail files
- Sends/receives mail
- Reviews mail

- Mailbox directory maintainance
- Runs system utilities
- Only communicates automatically with other Micro-Courier machines

Name: Transend
Distributor: Transend Corporation
2190 Paragon Drive
San Jose, CA 95131
Computer/Operating System: IBM PC, Apple
Description:

- Allows network building
- Built-in message editor

OUTLINING AND ORGANIZATION AIDS

Name: Questtext III
Distributor: Information Reduction Research
1538 Main Street
Concord, MA 01742
Computer/Operating System: IBM PC
Description:

- Uses boilerplates, templates, outlining, research note taking, CAI
- Interfaces with WordStar
- Three to five levels of branching, with only one level displayed on the screen at any one time
- Each branch can have 99 subbranches
- Line-oriented (line numbering) without word wrap

Name: Superfile
Distributor: FYI, Inc.
4202 Spicewood Springs Road, #114
Austin, TX 78759
Computer/Operating System: CP/M
Description:

- Free-format information retrieval system, filing program
- Creates files in a word-processing program, then assigns keywords
- Very fast
- Unlimited files can be cross-referenced up to 250 different ways

Name: ThinkTank
Distributor: Living Videotex, Inc.
                   2432 Charleston Rd.
                   Mountain View, CA 94043
Computer/Operating System: Apple, IBM PC
Description: Electronic outliner, allowing entry, editing, and rearranging of outline headings and subheadings. Headings may be filled in with paragraphs of up to 2,000 characters. Portions of the outline may be expanded or collapsed. Includes search and sort commands.

Name: ZyIndex
Distributor: Zylab Corporation
                   233 E. Erie
                   Chicago, IL 60611
Computer/Operating Sytem: IBM PC
Description: Treats text as a database, allowing searches for strings within a specified distance of another string (e.g., every occurrence of "Rogers" or "Whittaker" within 100 words of "wisdom").

PROMPTING FOR PREWRITING AND PLANNING

Name: QUILL Planner
Distributor: D.C. Heath and Company
                   125 Spring Street
                   Lexington, MA 02173
Computer/Operating System: Apple
Description:

- Menu-driven
- Helps with prewriting
- Can prompt by keywords, title and author, or entry numbers (entered by teacher or student)
- Prompts for information about a predefined topic

Name: SEEN
Contact: Helen Schwartz
               P.O. Box 911
               Rochester, MI 48063
Computer/Operating System: Apple
Description:

- Prompts for one type of paper: analysis of a character in a fictional work

- Bulletin board feature (pen names)
- Can down-load notes to word-processing programs like Apple Writer for further development
- Group notices disk, individual folders disk
- System manager disk for teacher

Name: TOPOI
Contact: Hugh Burns
Air Force Human Resources Laboratory
Lowry Air Force Base, CO 80230-5000
Computer/Operating System: DEC, Apple, IBM PC
Description:

- Personalized
- Asks for subject topic, then prompts for purposes
- Brainstorming tool

Name: Prewrite
Contact: Mimi Schwartz
4 Evelyn Place
Princeton, N.J. 08540
(or Boynton/Cook, P.O. Box 860, Upper Montclair, N.J. 07043
Computer/Operating System: Apple
Description:

- Includes prompting for prewriting and word processing functions
- Teachers can add, edit, and delete question prompts

PROMPTING FOR REVISING AND TEXT-ANALYSIS PROGRAMS

Name: Catch (currently being used for research purposes)
Contact: Colette Daiute
Harvard Graduate School of Education
Appian Way
Cambridge, MA 02138
Computer/Operating System: Apple
Description: Prompted revision program that includes grammar and style checking, and prompts to guide revising.

Name: EPISTLE
Developer: Lance Miller
          T.J. Watson Research Center
          Yorktown Heights, NY 10598
Computer/Operating System: IBM 370 family
Description:

- Uses parsing rules to detect fourteen classes of syntactic errors in sentences (from L.A. Miller, G.A. Hiedorn, and K. Jensen, *Text-critiquing with the EPISTLE system: An author's aid to better syntax*)
  —*Disagreement in*:
  number between subject and verb
  person between subject and verb
  number between determiner and noun
  number between quantifier and noun
  number between relative clause and head noun-phrase
  —*Use of*:
  object pronoun in predicate nominative position
  object pronoun in subject position
  subject pronoun in direct object position
  subject pronoun in indirect object position
  subject pronoun in prepositional phrase
  "who" for "whom"
  "whom" for "who"
  "of" for "have"
  improper verb form

Name: Grammatik
Distributor: Aspen Software
          P.O. Box 339
          Tijeras, MN 87059
Computer/Operating System: CP/M, IBM PC, TRS-80
Description:

- Prompts for errors in capitalization, punctuation, misused phrases (trite, wordy), sexist language
- Gives word/sentence length information

Name: Homer
Distributor: The Scribner Book Co.
          College Department
          597 Fifth Avenue
          New York, NY 10003

Computer/Operating System: Apple
Description:

- Revision program
- Reading analysis based on "para-medic method"
- Isolates prepositions, *to be* verbs, imprecise words
- Graphs sentence lengths, word types
- User or teacher can create word lists

Name: Punctuation & Style
Distributor: Oasis Systems
  2765 Reynard Way
  San Diego, CA 92103
Computer/Operating System: CP/M, MS-DOS
Description:

- Catches punctuation errors and unpaired format commands, doubled words
- Suggests alternatives for commonly misused or overworked phrases
- Shows where active voice can replace passive

Name: Writer's Workbench
Distributor: Bell Laboratories
  190 River Road
  Summit, NJ 07901
Computer/Operating System: UNIX
Description:

- Includes programs to proofread, comment on stylistic features of text, and reference information about the English language
- Can detect split infinitive, spelling and punctuation errors, overly long sentences, wordy phrases, and passive sentences
- Includes SUGGEST, STYLE, ABST, DICTION

READABILITY PROGRAMS

Name: Readability Analysis (School Utilities Disk #2)
Distributor: MECC
  2520 Broadway Drive
  St. Paul, MN 55013

Computer/Operating System: Apple
Description:

- Spache, Dale-Chall, Fry, Raygor, Flesch, Gunning-Fog tests
- Word list with number of syllables per word
- Numbers of sentences, words, syllables
- Words of six or more letters, three or more syllables
- Average sentence length, letters per word, syllables per word

Name: Readability
Distributor: Encyclopedia Britanica Educational Corporation
425 North Michigan Avenue
Chicago, IL 60611
Computer/Operating System: Apple
Description:

- Spache, Dale-Chall, Fry, Raygor, Flesch, Gunning-Fog, Smog tests
- Includes editor for on-screen changes

SPELLING CHECKERS

Name: Electric Webster
Distributor: Cornucopia Software
P.O. Box 6111
Albany, CA 94706
Computer/Operating System: CP/M, IBM PC/DOS, TRS-80
Description:

- 50,000-word dictionary
- Dictionary look-up feature
- Grammar and style checker
- Integrates with ten word-processing programs (WordStar, Spellbinder, Newscript, Lazy Writer, SuperScripsit, Electric Pencil, Copy Art, Superscript, Zorlof, Magic Wand)
- Hyphenation option

Name: Lexicheck
Distributor: Quark Engineering
1433 Willimas, #1102
Denver, CO 80218
Computer/Operating System: Apple IIe
Description:

- 50,000-word dictionary

- Compatible with Word Juggler
- Highlights words in context
- Allows creation of specialized dictionary

Name: Perfect Speller
Distributor: Perfect Software, Inc.
1400 Shattuck Avenue
Berkeley, CA 94709
Computer/Operating System: CP/M, IBM PC
Description:

- 50,000 words
- Integrated with Perfect Writer
- Allows in-context correction
- Allows creation of specialized dictionaries

Name: Random House Proofreader
Distributor: Digital Marketing
2670 Cherry Lane
Walnut Creek, CA 94596
Computer/Operating System: CP/M, IBM PC
Description:

- 50,000-word dictionary
- Screen-prompted

Name: Sensible Speller
Distributor: Sensible Software, Inc.
6619 Perham Drive
West Bloomfield, MI 88033
Computer/Operating System: Apple
Description:

- 80,000+ words
- Includes the *Random House Dictionary*, concise edition
- Compatible with almost all Apple word-processing programs

Name: SpellStar
Distributor: MicroPro International Corporation
33 San Pablo Avenue
San Rafael, CA 94901
Computer/Operating System: IBM PC, MS DOS, CP/M
Description: Works with WordStar

Name: Spell Wizard
Distributor: Datasoft Inc.
               9421 Winnetka Avenue
               Chatsworth, CA 91311
Computer/Operating System: Atari
Description:

- 33,000-word dictionary
- Allows for immediate correction

Name: The Dictionary
Distributor: Sierra On-Line, Inc.
               Sierra On-Line Building
               Coarsegold, CA 93614
Computer/Operating System: Apple II
Description:

- 28,000-word dictionary
- Compatible with Screenwriter II and other Apple word-processing programs

Name: The Word Plus
Distributor: Oasis Systems
               2765 Reynard Way
               San Diego, CA 92103
Computer/Operating System: IBM PC, CP/M
Description:

- 45,000-word dictionary
- Can look-up words on-line
- In-context viewing
- Specialty dictionary
- Word frequency count
- Alphabetizer
- Automatic hyphenation function

Name: Word Proof
Distributor: IBM
               P.O. Box 1328
               Boca Raton, FL 33432
Computer/Operating System: IBM PC
Description:

- 125,000-word dictionary
- Built-in text editor
- Thesaurus

SOURCES OF INFORMATION
ON LANGUAGE ARTS
SOFTWARE

Name: *The 1984 Book of Atari Software* and *The 1984 Book of Apple Software* (Los Angeles: The Book Company, 1984)
Description: Two separate books, with detailed descriptions of many programs for each machine.

Name: Classroom Computer Learning Directories
Distributor: Classroom Computer Learning
           5615 West Cermak Road
           Cicero, IL 60650
Description: Included with a subscription to *Classroom Computer Learning*, a directory of educational software, published quarterly.

Name: Educational Products Information Exchange
           P.O. Box 839
           Water Mill, NY 11976
Description: Nonprofit, consumer-oriented evaluation agency.

Name: Minnesota Educational Computing Consortium
           2520 Broadway Drive
           St. Paul, MN 55013
Description: Publishes its own line of educational software in many subject areas.

TYPING PROGRAMS

Name: Smartype by Colette Daiute
Contact: McGraw-Hill Book Company—Gregg Division
          1221 Avenue of the Americas
          New York, NY 10020
Computer/Operating System: Apple

Name: Typing Tutor
Distributor: Microsoft Corporation
           10700 Northup Way
           Bellevue, WA 98004
Computer/Operating System: Apple, IBM PC

Name: MasterType
Distributor: Lightning Software, Inc.
         P.O. Box 11725
         Palo Alto, CA 94306
Computer/Operating System: Apple, Atari

Name: Type Attack
Distributor: Sirus Software, Inc.
         10364 Rockingham Drive
         Sacramento, CA 95827
Computer/Operating System: Apple, Atari, IBM PC, Vic 20

Name: Touch Typing Tutor
Distributor: Taylormade Software
         Box 8732
         Lincoln, NE 68505
Computer/Operating System: Vic 20, Commodore 64

Name: Typing Teacher
Distributor: Instant Software
         Route 101
         Peterborough, NH 03458
Computer/Operating System: TRS 80

PERIODICALS TO CHECK
FOR SOFTWARE AND
RESEARCH UPDATES

AEDS Journal and AEDS Monitor
Association for Educational Data Systems
1201 Sixteenth Street, NW
Washington, DC 20036

Classroom Computer Learning
Subscription Department
5615 W. Cermak Road
Cicero, IL 60650

Computer Update
The Boston Computer Society, Inc.
1 Center Plaza
Boston, MA 02108

Computers in the Schools
The Haworth Press
28 East 22nd Street
New York, NY 10010

Computers in Reading and the Language Arts
CRLA Department M
P.O. Box 13247
Oakland, CA 94661-0247

The Computing Teacher
The International Council for
  Computers in Education
University of Oregon
1787 Agate Street
Eugene, OR 97403-1923

ECTJ—Educational Communications and Technology
Association for Educational Communications and Technology
1126 Sixteenth Street, NW
Washington, DC 20036

Electronic Learning
Scholastic, Inc.
902 Sylvan Avenue, Box 2001
Englewood Cliffs, NJ 07632

Journal of Computer-Based Instruction
International Headquarters
Miller Hall 409
Western Washington University
Bellingham, WA 98225

Journal of Educational Computing Research
Dr. Robert H. Seidman
Graduate School
New Hampshire College
2500 N. River Road
Manchester, NH 03104

Personal Computing
Hayden Publishing Company, Inc.
50 Essex Street
Rochelle Park, NJ 07662

Research in Word Processing Newsletter
Editors, Dr. B. Morgan and Dr. J. Schwartz
Liberal Arts Department
S.D. School of Mines and Technology
Rapid City, SD 57701-3995

School of Microcomputing Bulletin
Learning Publishing, Inc.
Department SMB-84, P.O. Box 1326
Holmes Beach, FL 33509

School Uses of Microcomputers
Center for Social Organization of Schools
The Johns Hopkins University
3505 N. Charles Street
Baltimore, MD 21218

Glossary

This glossary gives basic definitions of technical terms, many of which name complex processes with levels of meaning and a variety of nuances that must be collapsed when they are presented in a few sentences. When examples or specific focuses are necessary, they usually relate to uses of computers for writing or other linguistic activities. Readers who are interested in more detailed descriptions of computer hardware and computer processes should consult basic computer science books.

Append   To add text to the end of a *file*.

Authoring language   A high-level computer programming language that guides users with no programming expertise in writing computer programs. Because they provide the general structure and process for a program, authoring languages are designed for specific uses, such as creating question-and-answer drill programs. PILOT is an example of an authoring language designed for educational purposes.

Bidirectional printer   A printer that prints in two directions, rather than only one, thereby accelerating the printing process. After printing from left to right, the print mechanism moves down to the next line and prints it from right to left.

Bit   The basic unit of computer *machine code*, represented in the binary notations 0 and 1. A bit is a pulse of high or low voltage. Bits function in groups known as *bytes*.

Block move   A sequence of commands in a *word-processing program* that the writer uses to reorganize texts. The typical block move procedure involves moving a section of text to a temporary storage space—the *buffer*—and then reinserting the section in the desired position elsewhere in the text. The boundaries of the section are identified by the *mark* that the user inserts in the text and the cursor position.

Boilerplate   A precomposed format stored for multiple uses when composing texts with frequently repeated formats. Boilerplates may also contain substantial amounts of text that is repeated from draft to draft.

Branch   A sequencing option in the flow of a *program*, determined automatically according to a record of the pattern of responses by the program user and stored in the program. For example, if a student using a spelling drill program makes repeated mistakes on the *ei* sequence, the program would branch to present a rule and/or additional practice on words with that sequence.

Buffer   A temporary computer storage space with several functions, including holding data and compensating for changes in the flow of data between components of the computer, such as the keyboard and the screen. A buffer in *word-processing programs* typically holds text sections as they are being composed or holds sections that will later be inserted into a draft of a text.

Byte   A string of eight high and/or low voltages symbolized as 0s or 1s (*bits*). Computers store and process letters, numbers, and other symbols encoded in uniquely ordered patterns of bytes.

Card   A stiff piece of cardboardlike material on which the integrated circuitry of a computer is arranged and linked.

Central processing unit (CPU)   The part of a computer that contains the circuitry for controlling and performing instructions.

Color plotter   A special printer that uses pens and colored ink to reproduce designs according to instructions from the computer graphics program or *graphics editor*.

Command   A signal or set of signals to indicate an operation for the computer to perform. Commands are one of the main forms of communication from the computer user to the program and the computer. Pressing the CTRL key and the S simultaneously, for example, is a command used on some computer systems to tell the computer to stop presenting screensful of text in fast sequential order. Programs also include commands that are given automatically when the program is in operation.

Communications card   A *card* that provides special circuitry for transmitting data between computers and has a series of prongs—a serial port—to which a communication cable can be attached. Such a card sometimes has a *modem* on it.

Communications software   A computer program that monitors interactions between computers by directing data transfer, controlling the order in which messages are sent, stored, and processed, and checking and maintaining the accuracy of data transmission. Communications software is necessary for using a microcomputer as a *terminal* to connect to a large computer and sometimes for *networking* microcomputers.

Computer   A device that can accept information, perform specified operations on the information (for example, via computer programs), and present the results of these operations. The term can refer to the information-processing circuitry (computer chips) or to a combination of chips integrated on *cards* and placed in a housing with other components that allow communication with the chips. Computer systems usually include input devices, such as keyboards; output devices, such as visual display screens and printers; storage devices, such as *disks*; arithmetic and logical units; and processing devices.

Computer-aided instruction (CAI)   Programs that systematically present material from a discipline, usually in a question-and-answer format, and require some feedback from the person using the program. Such programs are sometimes referred to as computer-assisted instruction or computer-based instruction (CBI) programs.

Computer-managed instruction (CMI)   Programs that integrate *computer-aided instruction* with features that keep track of administrative aspects of instruction, such as time on task, students' responses, and grades.

Computer memory   A device that holds information as it is entered into the computer, as it is running or being processed in the computer, and/or as it is stored. The power of a computer is determined partially by the size of its memory, which is measured in *bytes*.

Concordance   A computer program that creates a list of words from a text and includes the numbers of the pages on which each word appears.

Configure   To customize a computer program so that it meets requirements of the *hardware* on which it is to run.

Control (CTRL) key   A key on the computer keyboard that is part of a command sequence. For example, pressing the CTRL key simultaneously with another key gives commands for operations, such as moving the cursor on the screen, deleting a word, or saving a text.

Conversion   The process of translating files stored or written in the appropriate code for one computer into the machine language for another computer. For example, there is conversion software that automatically translates files from the American Standard Code for Information Interchange (ASCII) into IBM's Extended Binary Coded Decimal Interchange Code (EBCDIC), which is used on some IBM computers.

Cursor   A light on a visual display screen, often formed as a line or small square, that indicates where the next input will be recorded.

Daisywheel   A type of impact printing device that is faster than the familiar ball mechanism on electric typewriters; the symbols are printed from raised images at the ends of spokes radiating from the center hub of this printer wheel. Daisywheels are typically used on *letter-quality printers*, and they must be replaced periodically.

Database   A block of information that is organized into a specified set of categories and entered into a computer in a consistent format so that a program can be used to search, sort, merge, and update the data. Information in a database is usually accessed via a database search or management program by typing keywords—names of information categories and/or items in specific entries.

Database management system (database program)   A *program* that accepts, formats, organizes, and updates information in relation to specific categories set up by the program user. The program requires the user to label *fields* of information categories, including a category label and the maximum length of an entry into the field. The program has sophisticated functions for updating a *database* that allow the user to add and delete fields, leaving reorganization up to the program. Distinctions between the terms *file management system* and *database management system* are often blurred, because even the experts do not agree on the exact specifications for programs that manage databases.

Data line   A line at the bottom or top of the screen where status messages, such as the direction of a search in a *word-processing program*, or command *prompts*, such as the word to search for, are displayed by the program. Such a message area is also referred to as an echo area or mode line.

Default settings   A series of commands automatically given to a computer as specified by a program or the program user, usually because the operations the commands represent are frequent. For example, commands to print text with 72-character lines and straight right margins are defaults in many *formatting* programs. In many systems, users can specify ther own default settings, which are stored in the program or in a separate data file, depending on the program.

Delete key   A key on the computer keyboard that moves the *cursor* one place to the left and erases the symbol in that position. The key that functions in this way is labeled DELETE or DEL on some keyboards but may, instead, be represented by a back arrow.

Directory   A catalog of the *files* on a storage device, such as a *diskette*. The amount of information presented about these files varies between operating systems. Some systems display information such as the size of each file (in *bytes*). This term is also used to refer to the storage space and access privileges of specified users of a computer system, usually a *time-sharing system*. For example, in many college settings, students apply and pay for a directory on the computer.

Disk   A storage device for magnetically stored, computer-readable data and programs. Disks vary in size, in the amount of storage space they contain, and in the material of which they are made—some are metal, some are plastic. Two types of disks are *diskettes* and *hard disks*.

Disk drive   The device that transfers information between the computer and the external storage *disk*; the transfer processes are often referred to as "reading" information from and "writing" information to disk. A typical disk drive has a moving head—similar to an audio or video recording head—that records or retrieves magnetic information on the disk at high speeds and in the order specified by the user.

Diskette   A thin, flexible platter that is treated with a substance capable of storing magnetic material. Diskettes are used to store information from and transfer information to computers. Sometimes called *disks*, they come in standard sizes (3½, 5¼, and 8 inches) and are the most popular storage devices used on micro-computers.

Document design program   A *program* that provides the format for a specific type of document, such as a business letter.

Dot matrix printer   A printer that uses several (often nine) pins to create patterns of dots in many shapes, such as letter shapes, numbers, and designs created in a graphics program. The paper copy produced on a dot matrix printer is readable but is not referred to as letter-quality; that is, it is not considered polished enough to be sent to readers.

Edit mode   A section of a *word-processing program* that responds to commands for moving the cursor and changing the text.

Electronic mail   Messages sent and received on a computer system. Electronic mail programs are typically used on *time-sharing* or *networked* systems that are shared by many individual users. Electronic mail programs provide options for setting up a message and transferring it from one user's storage space (*directory*) to the other's, and a variety of other options, such as time-stamping and editing functions, depending on the system.

Embedded commands   Program or machine-readable symbols in a text that may or may not be visible but that control the way a text will be formatted.

Error message   A message presented to alert the user to a problem the computer is having in carrying out an instruction. Programmers insert such messages into programs to advise the user of a variety of predictable mistakes in writing computer programs or in interacting with a computer. Error messages vary in clarity, directness, and appropriateness.

Escape (ESC) key   A key—like the *Control (CTRL) key*—on the computer keyboard that signals a change in the meaning of one or more of the keys that are pressed after it. The ESC key is also used to change the current mode of program operation. The ESC key is often used for commands of a relatively high level, such as *search* and *replace* commands, rather than for commands that operate on a lower level, such as deleting characters—which is often done with a CTRL key sequence.

Field   One or more characters treated as a whole. The term is commonly used to name a defined category in a database, such as the name field and the address field in a database of members of an organization.

File   A collection of related items of data, such as lines of a text or a list of addresses, that has been given a name by a user, that is stored in memory or on disk, and that is treated as a unit.

File management system   A program that provides codes for creating, deleting, retrieving, and updating files or sections of files. The user's coding in such a system is more general and on a higher text level than the coding used in a *database management system*. For example, in a file management system, the user might define names and topic headings for sections of text after they have been entered into the file, rather than before, as the user does in a database management system.

Fill (filling function)   A word-processing function that arranges text into standard prose form, with words appearing consecutively on lines of text rather than as a list, for example. The filling function in specific *word-processing programs* might vary for specific settings, such as the length of the lines.

Find (search)   A word-processing operation that identifies a character or string of characters specified by the user.

Firmware   Programs that are part of the computer hardware, such as programs on special-purpose *cards* that are inserted into the computer. Frequently used programs are designed in this way to bypass the step of loading *software* from an external storage device, like a *disk*, into the computer memory for processing.

Formatting   Automatic arranging of data, such as text, for placement to or from a computer display screen or printer. Many *word-processing programs* include formatting sections, but there are also programs whose sole function is to arrange words in a computer text file according to specific formatting instructions. Formatting options include centering, spacing, page length, line length, underlining, indenting, and other similar features of text presentation. Formatting also refers to the preparation of *disks* for storing data. For example, the user must run a formatting program on a microcomputer *diskette* before attempting to store any files on it.

Freewriting   The technique (advocated by Peter Elbow) of writing, without editing, whatever thoughts come to mind in a manner as close to stream-of-consciousness thinking as is possible with the slow and structured act of writing.

Global   Signifying the scope of a command sequence that will automatically be repeated until every instance to which it applies has been carried out.

Graphics editor   A computer program that allows users to create, store, and change designs.

Graphics tablet   A flat peripheral device connected to the computer that translates images drawn on its surface with an electronically coded penlike device. The tablet and additional *software* record the lines drawn on the tablet into coordinate markings, which are then translated into digitized code that can be stored and edited in much the same way the text stored in the computer can be edited.

Hacker   A term describing an individual who spends many hours working on computers, inventing clever ways to write computer programs, and debugging programs. The term has become an affectionate name for people who are part of a subculture of frequent computer users.

Hard copy   A copy of data, such as text, from a computer file that is printed on paper.

Hard disk   A storage device—generally an aluminum drum—that is coated with a substance capable of storing magnetic information. Hard disks are often preferred over *diskettes* because they can store larger amounts of data, but they are less portable and more expensive than diskettes.

Hardware   The physical elements of a computer system, such as integrated circuits, wires, terminals, printers, cabinets, and motors.

Impact printer   A printer that produces images by pressing a raised mold of the desired symbol against an inked ribbon.

Information utility   A service offering subscribers access to databases of electronically stored and delivered information, computer programs, and electronic mail, among other services. The Source, CompuServ, and the New York Times Information Service are examples of such systems.

Joy stick (game paddle)   A lever-type device connected to a computer; when tilted in various directions, it controls the movement of the *cursor* on the screen. These devices are often used with graphics packages and with computer games.

Justification   An alignment of text with straight left and right margins.

Kilobyte (K) 2^{10} or 1024 bytes.

Letter-quality printer   A printer that produces the same print appearance as a high-quality electric typewriter. The images from such a printer are clear and sharp compared to the fuzzier appearance of images from *dot matrix printers*.

Light pen   A pen-shaped device that is connected by a cable to a computer. This device, which can be used like a pen, transforms sensed light waves on the monitor into digital signals read by a computer. Light pens are used to draw or move images on a computer screen.

Line-based editors   The most basic form of *word-processing program* or text-editing program. These primitive programs number each line of text and restrict the range of editing opreations to a line or group of lines of text at one time.

Link   *Software* on *time-sharing* computers that allows several users to work in the same memory space at the same time. The term also refers to the connection of a program part with the main program and the joining of two separately written programs.

Loading   The transfer of *software* from an external storage device, such as a *disk*, into the internal computer memory.

Machine code (language)   The series of 1s and 0s that are translated into high and low voltages in the computer circuitry. High-level programming languages (which often use words of natural languages) and all information that the computer stores and/or processes must be translated into machine code to be used by the computer.

Mail merge A program that stores, manipulates, and sends entries from a mailing list database out to a printer to be printed on letter headings and envelopes.

Mainframe A large, *time-sharing* computer that can fill a room. A mainframe typically has faster and larger processing than minicomputers and can support more users simultaneously.

Mark A code in a text file that identifies a section for some *program* operation. For example, the *block move* operation looks for a mark to determine the boundary of a section of text to be moved. Although the user identifies the mark by pressing a "set the mark" command, the mark is usually invisible. In computer communications, this term names an impulse that closes or changes the direction of a process.

Memory chip An electronic chip that stores digital information.

Menu A list of command descriptions, usually presented in an abbreviated form, that allows users to choose which part of a computer program they want to use.

Merge The process of taking sorted data or files and recombining them in a newly defined logical order, such as alphabetical order.

Microcomputer A complete small computer system in which the processsing power and storage device, as well as the keyboard and display screen, are devoted to one user at a time. Microcomputers have less processing power and space than *minicomputers*, but they also cost less.

Minicomputer A *time-sharing* computer that has more processing power and space than a *microcomputer*. Although minicomputers may be very fast, they typically support fewer uses at one time than *mainframes* do.

Mode A method or environment of operation in a computer program. For example, many *word-processing programs* have separate modes or sections of *programs* that accept *commands* to insert or edit text.

Mode switching Changing between two methods of operation that are mutually exclusive, such as changing from a section of a program that replaces letters on a screen with letters typed at the corresponding cursor position to a section of a program that is devoted to inputting new text.

Modem A device used to connect a *terminal* or *microcomputer* to another computer via phone lines. The modem *mo*dulates the digital code that computers use into the sound waves that phone lines are constructed to carry and *dem*odulates sound waves into the digital high and low voltages (1s and 0s) in the computer.

Monitor A cathode ray tube (CRT) that looks like a television screen and displays data input to a computer. Some computer systems can be set up with television sets as monitors.

Mouse A mechanical device, a little larger than a hockey puck, with one or two buttons on top, which, when moved across a flat surface, causes the cursor to move in the direction of that movement on the monitor. The buttons provide a small set of commands that operate at the cursor position identified by the mouse position and movement.

Multiple-window feature (two-window feature) The capacity to split the computer screen into two or more sections that can each display data from different files or different sections of a file. The computer operates in the window where the cursor appears, and the program provides commands for moving the cursor across windows. The multiple-window feature is a valuable but not yet standard feature in word-processing systems.

Network   The connection of two or more computers for sharing and transmitting data across different computer systems.

Numeric keypad   A small keypad including numbers and sometimes symbols for arithmetic operations. The numeric keypad is often placed on the far right of the computer keyboard.

On-line   A situation in which peripherals, such as the keyboard and *monitor* are under the control of the *central processing unit* of the computer. When working on-line, a user interacts with the computer system as operations occur, rather than setting up an activity that runs at a later time or that runs with the minimal power of a local *buffer* in a *terminal*.

Operating system   The program that controls and manages the operations of the computer, including control of input/output procedures, data conversion routines, and file management operations.

Peripherals   A variety of machines that operate with the computer but are not contained in the main computer, as are more central parts, such as processing chips. Printers, disk drives, and light pens are peripherals.

Program   A set of instructions that specify to the computer patterns of electrical flow for carrying out specific tasks. Programs are also referred to as *software*, although they can be part of the physical circuitry of the computer. Programs are written in programming languages, such as BASIC, Pascal, and Logo.

Programmed function keys   Extra keys on the computer keyboard that are specifically programmed with commonly used commands. When a system has such keys, commands that would otherwise require multiple keystrokes can be carried out with single keystrokes, thereby simplifying and speeding up interactions with the computer.

Prompt   A message displayed on a computer screen that alerts the user to the present status of the program, asks for input from the user, or presents more general comments that do not require input.

Prompting program   A program that prints messages on the screen, either automatically, depending on prior program operations, or at the user's direction. Prompting programs have been developed to guide the writing process.

Record file   A file containing all of the keystrokes that were entered into the computer during a specified period of time; also called a log, dribble, or journal file.

Replace (search and replace)   A word-processing operation that identifies a string of characters specified by the user and replaces it with another specified string.

Save   A command that instructs the computer to record (write or dump) information currently in memory onto a designated permanent storage medium, such as a *disk*.

Screen-based editor   A sophisticated *word-processing program* that allows users to perform editing operations on large blocks of text. The writer working with such a program can also move the cursor to places in the text where operations should be performed, rather than having to refer to line numbers. Screen-based editors also provide formatting commands that are carried out directly on the screen as one writes, rather than via embedded commands that operate after the text file is run through a formatting program.

Scrolling The option to display pages of text sequentially on a screen, either backward or forward, as if the text were wrapped around a scroll.

Search See *find*.

Simulation A computer program that imitates the interaction of many variables in lifelike situations, such as on the control panel of an airplane. The program displays the effects of changes in one or more variables, such as indicating the speed of a plane at various points when altitude and atmospheric conditions change.

Software Computer *programs* that carry out a variety of activities on the computer.

Sort The process of arranging files, or data in a file, according to a defined logical order—for example, in alphabetical order.

Speech synthesis The production of natural language sounds and sound sequences by a computer.

Spelling checker A program that matches words in a text against a dictionary database and presents all nonmatches as words to check for misspelling. Spelling checkers vary in the number of words in their dictionaries and the methods of presenting and reacting to mismatches.

Spreadsheet A *program* that provides a structure and operations for entering and manipulating financial information in the computer.

Statistical package A *program* used for doing statistical analyses of data entered into files in specific formats.

Template A program or text file that provides a basic structure, such as a letter format. The user enters specific information in the template sections and, depending on the sophistication of the program, it can perform operations on the information. Document design programs and mail merge programs are templates.

Terminal A keyboard and visual display device that allows the user to interact with a computer. Terminals vary in the sophistication of their displays (for example, whether they can display graphics) and their keyboards (for example, how many programmable function keys they have).

Text-analysis program A program that analyzes various specific components of a text, such as number and placement of specific words, unnecessary words, like "sort of," and the number of words per sentence. Such programs cannot do detailed semantic analyses of texts.

Text editor A *program* that is like a *word-processing program* but does not include *formatting* options.

Time-sharing The running of more than one terminal from one computer, apparently at the same time. Since computers can process some kinds of information faster than people can, the computer can actually be transmitting and receiving information from each remote user, in turn, without any noticeable delay to any user unless the basic system capacity is overloaded. See also *minicomputer*, *mainframe*, and *network*.

Touch-sensitive screens Visual displays with special screens that can translate contact from the human body into commands to the computer.

Tutorial *Computer-aided instruction (CAI)* that presents instruction in a content area or process and that provides interactive practice for mastery of the material presented.

Two-window feature See *multiple-window feature*.

User   An individual who is interacting with a computer.

Videotex and teletext   Electronically presented textual and graphic information received by television receivers and displayed on screens. The information is frequently updated, and the user selects options by pressing keys on a *numeric keypad*. Videotex and teletext services include news, luxury services such as restaurant guides, and, occasionally, educational programs.

Voice input   Special components and *software* that allow a computer to convert sound waves that are spoken into a recording device on the computer into digital code that the computer processes in the same way as information input through a keyboard.

Word processor   A computer that has been designed primarily to allow users to compose, edit, format, and print texts. Since word processors are dedicated to one function, they tend to be easy to use, but they are usually limited and expensive.

Word-processing program   A *program* that accepts and manipulates text on command from the user. A word-processing program, as distinct from a text-editing program, usually includes *formatting* options.

Word wrap   A word-processing operation that automatically places words on the next line when a line of text exceeds a predetermined length, usually 37 or 72 characters.

Index

Abstracts, 288
Academic formats, usefulness of computer for, 224–225
Adolescents
  importance of free writing for, 209
  improving writing of
    with computer conferencing, 197–200
    with debates on diskettes, 197–199
    with electronic comments, 208
    with essay-building exercises, 199
    with exercises structuring debate files, 199
    with multiple-window comparisons of paragraph improvements, 208
    with parsers, 209
    with prompting programs, 206–207
    with rewriting exercises, 208
    with structured composing programs, 207
    with text-analysis programs, 207–209
  learning word-processing by, 193
  problems in teaching writing to, 194
  typical problems in writing of, 194–196
  and usefulness of computers, 197, 201
    for business letters, 211
    for discovering interests with electronic mail, 201
    for experimenting with alternate styles, 207
    for reorganizations, 199–200
    for resumés, 210–211
    deadwood files as tool for revising, 210
    for term papers, *see* Term papers
Adults, 220
  common writing problems of, 214–215
  effects of computer on writing skills of, 219

  as functional writers, 230–231
  improving writing of
    with drills versus writing practice, 215–216
    with text-analysis programs, 217
  learning word-processing by, 193
  mastering basic skills by, 230
  strategies for adapting computer to needs of, 242
  training of, 244–246
    example versus principles in, 216
    steps in program of, 245–246
  transfer of skills in, 219–220
  and usefulness of computers, 213–214, 231–237
    access as factor in, 233
    adult-appropriate software for teachers as factor in, 233
    for checking style, 238–241
    composing style as factor in, 241–243
    for drill in mechanics, 216
    ease of use as factor in, 234–236
    efficiency as factor in, 231–232
    file compatibility as factor in, 233–234
    for formatting papers, 218–219
    for professional formatting, 224
    for revising, 222
    for text organization, 221
    for writers in college and graduate school, 227
    for writing, 217–218
    see also Teachers
Alphabet programs, 146
Amsel, Eric, 229